The Wind of the Hundred Days

The Wind of the Hundred Days

How Washington
Mismanaged Globalization

Jagdish Bhagwati

The MIT Press
Cambridge, Massachusetts
London, England

This book was set in Adobe Palatino by Asco Typesetters, Hong Kong, in QuarkXPress®. Printed and bound in the United States of America.

Library of Congress Cataloging-in-Publication Data
Bhagwati, Jagdish N., 1934–
 The wind of the hundred days : how Washington mismanaged globalization / Jagdish Bhagwati.
    p.   cm.
 Includes bibliographical references and index.
 ISBN 0-262-02495-0 (alk. paper)
 1. United States—Foreign economic relations. 2. United States—Commercial policy. 3. Free trade. 4. Capital movements. 5. Globalization—Economic aspects. 6. Globalization—Social aspects. I. Title.
HF1455 .B48   2000
337.73—dc21   00-064596

For my teachers

Paul Samuelson
and
Robert Solow

and my student

Paul Krugman

Kindred spirits, seeking social good by combining deep scholarship
with effective public policy writing

Contents

I met the wind of the hundred days.
It covered all the nights with sand,
Badgered my forehead, scorched my lids.

Octavio Paz, "Happiness in Herat"

Preface

In writing these op-ed articles, essays, lectures, book reviews, and occasional letters to the newspapers, I have drawn on the help of many students, current and past. They have acted as sounding boards for my ideas; and they have tracked down all sorts of things on the proliferating websites that would have been well beyond my modest technological competence. I would like to thank, most of all, Maria Coppola and Bikas Joshi, enthusiastic and insightful aides who have worked beyond their contractual obligations, wonderful specimens of the "overworked Americans" who are making the news these days.

My MIT students—Robert Feenstra, Gene Grossman, Paul Krugman, Steve Magee, Jeffrey Frenkel, Maurice Obstfeld, and Ken Rogoff—all now extremely distinguished international economists, and also my later students at Columbia—Elias Dinopoulos, Kar-yiu Wong, Doug Irwin, Don Davis, Peter Rosendorf, Ian Wooton, Rodney Ludema, Vivek Dehejia, Pravin Krishna, and Devashish Mitra—already well known in the profession for their considerable scientific abilities, have provided ideas, directly or through their important research, that I have profited from as I have worked my way through the many complexities of international economic policy today.

My debt is equally great to T. N. Srinivasan, Arvind Panagariya, Koichi Hamada, Richard Brecher, and John Wilson, who have collaborated with me on a great deal of scholarly research without which the contents of this volume would have been intellectually the poorer. I have also learned much on trade policy from Robert Baldwin, Avinash Dixit, and Alan Deardorff.

Finally, my thanks go to Terry Vaughn, Economics Editor of the MIT Press, whose good judgment in trying to publish almost everything that I have written in the last decade cannot be faulted! Frankly, without his tender loving care and his patient nudge at critical moments of distraction, lavished without stint on this book and others, few of them would have seen the light of the day.

Introduction

A previous selection of fifty-six of my op-ed articles, essays, book reviews, letters, and lectures, *A Stream of Windows: Unsettling Reflections on Trade, Immigration, and Democracy* (MIT Press, 1998) was received with a warmth that exceeded all my expectations. It drew reviews in leading newspapers, magazines, and professional journals around the world, while winning the prestigious Eccles Prize for Excellence in Economic Writing.

That would be reason enough to go to the well once again. Few novelists, savoring the triumph of their first novels, are so timid or content that they will not write again. Indeed, success is likely instead to produce hubris and most of us will yield to the temptation to seek yet more. But that is not really why I have now put together yet another selection of my most recent popular writings. It is rather because I again have a unifying theme and an overriding message.

In *A Stream of Windows*, which had a broad intellectual range, the central conception (developed by me over nearly forty years of reflection and writing, from the time I returned to India from study abroad at Cambridge, Oxford, and MIT in the late 1950s) nonetheless was that the best economy and the better society was one that combined both markets and democracy. In that context, the virtues of freer trade and a more expansive policy on immigration were underlined and underlay much of what I had written.

Running intermittently through the long book, however, was also dissatisfaction with recent trends in U.S. policy, generally in regard to trade. In particular, the Clinton administration was faulted for:

occasional pandering to Japan-fixation and perhaps even Japan-bashing when Japan was considered omnipotent;

the embrace of preferential trade agreements (such as, and even beyond, NAFTA) instead of leadership aimed at strengthening the nondiscriminatory multilateral trade regime in general under the GATT then, and WTO now;

an inadequate and inappropriate response to the growing demands on the trading system by the environmentalists and labor unions; and

a growing surrender to, and witless encouragement of, the cries by these and other groups for "fair trade."

But while I was hinting at, even highlighting, the irony of the administration's flaws in trade policy despite the widespread perception of the administration's success with trade policy, the years since the Asian crisis broke in mid-1998 brought into sharp focus a yet different aspect of the Clinton administration's failings on the international front. For, while the shortcomings of the administration on trade policy were apparent only to the informed scholars, and even eluded many of the sophisticated journalists in the leading newspapers, the Asian financial crisis was too dramatic and obvious an episode to be dismissed from public attention without raising the suspicion that somehow the administration had blundered.

Was this huge failure President Clinton's *real* scandal? And if so, the irony would be that, even as the administration had chalked up great success in domestic prosperity, it had visited a fierce firestorm abroad, creating the worst man-made crisis in the world economy since the notorious Smoot-Hawley Tariff of 1931.

The paradox would then be the simultaneity of admirable domestic policy success and abysmal foreign policy failure. As it happens, that specific judgment, which I advance in this set of essays, is altogether arguable, even plausible, when we examine (as I do in many of my essays) the financial debacle in Asia and elsewhere without wearing partisan eyeglasses. But even my thesis of the presidential goof-ups on trade policy, a hard sell earlier, has now gathered more plausibility from the debacle in Seattle at the 1999 WTO Ministerial meeting in late November and early December, a failure that has been properly laid at President Clinton's door by critics everywhere. That disaster has been mitigated in no way by the successful House vote in May 2000 on the trade deal with China: the terms were so totally biased in favor of the United States that it was a no-brainer, and yet another loss by the president, despite the cards being stacked overwhelmingly to U.S. advantage, would have certified him and his administration as klutzes.

The Financial Debacle

President Clinton's foreign economic policy failure, especially the ravages wrought by the Asian financial crisis under his watch and even a result (partially, if not wholly) of his own men's prodding, defines the subtitle of the collection, while the evocative image of devastation in Octavio Paz's chilling line "I met the wind of the hundred days" has provided me with the title.

And the volume opens therefore precisely with an essay in *Foreign Affairs* (May/June 1998) that pointedly noted where the administration had gone wrong, while the five chapters that follow discuss how our errors helped change the Asian economic "miracle" of the last three decades into a debacle.

In particular, the *Foreign Affairs* essay has produced a worldwide following to the point where I was recently awarded the (first) Suh Sang Don Award, by a major Asian NGOs' World Forum, based in Taegu, South Korea, for alerting the world to the elements of asymmetry between the case for free trade and the case for free capital mobility and hence to the dangers that unregulated capital flows pose to countries. The subsequent writings in late 1998 on capital flow controls by Paul Krugman (in *Fortune* and elsewhere) and by Joe Stiglitz (from the World Bank) supported the position that I had taken. Over time, Barry Eichengreen, IMF's adviser on the subject, also appears to have had a change of heart on the matter.

My essay also introduced into the public domain and into the political-economy literature the nonconspiratorial concept of the "Wall Street–Treasury complex" with which I, in the spirit of Dwight Eisenhower's military-industrial complex and Wright Mills's concept of the "power elite," sought to explain how powerful lobbying "interests" on Wall Street, working within a network of like-minded people moving back and forth between Washington and Wall Street, had combined with a growing shift to markets imprudently extended to capital flows to push the developing countries into a hasty embrace of capital account convertibility without adequate safeguards.

The influence of this complex can be seen in the massive resistance it showed at the outset to admitting the mistakes that had been made; it is also manifest in the fact that U.S. negotiations on admitting China into the WTO were held up during the Chinese premier's U.S. visit in 1999, for the most part, by the failure to get yet more concessions from China on opening its financial sector, even as the Asian economies had not yet worked their way out of the devastation of the financial crisis. Indeed, many leading members of the Wall Street–Treasury complex have been keen to scapegoat the Asian financial crisis onto the Asians themselves, citing "crony capitalism" as being the cause of it.

Chapter 6 in this book argues that cronies are part of every political system. A little role reversal and examination of our own system with the spectacles that we wear when looking critically at others will convince the objective analysts that, by our criteria, President Clinton's cronies include Barbara Streisand, other Hollywood figures such as Alec Baldwin and Kim Basinger, and Terry MacAuliffe, who went so far as to bankroll in effect the Clinton's mortgage on their New York house in Chappaqua. Besides, cronies were totally compatible with rapid growth and transformation of these Asian economies in the previous three decades. I have rarely seen a satisfactory explanation of how the same institutional phenomena that produced economic miracles were suddenly to be regarded as the phenomena that ended them so shabbily!

Chapter 6 probes more deeply the question of corruption and development, in the process also distinguishing between two types of corruption: "rent-seeking" and "profit-sharing." The former occurs when monopolies are created and policies pursued by the state such that "rents" are earned on artificial scarcities and these are then given to one's friends and political supporters, examples being President Suharto's and Prime Minister Indira Gandhi's sons enjoying the proceeds of special protection on their pet car projects vis-à-vis rival foreign and domestic car producers. Such "rent-creating" corruption has high economic cost. But where the corruption takes the form of "profit sharing" so that, as in China (especially in the Guangdong provinces on the coast where economic activity has boomed for long) and (partially) in Indonesia, the well-connected are paid off by being given a share of the profits, the incentive to earn profits is great and economic incentives and allocative efficiency tend to be the way things are done. Such "profit-sharing" corruption is then economically compatible with rapid growth of the economy and its costs are more political (since corruption siphons off some of the profits to the undeserving) than economic. The corruption in hegemonic countries like the United States also takes generally the profit-sharing form and none are rewarded through creation of rents: Cronies such as the Spielbergs and Streisands are rewarded, not by giving rent-creating domestic monopolies to their films and songs, but by rewarding them and Hollywood and the United States generally at other (frequently poor) countries' expense through forced opening of markets (which often lead to legitimate complaints about the United States ignoring other countries' cultural concerns) and through tough enforcement of excessive intellectual property protection in all sorts of ways.

The Trade Debacle

While therefore it is hard to maintain that the Asian financial crisis was homespun in Asia, and the accusatory finger can be properly directed at the U.S. administration for its principal role in this policy disaster, the failure to understand and manage the question of free trade today has been a failure of almost equal magnitude.

The bulk of this volume addresses the challenges that have repeatedly faced this administration, and its often-inadequate and even inappropriate policy responses and outcomes, on several specific matters such as NAFTA, its extension to South America, the desire to get fast track authority renewed, the intended launch of multilateral trade negotiations in Seattle, taking on Japan's trade policy, the accommodation of demands from the unions and the environmentalists, and the issues raised by human rights activists on China's MFN renewal with the United States and the question of its admission to the WTO.

Underlying these themes, however, is a central critique of the trade policy of President Clinton that I may stress. The American scene by now has become dominated by the notion that trade must be "fair," not just "free." This is, of course, a convenient route to protectionism since, if you say you want protection because you cannot hack it against your foreign competitors, it is a trifle difficult to get protection: after all, we economists have succeeded in convincing most politicians that protectionism is, next to four-letter words, a temptation to be avoided if they wish to promote the social good. But if you can say that your rival is an "unfair" trader, that works wonders, particularly in a society that prides itself on equal opportunity rather than equal outcomes, on equality of access rather than equality of success. This is a principal reason that economists have argued against the use of antidumping (AD) actions by firms facing increased import competition as a way of getting import relief: these AD actions invoke, by arguing that "dumping" (a pejorative word) is taking place, the notion of "unfair trade" and hence typically work to secure protection more effectively than other import relief procedures such as the use of simple "market disruption" provisions.

Fairness, like beauty, is of course in the eye of the beholder. It is apparent therefore that if one starts down the road of claiming that "trade must be both free and fair" or, more emphatically, that one must have "fair trade before free trade," then one has inevitably played into the hands of the protectionists. What President Clinton should have been doing therefore is to challenge these dangerous slogans, recognizing them for the subversive verbiage they represent. Instead, he and his administration actively encouraged them, lending them respectability.

Thus, President Clinton came into office in 1992, riding on a wave of Japan-bashing. Supported by the Silicon valley that endorsed him, appointing Laura Tyson (obsessed with Japan at that time) as the chairperson of the Council of Economic Advisers, putting at the center of his trade agenda the confrontation of Japan with a revived Super 301 policy that would enable us to condemn Japan as an "unfair trader" and subject it to tough retaliatory action, Clinton was elevating "unfair trade" to center stage. My earlier collection of essays, *A Stream of Windows* (MIT Press, 1998), contains extended documentation and analysis of this folly, which accelerated the notion in the United States that Japan was an unfair trader, and that indeed we were virtuous and others were in sin when it came to open markets and fair practices. Chapters 7–9 in this volume underline the problems that this self-inflicted wound has caused the president in moving toward freer trade.

But Japan was not the only cause of the phenomenal rise of fair trade arguments in the United States in the Clinton years. NAFTA also aided in this process. This happened because bilateral and regional trade agreements enable the protectionists to zero in on this form of trade liberalization by converting nontrade into trade issues. Thus, if Mexico is being brought into freer trade with us, the protectionists will go to town and say, with apparent plausibility, that Mexico is not entitled to free trade with us because "Mexico is not a democracy," or "Mexico has bad environmental standards," or "Mexico's labor laws are not adequate." In short, any warts, real or imagined, on Mexico's face become weapons to destroy a trade pact with it. And if this is not done, and you manage to make Mexicans raise their standards, you at least manage in turn to raise the costs of production there to moderate the competition that you fear from NAFTA as a protectionist. But the net result is that all kinds of nontrade issues that have little to do with trade liberalization are then elevated in the public debate and imagination to the status of "fair trade" preconditions for free trade. I can speak from my own experience in public debates, on the multilateral trade liberalization under the Uruguay Round, at the same time as NAFTA, that few protectionists thought it fruitful to attack the Uruguay Round on such nontrade grounds: It would have been much harder to do so, with too many countries and too many issues at stake and with no easy way to zero in therefore on one country's warts and exploit them to advantage. So, both the Japan-bashing of the Clinton administration, which legitimated a number of "unfair trade" complaints that extended to domestic policy measures and institutions (e.g., keiretsus, retail distribution systems, savings habits) in foreign nations whose fault was merely that they were different from ours, and its witless backing of NAFTA (which was after all a preferential trade agreement with all its disadvantages vis-à-vis multilateral trade liberalization under GATT auspices, an issue that I discuss in chapters 25–28), and hence the legitimation of yet other complaints about "unfair trade" (on labor, on environment, on governance), would leave a legacy that was to prove difficult for the administration when it sought new initiatives for trade liberalization.

In each case, the president and his advisers played drafts, settling for options that would apparently win a battle. But they never looked ahead, playing chess, to win the war. Fair trade notions played well in Peoria, and with lobbies including certain vocal NGOs; but they defined and set in cement the ethos of fair trade that would hobble new trade initiatives.

Now, these lobbies are very much on the trade scene, causing the president to lose the fast track and also contributing to the Seattle debacle in December 1999. Demands to eliminate unfair trade by introducing a Social Clause on labor and environmental standards, for example, are rejected by the developing countries, which see them as daggers aimed at their exports.

Presented also as moral agendas for other countries, these demands make little sense because they are always framed in a way that singles out the poor countries for moral lapses, not the rich ones. Besides, if such "empathetic" desires are behind the demands for a Social Clause at the WTO, it is easy to show that these agendas are better advanced by shifting to nontrade methods and programs at other, more appropriate agencies such as the ILO. For instance, with nearly 200 million children at work, and with only 5 percent of their output exported according to the best available estimates, trade sanctions (as implied by putting the use of child labor as a ground for market access suspension into the WTO through a Social Clause) will most likely bounce children engaged in exports into other occupations, even into prostitution, as happened with children in textiles in Bangladesh when the U.S. Congress was considering the Harkin bill on Deterrence of Child Labor. Child labor is thus, in the words of the remarkable British Minister Clare Short," a development, not a trade, problem." Better measures can be devised that do not use trade sanctions and advance more effectively the reduction of child labor in the poor countries. But these measures, which require working with local NGOs, with aid programs, with local governments, and with sustained dedication are indeed starting at the ILO, which is the more appropriate agency, and the demands for trade sanctions at the WTO are simply wrong, even morally wicked. In supporting the latter rather than urging a shift to the former just because misguided unions want the latter, and in thus prompting the poor countries to walk away and causing a failure of the Seattle talks on launching a new round of multilateral trade negotiations, President Clinton regrettably betrayed a cynicism, indeed an abdication of moral responsibility toward others, that has almost become the hallmark of his international economic policy. That is the burden of chapters 31–35 on the Seattle debacle: These essays spell out precisely why the administration's trade policy has been a disaster waiting to happen and why the disaster has happened.

To state it unequivocally, these define then the central theme of this volume: The huge financial and economic failure in Asia and the tragic debacle in Seattle mark this administration as ironically guilty of colossal mistakes, of economic policy and architectural design of the financial and trading system. The story is that of a Greek tragedy: disasters brought on itself by an administration supremely oblivious to warnings and advice, hooked on focus groups and on the polls, never leading and heading off the impending disasters through prudential but creative thinking.

There are other related themes in the chapters. In particular, in part VII on globalization, I note how President Clinton's lazy echoing of the ill-informed views that one heard again on the Seattle streets, that "globalization needs a human face," has been an implicit surrender to the view that globalization *lacks* a human face. Thus, he neglects the abundant evidence that globalization (on the trade and direct foreign investment fronts) has been a force for good, not evil, as chapters 4, 11, 12, 40, and 46 in particular argue from available evidence. I similarly challenge the platitudes against globalization and liberal market reforms as being irrelevant to poverty reduction, and the populist charge that they constitute "trickle-down" economics that does not work. I argue that these reforms produce growth, which is an important "pull-up" strategy to bring about poverty reduction through increases in gainful employment of the poor.

These chapters provide a blunt attack on economists whose writings have implied the contrary, and whose platitudes about poverty reduction and feel-good but inappropriate policies based on them are likely to accentuate the very poverty that they deplore. Indeed, in countries such as India, the economists who profess to worry today about poverty and India's abysmal experience with its reduction are themselves the cause of it, having opposed economic reforms during nearly a quarter of a century when the autarkic and inefficient-public-sector-dominated economy, blessed with these very economists' accolades, was growing at an average of about 3.5 percent annually and naturally failed to reduce poverty.

A fierce recognition of these failings of the antiglobalization and the antimarket policies needs to be kept in view, and reforms in these areas by the developing countries need to be fully and continually nurtured if they are to take hold. The reforms are still fragile and could be undermined by institutions such as the World Bank whose aid-dispensing power is large enough to overwhelm good with bad policies. The gift horse of aid under the Bank's present leadership, is in real danger of turning into a Trojan horse.

Hence, I have turned a critical eye on Mr. Wolfensohn's dangerously naïve pronouncements and policies in a letter to the *Financial Times* (chapter 43) that generated a large outpouring of critical letters on Mr. Wolfensohn. All in a good cause; besides, coming from India and having worked for four decades on problems of poverty and development, I may be forgiven for presuming that I perhaps know, and care, more than Mr. Wolfensohn, a boutique investment banker by profession and a recent novice in the complex task of development, about what we next need to do in both India and other developing countries.

I

The Two-Edged Sword: Capital Flows

1

The Capital Myth: The Difference between Trade in Widgets and Dollars

In the aftermath of the Asian financial crisis, the mainstream view, indeed the prevalent myth, that dominates policy circles is that despite the evidence of a crisis-prone world of freer capital mobility as inescapably brought to our attention by the 1994 Mexican peso debacle and the current Asian tragedy, a world characterized by full capital mobility continues to be not just inevitable but also immensely desirable.[1]

Instead of returning to a world of carefully restricted capital mobility, we are told that the only sensible course before us therefore is to continue working toward unfettered capital flows; the favored solution is to do this principally through the IMF, by turning it even more firmly into an international "lender of last resort" that dispenses bailout funds to crisis-afflicted countries. In fact, while the obligations originally listed for member countries of the IMF in Article VIII of the Articles of Agreement included only "avoidance of restrictions on payments for current transactions" and did not embrace as an obligation or even a goal the embrace of capital account convertibility—which means that you and I, nationals or foreigners, can take capital in and out freely, in any volume and at any time—the Interim Committee of the IMF issued a statement virtually endorsing an eventual move to capital account convertibility by the IMF members, at the Hong Kong meetings last September.

This is a seductive idea: freeing up trade is good, so why not also let capital move freely across borders? But the assertion of the huge desirability of free capital mobility fails to persuade: substantial gains from free factor mobility have been asserted, not demonstrated; the gains

An abbreviated version of this chapter appeared in *Foreign Affairs* 77, 3 (May/June 1998): 7–12. Copyright 1998 by the Council on Foreign Relations, Inc. Reprinted with permission.

from transnational capital flows can be obtained mostly by (direct) equity investment instead; and there are good reasons to believe that even a resource-augmented IMF and attendant changes in its methods of operation will not rule out crises or reduce their costs significantly. The myth to the contrary has been created by what I shall christen, implying not a crude conspiracy but only a nuanced networking ethos, the "Treasury–Wall Street complex," following in the footsteps of my erstwhile colleagues at Columbia University: President Eisenhower, who had talked of the "military-industrial complex," and the sociologist C. Wright Mills, who had written of the "power elite."[2]

Capital Mobility Ideology

Until the Asian crisis sensitized the public to the reality that free capital mobility could repeatedly generate crises and attendant costs, many assumed that free capital mobility among all nations is exactly like free trade in their goods and services, a mutual-gain phenomenon. Hence restricted capital mobility, just like protectionism, is harmful to economic performance in each country, whether rich or poor. That the gains might be problematic because of the cost of attendant crises was not considered.

Now that the crises cannot be ignored, the myth has been weakened and modified to address this problem. It is conceded now that this downside exists. But it is claimed that it can be downsized, if not eliminated, and free capital mobility's immense advantages be enjoyed by all by simply fixing the system. The conservatives would do this by "letting the markets rip," untended by the IMF, which would then be sidelined or even disbanded. The liberals would do it instead by turning the IMF into a supremo, the world's lender of last resort, dispensing funds during crises with conditionalities of several sorts, and overseeing, buttressing, and managing the world of free capital mobility.

It is necessary to understand why the stronger myth, which propelled the above noted adoption by the IMF of capital account convertibility as a sensible goal for all member nations, was just that. True, an economist is certain to say that there is a correspondence between free trade in goods and services, and free factor mobility: interfering with both will surely produce inefficiency losses. But equally, only an untutored economist will argue that, therefore, free trade in widgets and life insurance policies is the same as free capital mobility. Capital flows are characterized, as the economic historian Charles Kindleberger of MIT has noted in an influential work, by "panics" and "manias."[3]

Each time a capital-inflows-related crisis hits a country, it typically goes through the wringer. The debt crisis of the 1980s cost South America a decade of growth. The Mexicans, who were vastly over-exposed through short-term inflows, were devastated in 1994. The Asian economies of Thailand, Indonesia, and South Korea, all heavily burdened with short-term debt, went into a tailspin nearly a year ago, drastically lowering their growth rates. Sure enough, economic "crises" can arise at times without short-term exposure; macroeconomic mis-management in Japan has reduced its growth rate over nearly seven years by now, and Japan is a net lender of capital. But it is a non sequitur to suggest, as the defenders of free capital mobility do, that this somehow undermines the view that short-term borrowings under free capital mobility will be, and have been, a source of considerable economic difficulty.[4]

Downsizing Gains

When a crisis hits, the downside of free capital mobility arises. Martin Wolf has described well the huge gyrations of exchange rates, and re-sulting internal turmoil, that have been imposed on countries that were hit by crises that reversed their short-term capital inflows.[5] To ensure that capital returns, the afflicted country must do everything that is supposed to restore the confidence of those who have taken their cap-ital out. This typically means higher interest rates (as imposed by the IMF on Indonesia), which in turn have decimated in the Asian case the many firms with high debt exposure. It also means having to sell do-mestic assets, greatly undervalued because of the credit crunch, in a fire sale to foreign buyers with better access to funds when, in fact, the conventional advice has been the exact opposite: restrict foreign access to your assets when your credit has dried up but not that of others! Thus, Thailand and Korea have been forced, as if they were actors in the Theater of the Absurd with the IMF playing the role of the Italian Nobel Laureate Fo, to further open their capital markets, even though the short-term capital inflow (resulting from borrowings under a par-tial move to capital account convertibility) played a principal role in their troubles in the first place!

And one should add to such economic losses the loss of political in-dependence to run your own economic policies as you deem fit. That you lose it, not directly to foreign nations, but to an IMF that increasingly is extending its agenda for borrowing nations and is being geared up, at the behest of the U.S. Congress, to invade domestic policies on matters of social policy as well (as with the acceptance by the Treasury of the Frank Amendment which seeks to attach environmental and labor standards conditionalities to the proposed augmentation of bailout funds), is small consolation indeed.[6]

Thus, any nation contemplating the embrace of free capital mobility, as acceptance of capital account convertibility would obviously imply, must reckon with these costs and weight them by the not negligible probability of running into a crisis. The gains from economic efficiency that would flow from free capital mobility, in an impossible but hypothetical crisis-free world, must be set against this loss if a wise decision is to be made concerning the adoption of capital account convertibility.

But I should also emphasize that none of the proponents of free capital mobility have ever estimated the magnitude of the gains from capital mobility that they expect to materialize, even leaving out the losses from crises that can ensue. For free trade, numerous studies have measured the cost of protection. The overwhelming majority of trade economists would judge the flip-side gains from free trade to be significant, lying somewhere between Paul Krugman's view that they are too small to be taken seriously[7] and Jeffrey Sachs's view that they are huge and cannot be ignored. But all we have from the proponents of capital mobility is banner-waving, such as that of Bradford De Long, the distinguished Berkeley economic historian and former deputy to Lawrence Summers at the Treasury:[8]

Now we have all the benefits of free flows of international capital. These benefits are *mammoth*: the ability to borrow abroad kept the Reagan deficits from crushing U.S. growth like an egg, and *the ability to borrow from abroad has enabled successful emerging market economies to double or triple the speed at which their productivity levels and living standards converge to the industrial core.* [italics added]

And of Roger Altman, the investment banker:[9]

The worldwide elimination of barriers to trade and capital ... have created the global financial marketplace, which *informed observers* hailed for *bringing private capital to the developing world, encouraging economic growth and democracy.* [italics added]

These assertions assume, without evidence, that free capital mobility is hugely beneficial, while simultaneously failing to evaluate also its crises-prone downside. But, even a cursory glance at history suggests that these gains may be negligible. After all, China and Japan, both different in politics and sociology, as well as historical circumstance, have registered remarkable growth rates over long periods without capital account convertibility. Western Europe's return to prosperity was also without capital account convertibility. Except for Switzerland, capital account liberalization was pretty slow at the outset and did not gain strength until the late 1980s, and some European countries, among them Portugal and Ireland, did not make it until early 1990s.

Besides, even if one believes that capital flows are greatly productive, an important difference remains between embracing free capital mobility and having a policy of attracting direct equity investment. Maybe the amount of direct foreign investment that a country attracts will be reduced somewhat by not having freedom of capital flows, but there is little evidence for this assertion. Even then such a loss entailed by foregoing free capital movements would be a small fraction of the gains from having a pro–foreign equity investment strategy.

But that brings us to the issue raised by the *weaker myth*: that the downside of the crises under capital account convertibility can be eliminated. We have, of course, heard this assertion before, as each crisis has been confronted, and then we have been hit by yet another one! Like cats, crises have many lives, and macroeconomists, never a tribe that enjoyed a great reputation for getting things right or for agreeing among themselves, have been kept busy adding to the taxonomy of crises and their explanations. None of the solutions currently propounded can give us the confidence that we will finally and fully rid the system of free capital mobility of its crisis-proneness.

Thus, while no one can disagree with Secretary of the Treasury Robert Rubin's contention that greater transparency and reform of the banking systems around the world will help, few should agree with him that this will eliminate the crises that unregulated capital flows inherently generate. Nor can the abolition of the IMF and its "lender of last resort" bailouts eliminate crises be the magic bullet: there were crises before Walter Bagehot invented the domestic "lender of last resort" function for central banks in the nineteenth century.[10] Nor can making the IMF a more powerful lender of last resort kill the crises or give it the nonexistent macroeconomic wisdom to manage them with least cost when they arise.

In short, when we penetrate through the fog of implausible assertions that surround the case for free capital mobility, we realize that the idea and the ideology of free trade and its benefits—and this extends properly to the continuing liberalization of trade in goods and in financial and other services at the World Trade Organization (WTO)—have, in effect, been hijacked by the proponents of capital mobility and used to bamboozle us into celebrating the "new world" of "trillions" of dollars moving across "daily" in a "borderless world," creating gigantic economic gains, rewarding virtue, and punishing profligacy. The pretty face presented to us is, in fact, a mask that hides the warts and wrinkles underneath.

The Wall Street–Treasury Complex

The question, then, is why the world has nonetheless been moving in this direction.[11] The answer, as always, reflects ideology and interests (i.e., lobbies).

The ideology is clearly that of markets, and the steady move away from central planning, overregulation, and general overreach in state intervention toward letting markets function has now reached across many sectors and countries. This is, in my view, all to the good and promises worldwide prosperity. But this tidal wave has also overwhelmed many economists and policymakers into complacency about the pitfalls that certain markets inherently pose even when these were understood in the classroom: free capital mobility is just one supreme example of this unwarranted attitude. Indeed, Stanley Fischer, the deputy managing director of the IMF, admitted as much in a recent appearance on *The Charlie Rose Show* on PBS: yes, he had underestimated the probability of such crises arising in a world of capital mobility.[12]

But interests have also played a central role. Wall Street's financial firms have obvious self-interest in a world of free capital mobility since it only enlarges the arena in which to make money. It is not surprising therefore that Wall Street has put its powerful oar into the turbulent waters of Washington political lobbying to steer in this direction. Thus, when testifying before Senators Hank Brown (Rep.) and Diane Feinstein (Dem.) on the Senate Foreign Relations Committee on South Asia in March 1995, right after the Mexican peso crisis of 1994, I was witness to the grilling of Undersecretary of Commerce Jeffrey E. Garten on why India was not fully open to U.S. financial firms (implicitly, as under capital account convertibility). To his credit, Garten said that this was not an exactly propitious time for the United States to pressure India in this direction!

I should also recall that, right before the same Mexican crisis, the CEO of a major Wall Street financial firm, sitting next to me at the annual dinner of a Washington think tank, lectured me on how Mexico was the best developing country in the world because it had capital account convertibility, so that he could freely take his money in and out. Of course, a few months later, he did take it out, and the rest is history!

Then again, Wall Street has exceptional clout with Washington for the simple reason that there is, in the sense of a power elite à la C. Wright Mills, a definite networking of the like-minded luminaries among the powerful institutions—Wall Street, the Treasury Department, State Department, the IMF, and the World Bank most prominent among them. Even a casual glance will show that Secretary Rubin comes from Wall Street and will likely return there; Roger Altman went from Wall Street to the Treasury and back; Nicholas Brady, President Bush's Secretary of the Treasury, is back on Wall Street as well; Robert Hormats went from State to Goldman Sachs; Ernest Stern, once acting president of the World Bank, now heads J. P. Morgan; James Wolfensohn, an investment banker, heads the World Bank today: one could go on.[13]

This powerful network, which may aptly, if loosely, be called the Wall Street-Treasury complex, is unable to look much beyond the interest of Wall Street, equating it optimistically with world good. Thus, the IMF has been relentlessly propelled toward embracing the goal of capital account convertibility. The Mexican bailout of 1994 was presented as necessary, which was true. But so too was the fact that the Wall Street investors were bailed out as well, which was not. Surely, other policy instruments could have been deployed simultaneously to punish Wall Street for its mistakes but were never considered. Even in the current Asian crisis, our banks could have been all forced to the bargaining table, absorbing far larger losses than they did, but were cushioned by the IMF bailouts where the IMF virtually acted as a lender of first, rather than last, resort: certainly in South Korea.

And despite the evidence of the inherent risks from the crisis-proneness of free capital flows, the Wall Street-Treasury complex is currently proceeding on the self-serving assumption that the ideal world is indeed one of free capital flows, with the IMF and its bailouts at the apex in a role that (it must not be forgotten) guarantees its survival and enhances its status. On the other hand, the weight of evidence and the force of logic points in the opposite direction: toward restraints on capital flows. It is time to shift the burden of proof from those who oppose to those who favor liberated capital.

Notes

1. Sure enough, there are a few cracks. Thus, for example, skeptical views were expressed by me as early as in an interview in *The Times of India* (New Delhi), December 31, 1997; and most recently, a powerful case for regulation of capital flows has been made by Martin Wolf in "Flows and Blows: After the Asian crisis, the question is not whether capital flows should be regulated but how," *The Financial Times*, March 3, 1998. But, as typified by the writings of Stanley Fischer of the IMF and of Lawrence Summers of the U.S. Treasury, also in *The Financial Times*, the preponderant view is the myth I describe in the text.

2. Eisenhower's famous 1961 speech on the military-industrial complex said, among many things, that "This conjunction of an immense military establishment and a large arms industry is new in American experience ... we must not fail to comprehend its grave implications ... we must guard against the acquisition of unwarranted influence, whether sought or unsought, by the military-industrial complex." Cf. Dwight D. Eisenhower, *Public Papers of the Presidents*, ed. Alfred D. Chandler Jr. Stephen E. Ambrose, associate editor. (Baltimore, MD: Johns Hopkins Press, 1970), 1035–1040. C. Wright Mills had written already in 1956 in *The Power Elite*, (London: Oxford University Press), in a far more penetrating and persuasive way of the growth of a powerful elite in the United States. Thus, he wrote: "The conception of the power elite and of its unity rests upon ... coincidence of interests [and also] upon the similarity of origin and outlook, and the social and personal intermingling of the top circles from each of these dominant hierarchies" (292).

3. Cf. Kindleberger, *Manias, Panics and Crashes* (New York: Basic Books, 1978).

4. Cf. Lawrence Summers, "Go with the Flow," *Financial Times*, March 11, 1998. Summers argues that "before we turn the clock back in favour of new controls on foreign borrowing, we should remember that a good number of countries that have recently got into difficulty have been exporting capital."

5. Wolf, "Flows and Blows."

6. I agree with Martin Feldstein's complaints about the IMF's expanding conditionalities in both economic and social directions unconnected immediately with macroeconomic bailout, as expressed in his brilliant 1998 article, "Refocusing the IMF," *Foreign Affairs* 77, 2 (March/April): 20–33. (http://www.nber.org/feldstein/fa0398.html)

7. See his "Protectionism: Try It, You'll Like It," *The International Economy* (June/July 1990): 35.

8. Bradford De Long, "Asia's Flu: A History Lesson," January 11, 1998, from his homepage on the Web site http://econ161.berkeley.edu or email him at delong@econ.berkeley.edu.

9. Roger Altman, "The Nuke of the 90's," *The New York Times* (Sunday Magazine), March 1, 1998, 34.

10. Cf. George P. Schultz, William E. Simon, and Walter B. Wriston, "Who Needs the IMF?," *The Wall Street Journal*, February 3, 1998.

11. This question has been posed also in a recent, splendid analysis by Robert Wade and Frank Veneroso, "The Asian Financial Crisis: The High Debt Model and the Dangers of IMF Strategy," Russell Sage Foundation, Working Paper #128, February 10, 1998. Available from the Russell Sage Foundation, 112 E. 64th Street, New York, N.Y. 10021.

12. In jargon, he referred to "multiple equilibria" as characterizing this market. Indeed, such analysis dates back almost two decades, starting with Robert Triffin's seminal work on capital mobility and its downside.

13. Cf. Mills, *The Power Elite*: "The inner core of the power elite consists, first, of those who interchange commanding roles at the top of one dominant institutional order with those in another" (288); and "As an elite, it is not organized, although its members often know one another, seem quite naturally to work together, and share many organizations in common. There is nothing conspiratorial about it" (294).

2　Why Free Capital Mobility May Be Hazardous to Your Health

Since I am unable to return from Chile in time for this Conference, Marty Feldstein has asked me to put on video my views on Free Capital Mobility (FCM), namely, on full-blooded capital account convertibility, as expressed originally in my May 1998 *Foreign Affairs* article (chapter 1).

Presumably, this is because the article has attracted an inordinate amount of attention. I am told by the *Foreign Affairs* editors, who provocatively titled it "The Capital Myth," that it is possibly the most reprinted and translated economics article in their magazine in recent years. I also notice that, in the latest issue, almost eight months after mine appeared, the IMF has gotten its External Publicity Director, Shailen Anjaraia, to write a rather feeble two-page riposte: a sure sign that the IMF regards the article as particularly potent in view of its being cited by all sorts of G-somethings that are part of the IMF's clients and patrons!

I guess my views concerning the acute problems raised by FCM, and the contrast I raised with free trade (FT), which is free from these problems, are not particularly bizarre or off the curve. Indeed, I have held these "asymmetric" views about FCM and FT for as long as I remember. Indeed, they were expressed, by reference to Chilean experience, in the Report on India's Economic Reforms that I and T. N. Srinivasan prepared for the reformist Indian Finance Minister in 1992–93. But somehow, the public expects that if you are for one sort of globalization, you must logically be for another: that free trade, free DFI, free capital flows, free immigration, free love, free ... whatever should go together! Well, they are wrong.

Based on remarks prepared for the NBER Conference on Capital Controls, Cambridge, Massachusetts, November 7, 1998.

But this *unwarranted link* between FT and FCM is a major source of problems for FT today, as I discover in increasing numbers of debates with FT's opponents such as Ralph Nader just a few weeks ago at Cornell: the sins of FCM are visited on the virtues of FT. Even Dani Rodrik, one of us, in a recent essay in *The New Republic*, seems to draw sustenance illogically from the social consequences of the financial crisis to condemn the "myths and half truths" of FT and for an alleged disregard of the social consequences of FT (which is another matter altogether). And so, FCM has imperiled the cause of FT in an insidious but potent fashion.

The issue of FCM is therefore of great importance. But if I argue that FT and FCM are asymmetric, it does not follow that I am all for capital controls either. I shall take this opportunity to recap and explain my position through a succession of six propositions.

Proposition 1

Although similarities exist, the case for FT is different from the case for FCM. Specifically, capital flows are subject to what Kindleberger has famously called panics, manias, and crashes. In theoretical terms, we would say that destabilizing speculation can, and does, break out where the speculators can emerge unscathed even when they are betting against fundamentals because these fundamentals shift as a result of the speculation, validating the speculation. (The original Friedman argument that destabilizing speculation would punish the speculators is therefore not correct. The first known argument to that effect, I believe, is by Triffin, then by Aliber, and later the argument has been formalized by a number of theorists, principally Maurice Obstfeld, who naturally show that multiple equilibria can obtain in this game.)
    No one of sound mind can seriously sustain the notion that either trade in goods and services leads to such problems or we have the macroeconomic expertise, indeed the alchemy, to eliminate this important, inherent downside of free capital flows.

Proposition 2

Therefore, this downside of FCM must be put against the upside of FCM. The upside consists, of course, of two important and well-known arguments: (1) freedom to buy and sell, as also to move capital, is a value in itself (but, of course, it does not follow that, like the freedom to shout "fire," it must necessarily be left unregulated and unconstrained if the consequences are immensely harmful to society at large); and (2) anytime you free up a market, there is a presumption of dead-weight gain in efficiency.

But two qualifiers must be added. First, Richard Cooper has argued that, drawing on the celebrated Brecher-Alejandro argument, free capital flows in the presence of trade distortions can be immiserizing (or, at least, would have less than apparent value). There are, of course, still many tariffs in place around the world. So, Cooper's caveat certainly has some relevance. I would draw from it the policy judgment, not that FCM is bad, but that it must be preceded by substantial trade openness. I return to this later, arguing that it is better to have many developing countries not yet on FCM to concentrate their energies instead on pushing further toward FT.

Second, as I said in the May/June 1998 essay, the gains to developing countries from capital inflow, and more, can be obtained by encouraging the inflow of DFI, which also brings in skills and technology and is pretty much regarded today, and properly so, as a source of mutual advantage, like FT. DFI can be attracted by granting convertibility to the firm's earnings and capital; this is a much restricted and targeted form of capital account convertibility that does not extend to the ability of nationals and non-nationals to take capital out of a country in any magnitude, or letting firms and banks borrow short-term capital freely, precipitating and intensifying crises. True, if you had the latter, namely, full convertibility, perhaps there might be more DFI; I doubt, however, that this loss is large.

Proposition 3

The gains from FCM, measured at "crisis-free" value, must in any event be set against the expected value of losses during a crisis. The latter obviously reflects the probability of a crisis setting in and the expected value of the losses during the crisis.

Proposition 4

First, what then can we say about the "crisis-free" gains? Here, I am afraid that we have really do not have, to my knowledge, any studies that suggest that the gains from FCM are "mammoth" as Bradford De

Long has argued. I am not suggesting that capital flows, per se, could not have a beneficial effect, ceteris paribus. But even this likely outcome has to be discounted by the fact that inflowing capital may well be put to bad use: a possibility that may be linked to the fact that short-term inflows tend to increase sharply in the presence of unsustainable asset price booms.

Also, the question before us is really not whether capital inflows are productive, but rather whether FCM—namely, capital account convertibility—is associated with rapid growth and prosperity. Here, surely the answer is even tougher to provide. We have had hugely successful economic growth in China and Japan, for instance, without FCM. Dani Rodrik has bravely tried to look at the empirical issue by using multicountry regressions and finds no relationship between capital account convertibility and growth. While I must confess to a prejudice that I find this kind of analysis too unsubtle to have much value—I talk about "endless" regressions, whereas Bob Solow is more brutal and calls them "mindless" regressions—, it may nonetheless be used as one more reason to look some of the more extravagant claims regarding the gains from FCM in the eye.

Second, reinforcing this skepticism about "mammoth" gains from FCM, we would have to reckon also with the fact that, as the latest Asian crisis demonstrates, the probability of being hit by a crisis (once you have FCM and hence the possibility of excessive short-term exposure and associated possibility of herd-behavior-driven panics for instance) is not exactly "low."

Until we have had the new Bretton Woods conference everyone is talking about, and we have decided what is the new international architecture that we are going to have, it is not even clear that much can be done to effectively reduce the probability of being hit by the crises and to increase the efficacy of dealing with them adequately when they arise. The latest IMF/World Bank meetings revealed how much we need to know what the right solutions are and (sadly) how little we know what they are!

Proposition 5

Add to all this the fact that the IMF can, and indeed did in the current Asian crisis, get its conditionality badly wrong as well. I am persuaded by Sachs and Radelet's arguments,[1] and by a recent brilliant essay by Max Corden,[2] that the IMF should not have gone in for deflationary policies but should have instead undertaken a Keynesian-style re-flationary policy to offset the initial and induced deflationary effect of the capital outflow. True, one can make several arguments for what the IMF did; and it is inherent in the macroeconomic game that the assumptions one makes about responses of agents to policies may turn out to be either wrongly signed or badly off on the parameters. But the fact is that the IMF did get things wrong, according to even impartial observers who have nothing against the IMF and do not proceed on the assumption that whatever the IMF does, the opposite must be the right policy.

So, when the crisis hits, you are not even sure that it will not be compounded, instead of being eased, by those whose job it is to assist you! So that increases yet further the likelihood of significant costs from the crisis when it hits you.

But these are only the economic and social disruptions that can get you politically. What happens when the IMF starts telling you to change your "structural" policies, which have little to do with the crisis at hand, or else? When you look at the conditionalities imposed on Indonesia and South Korea, for instance, you can't help but raise this question. Marty Feldstein, in his *Foreign Affairs* article,[3] also greatly influential, raised this question trenchantly. And I agree with his view that this was an unwelcome development. Besides, how does one know that the IMF's judgments about structure were correct, being given to countries whose track record on growth has been so substantial that it has been described correctly as a "miracle"? It needed chutzpah, or deep concession to Washington's longstanding demands to remake Asia in its own image, to ask for these kinds of changes. As Marty has noted, these are questions to be decided by sovereign nations. In short, to the immediate economic costs of wrongheaded early IMF conditionality, we must add the political costs of unjustified loss of sovereignty and even the long-term costs of possibly ill-advised and politically driven demands for changed policies in place of ones that these afflicted nations preferred and may well have aided in producing their high growth rates.

In addition, I must note specifically, as many have, that the IMF's and Treasury's continuous hammering of the theme that these countries were characterized by "crony capitalism," "corruption," "inefficient" policies, and every other sin in the Book of Virtue, to the exclusion of the role played by what I have called the Wall Street–Treasury Complex (in a nonconspiratorial sense), was a self-serving analysis. This only aggravated the panic that started and fueled the crisis; it was thus not merely wrongheaded but also accentuated the problems both for the afflicted countries and, in turn, for the IMF itself.

Proposition 6

So, if we are to draw any lessons concerning FCM at the present time, I would make the following two observations:

First, there are many developing countries that are still not on FCM. The IMF, and indeed the Wall Street–Treasury Complex, had been pushing aggressively for greater shift to FCM. True, the IMF's splendid economists cannot have been unaware of the reasons to go easy on this; but the political pressures and the euphoria were huge enough to make even the IMF drop its guard de facto. I believe that there is now more prudence on this question. So, for these countries, for whom the question is not one of adopting capital controls but of dropping them, I would say: Cease and desist from moving rapidly to FCM until you have gained political stability, economic prosperity and substantial macroeconomic expertise—and not just "transparency" and better banking supervision. Concentrate instead on freeing external trade barriers and implementing internal reforms such as privatization.

Second, for the few developing countries that had embraced FCM more or less, and that have run into the current and the earlier crises, the question is rather different: should they, like Malaysia, make a 180-degree turn and abandon FCM for a slew of capital controls? Here, I incline to an asymmetric answer from that to the preceding question. Using an analogy, I would say that if you have joined the Mafia, you do not go up to Mr. Gambino and just tell him that you are leaving; if you do, you will leave in a coffin. What you do instead is to call up the FBI, get into the witness protection program, and so on. Similarly, the countries already in the FCM game must exercise caution instead of making a U-turn precipitously to capital controls. More specifically, I would distinguish among three groups of countries.

1. Once you have been on FCM more or less, and you experience reversal of capital inflow of the order that added up to over 10 percent of GNP for the five afflicted Asian countries, the main problem surely has to be: how do you get some or most of this capital back in order to ease the inevitably serious problems caused by this huge loss of resources. (If I recall correctly, the income loss imposed by the oil price increases of 1971 and 1973 on OECD countries was of the order of 3 percent of

GNP and was sufficient to unsettle these advanced countries' macro-economics almost through the 1970s.)

So, restoring confidence is essential. Capital controls, especially in a sharp turn, surely cannot provide, and will only undermine further, that confidence in my view. True, as Krugman has reminded the advocates of such a policy, you can lower interest rates with controls and then revive the economy.[4] But, if the diffidence has worsened, who will borrow to invest? I therefore think that Malaysia's option should have been to stay the course and to work with a chastened IMF, which has reversed course and begun to back reflationary policies in the region. And I would advocate the same for all those who are already in the game of FCM in a significant degree and have gotten into trouble.

2. For the countries on FCM that have fortunately not gotten into trouble because they were prudential and watched their short-term debt exposure and regulated it Chilean style as called for, my advice is to stay the course and continue doing more of the same.

3. And for those countries on FCM that have unwittingly managed to avoid getting short-term flows in any significant degree, the best policy advice is to be prudent for the future: introduce monitoring and review of future inflows, while keeping Chilean-style control mechanisms in place for use *as necessary*.

Notes

1. See Steven, Radelet, and Jeffrey D. Sachs, "The Onset of the East Asian Financial Crisis." Working Paper #W6680. Cambridge, MA: National Bureau of Economic Research, 1998. (http://papers.nber.org/papers/W6680.pdf)

2. See Max Corden, "The Asian Crisis: Is There a Way Out? Are the IMF Prescriptions Right?" Mimeo, School of Advanced International Studies, Johns Hopkins University, 1998. (http://www.sais-jhu.edu/faculty/econ/crisis.pdf) Reprinted in *The Asian Crisis: Is There a Way Out* (1998). Singapore: Institute of Southeast Asian Studies.

3. See Martin Feldstein, "Refocusing the IMF," *Foreign Affairs* 77, 2 (March/April 1998): 20–33. (http://www.nber.org/feldstein/fa0398.html)

4. See Paul Krugman, "Saving Asia: It's Time to Get Radical," *Fortune*, September 7, 1998. (http://www.fortune.com/fortune/investor/1998/980907/sol.html)

3   Free Trade, Yes; Free Capital Flows, Maybe

The Asian, and now international, financial crisis has led to a perception that the financial system has put capitalism itself at risk. Because of the role short-term capital flows played in precipitating the Asian crisis, many critics are calling for capital controls. Free-market types largely reject the idea of capital controls, seeing it as a form of protectionism. But the case for free capital flows and the case for free trade are not identical.

In fact, there is no compelling reason why if one is for free trade, one should also be for free direct foreign investment, or for free capital flows, or for free immigration, or for free anything for that matter. For reasons both political and economic, these different policies should be considered separately. The political point is obvious: The difficulties in winning support for free trade, free direct foreign investment and capital inflows, and free immigration rise as we go down that list.

On the economic dimension, free trade and free capital flows have striking differences, not just similarities. These differences reflect a unique downside to a policy of free capital flows.

Freedom to Transact

The similarities between both policies are well understood. They relate to the upside of both trade and capital flows. Freeing both affirms the freedom to transact where and how one wishes. At the same time, any time you segment a market, you lose efficiency. Barriers to capital mo-

---

bility thus carry the presumption of economic losses, just as barriers to trade do.

But here's the downside: Capital flows are subject to what the economic historian Charles Kindleberger of MIT has called "panics, manias and crashes." In a classic response to these concerns, Milton Friedman famously argued that speculative flows would tend to be "stabilizing," hence welfare-enhancing, because the speculators who betted against "fundamentals" would be wiped out in the marketplace. But the unfortunate fact is that speculation can be self-justifying: The fundamentals may change to reflect the speculation. Is this not what most likely happened when, out of panic, investors fled from what they perceived as weakened Asian economies, weakening them when they were originally strong?

The case for free trade is overwhelmingly powerful, thanks to both economic logic and the empirical demonstration of the postwar success with outward trade orientation. But if we are to back free capital mobility with the same confidence, we have to be assured on two counts. First, the costs of these crises should not be of the order seen in Indonesia. Second, the probability of such crises must be greatly and credibly diminished.

The costs of the crises to date have been unusually large. They were huge in Asian countries because substantial short-term inflows suddenly went into reverse. For the five countries—Indonesia, Malaysia, the Philippines, South Korea and Thailand—the effect was a loss of resources estimated at over 10 percent of their combined gross domestic product. Just recall the macroeconomic difficulties the United States went through in the 1970s, as increased oil prices led to a reduction in the nation's resources that was a mere 3 percent of GDP.

As these countries (except Malaysia) turned to the IMF, matters worsened. Excessively deflationary, and ignoring the strong fundamentals of basically sound economies, the IMF should have instead counseled reflation. So, to the inherent costs of a crisis, there were added the gratuitous costs of mistakes by those whose job it is to assist during crisis.

But that is not all. The IMF fueled the panic by extravagant charges of "crony capitalism," "corruption" and every other sin in the Book of Virtue, going on to insist on "structural" reforms that had little to do with the crisis. So it also began the era of unwarranted intrusion into economic choices that are properly within the crisis-afflicted countries' sovereign domain.

But if these economic and political costs of crises are big, the chance of successfully changing the Bretton Woods infrastructure to make such crises improbable is small. The recent IMF-World Bank meetings in Washington revealed agreement on the easy issues. Who could oppose apple-pie demands for "transparency" and better banking standards and supervision? But it also demonstrated fundamental division on difficult issues, such as the choice between fixed and flexible exchange rate regimes as antidotes to financial and currency crises, and whether the IMF is the problem (as former Secretary of State George Shultz and economist Allan Meltzer argue) or the solution (as Treasury Secretary Robert Rubin and his deputy, Lawrence Summers, believe).

Facing this reality, and recognizing that zealous overconfidence in announcing the end of the crises has never been in short supply, I believe that prudence and caution concerning free capital mobility are in order. For many developing countries today, including India and China, the question is not whether to impose capital controls but whether to drop them. To them, I say: Cease moving toward free capital flows until you have political stability, sustained prosperity and substantial macroeconomic expertise. Concentrate instead on internal reforms such as privatization and external reforms such as freer trade. Allow "targeted" convertibility for dividends, profits and invested capital for direct foreign investment. It brings capital and skills and is more stable than short-term capital flows.

For the countries that had already freed capital flows substantially and are currently afflicted by panic-driven outflows, my advice is the opposite: Do not jump into capital controls.

These countries need to restore confidence. The imposition of capital controls, as in Malaysia, would not establish, and could easily undermine, that confidence. True, you can lower interest rates with capital controls and hope to revive the economy quickly. But this textbook analysis ignores the obvious: If diffidence has increased, who will borrow to invest?

Stay the Course

They should rather stay the course, eschewing capital controls whose efficacy, in any event, is likely to be short-lived—since playing the game of capital-account convertibility has already produced players who have the knowledge and expertise to evade the controls.

And when back on track with capital account convertibility, these countries need to learn from their recent afflictions that they must be prudent, watching their short-term debt exposure and being prepared to regulate and moderate it as necessary. In short, gung-ho financial capitalism, letting capital flows rip, is far too risky—a sure-fire way of betting the company.

II

From Miracle to Debacle:
The Asian Drama

4

The "Miracle" That Did Happen: Understanding East Asia in Comparative Perspective

I am honored by the invitation to give the keynote speech at this celebratory conference in honor of Professors Liu and Tsiang.[1] But I am also intimidated. The many distinguished economists assembled here are scholars who know so much more than I do about the subject that I have been asked to address that my participation in the conference will earn me an unrequited transfer rather than mere gains from trade.

Perhaps the most productive task I might undertake would be to address the lively debate in recent years over the issue of the East Asian "miracle," in which Taiwan has been a major player. What factors explain this phenomenon? What lessons can the laggard, reforming countries draw from this analysis? Drawing on a historical contrast between India, whose experience I know fairly well from my own research, and East Asia, whose experience I know almost as well from others' research, I plan to argue the following (among many other things):

• that the contention (by Paul Krugman, drawing on the Alwyn Young calculations of total factor productivity (TFP),[2] but in fact going back, as I say below, to T. N. Srinivasan in his comments, based on Jong-Il Kim and Larry Lau's calculations instead, on the World Bank study of East Asia) that there was no "miracle" misconstrues what is miraculous about the East Asian growth experience;

• that the miracle consisted in the enormous growth in rates of private investment in these countries, to levels that are almost certainly unparalleled in the experience elsewhere, now or historically;

Based on the keynote speech delivered at the Conference on Government and Market: The Relevance of the Taiwanese Performance to Development Theory and Policy, Cornell University, May 3, 1996.

• that this "fundamental" cannot be explained without assigning a major explanatory role to the region's outward orientation, namely, to its "export promoting" (EP) as distinct from an "import substituting" (IS) trade strategy;

• that, in turn, the growth of export earnings also led to this investment being "implemented" with increasing imports of newer-vintage capital equipment, which embodied significant technical change, whose social contribution exceeded its cost, providing therefore a double whammy (i.e., both high rates of private investment induced by exports and returns from technical change embodied in imports) that raised growth to "miracle" levels over a sustained period;

• that the excess of the social contribution by newer-vintage-capital-goods over their international cost was the larger because of the phenomenally high levels of literacy and education that characterized the East Asian countries, thus reinforcing the second source of contribution to growth noted above;

• that direct foreign investment (DFI), like trade, was equally productive in East Asia, reflecting the high returns to the EP strategy, whereas the IS countries both attracted less sustained inflows of DFI and got less therefrom;

• that "industrial policy," or what Alice Amsden has called "getting prices wrong," has little to do with East Asia's growth and may have even harmed it;

• that this mighty engine of growth, based on outward orientation, must be contrasted with the sluggish locomotive that India's IS-strategy-burdened economy registered, to appreciate the thesis I advance; and

• that the East Asian "model" has already been adopted with dramatic results by the NECs, having traveled west from the NICs, and India in South Asia stands poised to profit from a shift to it as the reforms initiated in 1991 are intensified.

A Miracle or Not?

At the outset, permit me to examine the issue whether there was a miracle or not.[3] To my knowledge, many of us christened the East Asian experience of near and actual double-digit growth rates over nearly a quarter century a miracle; and I have often thought that ours must be a dismal science indeed if anytime a country does remarkably well, we call it a miracle!

Some of the recent critics who contend that the East Asian miracle is a myth seem to take the theological view that a miracle is a phenomenon that cannot be explained. Since growth accounting suggests (what cannot but have been apparent to the scholars of East Asia) that the remarkable growth performance can be explained overwhelmingly by high rates of investment, the miracle ceases to exist: a miracle dissolves the way a paradox is lost as soon as it is explained.

But then there are also those who argue more substantively that the central role played by investment and the absence of significant TFP gains in East Asia means that there was no "miracle" in the different sense that we do not need to invoke or infer some silver bullet or an alchemy such as a wondrous "industrial policy" that we must all imitate or Max Weberite "Asian values" to account for East Asia's special performance.

Thus, let me cite T. N. Srinivasan, who fully anticipated the later Krugman contention that there was "no miracle." In a forceful commentary on the draft of the World Bank study on the East Asian miracle, he argued as early as July 1993:[4]

the analysis of Jong-Il Kim and Larry Lau suggests that there was no TFP growth in the NIC's. They conclude that "the hypothesis that there has been no technical progress (or increase in efficie~ ., in the Newly Industrialized countries during the post-war period cannot be rejected. By far the most important source of economic growth ... is capital accumulation accounting for more than 80 per cent of their economic growth." (Jong-Il Kim and Lawrence J. Lau, "The Sources of Economic Growth of the Newly Industrialized Countries on the Pacific Rim," Stanford University (processed), December 1992.) ... Thus, one does not have to look beyond the neoclassical explanations based on fundamentals ... to understand East Asian growth. **There is no mystery or miracle.**

And, in a subsequent letter to Michael Bruno, a few months later, he went on to argue that, therefore, "the 'culture' and 'authoritarianism' hypotheses ... ought to be firmly rejected," and that, in any event, other direct arguments could lead one to reject such "exceptionalism" hypotheses.

Equally, Ian Little, in an illuminating recent pamphlet on the subject, has argued that "exceptionalism" in the shape of "industrial policy" need not be cited to explain the East Asian miracle, given the enormous and conventional role of investment, while also claiming that, as I say below on the basis of his persuasive arguments, direct analysis of the role of industrial policy suggests that it was neither necessary for East Asia's performance nor harmless to it.[5]

My own view is that, even if the TFP calculations are taken seriously, the East Asian miracle, in the sense of "exceptionalism of outcomes" simply gets to be the miracle of East Asia's phenomenal increase in investment rates, namely, it becomes an "exceptionalism of the fundamental of investment."[6] More to the point, since the East Asian investment rate increased in the private sector (whereas similar rises in investment rates occurred in the postwar period in the public sector in the former socialist countries, the latter resulting in blood, sweat, and tears but not in growth), the real miracle that requires explanation is that of the phenomenal rise in private investment rates on a sustained basis to high levels, unparalleled as far as I know in any other region or historical period.

Explaining the Miracle: A Synopsis of My Thesis

In providing this "exceptional-private-investment"-centered explanation, which must be the critical starting point in any explanation of East Asia's miracle or exceptional performance, I will turn today to the region's outward orientation, especially to the adoption of the export-promoting (EP) strategy, and the substantial inducement to invest that the increasingly accessible world markets provided, while contrasting it with the adoption of the import-substituting (IS) strategy in India which, I shall argue, impaired instead the private inducement to accumulate by limiting it to that provided by the demand generated by the domestic (agricultural) growth rate.[7]

In turn, I will also argue that the flip side of the EP strategy was the exceptional export earnings that enabled the increased private investments to absorb increased imports of newer-vintage capital equipment whose social marginal product exceeded their international prices, yielding a "surplus," and hence an added boost to the East Asian growth.

Then again, this surplus must have been increased, and the miracle enhanced, by the increment in the social marginal product resulting from the high levels of primary education and literacy, as also the increases in higher education, that could interact meaningfully with the accumulation and imports-of-embodied-technology process that the outward orientation had unleashed and fed.

Dismissing Conventional Exceptionalism Arguments

But before I develop this argument, let me mention, only to reject, some of the conventional "exceptionalism" arguments that surface from time to time, especially those concerning the region's authoritarian politics, Confucian culture, or industrial policy.

The exceptionalism cited to explain away the East Asian performance has taken some strange forms. For instance, it used to be asserted that Hong Kong and Singapore were small "city states" and therefore somehow not subject to the economic laws applying to other "normal" nations. Of course, many nations around the world are even smaller on dimensions such as population. Again, coming from India, I recall exceptionalism being applied similarly to explain India's lack of performance: we were an exceptionally "large" country, so what could we expect? Of course, we then had to contend with Brazil and, now, we see China, which is even larger (in population), pushing ahead rapidly. But the less outrageous claims of exceptionalism are no more persuasive.

Authoritarianism

The commonest and superficially plausible assertion, of course, is that East Asia prospered because it had authoritarian rule and that democracy is inimical to growth. It is hard to see authoritarian rule, however, as either a necessary or a sufficient condition for efficiency or for growth. Indeed, the historical record, as well as recent postwar experience across nations, underlines the tenuous, even false, nature of such claims.

I suspect that these claims were a result of the Harrod-Domar style of thinking when the postwar period of planning began.[8] If one treated the marginal capital-output ratio as more or less a technological parameter, as the major development economists of the time such as Paul Rosenstein-Rodan and Jan Tinbergen did, then all policy action was concentrated on raising the average savings rate to increase investment and hence the growth rate.[9] If public-sector saving was considered to be the principal agent for raising the savings ratio, then it was evident that the authoritarian states would be at an advantage over democracies: the former could create the necessary surplus through heroic fiscal efforts that the latter, dependent on popular support, could not.

Interestingly, both the Marxist and the Harrod-Domar models produced the same presumption.

But, of course, the reality turned out to be otherwise. For one thing, the East Asian miracle reflects private, not public, savings and investment: its sustained and extraordinary increase itself must be explained by reference to the East Asian policy framework. At the same time, more generally, the variations in growth performance across countries have tended to reflect not just differences in rates of investment, but also dramatic differences in the marginal capital-output ratio. The latter, in turn, reflects the policy framework and its effects on efficient use of resources. Again, I would argue that the policy framework relevant here includes incentives and democratic processes that both enable and motivate effective participation by the citizenry in the growing economy.

Returning to East Asia, I would still argue that authoritarian structures permitted these countries to make the right policy choices, uncluttered by democratic pressures. So, if I believe that the EP strategy was at the heart of the East Asian miracle, then the choice of this strategy and its execution with a steady hand must be attributed to the authoritarian structures. But the choice of policy by these nondemocratic governments could well have been for the IS strategy, as was the case in many other countries in Africa, Latin America, Eastern Europe, and within Asia itself (as in Indonesia).

I have seen no truly compelling explanation of why the East Asian nations, uniquely among the developing nations at the time, chose the EP strategy, on which I have made plain that I plan to lay heavy duty to explain the miracle. Do not count out luck, however. Pertinent examples include the fact that the economists we honor today happened to render the right advice to Taiwan; that Saburo Okita, as Head of the Economic Planning Agency, propelled Japan itself toward exports-orientation in the late 1950s despite widespread export pessimism; that, by contrast, the influential Indian planner P. C. Mahalanobis in the late 1950s,[10] aided by some of India's distinguished economists, propelled the economy toward the harmful IS strategy precisely by taking export pessimism too seriously.[11]

Did East Asia's proximity to Japan, which has followed a similar EP strategy historically, help by diffusing the ideas more readily to the region? But, if so, why did that influence stop right at the four "little tigers"? Besides, the region is proximate also to China which, at least at the time, was considered with India to be a potential superstar in development, so that the IS strategy might have been considered to be equally diffusible to East Asia!

Similar objections can be raised against the hypothesis that these were "island" economies that "naturally" looked outward, like Japan, and thus embraced the EP strategy. Have we not heard of Jamaica under Manley or of Indonesia under Sukarno and the early Suharto? If all these hypotheses collapse under the weight of scrutiny, it is easy to understand the implausibility of the more farfetched contention that authoritarianism explains the choice by East Asia of the EP strategy; nothing more needs to be said on the subject.

Confucian Values

The notion that "values" have provided the necessary fuel to ignite the East Asian miracle has appeal to the Webcrites and to Prime Minister Lee Kuan Yew of Singapore. It is not that values *don't* matter in affecting economic performance: that would be a vulgar and untenable position to take. The problem is rather that the very same Confucian values that were supposed to be a hindrance to development in the Far East are now advanced as having been the engine of growth there: an ex post explanation that seems contrived rather than compelling. Indeed, culture and values rarely seem to provide a strong causal explanation of economic performance and are generally overwhelmed by conventional economic factors in producing or inhibiting economic performance.

Thus, contrast South with North Korea: surely both had identical values at the outset. Or compare East and West Pakistan, both Islamic: the contrasts in their performance before the creation of Bangladesh were striking. Or array the European and Latin American Catholic countries on their growth rates in the postwar period: the differences among them are again quite striking, just as they are among the aggregated Christian countries.

Moreover, an acquaintance with the literature on what the culturalists have said about the critical importance of culture and values to development will make economists generally skeptical of the assertions in regard to the claims in behalf of cultural determinism and its iron grip on development. In particular, many of these claims turn out to be specious, the alleged differences being themselves a product of differences in economic opportunity and circumstance. Thus, for example, in the context of Japan, James Fallows had argued, in a series of influential articles on Japan where he sought "containment" of Japan and (citing Rudi Dornbusch's earlier proposal in the New York Times to give Japan import targets and to whip it with across-the-board tariffs in case of noncompliance) asked for punitive tariffs on Japan of 20–25 percent,[12] that one cannot expect Japan to open markets through rules and must instead impose import targets (i.e., VIEs) on them because the Japanese are not into abstract thinking and prefer to deal with concrete quantities (such as VERs in trade) rather than rules (as at the GATT). Of course, as anyone familiar with Japanese trade history knows, the VERs were imposed on Japan, starting in the 1930s, because we did not wish them to trade by rules: their exports were growing too fast for our industries' comfort. The Japanese learned to trade by quantities rather than by rules, because we would not let them export by rules: it was our demands, not their culture, that was the culprit.[13]

Let me also cite my favorite quote on misguided cultural inferences. In 1915, an Australian productivity expert invited to Japan had the following to say to the government about the Japanese work force:

My impression as to your cheap labor was soon disillusioned when I saw your people at work. No doubt they are lowly paid, but the return is equally so; to see your men at work made me feel that you are a very satisfied easy-going race who reckon time is no object. When I spoke to some managers, they informed me that it was impossible to change the habits of national heritage.[14]

Such examples could be multiplied readily from our own time, of course.

Industrial Policy

It is harder to dismiss, however, the exceptionalism attributed by some, especially Robert Wade and Alice Amsden,[15] to the industrial-policy interventions of East Asia. I do think that there is a beneficial role to be assigned to governmental interventions in the East Asian miracle, in the early take-off period of the 1950s when these economies (as also India) were being kicked up into a bastardized, Rosenstein-Rodan-Vishny-Schleifer, superior equilibrium, as I will argue below. However, the notion that interventions, especially in the nature of industrial policy, played a systematically beneficial role for decades thereafter (and furthermore that outward orientation played a passive, not an active, role in explaining export and economic performance) is not persuasive to me, though it has gained my colleague Dani Rodrik as a convert or, perhaps I should say, as a victim.

With Alice Amsden at this conference, I realize that I am bearding the lion in her own den, if I may mix my metaphor genderwise. But let me make two critical observations. First, even if industrial policy was important, her phrase that it amounts to "getting prices wrong" is inappropriate. Two propositions are essential to making good policy: one must always get one's prices right; and, in the presence of market failures, the right prices that economists call shadow prices will generally differ from market prices. To combine those propositions into the proposition that one must generally get prices wrong (because presumably there are market failures) is to add two positives to get a negative: a generally invalid procedure despite the philosopher Sidney Morgenbesser's classic response in rich Yiddish to Noam Chomsky (when Chomsky argued that two positives did not make a negative in any language): Ya, Ya?

But linguistics aside, I have a more serious reservation. Of course, contrary to the claims made by the revisionists who embrace industrial policy, the fact that the East Asian superperformers, with the exception of Hong Kong, had interventions, including in the credit and trade markets, was familiar to many of us who wound up assigning little role to this bit of information in the well-known OECD studies directed by Ian Little, Maurice Scott, and Tibor Scitovsky in the late 1960s and in the NBER studies in the early 1970s directed by me and Anne Krueger. We may have been wrong, but we were certainly not ignorant.

The real issue is therefore whether these interventions can be regarded as having had a substantial, and a positive, effect. Here, the Bhagwati-Krueger NBER project finding for South Korea was that, when quantified into ad valorem equivalents—a procedure I admitted was not very satisfactory from an analytical viewpoint—the diverse quantity interventions and subventions did not significantly alter the pattern of incentives that world market prices would have provided.[16]

The World Bank analysis of the East Asian miracle[17] has subsequently argued that, contrasted with expectations of sectoral patterns predicted from endowments (as estimated in ways that can be disputed), there is no conclusive evidence that the sectoral developments were different from the predictions and, for South Korea, the evidence is conclusively so since the sectors growing most during 1968–1988 were the labor-intensive ones whereas the governmental interventions were, if anything, in favor of other sectors. The World Bank study thus concluded: "The quantitative importance of government intervention to alter the structure of production is not confirmed at the sectoral level."[18]

This conclusion, of course, is correct as a "central tendency" and does not mean that specific sectors were not influenced by the activist industrial policy. Thus, Little has argued that "common sense tells one that the timing, scale and pattern of investment in heavy industry— especially cars, shipbuilding, and petrochemicals—was markedly different from what would have occurred under laissez faire (or under some non-selective industrial promotion)." It is pertinent therefore that the sectors favored by the industrial-policy proponents in South Korea are precisely the ones with lagging productivity performance. Little quotes the recent Dollar and Sokoloff finding that "TFP growth in the most capital-intensive sectors (many the object of industrial policy promotion) was less than half that in the most labor-intensive sectors. Electrical goods; rubber, leather and plastic products; furniture; and clothing and footwear all show above average TFP growth."[19]

In addition, I find particularly compelling Little's qualitative arguments, based on his intimate knowledge of Taiwan and South Korea, which militate against the thesis that industrial policy was both comprehensive and, where applied, also beneficial. Thus, let me cite just a few of the many telling examples he gives for South Korea, right after he has measured the social returns from Korean heavy industry and found them to be "bad news for heavy industry fundamentalists, and those who stress the importance and value of the government's industrial policies":[20]

In 1975 I led a small team which investigated on behalf of the Asian Development Bank the performance of 28 randomly selected medium-size firms which had received loans from the Medium Industry Bank. Since the bank was government-owned it might be thought that our sample firms were selectively promoted. This was not so. The government's guidelines to the bank gave priorities which covered every kind of industry except non-traded luxury consumer goods. (The bank agreed that confectionery was probably the only exclusion.) This, incidentally, suggests that the extent to which the government directed finance (because it owned the banking system) is sometimes exaggerated by the revisionists.

The main steel company, POSCO (the only important state enterprise in the industries mentioned), has had low financial returns throughout its 20 year life despite heavy subsidization of its non-traded inputs, including the real interest rate which has been negative throughout most of its life. It has also received protection (the import tariff on steel was 25% until recently). Despite this, pre-

tax income as a percentage of assets averaged only 4.6% from 1973–87....
POSCO may even have had negative social returns.

I find myself therefore in sympathy with Little's conclusion that industrial policy in South Korea cannot be regarded as successful. His retort to Wade seems quite persuasive to me:[21]

[The revisionists] do not question the proposition that industrial policy was successful [because government leadership fixed some market failure or another]. To quote Wade (1990, pp. 305–6): "... the balance of presumption must be that government industrial policies, including sectoral ones, helped more than hindered. To argue otherwise is to suppose that economic performance would have been still more exceptional with less intervention which is simply less plausible than the converse." Since the less interventionist Hong Kong, Singapore, and Taiwan grew faster than Korea, it is unclear why Wade thinks it simply less plausible that less intervention would have been better, given also the widespread failure of government industrial policies elsewhere. I find it simply more plausible that Korea grew fast despite its industrial policies, than because of them.

Why the Miracle Happened

So, having assessed and found unpersuasive the three most popular views about the miracle's source, let me turn to my own thesis, which I sketched earlier.

I must confess that it was suggested to me while contemplating the contrasts between the Indian and the East Asian experience. I hope to persuade you that this sort of "comparative economics" is revealing in a way which many-country regressions (regressing, say, growth rates in 100 plus countries on proxies for natural resources, openness of the economy, and others on the RHS of the estimated equation) are not. I find it difficult to see what I can reliably learn by putting Poland, Outer Mongolia, Venezuela, India, and Singapore, among many others, on one regression line. While running such regressions can be suggestive of hypotheses one has not thought of, I am afraid that their ability to persuade is crippled by the twin facts that the cross-country data are generally not conceptually commensurate and comparable whereas the context within which these data must be understood and assessed is vastly different across countries. The inevitable destiny of such regressions across 100-plus countries is thus to be dismissed by serious scholars as irrelevant when they do not conform to one's intuitions and theories, and to be cited as corroboration when they do.

I believe that the stylized "story" of the East Asian miracle, and its absence in India, can be told in two phases. I emphasize the fact that my account is a sketch of what I think to be the essential elements of the analysis; it therefore builds on stylized facts as I understand them, whereas a complete account would have to bring in many details that I cannot possibly encompass or even claim to know.

Phase 1

The first phase of enhanced Indian, and East Asian,[22] growth during the 1950s must principally be explained, I believe, by reference to the Rosenstein–Rodan argument that has now been formalized by Vishny and Shleifer in their important article in the *Journal of Political Economy* as a case of multiple equilibria. In his classic 1943 *Economic Journal* article, arguably the most beautiful piece of creative writing on development, Rosenstein-Rodan contended that for developing countries stuck in a Nash equilibrium with low levels of investment, there existed a superior cooperative equilibrium with higher levels of investment and growth.

The Indian planners, in formulating the First Five Year Plan (1951–56), basically were exploiting this insight. This was an indicative plan, without the straitjacket of controls and targeted allocations that would presumably reflect the contours of the superior equilibrium. In fact, it is absurd to imagine that anyone, either in India or East Asia, could have worked out such a Rosenstein-Rodan-Vishny-Schleifer equilibrium even if there had been complete information to do so! What did happen instead was that the large component of public spending on infrastructure that was built into these indicative programs made the government's commitment to kicking the system up into some bastardized version of the Rosenstein-Rodan-Vishny-Shleifer equilibrium quite credible to the private sector, triggering the self-fulfilling private-sector investment response that lifted the economy into higher investment and growth rates.[23]

Phase 2

But, at the end of the 1950s, the policies of the two regions diverged in ways that would set them apart dramatically in their economic performance. The critical difference was that India turned to the IS strategy, East Asia to the EP strategy.

1. *Inducement to Invest:* India thus handicapped the private inducement to invest, while East Asia wound up enhancing it. India turned inward, starting with the balance of payments crisis in 1956–57, which precipitated the imposition of exchange controls that then became endemic to the regime, reflecting the currency overvaluation that implies the effective pursuit of an IS strategy. Again, the explicit pursuit of an IS strategy was also desired, reflecting the economic logic of export pessimism that characterized the thinking of India's planners.

The result was that the inducement to invest in the economy was constrained by the growth of demand from the agricultural sector, reflecting in turn the growth of that sector. But agriculture has grown almost nowhere by more than 4 percent per annum over a sustained period of over a decade, so that increment at the margin in India's private investment rate was badly constrained by the fact that it was cut off from the world markets and forced to depend on inevitably sluggish domestic agricultural expansion. Thus, it became customary for Indian economists to talk about "balanced growth" and about the problem of raising the investment rate that, by the mid-1980s, was still in the range of 19–20 percent.

By contrast, the East Asian private investment rate began its takeoff to phenomenal levels because East Asia turned to the EP strategy. The elimination of the "bias against exports," and indeed a net (if mild) excess of the effective rate for exports over the effective exchange rate for imports (signifying the relative profitability of the foreign over the home market), ensured that the world markets were profitable to aim for, assuring in turn that the inducement to invest was no longer constrained by the growth of domestic market as in the IS strategy. Private domestic savings were either raised to match the increased private investment by policy deliberately encouraging them or by the sheer prospect of higher returns.

This argument is not easy to defend once you face up to what my former student Don Davis, now at Columbia, has called the "tyranny of Stolper-Samuelson": for, when this theorem holds, wages and rentals on capital are inversely related.[24] When exports are labor intensive, the EP strategy may be expected to raise the wage of labor but depress the return to capital, thus depressing, not raising, the inducement to invest. Clearly, therefore, the force of the Stolper-Samuelson argument must be broken, as indeed it can be by relaxing one or more of the assumptions underlying that theorem.

Thus, Davis suggests that the forces of comparative advantage may be argued to have been sufficiently strong as to make East Asia specialize in the production of the labor-intensive goods. This "decouples factor returns from the factor price frontier for the capital intensive good, leaving wages and rentals dependent only on productivity in the labor intensive good and the price of that good. In moving from autarky to free trade, both factor prices can rise, inducing an accumulation 'miracle.'" Another way out would be to assume productivity differences across countries, as in Ricardian theory. In this case, "if we assume that the relative productivity gap of East Asia relative to the rest of the world is largest in the capital intensive sectors, and that trade serves to close this gap, then it is again possible for both wages and rentals to rise."[25]

While it is possible therefore to formalize the argument I have made that the EP strategy increased the inducement to invest, I must also address Dani Rodrik's recent objection that exports were a relatively small part of the economy at the outset so that EP strategy could not have resulted in any significant impact, and therefore the source of the investment must be found in governmental subventions and interventions whereas the growth of trade is simply a passive result of the growth induced by these other factors. But this argument is totally unpersuasive because East Asia would have run into precisely the problem of demand constraint that India was afflicted with if an IS strategy had been followed, with the efficacy of these other policies in generating investment seriously impaired. Moreover, the ultra-EP strategy, with its mild bias in favor of the export market and the policy-backed ethos of getting into world markets, meant that the export incentives must have played a major role in influencing investment decisions, not just in the exporting industries, but also in the much larger range of nontraded but tradeable industries.[26] In any event, the growth of exports from East Asia was so phenomenal that the share of initial exports in GNP quickly rose to levels that would lay Rodrik's objection to rest, even if it were conceptually correct.

2. *The Imports of Newer-Vintage Equipment:* The flip side of the process was, of course, the generation of substantial export earnings that enabled the growing investment to be implemented by imports of equipment embodying new technical change.

Now, if the social marginal product (SMP) of this equipment exceeded the cost of its importation, a "surplus" would accrue as an income gain to East Asia and would also, as I argue below, boost the growth rate. For this argument to hold, however, the international cost of the newer-vintage equipment must not reflect fully its SMP for East Asia. In a competitive international market for equipment, therefore, I must assume that East Asia was a small player whose higher SMP did not pull up the world price to reflect the higher SMP—namely, that East Asia could, even without "piracy" and "theft" of intellectual property (which was widespread in the region until the new WTO regime), get embodied technology at bargain prices. This seems a reasonable assumption to make, especially when one sees that the world prices of the last-but-one vintage equipment fall drastically due to rapid obsolescence in the presence of quick product innovation: just think of your PCs. (To understand fully the foregoing point, note that an economy in 1970 such as Soviet Russia's, which was confined to using its own 1930s-vintage technology in equipment, would not lose to East Asia, which could use 1960s technology that was heuristically twenty times more productive if East Asia had to pay twenty times more for it. The surplus arises because East Asia pays, say, only five times as much in world markets for equipment that is twenty times more productive in East Asia.)

This argument is illustrated in figure 4.1 in a simple diagram, with the SMP curve for increasing imports of the vintage capital equipment for East Asia put against the international cost of importing it, the striped area then representing the surplus that accrues to East Asia.

But there may also be another reservation about this argument's effect on the growth rate, as distinct from its effect on income. It is fair to say that, thanks to the focus on the steady state in Solow-type models, it has now become fashionable to assert that the gains from trade, like any allocative efficiency gains, amount to one-time gains, not affecting the growth rate. This is, however, wrongheaded as a general assertion. Thus, consider the simple Harrod-Domar corn-producing-corn growth model with labor a slack variable. If allocative efficiency regarding land use (say, from one inefficient farm to another efficient farm) leads to a greater return to the total amount of ("invested") corn being put into the ground, the marginal capital-output ratio will fall, ceteris paribus, and lead to a permanently higher growth rate. Similarly, it takes no sweat for a first-rate theorist to construct models where trade in capital goods leads to higher growth rates, without building in externalities and relying exclusively on the fact that they can be imported more cheaply than constructed under autarky.

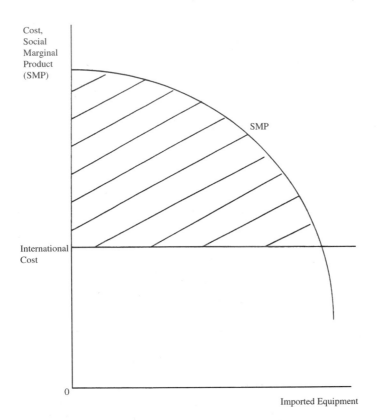

Figure 4.1

T. N. Srinivasan has extended the Mahalanobis-type putty-clay model to include trade and demonstrated precisely this.[27] Thus, he assumes (in place of just one capital and one consumer good in the autarkic version) that there are two of each class of goods, with the marginal product of capital constant in each sector as in the Harrod-Domar model. The social utility function and the function that transforms the output of the two investment goods into aggregate investment are Cobb-Douglas. There is no intersectoral (i.e., between the consumer goods and the capital goods sectors) as opposed to intrasectoral (i.e., between the two goods in each sector) mobility of capital: this is the clay assumption.

Assuming that all four goods are produced under autarky, that free trade is undertaken at fixed terms of trade, and that the share of investment going to augmenting capacity in each of the two sectors is fixed exogenously, Srinivasan then demonstrates plausibly that free trade in consumer goods (but with autarky continuing in investment goods) will raise welfare relative to autarky but not affect the growth rate of income or utility. On the other hand, freeing trade in investment goods will have a positive effect on transitional as well as on long-run (steady-state) growth effect, and also a beneficial welfare effect relative to autarky. The vulgar belief that trade gains cannot affect the growth rate is thus disposed of easily.

However, how does one reconcile the "surplus" argument with the findings that TFP growth has been a negligible factor in East Asia? So, is my story plausible but not borne out by the facts, as is often the case with our most interesting theories? I think not.

Consider the case where the imported equipment is twenty times more productive in period 2 than in period 1, but where its price is only five times as high. If the valuation of this equipment is at domestic (producer) opportunity cost, as it should be, then it will indeed be priced twenty times higher than the older-vintage equipment of period 1. Thus the measure of capital contribution at the level of the industry will rise commensurately, and I presume that the estimated TFP growth in the industry will be zero: in that case, my thesis about the surplus is totally compatible with measured TFP emerging as negligible. But, of course, if the equipment is priced at its international cost, then I presume that TFP growth will pick up three-fourths of the gain that accrues from the "surplus" of SMP over the international cost. My guess then is that, in East Asia, the former was the case. This might have been, not because the accountants were smart and valued period 2 equipment at domestic opportunity cost, but because I guess that much of the imported equipment may have gone through importing trading firms that collected the three-fourths premium rather than the producing firms.

Literacy and Education

The role of literacy and education comes in precisely at the stage of the second step in my story above. For, the productivity or SMP of the imported equipment would be greater with a work force that was literate and would be further enhanced if many had even secondary education. Thus, as shown in figure 4.2, the SMP curve could shift to the right with literacy and education, leading to greater surplus for any given international cost of newer-vintage equipment.

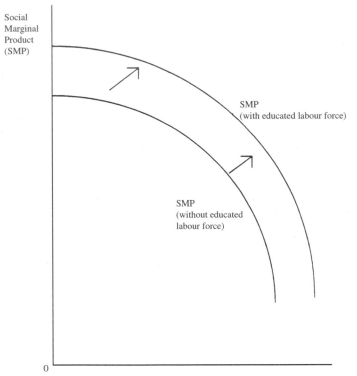

Figure 4.2

Here again, there will be much that is scholarly on this subject at the conference, but I may cite Little using the pretext that a lecture justifies the informality of argumentation that a conference paper does not:

It was largely from the experience of conducting this [1975, South Korean] survey, involving visits to the [28 randomly selected] firms ranging from 1.5 to 3.5 hours, that my own impressions of such matters as the acquisition of technology and skills on the part of the labour force... were formed. I also visited a number of high exporting medium-size labour-intensive firms in Taiwan in 1976.... Two points are mainly relevant in the present context. First the technology was simple, non-proprietary and easily acquired... Secondly, both Korean and Taiwan workers were very quick to learn. Employees would usually reach the expected high level of productivity within a few weeks. This would probably not have been the case if the standards of primary education had not been high. (P. 23)

Of course, as these economies grew rapidly, the demand for secondary and higher education in turn would rise, and a virtuous circle would follow: primary education would enhance the growth that the EP strategy brought, whereas the enhanced growth would demand and lead to a more educated work force. Therefore I see primary education and literacy as playing an enhancing, rather than an initiating, role in the EP-strategy-led East Asian drama, again contrary to what I think Dani Rodrik has suggested in yet another analysis of the role of education in development.

Thus, my story combines in its own way three major elements, in that order: (1) the enhanced inducement to invest due to the EP strategy; (2) the benefit from the surplus of domestic SMP over international cost of imported newer-vintage capital equipment; and (3) the raising of this SMP by the presence of a literate workforce. But if the main plot is this, the story has doubtless many subplots. I will end on just one of them, especially as the analysis dates back to the early 1970s and to the Bhagwati-Krueger NBER project, underlining the richness of the argumentation at the time that is hard to find in the somewhat caricatured accounts provided in the revisionist critiques.

Direct Foreign Investment (DFI)

First, in my synthesis volume[28] for the NBER project findings, I had noted that among the advantages of the EP strategy, which the project had found beneficial, one had to count the fact that trade barriers-jumping DFI in the IS countries was likely to be limited in these countries by the size of the domestic market by which it was motivated —there are shades here of the inducement-to-invest argument I have made today, but only in the faintest strokes. Second, such DFI as was attracted in the IS countries was also likely to be less productive because it would be going into economic regimes characterized by significant trade distortions that could even generate negative value added at socially relevant world prices—a possibility that was discussed by me (based on an extension to the DFI issue of the contribution by Harry Johnson to the theory of immiserizing growth in tariff-distorted economies)[29] and then nailed down into a certainty under certain conditions in well-known articles by Hirofumi Uzawa and by Richard Brecher and Carlos Diaz Alejandro independently.

I did say earlier that we all cite the many-country regressions when they go our way. So, let me mention that both these (thoroughly plausible in terms of their economic rationale) hypotheses have been examined, with some success, in cross-country regressions by another former student of mine, V. N. Balasubramanyam and his co-authors.[30] So, this element of explanation may also be added to the explanation of East Asia's superior performance relative to that of the IS-strategy-plagued countries.[31]

The Westward Diffusion

So, I conclude by noting that the East Asian alchemy seems to have been traveling westward, lifting the economic performance of countries such as Indonesia and Thailand, and India now seems finally poised, with its economic reforms in the direction of global integration, to profit from it almost a quarter of a century later.

The miracle of East Asia can thus be explained; and having explained it, we can reproduce it. In that sense, it is more magic than miracle. But I will settle for magic, which is no less a spectacle than a miracle, and more consonant with our rational age.

Notes

1. This is the text of the keynote speech delivered on May 3, 1996, at Cornell University. I am thankful for many discussions I have had over the years with Ian Little, Martin Wolf, Don Davis, Vivek Dehejia, Magnus Blomstrom and T. N. Srinivasan on the issues raised by the East Asian experience. In making the final revisions to this chapter, I have also profited from the contributions of many of the participants at the Cornell Conference, among them Irma Adelman, Erik Thorbeke, Arnold Harberger, John Cheh, Larry Lau, Gus Ranis, and Henry Wan.

2. Krugman has advanced this argument in a number of newspapers and magazines, but the chief source is his article "The Myth of Asia's Miracle," *Foreign Affairs* 73, 6 (Nov./Dec. 1994): 62–78.

3. T. N. Srinivasan, "Trade Orientation, Trade Liberalization and Economic Growth," Yale Economic Growth Center, mimeo, 1996, has recently suggested that the characterization of the Far Eastern performance as a miracle owes to Robert Lucas's lecture on "Creating a Miracle," followed by the World Bank's well-known study entitled "The East Asian Miracle," both in the early 1990s. However, Srinivasan is not correct. The characterization of the East Asian experience as a miracle, in the sense of an extraordinary performance, predates Lucas for sure. Thus, writing in the late 1980s in my book *Protectionism* (Cambridge, Mass.: MIT Press, 1988), I myself had remarked on the Far Eastern experience as a miracle, in the context of arguing that everyone tended to see the miracle as produced by their preferred prescriptions: "how could an economic miracle have occurred if policymakers had not followed our preferred policies? Recalling that public goods have the property that I can enjoy them without depriving you of your pleasure, I have formulated the following law: Economic miracles are a public good: each economist sees in them a vindication of his pet theories" 98. I have no doubt that others have also used the word "miracle" in this sense, both generally and in relation to the East Asian experience, much before Lucas and the World Bank.

4. This quote is from a widely circulated internal memo to the team in charge of the World Bank study, dated July 21, 1993. Italics are in the original; boldface has been added.

5. See the recent pamphlet by Ian Little, "Picking Winners: The East Asian Experience," Social Market Foundation Occasional Paper, London, 1996. I consider the subject of industrial policy in depth later in the lecture.

6. In my analysis below, I explain why the inducement to invest was so high as to yield this exceptional investment performance. However, the accommodating increase in domestic savings also had to be remarkable and hence may be treated also as part of the miracle. As far as I can tell, the governments played a role in facilitating this process.

7. This element of my thesis was outlined in a letter to the editor entitled "Private Investment and the East Asian 'miracle,'" The Financial Times (January 15, 1996), apropos of Michael Prowse's column that had mentioned the Krugman views in Foreign Affairs. Krugman is wrong in arguing that there is no miracle in East Asia because the high growth can be explained by reference to "fundamentals" such as investment, while forgetting that the miracle lies precisely in these fundamentals being so exceptional: the fundamentals are themselves to be explained. In drawing an analogy between the USSR and East Asia to argue that the latter will grind to a halt the way the former did, Krugman also misses critically important differences between the two areas. The Soviet growth reflected exceptionally high levels of public saving and investment, set within a policy framework where incentives to use resources efficiently and to innovate (both endogenously and through imported technology via trade and investment) were both crippled, so that we would experience quite rapidly the observed phenomenon of sagging and then sinking growth rates as illustrated dramatically by Padma Desai's figure 1.1 (especially for 1955–1979) in her well-known analysis, Growth Retardation in The Soviet Economy: Problems and Prospects (Oxford: Basil Blackwell, 1987). By contrast, the East Asian experience is strongly built on exceptionally high private investment and saving and high levels of absorption of foreign technology, explaining (in the manner outlined in the text) why the growth process has been sustained over a much longer period and the prospects are equally quite different from those that overtook the Soviet Union.

8. I have developed this theme at greater length in my 1994 Rajiv Gandhi Memorial Lecture, "Democracy and Development: New Thinking on an Old Question," published in a slightly abbreviated version in the Journal of Democracy (October 1995). The full text is published as chapter 40 in my book A Stream of Windows: Unsettling Reflections on Trade, Immigration, and Democracy (Cambridge: MIT Press, 1998).

9. That the marginal capital-output ratio would be constant in the Harrod-Domar model with slack labor force, which would be the case if we also assumed a Lewis surplus-labor economy, is consonant with the point I am making in the text about the capital-output ratio being taken by planners as virtually a technological parameter independent of the policy framework and its effects on efficiency.

10. See, in particular, P. C. Mahalanobis, "The Approach of Operational Research to Planning in India," Sankhya 16, no. 1–2: 3–130.

11. I can testify to Saburo Okita's role personally, having gotten to know him in Tokyo in 1962, and I discussed these questions in depth with him, when he and I were secretaries to the Japanese and the Indian Groups of Wise Men, respectively, to promote Indo-Japanese research collaboration, trade, and investment. Okita was head of the Economic Planning Agency at the time. The Indian economists who worked with models that for-

mally assumed elasticity pessimism to discuss developmental strategy, drawing policy lessons therefrom, and who therefore may properly be credited with the failures of India's developmental efforts, included K. N. Raj and Amartya Sen. For further discussion of the harmful role of economists in misguiding India's economic policy, see my Radhakrishnan lectures at Oxford, *India in Transition* (Oxford: Clarendon Press, 1993).

12. In a *New York Times* op-ed article on February 22, 1996, provocatively titled "What Buchanan Owes Clinton," I noted that Pat Buchanan had picked up his specific trade policy proposals from mainstream policy wonks and others, many uncomfortably close to the current administration. Thus, for instance, Buchanan has asked for a 10 percent across-the-board tariff against Japan, a moderate proposal compared to the 20–25 percent tariff argued for by Fallows, and in a tone that is less alarmist and accusatory than that adopted by the leading Japan-baiting economists.

13. I have discussed this issue in my Harry Johnson lecture, published as *The World Trading System at Risk* (Princeton: Princeton University Press, 1991).

14. See my "Development Economics: What Have We Learnt?," *Asian Development Review* 2, 1(1984): 23–38. Reprinted in Bhagwati, *Essays in Development Economics*. Volume 1: Wealth and Poverty (Cambridge: MIT Press, 1985), 13–31.

15. Cf. Alice Amsden, *Asia's Next Giant: South Korea and Late Industrialization* (New York: Oxford University Press, 1989); and Robert Wade, *Governing the Market: Economic Theory and the Role of the Government in East Asian Industrialization* (Princeton: Princeton University Press, 1990).

16. This finding was based on the South Korea study in the NBER project by Charles Frank, Kwang Suk Kim, and Larry Westphal (New York: Columbia University Press: New York, 1975) and discussed in my overall synthesis volume, *The Anatomy and Consequences of Exchange Control Regimes*, NBER, (Cambridge: Ballinger & Co., 1978).

17. World Bank, *The East Asian Miracle, Economic Growth and Public Policy* (New York: Oxford University Press, 1993).

18. Ibid., 333, quoted in Little, op. cit., 19.

19. Little, op. cit., 19, citing David Dollar and Kenneth Sokoloff, "Patterns of Productivity Growth in South Korean Manufacturing Industries, 1963–1979," *Journal of Development Economics* 33: 309–327.

20. Little, op. cit., 22; the following quotes are from pp. 22–24.

21. Little, op. cit., 12.

22. Phase I may be set in part of East Asia as dating into the early 1960s; but this is a matter of judgment and detail of little consequence to my argument. Besides, phase I may even be considered absent in Hong Kong, which had the unique advantages of an abundant entrepreneurial class and an entrepôt economy that was already outward-oriented from the outset. I might add that the notion that East Asia's investment growth in phase 1 did not depend on outward orientation or EP strategy in trade will come as no surprise to any scholar in the field, though it is sometimes presented as if it were a modern discovery that somehow discredits those who talk of the critical role of EP strategy (which applies, of course, to phase 2).

23. Dani Rodrik seems to share broadly this view of how private investment rose but seems to err in two ways. He seems to suggest, presumably in sympathy with the

Amsden-Wade thinking, that the bureaucrats could figure out the sectoral contours of the superior equilibrium, a presumption that I find ludicrous, especially having seen the best bureaucrats in India confess to their inability to choose industrial favorites on any rational grounds. Moreover, he extends the argument well beyond the 1950s whereas, as I argue later in the text, this makes little sense.

24. I am drawing here on the preliminary draft of Don Davis's paper, " 'Miracles of Accumulation': Models of Trade and Growth in East Asia," Department of Economics, Harvard University, January 1996.

25. Don Davis, ibid., 2. Davis proceeds to formalize these ideas in a dynamic framework, more appropriate to the accumulation problem at hand.

26. Rodrik also seems to think it pertinent that the export incentive, in the shape of the real exchange rate, did not continue improving. However, it is not necessary for it to be improving continuously for the export incentives to operate. Thus, an excess of the effective exchange rate for exportables over that for importables (as distinct from continuous increase in this difference) will suffice to provide a continuing incentive for the export over the home markets. Cf. Dani Rodrik, "Getting Interventions Right: How South Korea and Taiwan Grew Rich," *Economic Policy* 20 (April 1995): 53–101.

27. See his "Comment on 'Two Strategies for Economic Development: Using Ideas and Producing Ideas," by Romer, *Proceedings of the World Bank Annual Conference on Development Economics 1992* (Washington D.C.: World Bank, 1993). Srinivasan also makes the valid point that the Mahalanobis-Feldman putty-clay models are among the earlier examples of "endogenous" growth theory since the growth rate is determined by the discretionary policy choice of the share of investment goods being allocated to the capital goods sector. The neglect of the considerable literature on such models by the originators of the current endogenous growth theorists is to be attributed to the fact that these theorists have come to their models from the Solow model and have no acquaintance with the growth models that came up in the context of developmental problems in the 1960s. Of course, most of us are rediscovering great ideas all the time!

28. Bhagwati, 1978, op. cit.

29. See Jagdish Bhagwati, "The Theory of Immiserizing Growth: Further Applications," in Michael Connolly and Alexander Swoboda (eds.), *International Trade and Money* (Toronto: Toronto University Press, 1973).

30. See, in particular, V. N. Balasubramanyam and M. A. Salisu, "EP, IS and Direct Foreign Investment in LDCs," in A. Koekkoek and L. B. M. Mennes (eds.), *International Trade and Global Development: Essays in Honour of Jagdish Bhagwati* (London: Routledge, 1991), for the former hypothesis; and V. N. Balasubramanyam, M. A. Salisu, and David Sapsford, "Foreign Direct Investment and Growth in EP and IS countries," *Economic Journal* 106, 434 (January 1996): 92–105, for an indirect test of the latter hypothesis (explaining growth as the dependent variable).

31. Of course, as Magnus Blomstrom has reminded me, I should also note that there is considerable evidence at the micro level of beneficial spillover effects from DFI, including from several studies he has undertaken in developing countries. Reconciling this evidence with the contention that there is little evidence of TFP in the Lau-Young type studies remains an unresolved issue, however.

5

The Asian Economic Crisis: What Do We Know Now?

Introduction

The Asian economies have historically been a source of surprise to economists. Just consider two telling examples, one going back to the early postwar years, which few present today were witness to, and the other from the later, recent years we all have lived through.

In the 1950s, nearly all economists thought that the two sleeping giants, China and India, would wake up and become the super-achievers in the quarter century after the end of the Second World War and with the beginning of the new era in the 1950s of determined national and international efforts at accelerated development. Imagine then our astonishment that the winners in the race turned out instead to be the four little tigers of the Far East: Korea, Taiwan, Singapore, and Hong Kong.

Indeed, these NICs, the Asian Four, grew over a long period of nearly three decades at rates that exceeded the wildest expectations of anyone in the 1950s about the maximum potential growth rates anywhere in the world, no matter how splendid the policy framework. It seemed natural therefore to consider the East Asian performance to be one that should be called a "miracle," not in the sense that it was beyond explanation but in the sense that it was off the curve.

But then came yet another surprise. With the financial collapse of Thailand in mid-1997, and its immediate spread to Malaysia, Korea, and Indonesia (these are the new Asian Four, united by profound dis-

Based on the keynote speech delivered at the MITI Research Institute International Symposium, Tokyo, June 16, 1999. It also appears in Japanese, as chapter 1 ("The Asian Economic Crisis: Its Lessons"), in *The East Asian Economies and the Japanese Economy at a Turning Point*, ed. M. Aoki and J. Teranishi (Tokyo: Toyo Keizai, 2000).

tress whereas the old Asian Four were blessed by huge prosperity instead), the Asian miracle turned into an Asian debacle.

No one had predicted this, of course. My brilliant MIT student, Paul Krugman, is regarded as having foreseen the reverse because, in a much-cited *Foreign Affairs* article, he used the econometric work of yet another of my students (at Columbia University), Alwyn Young, to argue (along with Young) that the Asian miracle was a result almost entirely of increased investment. Hence, Krugman drew a parallel with the Soviet Union's decline (a matter that itself is dubious since distinguished experts on Soviet decline such as my colleague Padma Desai, the Harriman Professor of Comparative Economic Systems at Columbia University, have argued convincingly that the Soviet decline is far better seen as resulting instead from a progressive decline in technical progress and in economic efficiency), and he argued that increasing accumulation would lead to diminishing returns in Asia and hence to diminished growth rates and the end of the Asian miracle.

But it is wrong to assign prescience to Krugman for predicting the Asian debacle for two compelling reasons:

First, there are strong empirical reasons to reject Young's notion that total factor productivity (TFP) was negligible in the East Asian region as a source of growth. If you periodize the econometrics, it shows that the TFP did in fact increase with time. This is in fact what you would expect: technological maturity increases over time. Japan, for instance, progressed from shoddy manufacture, to quality manufacture, to minor product and process improvements, and, finally, to major ones. Young's work misses this element, I am afraid: the diminishing returns theory is therefore not consistent with the situation as we can see it plainly and as later econometrics seems to underline as well.

Second, and more pertinent, is the fact that Krugman's prediction of diminishing returns to capital accumulation would imply that the growth rate would fall gradually and continuously. Instead, the collapse was sudden, sharp, and discontinuous: and its causes were financial (though there is controversy about whether these were endogenous and internal to the Asian economies, taking the form of crony capitalism and weak financial structures, or were exogenous to them, and a product of speculative panic).

The diminishing returns hypothesis was thus not a plausible prognosis of a diminished Asian future, nor did it have anything robust to do with the grim outcomes since mid-1997. If I may then use a blunt analogy, assigning foresight to Krugman for the Asian debacle is akin to assigning credit to a Jesus freak, who has been walking the streets and declaiming that the end of the world is near because of a Biblical flood, for having forecast the end of the world when the world ends because of nuclear winter!

I say all this, not just to chastise my students, no matter how distinguished, when they go wrong—a habit that dies hard with professors —nor to remind you that economic forecasting, not merely for the short-term, is fraught with hazards, but because the reasons for the Asian miracle and then for the Asian debacle bear directly on the three questions that I wish to address today:

i. What were the causes, and hence what are the lessons for policy, of the Asian debacle both for the current recovery and for appropriate policies to avoid such shocks in the future?

ii. (Related to this), what is the prognosis for the pace of the afflicted Asian economies' recovery? and

iii. Will these economies return to the exceptionally high growth rates that marked the Asian miracle; or will they now rejoin the human race and settle for annual growth rates closer to, say, 7 than to, say, 10 percent on the average?

Since the miracle preceded the debacle, and its explanation has bearing also on the causes of the debacle, it is convenient to begin with the analysis of the last question first. I shall also, in the course of my analysis, have occasion to remark on Japan's economic predicament and the diagnosis and prescriptions that are routinely offered with a view to stimulating recovery.

The Miracle: Its Causes

Asia's miracle was clearly a product of *policy choices*. The remarkably high investment rates noted by many, and the steady absorption of technical progress that sustained these phenomenal growth rates, were a product, in my view, of the outward orientation of these economies in their trade, and for some countries (e.g., Taiwan and Singapore, not Korea), of their pro-DFI (direct foreign investment) policies.

Hong Kong and Singapore were certainly free traders, pretty close to nineteenth-century Britain. True, the others used trade barriers. But the results were still close to those promised by free trade because these countries managed, through other policies, to countervail the chief and fatal flaw of trade protection: namely, that your enterprises get addicted to sheltered home markets and then "goof off" into continuing inefficiency. This countervailing policy was the strong commitment to using export promoting measures such as export subsidies to make the external markets important as well, the continuous political emphasis on reaching world class in quality production, and accompanying emphasis on literacy and higher education as supportive policies.

The *outward trade orientation* furthermore meant that the inducement to invest was not limited by the domestic market, as was the case with import-substitution-oriented economies like that of India. Hence, investment rates could rise to, and be sustained at, much higher levels. With export earnings rising also due to export orientation, this also meant that the high investment took the form of imported capital goods that embodied the evolving technologies abroad, thus adding the benefits of technological absorption to those of capital accumulation. The emphasis on education in turn meant that the new technologies could be handled with great efficacy, and that over time there would also be elements of evolving domestic technical change of various kinds, both resulting in yet higher productivity gains (compared to countries where education was lagging behind).[1] In my view, none of these specific factors have changed for the worse as far as the basic Asian fundamentals are concerned.

In fact, the reason why one might even be more optimistic about the Asian resumption of high growth in the near future is that a segment of the reforms under way, specifically the introduction of better banking and accounting standards with bad debts increasingly targeted effectively for substantial reduction and an enhanced focus on transparency and good governance, should only strengthen the infrastructure within which high growth can proceed in a sustainable fashion.

This is not to deny that there are a few sources of pessimism about the continuation of the model underlying the miracle. One source of pessimism is the fact that the world is currently registering excess capacity in some sectors and a slowed growth in trade, so that, for the immediate future, the possibility of outward trade orientation as the key ingredient in Asian growth strategy is somewhat handicapped. But the postwar period has shown that trade is a pretty resilient phenomenon. The Asian countries, in particular, have demonstrated that markets can be found if there is no defeatism, and India has demonstrated by contrast that defeatism, in the form of export pessimism, is almost always a self-fulfilling phenomenon: if you assume you cannot export, you will not export. So, I would not set my sights for resumed growth, provided that the causes of the financial-crisis-caused debacle are set right.

Again, in a June 3, 1999, interview in Hong Kong with the editors of the *Far Eastern Economic Review*, I was asked by a pessimistic editor: in today's tight markets, should we not worry about the fact that if you export more, I will be able to export less? But that is a fallacy in principle. Unless you are accumulating reserves, if you export more, you also import more. So, as you take away markets, you replace them equally: it is simply wrong to accept one side of the phenomenon and not the other! This is, of course, not to deny the possibility that there could be adjustment problems if the new markets are for things different from the old markets: but that is a different, and far more tractable, problem.

Yet another source of pessimism about Asia's resumption of high growth rate, once the financial crisis is surmounted, comes from the pro-industrial-policy writers such as Robert Wade and Alice Amsden who thought that industrial policy was responsible for the high growth rate and that this will now be eliminated by pressures from the triumphant Americans and the conditionality-driven demands of the IMF. But, paradoxically, it also comes equally from the anti-industrial-policy reformers who feel that these reforms will take a long time to take hold. I believe that both are wrong. As I just argued, the principal driving force behind Asian economic performance lay elsewhere, the role (whether good or bad) of industrial policy, of *chaebols*, of "administrative guidance," of Japanese *keiretsus* and so forth being seriously exaggerated.

Whether these practices stay, and whether in an emasculated or robust mould, is therefore a matter of minor consequence in my view: however, I must say, I am willing to be persuaded by Professor Aoki, my host today, on this issue (though, I suspect that he is likely to side with those who will not immediately dismiss the Far Eastern industrial-organization practices as bad just because of current macroeconomic reverses).

I remain therefore unpersuaded by the notion that Asia's growth rate, once resumed, will run rapidly into diminishing returns. I might also remind the economists who subscribe to that school of thought (or perhaps thoughtlessness) that the interesting question they should ask instead is why diminishing returns did not strike these economies for three decades despite their phenomenal capital accumulation and growth!

The Debacle: Its Causes and Remedial Policies

So, I have answered in the optimistic mode the question of whether the Asian economies can return to fairly high growth rates, once they get past the current financial-crisis-fueled debacle. But how soon will they? The answer to that depends, of course, on our assessment of the causes of the crisis and therefore of the appropriateness of the remedies currently deployed. And then there is the related pair of questions: can similar, debilitating shocks be avoided in the near future? And if so, how?

Let me state at the outset that I subscribe to, indeed was among the earliest economists (in December 1997 in an interview in *The Times of India*, which was widely circulated by Robert Wade on the Internet), to propose that the chief underlying cause of the Asian crisis starting mid-1997 was to be found in the hasty opening to freer capital flows under pressure from what I have christened the "Wall Street–Treasury complex" in my much-cited and translated May 1998 *Foreign Affairs* article, provocatively titled "The Capital Myth" by the editors. Wall Street naturally wished to enlarge its sphere of operations; the U.S. Treasury reflected that lobbying pressure while also succumbing to the "ideology" of the market while forgetting that the capital funds market is not as innocuous as goods markets and needs to be monitored and regulated carefully. There has been a tendency in Washington to pretend that there was no such pressure; but just talk to any developing country's finance minister in the half decade prior to 1997 and you will get plenty of evidence to the contrary. In fact, Barry Eichengreen, the prolific friend of the IMF and of freer capital flows, has come around finally to much of what I had written about the hasty and imprudent opening of the capital account through financial liberalization and of the Wall Street-Treasury Complex's dominant responsibility for that outcome. Let me give some telling quotes:[2]

Only in recent years, in response to pressure from the International Monetary Fund and the United States, have governments (first in Europe and Japan, and later in most emerging markets) abandoned capital controls. The Asian crisis suggests that at least in the case of developing economies, this was a serious mistake.

After Mexico in 1994 and Asia in 1997, do we need a third reminder of the dangers of premature financial liberalization?

Pragmatism is the order of the day. Developing countries are simply not ready for prime time (in freeing up capital flows).

The U.S. Treasury needs to overcome the "Wall Street complex."[3]

This imprudent financial liberalization was followed by dangerous levels of short-term borrowing that, in turn, set up the Asian economies for the debacle. When the panic-driven reversals of the inflows came, amounting to a historically unprecedented levels of resource outflow for the Asian Four in quick succession, the IMF compounded the problem by imposing an anti-Keynesian prescription of high interest rates and deflation. Finally, in a third mistake, the United States and the IMF killed, even at a neonatal stage, the so-called Sakakibara plan to inject up to $100 billion from Japan into the afflicted Asian economies: the reasons were a mix of U.S. hegemonic concerns vis-à-vis Japan, the IMF-Treasury view that the IMF's hegemony to address crises must be left untouched, and the serious misreading of the crisis as one that would be fairly readily fixed anyway (the hubris coming from the success with the Mexican rescue).[4]

How wrong all this was! I am of the view that the U.S. administration really blew it. In fact, it is not unfair to say that Messrs. Rubin and Summers may well have presided over the largest man-made disaster in the world economy since Smoot-Hawley! Today, they are applauded for the turnaround that I shall shortly address: but that is a bit like, if you are a liberal Democrat in the United States, Mr. Kissinger being awarded the Nobel Peace Prize for the end of the war in Vietnam after having first prosecuted it to his countrymen's distraction and rage that is not yet spent.

None of this is to say that there were no weaknesses in the afflicted countries' economies. True, their banking systems were weaker than ours, though we can overdo this since Malaysia, for instance, had excellent standards and expertise. Again, there was indeed crony capitalism around. But neither cronies nor capitalism are unique to Asia: Washington has plenty of cronies around the White House and elsewhere who get a lot of press coverage; and not a week goes past without lurid tales of PAC-money corruption of U.S. politics. Besides, few of these critics who are eager to find scapegoats within these countries for errors of their own can tell us why precisely this crony capitalism could produce or be consonant with rapid growth over decades and suddenly became a cause of economic disaster. Crony capitalism of the Suharto variety is an abomination on grounds of income distribution and democracy; was it really incompatible with economic prosperity?

So, while I am quite enthusiastic about improving accounting standards and about the structural reform of banking systems overloaded with bad debts (caused, not necessarily by some failure hitherto endemic to Asia but by the crisis itself), I see little connection between other reforms such as the privatization of public enterprises and the prevention of financial crises or the recovery from the current one. Indeed, the recovery of South Korea, a little ahead of what had been anticipated last year, is consistent with lack of progress for instance on eliminating *chaebols*, which had been the target of U.S. and IMF criticisms. In fact, here I side totally with Martin Feldstein that the excessive conditionality being imposed by the IMF requiring all sorts of "reforms" is truly absurd, since it is based on a rejection of the "Asian" ways of doing many things when three decades of unprecedented growth under that way of doing things ought to make us at least a little more circumspect in these matters.

In this context, I recall reading in *The Financial Times* last year about Larry Summer's caustic remark about Japan, now regarded as a sorry spectacle but feared as omnipotent in the 1980s that (I quote roughly) "the last time Japan invented anything important was the Sony Walkman"! *The Financial Times* editors had mischievously run alongside that comment a story about how Honda had just announced a new engine that had cut emissions in half. So much for the hasty triumphalism of Washington. And for the resulting IMF's overreach on conditionality.

In my view, among the few robust policy prescriptions of a more general nature that relate to the emergence from the current crisis are the IMF's recognition that a deflationary response to panic-fueled capital outflows is likely to be counterproductive (even when it seems logical to do it in order to attract capital back) and the fortunate reversal of the deflationary policies of the IMF; and a recognition that the use of capital controls in times of crisis is not indefensible. Malaysia has not done dramatically better than, say, Korea with them; but it has not done notably worse either. Besides, Malaysia had to face a hostile IMF and United States; and it also shot itself in the foot by undertaking the ill-advised trial against Mr. Anwar that further alienated world opinion. So, we do not have a "controlled" experiment here of the advisability of using capital controls as a policy response when one has a capital-outflows crisis. Also, if you look beyond Asia, just consider the incredible rapidity with which Russia's IMF loan last year simply drained out in totality: could this have happened if the IMF had been wise enough to advocate the use of temporary suspension of capital account convertibility at the same time?

In addition, we now have an ongoing debate about the relative merits of different exchange-rate systems. As regards flexible rates and currency boards, the current orthodoxy seems to be that either is fine but what one cannot have is something in between, especially an adjustable peg or its equivalent—a currency whose value could predictably change under pressure. Unfortunately, this is not as simple as it seems. After all, even currency boards are man-made and therefore cannot be regarded as "unbreakable"; to pretend that they are unbreakable and therefore countries with such boards cannot be the subject of panic-fueled capital volatility is not quite plausible, I am afraid. In this area, there will continue to be endless debate.

On Japan's Travails: Foreign Economists among Them

What was the role of Japan in all this? Foreign economists, except for the truly informed Japan scholars such as Gary Saxonhouse and David Weinstein, have generally tended to lecture Japan as if it is run by witless idiots in the Finance Ministry who do not understand macroeconomics. In turn, these freewheeling critics have generally blamed Japan for the Asian crisis, or at least its great depth.

However, my sympathies are with Mr. Sakakibara who wrote in the *Wall Street Journal*, in response to criticism from Professor Rudiger Dornbusch, that Japan's main problem was that it was too polite toward freewheeling foreign economists with facile policy prescriptions based often on ignorance or simple prejudice. For instance, who cannot remember the relentless Japan-bashing by Mr. Dornbusch in the last decade, and his prescriptions for imposing import targets on Japan and the use of 301 tactics to make these targets stick? Of course, even a fool can be right by simple laws of chance: so perhaps Mr. Dornbusch and others could well be right about Japan's macroeconomic situation. But one begins to doubt that when one realizes that Mr. Dornbusch does not even have his facts right when he talks about seven years of Japan's stagnation. Mr. Sakakibara correctly notes that the 1996 growth rate in Japan was possibly the highest among the OECD countries (a fact which, when I included it in an article in *Nikkei* some months ago, even their well-informed editors had forgotten and made me document it, which I did!); and if you go back almost five years before that, the average growth rate of Japan, while low by Japan's earlier standards, was by no means miserable compared to that of other OECD countries. In fact, given the high growth rate during 1996 and Japan's high debt and annual budget deficit, the IMF and others advised Japan to begin reducing the budget deficit in order to meet the Maastricht criteria on budget deficits as a proportion of GNP!

What happened was that this widely approved deflationary impulse combined with the wholly unexpected deflationary jolt, however small, that came exogenously to Japan from the Wall Street–Treasury-complex-caused Asian financial crisis, throwing Japan off stride. Japan's recession in 1998 and 1999 is to be traced to this double whammy, in my view.

Concluding Observations

I should then like to end on a positive note, by making a few points:

• The Asian crisis is already bottoming out. Some necessary reforms in the financial sector are already on the way.

• Other elements of the Asian economies are probably productive rather than unproductive as claimed by some hasty critics in the West; their retention, or far slower attrition, is not to be lamented.

• When the recovery has finally taken hold, my analysis of the reasons for the Asian miracle suggests that Asia will resume growth rates that are impressive, if not phenomenal.

Notes

1. I have developed these arguments in chapter 4.

2. The first three passages are from "Capital Mobility: Ties Need Not Bind," *The Milken Institute Review, First Quarter 1999*, 29–38; the last one is from "A Practical Fix," *The International Economy* 13(3) (May/June 1999): 33.

3. Interestingly, whereas most analysts have now accepted my terminology of the Wall Street–Treasury complex, Robert Wade and associates have augmented it to include the IMF in the term whereas Barry Eichengreen seeks to reduce it just to the Wall Street. Both variations lack analytical justification.

4. Of course, there is no assurance that Sakakibara would have managed to get even $10 billion approved by the Japanese government. But the point is that the United States and the IMF acted together to kill the plan outright instead of even exploring it.

A Friend in the United States, but a Crony in Asia

Absolute power corrupts absolutely. Corruption is little better. Yet this statement is too gross. There is corruption, and then there is corruption.

The distinctions that we must make, and that I will now make, are prompted by the denunciations of "crony capitalism" in Asia following the devastating financial crisis there. These reflected, to some extent, a corruption of public dialogue. They constituted scapegoating by the true culprits, on Wall Street and in Washington, who would rather point the accusing finger at the victims themselves. Yet they raise questions that can be answered with illumination on how corruption must be analyzed.

Crony Capitalism

So, at the outset, we must ask: can we think of politics anywhere without "cronies"? Political cronies are, of course, the politicians' friends and supporters. We call them friends here and cronies over there. After all, we write the script and the check. But that does not alter the facts as we find them.

Thus, does President Clinton not have his cronies? Surely they include Barbara Streisand, Alec Baldwin, Kim Basinger, and Steven Spielberg in Hollywood. There are others he befriends on Wall Street. His new home in Chappaqua was to be financed, until public exposure and outcry threw a wrench in the works, by an indirect loan from a well-known crony, Mr. Terry MacAuliffe. One can therefore well imagine that an Asian intellectual, looking at Washington, would find our politicians with cronies just the way we find politicians with cronies in Asia. The play is the same; only the actors differ.

Originally published in *The Business Times* (May 25, 2000), Singapore.

Cost of Cronyism: Asymmetry between Us and Them

But the production of the play does vary enormously. Here we do have a major advantage, so that our cronies cost much less than others' cronies. Our cronies, who must be rewarded reciprocally here as elsewhere for the loyalty and cash they provide to the politicians, are given their compensation in ways that for the most part do not have social costs of the magnitude that obtain in Asia. Our institutions have evolved so as to give us a vigilant press, democratic practices, and a rule of law, all adding up to a firewall against rewarding cronies in expensive ways.

Thus, the Streisands and the Spielbergs are rewarded by giving them access to White House events. Pressuring others into greater market access and greater intellectual property protection rewards their industry, Hollywood, rather than the cronies themselves directly: these are options that a superpower can deploy. To many economists, the demands for intellectual property protection are not conducive to advancing economic welfare worldwide, contrary to the self-serving propaganda of our industries and our campaign-contributions-purchased politicians. But they do amount to an income transfer from the other, intellectual-property-using countries to us. So, we reward our cronies in such cases as the expense of *others*, not ourselves.

Rent-Creating versus Profit-Sharing Corruption

But if we can thus keep our cronies in comfort without hurting our economies in the process, this is not quite true in the newly independent countries, often without the historical evolution of institutions such as ours and also at times without even democratic governance.

But we need to distinguish between two type of corruption in these regimes: between rent-creating and profit-sharing corruption. Under rent-creating corruption, President Suharto of Indonesia rewards his cronies, including the members of his extended family, with monopolies in production or distributive activity. These create what economists call "rents," and the laymen call "windfall profits," based on artificial scarcity. These create, in turn, significant efficiency losses. Good examples are the creation of car-production privileges by Prime Minister Mrs. Gandhi of India and by President Suharto for their sons. Indonesia, before the financial crisis, appears to have had a fair share of such rent-creating corruption.

But consider the alternative form of corruption where, in profit-making enterprises, the cronies are given a share. With their fingers in the pie, the cronies have an incentive to make the pie as big as they can. Thus, efficiency is not impaired; instead, the incentive is to enhance it. This seems to have been the case partly in Indonesia where, along with rent-creating examples, one also reads of profit-sharing examples. Indeed the rapid growth of the Indonesian economy over nearly two decades prior to Suharto's downfall was with Indonesia embracing economic reforms, including general openness to trade and equity investments, often ahead of World Bank schedules (for such reforms) laid down under conditional aid inflows. It is also the story, I suspect, in the burgeoning openness of China's east coast where rapid growth took off.

But profit-sharing corruption, in the end, is not without cost. Profits, so siphoned off by cronies, could well cut into tax revenues that build useful infrastructure. On the other hand, they may be reinvested productively by the cronies whereas tax revenues may have been wasted. But the certain drawback of such corruption is political, though ultimately with deleterious economic consequences as well. Thus, as the people see the cronies siphoning off the profits and fattening on this undeserved largesse, they get cynical and the regime begins to lose legitimacy. When this happens on a large scale, with the passage of time, respect for the law disintegrates and political chaos may break out. It may also become difficult for the state then to do efficaciously elementary tasks such as the enforcement of taxation. The economic costs, if such a state is reached, can be substantial.

Possibly, Indonesia, just before the financial crisis hit it, was beginning to enter this phase. The crisis tore the ship of state apart, making it difficult to judge what might have happened in the course of normal evolution. But I would not be sanguine.

III

Free Trade: Fair Trade, Wages, and Human Rights

Free Trade and Fair Trade

Free Trade in the Twenty-First Century: Managing Viruses, Phobias, and Social Agendas

Let me begin by saying that I feel honored to have been invited to give the Summers Lecture today. The invitation also pleases me, and for both personal and professional reasons. I feel as if I have known both Anita and Bob for many years because, while I have often met Anita's celebrated and affable brother Ken Arrow, I have known Bob's brother Paul Samuelson very well indeed. He was one of my greatest teachers and then a most generous colleague at MIT; and he has remained a good friend even as the distance between Cambridge and New York now divides us. And, of course, I have known their son, Larry, over the years: I do not recollect him from my MIT classes but I am confident that he missed nothing since there is little that I could have taught this remarkably gifted young man. My Indian ancestors distinguished between "received" (or innate) and "heard" (or learned) knowledge: Larry is a fine specimen of the former!

But it is not just that Bob and Anita have a magnificent diaspora between their nuclear and their extended families; they are themselves accomplished economists of considerable repute. I am familiar with Anita's important work on educational policy, a critical component of a good society. At the same time, as an economist interested in trade and in developmental questions, I have been influenced by Bob's ground-breaking work with Irving Kravis and Alan Heston that has transformed the way we look at international prices and the manner in which we compute internationally comparable national incomes. Few of us can boast of such an enormous achievement.

And so, I think that no greater tribute could be paid by me to Bob and Anita than to talk today, within the broader context of problems

Based on the text of the Fifth Anita and Robert Summers Lecture, Wharton School, University of Pennsylvania, April 13, 1999.

faced by free traders as we end this millennium and enter the next, about the interface between their two interests: the pursuit of free trade and the pursuit of social agendas in the broadest sense so as to include the promotion of human rights, better environment, improved working conditions, and other elements of what might be called well-being. Unfortunately, the groups that passionately promote such agendas have now allied themselves with others coming from different directions and set themselves against free trade and its institutions such as the WTO, displaying not just skepticism but outright hostility.

Indeed, at a Cambridge Union debate with the leading English environmentalist, the younger brother of the late Sir James Goldsmith who was an impassioned protectionist, I found myself facing an intelligent man who nonetheless believed illogically and without evidence that free trade was responsible for damage to the environment, for the sorry state of women and children in society, for ills of all kinds that I lacked the imagination to lay at the door of free trade. So, being in England where wit rules supreme, I replied by recalling the 1831 novella of Balzac, *The Wild Ass's Skin* (in French, *La Peau de Chagrin*). The central character, Raphael, has a terrible condition: when he desires a beautiful woman, the talisman in the shape of the ass's skin that he has been tempted into accepting shrinks and, with it, his life span as well. So, to go to the opera where he cannot avoid seeing lovely women around him, Raphael carries a special "monocle whose microscopic lens, skillfully inserted, destroy[s] the harmony of the loveliest features and [gives] them a hideous aspect." Looking through this monocle, Raphael sees only ugly women and is able to enjoy unscathed the glorious music he loves. Mr. Goldsmith, I added, you seem to have with you a similar monocle except that when you use it and see us wonderful free traders, you find us turned into ugly monsters. Our angel's halo turns into the devil's horns!

It is tempting, of course, to dismiss Goldsmith and the Sierra Club, John Sweeney of the AFL-CIO and the unions, and countless other NGOs that regularly agitate against free trade and its institutions as nuisances to be ignored. Indeed, when I recently debated a militantly antitrade Ralph Nader at Cornell, with nearly a thousand students assembled, I had earlier addressed the faculty and graduate students at an economics seminar on the subject of free trade at a technical level and asked, which of you are going to the debate? And I was astonished to find that no one was. Their typical explanation was, why waste your time? But let me assure you that this is no waste of time. If the free traders among us do not figure out how to address and accommodate the pursuit of social agendas, and also how to confront and relieve the fears that create added opposition to free trade, in ways that preserve and advance the cause of free trade, we will certainly be overwhelmed.

If you do not believe me, just look at the expensive full-page ads that used to appear in *The New York Times* and *The Washington Post*, with declamations against free trade and denunciations of the GATT as GATTzilla, invoking both horror and the fear that Japan produced at the time.

Or simply recollect the high drama of a hapless President Clinton's defeat on his request to the Congress for renewal of fast-track authority to negotiate new trade-liberalizing agreements nearly two years ago. As always, there were other contributory factors, including in the days of the NAFTA passage failed promises to congressmen in exchange for their affirmative votes so that, having felt deceived, they did not find new presidential promises of largesse in exchange for support credible. But surely, a major role was played by groups that sought to advance social agendas by piggybacking them on fast-track and future trade treaties, and also by unions who feared that world competition would undermine their members' incomes.

I must remark that, astonishingly, this huge and impassioned hostility to free trade, afflicting the richest country today and present in some degree also in other rich nations, has come at the end of a half century of trade liberalization that was accompanied by unprecedented growth and prosperity. Begun by the rich nations, and led by us, this opening to trade was resisted by many of the poor nations. But in view of the failures of their own autarkic strategies and the success of those that turned outward, policymakers in many of the poor nations have come to recognize the folly of ignoring trade and have turned to greater openness in trade. A supremely compelling example is President Cardoso of Brazil, the celebrated sociologist known in the years of autarky as the proponent of the *dependencia* thesis and now the leader of Brazil's turn to integration into the world economy. So, we have what I call an *ironic reversal*: the poor nations have largely abandoned objections to freer trade today while the rich nations have embraced them.[1]

The key problem facing us therefore is the rise of this angst and hostility at our end, in our midst. And the key question for us therefore is, what can we do to confront it and to surmount it? In short, what do these developments at the end of the twentieth century tell us about the strategic ways in which we can advance the agenda of free trade in the twenty-first century, while recognizing and coping creatively with the new factors that seek to place obstacles in its path?

In addressing these questions today, I shall therefore not concern myself narrowly with the question of social agendas, a major issue on the trade scene; instead, I will broaden my analysis to include also some of the other ways in which free trade today is beleaguered.

Old-Fashioned Protectionism

Of course, old-fashioned protectionism has not died; it probably never will. Indeed, if one observes the Washington scene today, and the rise of protectionist sentiment in Congress over steel, for instance, it is evident that we are still witnessing the perennial war of import-competing or special interests with the social or general interest. Of course, one might cynically observe that, in public parlance, others' interests are special and one's own are general! But the fact remains that the general interest is served best by freer trade; and while ignorance and willful disregard of intellectual and empirical argumentation on the subject can produce the Buchanans and the Perots who are unashamedly protectionist, the congressmen, the Gephardts and the Boniors, who pander to protectionism are usually playing to special interests in their constituencies.

As you well know, Congress is particularly vulnerable to special interests. As a wit has observed, a Christian congressman in the United States feels constrained to provide a missionary for breakfast if a cannibal constituent demands it! The executive's role has usually been to countervail these special interests in Congress with a leadership that reflects the general interest. Unfortunately, President Clinton has, for several reasons, failed to provide that leadership.

Free Trade Afflicted by a New Virus: The Folly of "Fair Trade"

Among these reasons, we must reckon with his unfortunate surrender to the protectionist strategy to cast other nations increasingly as "unfair traders" and hence deserving of any trade barriers we might level at them. In a fundamental sense, fairness is a subjective, almost vacuous concept since anything can be declared unfair if it simply appears to us to be so. Besides, we also know that, generally speaking, it is absurd to deny ourselves the benefits of free trade simply because of what others do or do not do in their trade policy. As my old and grand and radical teacher, Joan Robinson, used to say, and I adapt and paraphrase a little: if others throw rocks into their harbors, it may be fair to throw rocks into ours, but it is damned silly to do so since we hurt ourselves twice over.

In fact, our Section 301 in trade legislation gives the authority, even lays down for the executive the duty in certain ways, to condemn other nations as "unfair traders" simply because they indulge in what we unilaterally list as "unreasonable" practices, and then to follow this up with threats of tariff retaliation. I have called this "aggressive unilateralism," and it stands condemned worldwide as an intolerable practice unworthy of a nation of laws.

True, President Clinton inherited the drift to claims of "unfair trade," but he accentuated them greatly. Thus, President Bush had largely refused to surrender to Japan-baiting, if not Japan-bashing, as Japan rose to be our rival in the world economy and there was talk of the twenty-first century being Pacific just as the twentieth century was American and the nineteenth had been British. But President Clinton came to the White House, rooting to go for Japan's jugular, literally surrounded by Japanophobes who cried foul at every opportunity. Japan was regarded by them as the mighty Superman and the evil Lex Luthor rolled into a fearsome juggernaut. Demonized, Japan was accused repeatedly by the administration during President Clinton's first term of being a wicked trader whose exports were predatory and imports were exclusionary.

President Clinton's second term only saw an intensification—this time however not with the administration's active complicity but rather with its weak effort at resistance, of this steady drift to the notion of others' "unfair trade"—with Mexico now being demonized as an "unfair trader." Messrs. Gephardt and Bonior worked the political circuit pretty thoroughly to almost defeat NAFTA by claiming that free trade with Mexico was "unfair" because its labor and its environmental standards were not as good as ours and that even its democracy was not up to snuff. Ironically, of course, the Canadian opponents of the Canada-U.S. Free Trade Agreement, the CUFTA, had earlier raised the same argument against free trade with the United States: that *our* social standards on health insurance and social security were lower than theirs. Remember also that the Europeans, thanks to their welfare state, often go further in their labor and social standards than we do, but I do not recall our fair-trade-minded politicians turning our public relations machine around to aim at our own trade as being unfair to the Europeans! But then, fairness is defined by all as it suits them; that is the name of the game.

The rot that has set in by now, from the advancing embrace of "fair trade," is manifest in the administration's response to the current demands for steel protectionism. Our spokespersons on trade, Ambassador Barshefsky and Commerce Secretary Daly, have endlessly complained in public about our increased trade deficit as a surefire sign that we have become the "importers of last resort" for the world's steel and that the EU and Japan have failed their responsibility by having inappropriate macroeconomic policies that have impaired their growth and hence their absorption of steel, thus compounding our problem. Thus, EU and Japan are as good, or perhaps I should say as bad, as unfair traders who must be blamed for the outbreak of our steel protectionism and even for the administration's difficulty in containing it.

This is truly ridiculous. Of course, if the EU and Japan were in fact using protection to contain their imports and thereby diverting imports onto U.S. shores, that would indeed be something we could complain about. But we are instead saying in effect: *your macro policies are not good enough and that is what makes you an unfair trader*. For anyone who knows how fragile our understanding of macroeconomics is, and how even the IMF and the U.S. Treasury with some of today's best macroeconomists unwittingly started, and then accentuated, the East Asian financial and economic crash, it must seem a foolhardy, if not a foolish, thing for us to consider macroeconomic failure to be tantamount to unfair trade! And yet that is exactly what the Clinton administration, from the President down to his trade deputies, is busy doing.

And so one must painfully conclude that these days our unfair-trade-obsessed politicians generally divide into two sets: the less disagreeable ones whose slogan is "free and fair trade" and the more disagreeable ones who insist on "fair trade before free trade," leaving only the rare few (like the distinguished Senators Moynihan, a Democrat, and Gramm, a Republican) who ask for plain free trade. I need only recall for you President Clinton's State of the Union address in January, calling for "a freer and fairer trading system for twenty-first century America"!

Indeed, at a recent trade summit organized by Senator Bob Kerrey in Omaha, Nebraska, I was struck by the widely shared sentiment that free trade was in crisis in the United States because we were confronted by a world of unfair traders! Conference speakers urged that only a militant crusade against other nations' unfair trade could save free trade. The plain truth, however, is that the ceaseless refrain of "unfair trade" has itself produced a public perception that free trade by us is both economically unwise and politically naïve. And so has the public support for free trade been seriously undermined.

This is ironic indeed; worse, it is tragic. If we are therefore to save free trade in the twenty-first century, our statesmen, as distinct from mere politicians, will have to learn painfully to confront and renounce, rather than accommodate and adopt, the rhetoric of fair trade, recognizing it for the deadly virus that it is.

On to Fears, and Social Agendas Reflecting Moral Values

But the folly of fair trade, and its corrosive effect on the pursuit of free trade, is not all that free traders in the United States face as they enter the twenty-first century. If I had to choose from the several flashpoints only the problems of perhaps the greatest significance, as I must in this lecture, I would select the following two:

i. the palpable fear that the unions have that trade with poor countries will produce poor in our midst; and

ii. the morally driven arguments that inform and prompt civil society institutions, not just ours, to set up the pursuit of social agendas as obstacles to the pursuit of trade liberalization.

I will say a little about each of these problem areas, and indeed most about the social agenda problem, arguing optimistically that the first is an unjustified fear, while showing you how economic analysis suggests solutions to the second that enable us to salvage free trade consistently with the pursuit of these other—what sophisticated economists call "noneconomic"—objectives.[2]

The Fear of the Unions: Threat to Real Wages

Our unions have a palpable fear of free trade: they are convinced that trade with the poor countries will produce poverty in the rich countries. The experience of the 1980s through mid-1990s, of a decline and then sluggishness in the real wages of workers, has produced this fear. As the Russian proverb states, fear has big eyes. In this instance, it has also had both ears of the administration for the reason, not necessarily of conviction, but of the exigencies of politics. For, while (as I shall presently argue) the evidence in support of the fear is far from compelling, and I myself believe that trade with poor countries actually helps moderate instead of accentuating the pressure on the real wages of unskilled workers that ongoing technical change imposes, the administration has never boldly espoused these views and challenged those of the unions in fierce intellectual debate for fear of losing their political support.

In fact, if you think back on the heroic battle for NAFTA that the administration fought, you will recall that the decisive turning point came when Al Gore slew Ross Perot in the celebrated TV debate. Of course, the outcome was astonishing, given Gore's unrivaled ability to simulate rigor mortis, until you realized that Perot was a knave so certain of his victory that he had clearly walked into the debate unrehearsed and armed only with an ego that made one recall Gore Vidal's famous witticism that the sweetest of all emotions is requited self-love. But when the president went for the fast-track renewal that he did not get, he could not pull off a similar defining moment. That would have required putting Al Gore on prime time against John Sweeney, and— well—that just would not do.

So, why do I think that the unions' fear is just that, with no substance? Let me take apart two main arguments that produce the fear.

First, as Paul Samuelson and Wolfgang Stolper showed in a classic paper over half a century ago,[3] if the price of imported labor-intensive goods falls in world trade, then ceteris paribus, the real wages of labor will fall too, under certain conditions which include our not reaching complete specialization (because it is manifest that any fall in the price of imports that have no import-competing production must benefit all factors that produce the exported goods). Hence, many fear that trade with poor countries will push prices of labor-intensive goods, and hence our workers' real wages, steadily down.

But if you look at the (relative) prices of labor-intensive goods in the 1980s, they actually rose, instead of falling, thus cutting off the Stolper-Samuelson argument at its source. When I started thinking about this empirical reality, I suddenly realized that it was not at all surprising. The reason is that some of the poor nations had become rich in the 1980s and had steadily moved up what the late Bela Balassa used to call the ladder of comparative advantage: they had become net importers of labor-intensive goods, absorbing the new exports of labor-intensive goods from countries poorer than themselves. This is the story, to some extent, in the 1970s when Japan's withdrawal from exports of labor-intensive goods absorbed much, but not all, of the exports of the four dynamic NICs: Taiwan, South Korea, Singapore, and Hong Kong. It is an even more significant story in the 1980s when the offset to China's entry as a major net exporter of labor-intensive goods is provided by the shift out of such exports by the NICs. Looked at directly in terms of underlying causes, capital accumulation and technical change in rapidly growing economies have put downward pressure on the production of labor-intensive goods—a conclusion that we know from general-equilibrium analysis of the output-composition changes from these phenomena when we hold goods prices constant— and so the tendency has been to raise, not lower, the world prices of labor-intensive goods.[4]

Second, unions often argue that the outflow of direct foreign investment (DFI) either "costs jobs" or drives down wages. But surely, whatever the purely economic merits or demerits of this contention, it cannot withstand the fact that, during the 1980s when the pressure on real wages was the most intense, there was also almost equal inflow of DFI into the United States. In fact, that DFI is a two-way street has been very much on the minds of international economists for nearly four decades; and there is no excuse really for having one's eyes trained only on the outflow. As always, concretizing this point helps. In their recent book *The Coming Prosperity*, *Wall Street Journal* reporters Bob Davis and David Wessel write how a stretch of I-95 going through North Carolina is now known as the Autobahn, with several top German multinationals having come in as the region lost textile factories to foreign locations. The low-paying jobs in textiles have vanished and the workers have wound up getting paid far more at Siemens and other German firms. They are now rooting for globalization, for investment and trade in the global economy.

Social Agendas and Free Trade: Burdening Trade with "Values-Related" Obstacles

These fears on the part of the unions have misled them into protectionism. At minimum, the unions have been lukewarm about fresh trade liberalization with the poor countries. There has even been talk at times of free trade only with "like-wage" countries.

But it has also made some of the unions, and the politicians sensitive to their concerns and demands, agitate for a social agenda (such as the raising of environmental and labor obligations) for the poor countries where their rivals are located. Why? Because, faced with competitiveness problems that you wish to moderate, you can either become a conventional, import protectionist, or you can try to moderate the competition by somehow raising the costs of your rivals abroad. I call this latter approach "export protectionism." Or, if the former is called "isolationism," the latter merits the epithet "intrusionism." An analogy might help. If a bull is charging at you, you can try to take it by the horns and stop it in its tracks; alternatively, you can (tortuously, for sure) reach behind the beast, hoping to seize it by its tail and to break its charge.

Despite all the protestations to the contrary, little doubt exists that many abroad (including some of the indigenous NGOs not indebted financially to our foundations and NGOs for their survival) see our efforts at including these social agendas into trade treaties and institutions as reflecting competitiveness concerns. And rightly so. Just ask the congressmen who voted to table the Harkin Child Deterrence Bill (which did not make it) whether they have a special interest in children's rights and welfare quite generally (as, say, Marianne Edelman's Children's Defense Fund has), whether they have a coherent and comprehensive policy to advance child welfare within the United States itself, and whether they have made any legislative efforts in Congress to get the United States itself to adhere more fully to the human rights law as based on the UN Convention on the Child (which categorically forbids, for instance, juvenile capital punishments as a barbaric practice that violates children's fundamental rights at their very core, when several of our states effectively permit it). I tried to probe the matter a little along these lines, calling up some of these congressmen only to get their staffs, whose willingness to explain their Congressmen's philosophy and practice on these matters was not exactly marked by enthusiasm.

But let me just add that morally motivated groups such as Human Rights Watch (with which I work on the academic advisory board to its Asia section), whose interest in social agendas has nothing to do with competitiveness or protectionist considerations, do exist. They would, for instance, oppose child labor on the moon, if Carl Sagan or Neil Armstrong had been able to find life there, even if we did not trade with the moon. They would show extended empathy for children everywhere, cutting across nation states. Morality sans Borders is their motto.

It is analytically helpful also to note that, in turn, these values-driven groups divide into two sets from the viewpoint of their objectives and how they impinge on free trade. The first set wishes to advance its social agendas abroad and would like to piggyback on trade treaties, believing that nations eager to trade with us will pay the price and accept obligations to extend the desired social agendas to their nationals. These groups seek to act strategically, using trade only as an instrumentality to advance their essentially trade-unrelated social agendas abroad.

Others, however, form a second set that does not necessarily share this consequentialist objective. Instead, they follow the moral principle that "I shall not sup with the devil even if all that happens is that I miss a free supper and the devil does not shed his horns." This viewpoint is particularly prevalent when, as I immediately discuss below, citizens feel that the products they are importing use production and process methods (PPMs) that they morally object to and hence demand that free trade in them be suspended. (I myself believe, however, that even these apparently nonconsequentialist groups, if you probed their sentiments deeper, are unlikely to be free from all traces of consequentialism and indeed do desire to reshape others in their own image, eliminating objectionable PPMs abroad.)

We also must distinguish among two entirely different levels at which these "values-related" objections to free trade arise. First, we may wish to embargo, altogether or by denial of trade privileges such as MFN status, entire nations that egregiously violate human rights: for example, apartheid in South Africa or the practice of gulag and the denial of democratic rights in China. Such dramatic embargoes are in practice driven by consequentialist groups and must be assessed as such.

Second, at a far less dramatic level but one that arises with far greater frequency in the public domain, we may want to proscribe only trade in specific products that use PPMs that offend our values: for example, the use of child labor, the use of purse seine nets that kill dolphins while catching tuna, the cruel raising of hogs in crowded pens and of chickens in cages, and the use of leghold traps in hunting for fur. Indeed, many such process-objections can be cited, ranging from niche or boutique values specific to one's own culture but puzzling to other cultures (e.g., passionately objecting to the killing of dolphins in the course of tuna fishing while happily eating mahi mahi) to the deeper values, which often are shared beyond one's own society and therefore tend to be embodied in multilaterally defined human rights law. In either case, the PPMs issue is raised by both nonconsequentialists who simply wish to proscribe such products in their midst and by consequentialists who would like to banish them elsewhere as well. And so, I will judge them successively by both criteria below.

Free traders should not, indeed I do not (despite astonishing claims to that effect by NGOs who cannot be expected to know better and some economists such as the Kennedy School's Dani Rodrik who surely should know better[5]), object to these values-related consequentialist and nonconsequentialist objectives as free traders though, of course, we can object to them as citizens who may find them unappealing or wholly unworthy. What free traders can, and should, object to instead is the inference that such objectives necessarily justify and require the suspension of the policy and pursuit of free trade. In particular, I believe that a cost-benefit analysis suggests that, generally speaking, there are more cost-effective ways of pursuing these objectives that permit the simultaneous pursuit of free trade. Let me explain.

Embargoes

Consider the case of embargoes (whose objective is almost always consequentialist: to deny benefits of trade and hence to pressure regimes into changing their ways). Now, as far as trade law today at the WTO is concerned, multilaterally shared goals and corresponding embargoes pose no real problem. It is perfectly possible for the entire trade of a member country to be suspended, at the WTO itself and also through UN procedures. The legal problem arises essentially when the decision to embargo the trade of WTO members is unilateral and lacks wide consensus. The WTO-illegality of such unilateral action creates resentment against the WTO and against free traders, when the embargo reflects strong outrage. But there are good reasons to think that the legitimation of such unilateralism is not desirable.

First, the legal ability to embargo trade freely and unilaterally with another WTO member, when a multilateral consensus has not been obtained (so that one's values are not effectively shared and hence their alleged universality itself may be called into question), could open up a number of uncontrollable disruptions of trade. More likely, it would result in the unequal and hence unjust resort to embargoes: the powerful nations would indulge them far more freely once all international safeguards and constraints on them have been lifted, whereas the weak states would feel constrained by prudence and intimidated by their relative lack of power in confronting the strong. In endorsing unilateralism, we would thus effectively be resurrecting the old adage "might is right" or the seductive doctrine of the strong that power and virtue go together.

Second, and this argument is more compelling, unilateral embargoes are generally likely to be ineffective. The reason is that embargoes are easier to evade when others have not joined us. This evasion reduces the cost of the embargo to the targeted country. But, since trade and investment get diverted to the nonembargoing countries, the effect is to set our own business lobbies against our unilateral embargo. So, we wind up with a fractious constituency for the embargo: the human rights and the business lobbies divide over the embargo, weakening the resolve and the sustainability of the embargo. Just recall the huge divisions over the renewal of MFN status for China, if not the current divisions over China's entry into the WTO.

So, it seems to me that we need to consider alternative ways of targeting the country whose human rights violations offend us. Surely, we are not without other policy instruments. These include the full articulation of our moral disapproval at the Human Rights Commission in Geneva, the moral and political support of NGOs such as Human Rights Watch that agitate against such violations, and financial support for dissidents in and from the offending country. These instruments may appear to be without teeth. But just as the Pope has no troops but wields much clout, these policies can embarrass, shame, and prod the offending regimes in the right direction, however slowly. After all, remember that China's communist regime has worked very hard to shut us up as far as our official articulation of dissent is concerned, suggesting that it takes our public criticism seriously.[6] Human rights and business groups are also more likely to unite on these instruments and hence make the sustainability of our pressure for change more certain.

"Values"-Related PPMs

Consider then the problems posed by values-related PPMs instead, taking first the nonconsequentialist argument that we merely object to products so defiled appearing in our own markets and next the consequentialist contention that we have instead a "social agenda" to advance elsewhere the elimination of the PPMs that we abhor.

Our Own Markets

The difficult issues here arise again when we *unilaterally* seek to deny or suspend market access to specific products that use PPMs that only we (or just a few) object to. It is tempting to argue that such unilateral action should be freely allowed, following only national legislation such as we have had in regard to the import of tuna caught with purse seine nets.[7]

But in granting such a freewheeling hunting license for unilateral trade-restricting actions, we run the danger of likely opening up a Pandora's box of trade barriers: any nation or society could in principle then assert that their moral values are offended by certain PPMs and hence suspend or deny market access without any restraints. I should also remind you that it would be terribly easy to devise legislation that appears neutral on the surface, objecting to products on the alleged ground that they use specific PPMs, while actually aiming the legislation at the moderation or elimination of uncomfortable competition in the products themselves. There are in fact many instances of GATT and WTO dispute settlement cases demonstrating precisely such abuse. Under freewheeling unilateralism, such cases would surely be impossible; that would be a pity.

So, again we must look for better alternatives. Indeed, these are possible. I would argue that labeling is precisely one such alternative that is rapidly gaining ground (even though it presents some difficulties); consumers can then make informed choices. We now have labels that say "Dolphin-safe Tuna," the Rugmark that says rugs have not been made by children, the Free Range Chicken label, and a possible resolution of the hormone-fed beef dispute between the United States and the EU through the device of labeling hormone-fed beef as such. This is surely a reasonable solution that dominates unbridled unilateralism. It is also a solution that acquires greater potency and appeal when we recognize the possibility of private boycotts, agitations, and educational campaigns—powerful weapons indeed.

Advancing Social Agendas Elsewhere

That brings me to those who would proscribe trade in products using objectionable PPMs with a view to advancing their social agendas elsewhere. This is clearly the motivation of the NGOs that back proposals such as the inclusion of a Social Clause, for instance, in the WTO—a proposal that the Clinton administration seems to have embraced but to which almost no developing country consents.

My main objection to the inclusion of such social agendas in trade institutions and treaties, or what is now known as the linkage issue, is that this amounts to trying to kill two birds with one stone—a recipe for missing both birds except in the fluke event where the two birds happen to lie on a common trajectory and Wonder Woman is hurling the stone into the sky with deadly force and accuracy.

We already know how the linkage proposed by the president divided the Republicans and the Democrats and was a factor in his loss of congressional support for fast-track renewal. And, even if it had cleared Congress, you can be sure that it would have been a divisive North-South issue, as indeed it is. All this, of course, slows down trade liberalization, thus missing that bird. But I would contend that linkage makes you miss the other bird as well; the social agendas themselves get compromised. Remember that when you take your moral agendas to the trade arena, the dominant players there are trade lobbies, and this context inevitably taints your program with the stench of competitiveness considerations. In fact, this distortion is very real. As many of us have observed, the objectionable PPMs that are currently specified in the Social Clause are, unsurprisingly, those where the competitive developing countries are expected to be the defendants, not the developed countries that fear the competition. Thus, you have child labor in the clause. But there is nothing there about sweatshops or the treatment of migrant labor. The former would destroy almost half of the U.S. garment industry, while the latter would deeply hurt U.S. agriculture if the occasional documentation of quasi-slavery on several farms using migrant labor is to be believed. So, the very choice of what you put into the Social Clause and what you leave out of it reveals the cynical reality that its moral face is a mask hiding the fear of competition. So you devalue the morality of your social agenda and hurt the cause, thus missing the other bird as well.

Linkage thus undermines both the freeing of trade and the advancing of our social agendas. We need another stone, or a number of pellets, to aim at a number of birds. Of course, this is the economists' theory of economic policy: generally speaking, we have to match the number of instruments to the number of targets. And we do have the possibility of fashioning new stones, as required. Thus, it is perfectly possible for us to pursue freer trade through WTO-led trade negotiations and treaties, while pursuing children's rights (including freedom from juvenile capital punishment) quite universally through UNICEF, child labor questions jointly between UNICEF and ILO, environmental improvement through UNEP, humane treatment of refugees through UNHCR, and so on. I have long proposed the creation of a World Migration Organization to oversee the ethical and economic dimensions of immigration flows quite generally, repairing this great lacuna in the international superstructure today. Impartial reviews of national policies by such institutions can be expected to assist in building pressure to amend policies that lack moral legitimacy today.

Moral and financial support of NGOs, in turn, can be important aids in mounting pressures for change, based on these impeccable and impartial reviews (as distinct from the biased and witless national reviews that, as with the State Department on Human Rights and the USTR on unfair trade, concentrate on others while turning a blind eye to our own failings). I am often told that the ILO, for instance, is toothless, its research incompetent and its structure unproductive. Even if this were true, surely the answer for a superpower such as the United States is to open the jaws and put in the missing teeth. If I may shift metaphors, we can successfully put our shoulders to the wheel.

Nor should we forget instruments such as aid and technology transfer. Thus, consider the recent WTO Shrimp-Turtle case to see how aid could well have solved a gratuitous conflict. When the WTO Appeals Court recently found against our legislation because it had, without prior efforts at negotiations, unilaterally excluded shrimps from countries that did not mandate the use of narrow-necked nets that would prevent turtles from being caught in them, U.S. environmentalist groups went ballistic against the WTO. But surely, this is ridiculous. The fishermen in the plaintiff countries (India, Pakistan, and Malaysia, with Thailand joining the case but having no shrimp fishing in dispute) could have been outfitted with the desired nets by the United States, which valued turtles, at something like $50.00 a net at Wal-Mart! The issue would have been off the front pages and the evening news, and the objectives of both freer trade and the turtle-protecting environmental groups would have been creatively reconciled at no social cost, if only a half dozen aid-financed boondoggle economics conferences in Bangkok and New Delhi had been canceled and the moneys diverted to such a program.

The same might be said of technological assistance. We all know how the global warming treaty has been facilitated by the use of technological transfer to the developing countries by the United States and other OECD countries. But let me tell you how the Save the Tiger campaign might also be aided by an ingenious use of technology to effectively supplement, if not substitute for, the use of trade sanctions. The danger to the tiger comes from the CITES-illegal demand for it by Chinese communities on the mainland and overseas because its organs are astonishingly considered an aphrodisiac by this otherwise sophisticated community. Consider also the case of Viagra now. It has of course swept America, which is no surprise. After all, faced with a choice between two Presidential candidates last time, one (Bob Dole) who needs Viagra and another (Bill Clinton) who needs an antidote, the country chose the latter! But if only this potent drug, which is surely more effective as an aphrodisiac and far cheaper than smuggled tiger parts, were made even more cheaply available by the EPA and USAID in South East Asia, we would have truly helped Save the Tiger. Or I fondly think so. And I do know that nothing would please Bob Dole more than to be our representative in Asia, doing well by peddling Viagra and doing good simultaneously by saving the tiger. Indeed, recalling Exxon's fetching slogan "Put a Tiger in your Tank," Bob Dole might embrace the ditty "Take a Viagra, hey; and Save a Tiger today."

So to return to my main theme, the administration has failed us is in not recognizing and proactively pursuing the numerous possibilities of fashioning alternative policies that are more cost-effective then burdening trade treaties and negotiations with social agendas as preconditions for the freeing of trade. The administration has thus failed to develop, and bring our citizens to its embrace, a clear conception of what I like to call *appropriate governance*—that is, how to accommodate creatively, while preserving the efficient pursuit of free trade, the different social or values-related agendas on the stage today. I submit that, instead of the intellectually lazy option of accepting the demands to pile everything on to the WTO and thus trying in a futile fashion to kill two birds with one stone, the President should be providing the leadership to argue forcefully and unequivocally that it is best to pursue (except when unavoidable interface exists) free trade and social agendas in different fora, with equal fervor.

Indeed, let him say that the pursuit of free trade, and indeed of economic reforms everywhere, is a moral agenda as well. For, without the prosperity that free trade and other reforms will engender, we can only carry our liberalism on the lapels of our jackets, not translate it into the reality that alone matters. So free trade is not an evil force that must be contained by social agendas; it is itself part of our overall moral agenda. And these different moral agendas, including better environment and respect for human rights, must be pursued appropriately, without sacrificing any one of them (except when this is totally unavoidable) by designing the tools of appropriate governance. Is that too much to ask of our leadership?

Notes

1. This is not to say that everyone in the poor nations is pro free trade today. Some of the civil society groups in the poor countries are also to be found arrayed against globalization generally, and sometimes against free trade specifically. But the preponderance of influential opinion is certainly changed to a pro-globalization agenda in the poor nations.

2. If I had more time, I would add an analysis of, and a solution to, two other issues of significance today: (1) the problems raised by the alleged conflict between trade and culture; and (2) the complaint that there is a "Democratic deficit" in the working of the WTO, with "faceless" bureaucrats running the trade rules, aided by international and national corporate interests.

3. See Wolfgang Stolper and Paul A. Samuelson, "Protection and Real Wages," *Review of Economic Studies* 9(1941): 58–73.

4. This argument is empirically supported by the work of the Australian economist Ross Garnaut. I have developed the argument more fully in chapter 11.

5. See my letter to the editor, commenting critically on Rodrik's article on the world trading system's flaws and his solution to them in *The New Republic* (chap. 18 in this volume).

6. True, some dictators are probably beyond the pale: for example, Stalin and Hitler. Mercifully, however, they are "outliers." And embargoes are equally unlikely to reform or deter them!

7. Dani Rodrik has recently suggested, as far as I can understand him, that such unilateralism should be permitted after an antidumping style "administrative" process that determines whether the legislation reflects a national moral consensus of sorts. This is, of course, a funny suggestion. I would have thought that the passage of the legislation itself demonstrates the expression of such a preference. Besides, imagine a process whereby quasi-judicial bodies sit in judgment over the legislation in this fashion! Rodrik also implies, in a recent pamphlet on globalization issued by the Institute for International Economics, that trade economists do not appreciate that PPMs matter. That view is, of course, based on ignorance of the massive literature on the subject (e.g., the two volumes edited by me and Robert Hudec on the subject with MIT Press in 1996). The problem is not that we do not understand that processes can be objected to but rather what to do about it in managing international trade sensibly.

Free Trade: Why the AFL-
CIO, Ralph Nader, and the
Sierra Club Should Like It

Last year, the president lost his bid for fast-track legislation, necessary for further trade liberalization within a framework of negotiations (as distinct from "going alone" and liberalizing unilaterally), for a variety of reasons.

Some had to do with himself. The credibility of his promises, relevant to the fast-track vote since he would have to "buy" support from skeptical Democrats, had been badly bruised by the fact that some of the promises he had made during the perilously close NAFTA vote had been forgotten and the betrayed congressmen had not forgotten.[1]

Others included a legacy from an unfortunate, if inherited but intensified, flirtation with regional and preferential as distinct from multilateral and MFN-based trade liberalization. While the president is widely credited by the pro-free trade media and by unsophisticated economists for his success on NAFTA (a preferential trade agreement par excellence and hence to be decried in itself by multilateral free traders such as myself),[2] it was in fact a Pyrrhic victory from the viewpoint of further trade liberalization. In particular, the NAFTA debate had crystallized, in a way that the multilateral (as distinct from preferential) trade negotiations such as the Uruguay Round rarely do, the fears of workers and the labor unions that freer trade with all but rich countries would imperil their real wages. Thus, the widespread perception that impoverished, illegal workers were streaming across from Mexico and driving down our wages had led many to argue, quite correctly from an analytical viewpoint, that freer trade with Mexico would be an indirect way in which this would happen. (In fact, in the impas-

Based on remarks made during an acceptance speech on the occasion of the award of the Seidman Distinguished Award in Political Economy, Memphis, Tennessee, September 18, 1998.

sioned national debate over the imposition of the first-ever national immigration legislation in 1905 by the English Parliament, the free traders were also free immigrationists, whereas the protectionists were also for immigration restrictions.)[3]

By contrast, the Uruguay Round raised few such worries: the diversity of issues, the multitude of countries, and the lack of political salience of the vastly greater poverty of countries other than Mexico, were guarantors of equanimity over the issue of trade with poor countries and its immiserizing effect on our own poor.[4] One serious legacy of NAFTA (whose advisability to a multilateralist such as myself is suspect anyway) therefore was the plague it visited on future trade liberalization, by accentuating and politicizing these fears (however unjustified, as I argue below) and by aligning the unions and their congressional supporters against the further freeing of trade and against the passage of fast-track legislation to advance such efforts without serious qualifications and safeguards that many of us would regard as creating new obstacles to trade.

As it happens, the cause of freer trade is under threat today from precisely such fears as those of the unions over the living standards of the workers and those of environmentalists who are afraid that free trade will harm the environment. John Sweeney of the AFL-CIO and the Sierra Club, among many NGOs, happen to be afflicted by these fears and have turned them into an anti-free-trade agenda. Complementing these fear-induced opponents of free trade are also the NGOs who seek to "piggyback" on trade institutions and trade-liberalization efforts to simply advance their social agendas, thus raising a very different set of threats to free trade.

But the protectionist viewpoint, never absent from the scene even in our classrooms ever since Adam Smith invented the case for free trade, is also to be reckoned with since it defines the broadly skeptical backdrop against which these fears are played out, especially by politicians such as Congressman Gephardt (though, I must say, he has lately begun to talk, perhaps for prudential reasons, less like a true-blooded protectionist who challenges the case for free trade and more like the fearful NGOs just cited).

And now the East Asian financial crisis, the Russian debacle, and the spreading contagion that is threatening the world economy have led to a new round of skepticism about, and often outright hostility to, the case for free trade, however illogical this inference is.

On this celebratory occasion, therefore, I would like to address my advocacy of free trade to all these groups, but treating the issues in the reverse order used above: first, the contagion from the recent financial crisis; second, the case for free trade and its serious professional critics; and finally, the recent criticisms stemming from fears and from advocacy of social agendas.

Contagion from the Recent Financial Crisis

Arguably, the most difficult challenge to Free Trade currently comes from the gratuitous spillover effect from the Asian financial crisis and its manifold ramifications in Asia, Russia, and in Latin America, all now threatening the continuation of the prosperity in the United States itself of the last several years. I have argued, in the May 1998 issue of *Foreign Affairs*, in an article that has made me as world-infamous as my trade research and writings have made me famous, that the essential feature of this crisis in Asia was the hasty shift to financial liberalization and the consequent overexposure to short-term capital borrowing that the IMF was presiding over in the last few years. Our clever economists at the IMF and the Treasury seemed to have forgotten the simple lessons that we had learned from Charles Kindleberger's brilliant historical book *Panics, Manias and Crashes: A History of Financial Crises* (New York: Basic Books, 1978) and from Robert Triffin's demonstration of successfully destabilizing speculation where speculators bucking the fundamentals would still survive since they would have changed the fundamentals through their speculation. So they behaved as if free trade in widgets and free capital mobility were equally good.

And they were helped along by the intense interest (read lobbying) of Wall Street where the financial firms wished to enhance their profits by extending their sphere of operations around the globe. So, between interests and ideology (of markets, with amnesia about market failures), the stage was set for the current financial crisis, as well as previous and future ones. I have attributed this outcome to the sociological and political phenomenon that I have christened, with some approbation and adoption, as the Wall Street–Treasury complex. I used this concept in the spirit of President Eisenhower's "military-industrial complex" and C. Wright Mills's "power elite," both of which were developed, not in the sense of a conspiracy, but rather in a nuanced way as a "networking ethos." Since both these men were at Columbia,

Eisenhower as the university president and Mills as a professor of sociology, some have now cast all three of us as the "Columbia trio." I guess this is the next best to becoming the Beatles or the Spice Girls!

But the fact is that, even as the IMF and the Treasury are trying to put the pieces together, the protectionists are busy throwing out the baby with the bathwater. I see no reason why the misfortunes visited on the world economy by an excessively hasty shift to freer capital mobility should make us doubt the wisdom of freer trade (or even of enhanced equity investments). I believe strongly, on grounds of both analytical argumentation and overwhelming empirical evidence, that noncoercive free trade brings benefits to all; I do not have to believe equally that this applies without any qualification to free capital mobility in the shape of capital account convertibility.

In short, if I am for free trade, I see no logic that requires me also to be for free capital mobility at the same time. To believe otherwise is the lazy man's approach, but I run into it everywhere, and the burdens of those who stand for free trade have doubtless increased at the present time.

The Theoretical Case for Free Trade: Why Protectionism Is Wrong

But if this deleterious "contagion effect" from the financial crisis is manifestly illogical and gratuitous, many challenges in the long history of free trade have been more serious and less easy to meet. Indeed, ever since Adam Smith invented the case for free trade over two centuries ago in *The Wealth of Nations*, and founded in the same great work the science of economics as we know it today, international economists have been kept busy defending free trade. A children's story by Dr. Seuss, popular in the United States, has the refrain "And the cat came back." The opponents of free trade, ranging from hostile protectionists to the mere skeptics, have kept coming back with ever new objections.

The critiques we have had to confront have often come from those who fail to understand the essential insight of Adam Smith: it pays me to specialize in what I do best compared to you, even though I can do everything better than you do. Economists call this the law of comparative advantage: each nation would profit from noncoercive free trade that would lead to such specialization. When asked by the famous mathematician Ulam "What is the most counterintuitive result in Economics?" the Nobel laureate Paul Samuelson chose this law.

Skeptics within Economics

But I must admit that the most compelling skeptics have come repeatedly from within the discipline of economics itself. To see why, it is necessary to understand that the case for free trade is, at an essential level, the case for markets. Adam Smith's Invisible Hand will guide you to an efficient allocation of resources only if the markets yield prices that reflect "true" social costs. If there are market failures, as when a producer pollutes the air but does not have to pay for this pollution, then the invisible hand can lead you in the wrong direction. Or to put it in flamboyant terms, free trade can immiserize you.

So, in virtually each generation, economists have discovered new, or focused anew on old, market failures that will undermine the case for free trade. In fact, John Stuart Mill, over 150 years ago, stated the case for infant industry protection succinctly though naturally not with the sophistication that it commands today: the losses faced by such an industry were presumably outweighed by the social gains from supporting it.

Then again, we all know how, when the world economy was afflicted by the Great Depression, John Maynard Keynes broke ranks with England's free traders. When you have massive unemployment due to lack of aggregate demand, tariffs can switch demand from foreign to domestic goods and thus create employment and income; in formal terms, market wages no longer represent the true social cost of (unemployed) labor.

And, when Edward Chamberlin of Harvard University and Joan Robinson of Cambridge University of developed their new theories of monopolistic or imperfect competition in 1929 and 1931 respectively, and also directly addressed (even if unsatisfactorily) oligopolistic competition among firms (in what was then called the case of "small-group" competition), it was immediately obvious that such imperfections constituted market failures, so that any belief in their practical importance would tend to undermine the faith in the doctrine of free trade. As a result, the 1930s were characterized by what John Hicks, a free trader and later Nobel laureate, described as "nihilism": if markets were imperfect, it was no longer possible to believe in the efficiency of free trade.

What we witnessed in the 1980s, with assertions that "strategic trade theory," based on oligopolistic competition, had undermined the case for free trade, was in essence then merely a replay of this "crisis of free trade" that Hicks described so eloquently in 1951 in a lecture to the Manchester Statistical Society as follows:

The Monopoly-Competition argument [against Free Trade] ... is of much less practical consequence than the others [such as the macroeconomic argument that led to Keynes's defection], but it deserves at least a passing mention, because of the undoubted influence which it undoubtedly exercises—in a negative sort of way—upon the minds of economics students ... If apparent costs [as reflected in market prices] only equal true [social] costs under conditions of perfect competition, and competition hardly ever is perfect, the bottom seems to drop out of the Free Trade argument. This is in fact a fair description of the state of mind which quite a number of economics students seem to have reached.

The difference between the 1930s and the 1980s was that the production of the same play more recently was more garish and dramatic. Whereas Hicks had described the damage to free trade as minor, the damage to it in the 1980s was more potent. Partly, the arguments fell this time into a context of what I have called the "diminished giant syndrome" in the United States, where the rise of Japan, and the fear that the oligopolistic competition among the giant firms of the trilateral powers would be won by countries whose governments aided the competitive strength of their "national champions," focused attention fiercely on imperfect competition and on how protection would, or could, aid governments in this "strategic" competition.

This renewal of 1930s worries was aided analytically by the fact that developments in the theory of industrial organization had prepared the profession to analyze the implications of oligopolistic competition much better than ever before. Helping the entire process, where free trade was widely denounced in the media and policy circles as an obsolete theoretical doctrine, was the activism of some of the proponents of the trade theory built on imperfect competition. Among them, the most prominent was my distinguished pupil, Paul Krugman, fortunately now an articulate convert back to free trade, who extensively wrote and lectured on how the "new" theory of trade under imperfect competition had shown that, at a theoretical level, the case for free trade was "passé." One of my many other pupils who was clearing his files recently sent me a 1991 article of Krugman from an influential Washington magazine, with the title: "Protectionism: Try it, You Will Like It"![5]

The Return of Free Trade

If you survey the academic scene in the 1990s, however, the economist defectors from the doctrine of free trade have returned to the fold; indeed today, there is harmony of agreement among the major economists on this policy position. A huge part of the reason is that the theory of free trade, and here I may self-indulgently on this prize-receiving occasion lay some claim to authorship of the idea, now distinguishes between two propositions:

1. if market failures remain unfixed, free trade can harm rather than help; and

2. if market failures are fixed through suitable policy intervention, then free trade can once again be used to exploit best the gains from trade.

Within the second proposition, economists also emphasize the following:[6]

If the market failure arises in domestic markets, then the appropriate policy intervention is the use of domestic policy directly targeted at the market failure, while free trade is maintained externally.

So, in a very sophisticated sense, international economists today have come around to looking at market failures very differently from their predecessors. Whereas the earlier economists drew away from free trade and accepted protectionism in a knee-jerk fashion when faced with market failures, today's economists say: fix those failures through appropriate policies and simultaneously get on with free trade. Free trade and these market-failure-fixing policies then become bedfellows.

I have often suggested (as in the previous chapter) that it is illuminating to remember that you generally cannot kill two birds with one stone. If you seek to do that, you will likely miss both birds. Nowhere is this better illustrated than in the debate between environmentalists and free traders (I shall return below to other dimensions of that debate). An important set of differences among the two arise simply because many environmental groups fail to appreciate that if market failure afflicts pollution because there is no enforcement of the polluter pay principle, we free traders realize immediately from our theory that:

1. free trade can hurt both income and the environment; but we also realize that so can protection (compared to free trade); and that

2. (the two targets of) income and the environment will be efficiently pursued by a simultaneous adoption of (the two policy instruments) free trade and the polluter pay principle.

So, by invoking simultaneous adoption of *suitable* market-failure-eliminating policies, we can rescue free trade finally from the iron fist aimed at it by the conventional market-failure critics over nearly two centuries. Thus, for instance, the answer to Keynes is that, if you manage to reflate and increase aggregate demand directly, you can return to free trade. Using tariffs to switch given aggregate demand from others to your own goods is to use a policy that simply switches employment from others to us but does not increase world employment, while damaging gains from trade by cluttering up the trading system with restrictions and, almost certainly, retaliatory trade restrictions by others trying to switch employment back to their own goods in a process that Joan Robinson called "beggar my neighbor" policies!

In fact, that prompts me to admit that the theoretical case for free trade with appropriate other nonprotectionist policies aimed at fixing market failures directly has one problem: the market failure in question may itself require an appropriate response in the form of trade tariffs. Theoretically, that does happen to be the case when there is imperfect competition in product markets: trade tariffs or subsidies can be shown to improve national welfare over what free trade would yield. In fact, this is only a sophisticated extension of the case made by Robert Torrens, again over 150 years ago; like a monopolist who restricts his sales to increase prices and profits, a nation enjoying monopoly power in world markets can do the same. In short, if the nation adopts free trade instead, it is not maximizing its own income by not fixing a "market failure" under free trade—namely, its failure to exercise monopoly power. So, here we do have a hole in the reinvigorated case for free trade.

But then, much in the spirit of the rejection of Torrens's argument when free trade was embraced by British Prime Minister Robert Peel with the repeal of the Corn Laws in 1846, we can still retain free trade as a reasonable policy by citing three quite persuasive arguments:

• "There is no beef": We could argue, as theorists of imperfect competition in trade (such as Avinash Dixit and Gene Grossman of Princeton) have done, that there is no evidence of significant enough imperfections for us to abandon free trade.

• "The Visible Hand will make matters worse": Or, we could take the stronger, definitely conservative, position (as Paul Krugman, among many others, has done) that if protectionist intervention is attempted, it will make matters worse because governmental interventions will reflect lobbying rather than social advantage.

• "Retaliation will ruin any chance of one's protection paying off": As a corollary of the preceding argument, it is not from one's own folly in choosing protection unwisely that we will hurt ourselves by abandoning free trade, but it is because other nations will retaliate and everyone will lose, in varying degrees, from the breakdown of free trade.

And, so, between the new theoretical arguments where domestic market failures can be fixed best through nonprotectionist domestic policies while retaining free trade as the best trade policy, and the new (essentially but not exclusively) empirical contentions that intervention is unnecessary or counterproductive when the market failure spills over into the external markets and must itself be fixed in principle through protection (singly or in conjunction with other policies), economists today have returned in hordes to free trade. The latest revolt, of the 1980s, has died down. Only neanderthals among the economists now militate against free trade: unfortunately, they will never lack an audience, but fortunately they have little effect presently.

Current Fears, Concerns over Fair Trade, and Trade-Linked Pursuit of Social and Moral Agendas

The real threats to free trade today come, in my view, from three altogether different directions that I identified at the outset. They are:

• Trade Hurts Wages: There is widespread concern that trade with poor countries will produce paupers in the rich countries; and

• "Fair Trade" before Free Trade: There are increasing concerns that free trade between countries that are different on a host of conventionally "domestic" institutions and policies is "unfair," and hence preconditions concerning harmonization of standards must be required of trade treaties.

• Advancing Social Agendas by Linking them to Trade: Many environmental and labor-rights NGOs seek to piggyback on trade treaties and institutions to advance social agendas.

Trade and Wages

A furiously compelling worry about free trade (and investments) has come from the fact that it is a prime candidate for explaining the phenomenon that, since the 1980s until very recently, the real wages of unskilled workers in the United States have fallen and then stagnated. In Western Europe, the pressure on the working class is believed to take instead the form of high unemployment because the labor markets are far more flexible in the United States.

The argument is not the old fallacy that free trade with poor countries is bad for your aggregate income, that your country will be immiserized by such trade. Rather, it is an income-distributional argument: while the country gains, the poor will be immiserized and actually get a smaller slice from the enlarged pie. The mindset behind this argument, of course, is that the progressive inclusion of the poor countries into the world trading system will effectively expand the unskilled labor force in the world economy, driving down the real wages of workers. In fact, Paul Samuelson had written a pair of articles in 1948 and 1949 on what economists call the Factor Price Equalization (FPE) theorem where free trade would drive wages into equality everywhere.

Regarded as a theoretical curiosum with no policy relevance at the time, the FPE theorem is now thought instead to provide the compelling reason for the immiseration of the rich countries' proletariat: in an ultimate irony, Marx, whose prediction of falling wages of workers was proven false by history for the nineteenth century, is now striking again with the aid of a neoclassical economist, Paul Samuelson! But I believe that Marx is destined to fail again. The evidence for the assertion that it is trade with poor countries that is increasing the numbers of the poor and accentuating their poverty in turn is simply not compelling.

Needless to say, this is a matter that has engaged the analytical attention of numerous economists. Many (but not all) trade economists have argued that the contribution of trade to the phenomenon is negligible whereas my own research has led me to believe that trade has actually had a favorable effect, moderating the fall in real wages of the unskilled that is being driven by technical change that economizes greatly on the use of unskilled labour.[7] It is hard therefore to believe how economists, among them Dani Rodrik in his unpersuasive but popular 1997 pamphlet "Has Globalization Gone Too Far?" issued by

Mr. Bergsten's influential Institute for International Economics in Washington, DC, can write that there is some sort of consensus among economists that trade accounts for 15–20 percent of the fall in real wages in the 1980s and beyond! Needless to say, this groundless assertion has been seized upon by protectionist congressmen such as Sander Levin of Michigan to argue that trade with poor countries is perilous and its force must be moderated through cost-raising equalization of foreign and domestic standards.

But if trade with the poor countries, or for that matter investments in them, should not be a matter for concern in regard to its income-distributional effects, and we can revert to accepting the benign view that the favorable influence of trade on aggregate incomes is a sufficient index to the virtues of free trade, I do believe that trade altogether (i.e., not just with poor countries) is today a phenomenon that creates economic insecurity.[8] Today, comparative advantage is relatively "thin." Many industries are "footloose," meaning that slight changes in costs abroad can undercut their competitiveness. The reason is that financial markets have integrated a lot so that interest rates at which you borrow don't vary as widely across countries as they used to. Technology also diffuses quickly and has converged rapidly among the OECD nations, for sure. Multinationals also move around, seeking small but significant cost advantages. Rival producers in a product or industry in many nations therefore face closely spaced costs and hence actual or potential loss of markets due to sudden, small, but effective shifts of comparative advantage. There is no great "buffer" or cushion of cost advantage today in most industries. The result is greater volatility in comparative advantage, driven by small changes in costs that are a fact of life. I call this the new phenomenon "kaleidoscopic comparative advantage." A flip side of the phenomenon is the widespread notion that "international competition today has been greatly intensified."

What this has done is to contribute to the greater labor turnover that has been observed; and this itself may have put some pressure on the real wages of the unskilled workers since, just as a rolling stone gathers no moss, a moving worker gains no on-the-job skills that lead to increased earnings. But, another effect of this is to create an accentuated need to make institutional changes to assist workers in coping with this turnover: adjustment assistance programs, portable health insurance benefits when these are provided by employers (as in the United States), and so forth. This reinforces the view, expressed forcefully in my 1988 book *Protectionism* (MIT Press), that we need to accompany the freeing of trade and the growth of trade with the institutional changes that increased exposure to international trade necessitates.

"Fair Trade" as Precondition for Free Trade

I must say that it is precisely the kaleidoscopic nature of current comparative advantage, with the narrowing or thinning of comparative advantage that it signifies, that has contributed enormously to the demands for "fair trade." Since even a small cost advantage enjoyed by your rivals abroad can be fatal to your health, you will begin to look over their shoulders to see if any difference in their domestic institutions or policies gives them that extra cost advantage: and you will lobby to iron it out, to harmonize standards or "cost burdens." Hence, when there are objections to Japanese *keiretsus* or to South Asian use of child labor, for instance, the objections are principally motivated by competitiveness considerations. And, in fact, it is astonishing how many such differences, which we would never have imagined to be relevant to trade issues, have now become part of the trade agenda. More such "fair trade" arguments are just around the corner. For instance, I would not be surprised if down the road, despite how ludicrous it appears now, population policies also became part of the trade agenda as rich countries object to "unfair trade" in labor-intensive goods by poor countries that have poor control over their population growth.

But, in conjunction with these demands, some morally driven demands exist for certain harmonization; for example, human rights groups will object to the use of child labor even if the children are the progeny of green men from Mars and the Earth does not trade with Mars.

These two principal, but wildly different, reasons for "fair trade" and harmonization as prerequisites for free trade raise two issues that have bedeviled the move to free trade and need to be resolved with clarity:

First, it is necessary to understand that, when trade is considered "unfair" because of differences in cost burdens due to differences in, say, environmental or labor standards, this is generally speaking a conceptual error. For example, even if we accept the polluter pay principle, there is no reason whatsoever why the payment for a unit carcinogen should be the same in India as in Switzerland. Or, if clean air and clean water are both highly prized, Mexico may well choose to devote its resources and energies to getting clean water first and clean air next as a suitable priority whereas the United States may well choose to go the other route. In each case, the cost burden will differ for the same industry across countries, and for perfectly sensible reasons. It is illegitimate, even unfair, then to force your own standards down the throats of others on grounds of unfair trade.

Again, even if this is granted, there might be a worry about a "race to the bottom" that may lead to a reductions of one's own standards even when one does not care about unfair competition per se. This race refers to the high-standards country forcing down its own standards to retain or attract investment that would otherwise move to low-standards countries. Theoretically, this is possible, of course, and a co-ordinated, cooperative solution can yield higher incomes and even standards for each country than under a noncooperative equilibrium (though, it must be emphasized that this cooperative equilibrium does not generally involve harmonization of standards). But much empirical literature shows that this theoretically correct fear is of little empirical relevance since multinationals typically seem to use the more environmentally friendly technology even when not required, and little evidence exists that governments actually lower standards in order to attract investments. Rather, the race to the bottom occurs typically on the fiscal dimension where developing countries, or states within federal nations, competitively offer cheaper land, subsidized inputs, tax holidays, or tax breaks in order to attract investments.

Hence, on the usual "unfair trade" grounds, reflecting competitiveness considerations, I see no reason to make harmonization or upgrading demands for standards and for other domestic institutional and policy structures part of the trade agenda. I am therefore against "linkage" of "fair trade" to free trade agendas and treaties as far as the competitiveness rationale is concerned.

Advancing Social and Moral Agendas

Second, however, linkage is also demanded at times for moral imperatives. Trade with countries that systematically violate civil and political rights, as China does, may be considered anathema by human rights activists, for instance, as was apartheid. Similarly, at the "micro" level of products produced by processes that are considered ethically unacceptable—for example, fur produced with leghold traps, chicken produced in coops, hogs raised in crowded farms, tuna caught in purse seine nets, and so forth—trade in such products may be denied.

These denials of trade may not be consequentialist in the sense that they are aimed at, and judged by, their success in changing these unacceptable practices. I may decide not to sup with the devil although the only consequence of that is that I lose a free meal. But most who wish to deny or suspend trade with others do look for efficacy of their actions in changing processes or practices abroad.

Either way, the question that arises with trade treaties is one that has brought environmentalists and other NGOs into conflict with free traders. These conflicts are twofold.

i. Free traders, and the WTO in fact, argue that if trade can be automatically and unilaterally suspended by a contracting party on moral grounds, then trade could fall into chaos because morality is subjective and can be indulged without constraint (e.g., there is no scientific test to constrain its use, as in the hormone-fed beef dispute between the EU and the United States). On the other hand, they recognize that morality is important and that you cannot get a country to eat "defiled" products, for instance, if it does not want to. The days of opium wars are not gone altogether, but the WTO surely cannot be built on those principles! So the sensible answer is to throw some sand into the tank of unilateral moral denials of market access. The GATT/WTO technique is to require that you pay some "compensation" or allow for "retaliatory" tariffs as Ambassador Carla Hills used in the EU hormone-fed beef dispute while the EU held on to its unilateral ban on such beef imports (and domestic production as well). While one can argue with the wisdom of some of the permitted measures (and in chapter 22 I do precisely that, suggesting better alternatives), this is surely the correct approach to the problem. And frankly, the current Shrimp-Turtle decision against U.S. legislation unilaterally suspending WTO members' market access for shrimps harvested without the turtle-protecting devices is also sensible in my view, since it will prompt the United States to sit down with the four plaintiffs who have won and will, in turn, lead to a negotiated settlement in terms of continued U.S. legislation and attendant U.S. compensation that could well take the form of financing the relatively inexpensive (for rich countries) protective devices that fishermen in these countries are being asked to use. The hysterical bridge-burning reaction of lobbies such as Ralph Nader's Public Citizen in this as in other instances, as opposed to bridge-building solutions favored by the less militant environmental groups working with the trade community, is exactly what we need in this area.

I might remind you also that when the action is not unilateral, but you can get a large enough majority to go along with your moral views, then you can suspend the entire trade access of a WTO member, or any specific offensive part thereof, through majorities set forth in the articles of the WTO. And then again, as with apartheid, which was against a GATT member, South Africa, United Nations embargo procedures are also available. So, again, the agitated propaganda against the GATT as Gattzilla and the WTO as trampling on countries' rights to pursue social and environmental agendas is just that.

ii. But, while these conflicts relate to existing trade treaties such as the WTO, and the rights and obligations that follow from them, there is the rather more dramatic conflict that has arisen in the context of freeing trade as at a new MTN Round or in the context of the extension of NAFTA to South America. Again, the labor and environmental lobbies argue for linkage to advance standards abroad. But economists such as myself—and many agree with me, as we petitioned President Clinton on this very issue during the recent fast-track debate which he lost —argue that the advancement of such agendas on moral grounds through linkage to trade treaties is plainly inefficient.

Here we return to the "killing two birds with one stone" analogy. Such linkage creates obstacles to freeing trade when trade treaties should be about removing them. So, you clutter up and slow down the freeing of trade, thus missing one bird. At the same time, as citizens advancing the social, environmental, and human rights agendas, we lose because the choice of the precise content of these issues to be included in trade treaties will inevitably reflect competitiveness considerations. For example, child labor is included in the proposed Social Clause at the WTO, but not sweatshops or migrant labor rights that afflict the United States itself pretty badly and where the consequence of their inclusion in the Social Clause would have a disastrous impact on U.S. textile and agricultural trade. So, by distorting the social and human rights agendas, we miss the other bird as well. In other words, we underachieve both trade liberalization and progress on social and human rights and on environmental objectives.

The efficient answer then is to use trade treaties to advance freer trade and to reap the gains from trade, while pursuing the other agendas proactively at different and appropriate institutions. Thus, UNICEF could pursue not merely child labor issues but also several other issues relating to children's rights: for example, the right to avoid capital punishment, which is not available in the United States in several states that have passed legislation permitting adults to be executed while also treating children as adults in certain cases. The ILO could pursue rights at work. The UNEP could pursue environmental agendas. True, these agencies are not equipped adequately to undertake these tasks. But then we need to strengthen them. I would even urge that they address themselves to impartial and effective monitoring and review of nations' practices in regard to their conformity to conventions, norms, and so forth, much as the WTO now undertakes trade policy reviews with great effect. The mere exposure of a country's policies in a coherent and impartial fashion can bring moral pressure to bear for change in the desired direction. I call it the Dracula effect:[9] expose evil to sunlight and it begins to shrivel and then die.

The Free Trade Agenda Now

That brings me to the principal task before us today. Faced with demands from civil society, often talking in uncivil terms, politicians have begun to think of accommodating the demands on the trading system in the only terms that they can usually appreciate; what can be done to buy peace minimally from these groups and get along with the important task of freeing trade?

But that is exactly the wrong way to set about these problems. Both agendas are of the utmost importance, and each must be pursued aggressively and also efficiently, free from crippling linkage.

As an economist, I want to see free trade advance efficiently and fully. I must add that I also see free trade as an important moral force for good since we cannot effectively rescue the world's millions from continuing deprivation and poverty without pursuing wealth-generating policies—I call growth the activist "pull up" strategy as opposed to the passive "trickle down" strategy. Growth will also, over time, likely induce values and institutions such as democracy and respect for human rights.

But as a citizen, I want the social and human-rights agendas advanced with all speed, instead of relying simply on these long-run processes. If a hapless woman is screaming for help as her husband beats her, it is ludicrous to say, Hang in there. As incomes grow, things will get better for you. No, you have to get in right there and nail the husband to the wall.

And, so, free traders must now walk hand in hand with the civil society groups seeking the social agendas. It is not as difficult a task as the first shock of discovering each other seemed to suggest. In fact, it is the task for the first decade of the next millennium.

Notes

1. Unfortunately, with the president's general credibility having been compromised as well by now by personal scandals that will not go away, it is dubious whether any future request for fast-track authority during the rest of his term will fare better on this account.

2. I bypass today the entire set of questions raised by the Clinton administration's embrace of a pro-PTA position in world trade policy, firming up a trend that was already beginning to emerge under the Bush administration. I have written extensively on this question, opposing this policy shift at both media and theoretical levels, in numerous publications. See, for example, chapters 25–28 and the extended analytical treatment in Jagdish Bhagwati and Arvind Panagariya, *The Economics of Preferential Trade Agreements* (Washington, D.C.: AEI Press, 1996), and Jagdish Bhagwati, David Greenaway, and Arvind Panagariya, "Trading Preferentially: Theory and Policy," *Economic Journal* (July 1998): 1128–1148.

3. It is noteworthy that the young Winston Churchill was for both free trade and free immigration. Economists and political scientists may find it interesting that, because immigration concerns had arisen over the influx of central European Jewry and hence the agitation for immigration restrictions had a tinge of anti-Semitism associated with it in some quarters, Churchill's stand was regarded with approbation by British Jewry. So, when this stand cost Churchill his parliamentary seat, he was offered a constituency from Manchester by Harold Laski's father, who was a prominent Jewish leader at the time.

4. Thus, when I debated Jeff Faux, President of The Economic Policy Institute, a unions-oriented think tank in Washington aided by Robert Reich and Lester Thurow, on the merits of free trade at Williams College, when both NAFTA and the Uruguay Round were up for passage, he clearly said to me, You can have the Uruguay Round but I will fight NAFTA tooth and nail

5. I must note that the titles of essays in magazines and newspapers are almost always chosen by others. But in this instance, as also others written by Krugman in these years (e.g., in *The Washington Post* where the burden of the argument was that the cost of protection was badly exaggerated), Krugman's conclusions were broadly consonant with the title quoted in the text above.

6. This is known today as the theory of Domestic Distortions and Policy Intervention.

7. I have presented my favorable findings in chapter 11.

8. The argument summarized below has been advanced at greater length in chapter 1 (based on a book-review essay in *The New Republic*) of my latest book, *A Stream of Windows: Unsettling Reflections on Trade, Immigration and Democracy* (Cambridge, MA: MIT Press, 1998).

9. Cf. Bhagwati, *Protectionism* (Cambridge, MA: MIT Press, 1988).

President Clinton is widely credited with a successful trade policy. But nothing is further from the truth. His successes, principally with the Uruguay Round, reflect the completion of initiatives begun by his predecessors. His failures, dramatic indeed, have been his own.

Mr. Clinton's trade policy during his first term was marred by an obsession with Japan. It resulted in the failure of the 1994 Hosokawa-Clinton summit in Washington as Japan turned down the administration's "managed-trade" demands for import targets. Washington also started and lost badly the high-profile dispute over automobiles.

The president's second term has been no better. What else can one conclude from the first-ever failure by a president to secure fast-track authority from Congress?

No Surprise

It should therefore come as no surprise that this administration is currently embroiled in a variety of disputes with foreign trading nations. It complains and fights over steel with Russia and Japan, bananas and hormone-fed beef with the European Union, genetically modified products with many nations, the insertion of a Social Clause into the World Trade Organization agreement with developing countries, cultural restraints with Canada, macroeconomic policies with the EU and Japan ... the list, already frighteningly long, keeps expanding. Ironically, this is at a time when the United States enjoys unique prosperity in a world economy mired in the aftermath of the Asian financial crisis. America should, by all historical reckoning, be feisty about its trading fortunes rather than frustrated and fearful. Where have we gone wrong?

It is tempting to argue that trade policy has been captured by lawyers and trade negotiators. The former aim to win cases and the latter seek concessions; both thrive on strategic confrontations, and neither has a sense of trade architecture. I once heard former U.S. Trade Representative Mickey Kantor profusely compliment a bureaucrat for having negotiated "several trade agreements"—all of which were bilateral textile accords that *restricted* trade. Some of the administration's key players in trade today, including the ambassador to the World Trade Organization, cut their teeth on such textile bilaterals.

But this theme can be overdone. After all, it is the political system that has chosen the lawyers and set them off on their mission. The underlying problem is the pervasive notion that the rest of the world engages in "unfair trade." The notion of "fair trade" is inherently vacuous. Economics teaches us that we generally gain from trade regardless of what our partners do. As the Cambridge economist Joan Robinson observed, we may think fairness requires that we throw stones into our harbor because our trading partners throw stones into theirs, but doing so only compounds our losses.

Yet the idea of fair trade guides U.S. trade policy, instilling officials with a false sense of moral authority that sparks impatience and unilateral threats and actions. Protection-seeking lobbies love the concept because it is elastic and arbitrary enough to make virtually any trade look unfair if the going gets tough; and it also has political resonance in a society that prides itself on equal opportunity and fair competition.

The objections to "unfair trade" by U.S. trading partners began in the 1980s, reaching a crescendo in the Clinton years. When Japan emerged as a major rival, American politicians began to demonize it as a wicked trader whose export policies were predatory and import policies exclusionary. When U.S. unions and politicians opposed the North American Free Trade Agreement, they condemned Mexico as a country with which free trade would be unfair because its environmental and labor standards were not up to snuff.

This distrust of trading partners actually has the force of law. Section 301 of the U.S. trade law authorizes retaliatory tariffs against countries whose trade policies the U.S. deems "unreasonable." Not surprisingly, other countries hugely resent this law. The EU, with Japan's support, has asked the WTO to rule on whether Section 301 violates the organization's rules.

The administration's handling of the clamor for protecting steel exemplifies the folly of "fair trade." The administration's two attack dogs on trade, Trade Representative Charlene Barshefsky and Commerce Secretary William Daley, have ceaselessly complained about America's increased trade deficit, a sure sign, they claim, that the United States has become an "importer of last resort" because the EU and Japan haven't "done enough" to accelerate their growth through appropriate macroeconomic policies. This has encouraged the notion that EU and Japan are therefore not playing fair, and that the responsibility for the out-break of steel protectionism, and its indulgence by the administration, lies with these other nations.

How absurd can you get? These are the best of times for the United States, and the administration should focus on that and tell the public that the trade deficit is irrelevant to the total job situation right now. What's more, to add to the list of "unfair trade practices" the inadequacy of macroeconomic policies abroad is plainly foolish. An administration whose misjudgments helped create the Asian financial crisis, the worst manmade economic disaster since the Great Crash of 1929, should at least understand that macroeconomic-policy correctness is an elusive concept.

If it is politically unavoidable to offer some protection for U.S. steel producers, the administration could have done so without zeroing in on specific suppliers, such as Russia and Japan, demonizing them and adding to the hysteria over unfair trade. Invoking Section 201, the Safeguards Clause, would permit legal restriction of imports in a neutral fashion without discriminating against particular suppliers.

Hormone-Fed Beef

The skirmish with the EU over hormone-fed beef is another example of the administration converting a manageable trade issue into an unmanageable "unfair trade practice." Although the United States has won the battle at the WTO, the fact is that the Europeans were not being protectionist. They can use hormones as well as we can, but they face a consumer movement that simply will not let hormone-fed beef be sold in European markets. Rather than force the Europeans to shape up or accept retaliatory measures, surely it is in America's interests to assume that over time these consumer sentiments will abate. In the meantime it is sensible to propose a labeling solution that the

Europeans must be urged to accept in lieu of hugely disruptive tariff retaliation.

Ms. Barshefsky has recently made noises in this direction. But she cannot have been serious when she reportedly said that, rather than use the label "Hormone-Fed Beef," the administration would propose that we be allowed to say "Made in USA" since everyone knows that Americans use hormones. That's like saying "Made in India" is the equivalent of "Made with Child Labor," because everyone knows that India has child labor.

Look at each trade skirmish and you will find American suspicion of "unfair trade." At times, this prompts a rush to unilateral action—as in the banana dispute with the EU, in which Washington refuses to wait for the legal process at WTO to run its course. It is time for the president to assert his leadership and restore a vision and coherence to trade policy—one that abandons the empty notion of fair trade and champions trade that is truly free.

10   Is Free Trade Working for Everyone?

Dear Jagdish Bhagwati,   26 October 1999

It is generally assumed that Adam Smith's *The Wealth of Nations*, published in 1776, provides an irrefutable justification for free trade as it is practised today. Nothing could be further from the truth. Smith did not advocate free trade as such, but free trade in conditions which are very different from those that prevail now.

Smith assumed that the market would be in the hands of small companies—too small to influence the market price. He abhorred monopoly power, especially if it was achieved by protecting trade secrets (what we now call "intellectual property"). He also assumed that investors would run their own businesses (being more motivated to do so than managers) and would invest at home rather than abroad.

Smith would have been horrified by the global free trade economy established by the World Trade Organization (WTO) and dominated by uncontrollable, quasi-monopolist, transnational corporations, which derive their funding from all over the world, no longer have any obligations to the society they are based in, and are willing to move anywhere on the globe if costs are lower, environmental controls laxer and subsidies higher.

Free trade seeks to establish a level playing field on which rich countries and poor countries, huge transnational corporations (TNCs) and small local companies compete as equals. But they are far from equal and to remove the protection that small countries and companies require is to seal their fate. If I had to confront Mike Tyson I would not want to do so on a level playing field.

Originally published in *Prospect* (Dec. 1999): 16–20, as a debate with Edward Goldsmith, editor of *The Ecologist* and co-editor of "The Case Against the Global Economy." Reprinted with permission.

Free trade was first imposed on the trading nations of the world by Britain in the middle of the 19th century. At that time, Britain was the workshop of the world. It produced two thirds of the world's coal, about half its iron, and one third of its manufactures. In addition, the City of London was the world's financial centre and was alone capable of financing the industrial expansion that free trade would make possible. But in the 1870s free trade was largely abandoned. There had been a long economic depression and Britain was losing its competitive edge. New markets had to be found abroad, and companies turned towards the markets of Africa, Asia, Latin America, and the Pacific. Hence the scramble for colonies. Promoters of colonialism, such as Cecil Rhodes, made no bones about it.

But the colonial system could not last forever and it became clear before the second world war broke out that a substitute had to be found. By this time it was the United States, not Britain, which dominated the world's politico-economic scene. Foreign policy professionals and heads of large corporations began to meet in Washington as early as 1939, to establish how the postwar, post-colonial world economy could best be shaped. The answer was to "develop" the third world. Three institutions were set up to achieve this objective: the World Bank, the IMF and the General Agreement on Tariffs and Trade (now the WTO).

The meaning of free trade underwent another dramatic change with the signing of the Uruguay Round in 1994. Free trade no longer simply means eliminating tariffs, which had already fallen from an average of 40 percent after 1945 to about 5 percent before the Uruguay Rounds began. It now means eliminating "non-tariff barriers," namely any domestic regulations which can be construed as interfering with trade by increasing costs to industry. Whether a regulation constitutes a non-tariff barrier is decided by a secret panel of the WTO. So far, every decision has been in favour of the corporations in their efforts to make themselves more "competitive," regardless of human, social and ecological costs.

It is not so much trade that is being freed, but the corporations which control it. They are acquiring the freedom to cut down virgin forests in order to produce plywood, lavatory paper and the Sunday edition of the *New York Times*; the freedom to erode, salinise and waterlog agricultural land so as to produce cheap raw materials for the food-processing industry; the freedom to pillage the oceans with trawlers which annihilate fish populations with "wall of death" drift nets; the freedom to churn out ever greater amounts of ever more toxic chemicals to spread on our fields and release into our rivers; the freedom to extinguish thousands of species every year to satisfy the short-term interests of the TNCs and the bureaucrats and politicians who live off them. What would Adam Smith have thought?

Yours,
Edward Goldsmith

Dear Edward Goldsmith, 30 October 1999

If free trade were as destructive as you claim, I would be at the barricades with you, AK-47 in hand, seeking its downfall. But I cannot understand how you have reached these alarmist conclusions about what is in reality a powerful engine of increasing well-being for everyone on the planet. I say this not just because Adam Smith, whom you misread, spoke so eloquently about the virtues of free trade. More importantly, the case for free trade has been reaffirmed by theorists over the two centuries since Smith wrote, and our practical experience has underlined the wisdom of his intuitions.

You are right to say that monopolies undermine the case for markets, and hence for free trade. But you are wrong in ignoring more than fifty years of economic analysis which has taught us that large corporations rarely have the monopoly power that the naked eye perceives: the possibility of being challenged by other corporations if you exert your monopoly power usually prevents you from doing so. And freer trade, by increasing the possibility of market entry by competitors from around the world, is the most effective antidote to monopoly —protection has long been known to be the main ally of domestic monopoly.

Your "Mike Tyson" analogy does not work. Small countries and small companies *can* compete. If you go down New York's Fifth Avenue, you will see small hot dog vendors thriving, despite the giant retail stores beside them. The case for free trade is compatible with different sizes of economic agents or nations as long as trade is noncoercive. The exceptions are where the nations are both hegemonic and coercive, such as the former Soviet Union in its trade with eastern Europe. The history of the US is more altruistic. For nearly four decades, until the late 1980s, the US was benign towards most of the developing countries that wished to keep their markets closed, letting them enjoy the benefits of trade liberalisation without reciprocal opening of their markets. In fact, since I believe (and so do they, now) that they would have been better off if only they had opened up their markets to freer trade, it is a pity that the US did not apply more pressure for reciprocity.

The postwar evidence for many of the newly independent and developing countries favours the claim that autarkic policies do not pay off. This is why many of them have now turned to liberalisation. The most dramatic individual case is the transformation of Fernando Cardoso, who as a dependency theory sociologist had warned the third world of the dangers of trans-national corporations (TNCs), but as President Cardoso of Brazil has been seeking to integrate his country into the global economy he once feared and despised.

You also seem to forget that, no matter how self-serving the actions of economic agents, the outcome may still be socially productive, especially when the institutional framework is well designed. The fact that nations and corporations pursue markets and profits in their own interests does not prove the venality of free trade and investment. For these policies have produced huge progress. It is not just the size of the total pie which has increased; by increasing prosperity, free trade has also helped to reduce poverty. And the wealth which liberal policies promote is not passive "trickle down" wealth; rather, it is an active, "pull up" strategy for sweeping up underemployed and poor people into gainful employment. The experience of India, which has the most poor in the world as a result of 30 years of abysmal growth under autarkic policies, is ample proof.

Even social policies, such as reducing illiteracy and extending women's rights, generally benefit from prosperity and hence from the liberal policies that you dislike. The existence of more jobs encourages poor parents to forgo current income and to send children to primary schools. Legislation forbidding a man to beat his wife means little until, when beaten, the wife can walk out, find a job and survive. Liberals sometimes say rashly that "all good things go together." In this instance they are right.

You say that the WTO is enabling TNCs to "cut down virgin forests" and so on. But African "slash-and-burn" agriculture long precedes both you and me, let alone the WTO. Forests have long been cut down—probably even where your offices are. The issue which comes up before the WTO's dispute settlement panels is whether Britain or Denmark can unilaterally decide to suspend trade in "lavatory paper and the Sunday edition of the *New York Times*"—simply because their NGOs do not want forests cut down in Malaysia or Brazil. Originating from India, I see here the quasi-imperialist notion that you and your friends can decide what we should or should not do. Harvesting forests in western countries is all right, but if you cut down "rain" or "virgin" forests which happen to be "over there," that must be stopped. But the days of gunboat diplomacy are long gone, and rich country NGOs cannot resurrect them by simply hanging a halo on their walls. That is what the fights at the WTO are mostly about.

I am no friend of the big corporations, but I reject the claim that they are promoting a "race to the bottom" on environmental and other standards. Where is the evidence? Studies indicate that big companies, jealous of their reputations (which can be swiftly damaged by NGOs, CNN and the internet), will not exploit lower standards, say, south of the Rio Grande on the US-Mexico border. Moreover, democratic countries play the game of attracting capital not by inviting investors to come and pollute their rivers, but by offering tax holidays. None the less, your fears are widely shared and the simplest answer to such fears is to insist that TNCs apply our environmental and labour standards when they go abroad: "Do in Rome as the Londoners do, not as the Romans do."

Yours,
Jagdish Bhagwati

Dear Jagdish, 31 October 1999

You accuse me of not providing evidence for my "alarmist" assertions. Let me do so by challenging your assertion that "large corporations rarely have the monopoly power that the naked eye perceives." As I see it, the power of big corporations is increasing by the day. Already fewer than four or five TNCs control 40 percent of the main commodities traded on the world market (tea, wheat, maize, sorghum and so on). In 1994, two companies, Cargill and Continental, shared 50 percent of U.S. grain exports, and a few weeks ago the press revealed that Cargill planned to buy Continental's grain division.

Similar trends are occurring with other food crops. Furthermore, in 1994 the U.S. exported 36 percent of the wheat traded worldwide, 64 percent of the corn, barley, sorghum and oats, and 40 percent of the soya beans. This means that the world price for these commodities is the U.S. price—and the U.S. price is fixed by huge corporations with monopolistic powers.

As for your claim that small and large companies can co-exist, it is perverse to choose an example from retailing. Today we are witnessing the annihilation of small retailers across the world. In Britain, 95,000 food shops closed down between 1961 and 1983. Grocers, greengrocers, fishmongers and butchers have been squeezed out by a supermarket network which in 1993 accounted for 83 percent of all food sold in this country. In 1997, five transnational food giants accounted for 80 percent of the grocery trade in Britain.

I also find it hard to accept that free trade is an antidote to monopoly. Transnational corporations now influence government trade policy, either directly or via the WTO, the World Bank and the IMF. Thus the new forestry policies to be proposed at the WTO meeting in Seattle are those imposed on the U.S. administration by the forestry giants—International Paper, Weyerhaeuser, Georgia-Pacific and Boise Cascade—whose combined turnover is around $50 billion.

Of course, politicians should never have handed over so much power to the WTO. But let's be realistic: the WTO is there, and written into its constitution is the principle that all member nations must modify their laws to conform with its own rules. It has in effect become a world government—especially as it is now branching out into other areas of policy-making such as education and health.

Nor can I accept your statement that the United States allowed third world countries to enjoy the benefits of progressive trade liberalisation without reciprocal opening of their markets. Walden Bello, the Filipino economist, has shown how the World Bank set out in the mid-1970s to bring his country within the ambit of the global economy. To do this meant first transforming the peasantry into a rural proletariat, then replacing the local middle class with the executives of TNCs geared to the global economy. This required a social and economic transformation so drastic that only a dictator such as Ferdinand Marcos—furnished with the required international aid—could impose it.

Third world countries did not abandon autarky because it did not pay. They were made to do so. The World Bank imposed large infrastructure projects on many of them, which then had to be repaid in foreign exchange, which in turn required entering the world economy. The World Bank also encouraged many countries to produce a very limited range of export crops which the market could not absorb. And the developed world has been less open than you imply: according to Oxfam our trade barriers cost poor countries $700 billion a year, 14 times what they receive in aid.

Finally, you would not expect me to agree that development is solving social problems. On the contrary, it is bringing with it the "diseases of civilisation"—crime, drug addiction, cancer, and so on. Crime, for example, is largely the product of family and community disintegration. This cannot be solved by faster growth, because it is economic development which is undermining traditional social institutions.

Yours,
Edward

Dear Edward,   2nd November 1999

You assume that monopoly power has increased just because the share of the larger companies in some industries has increased. But this is not the way to measure monopoly power. If a company exercises its monopoly power and makes monopoly profits, other corporations will soon enter the market, seeking those excess profits, like bees to the honey-pot. Economists, therefore, no longer look at market share but instead ask how "contestable" a market is.

Thus, even if Cargill and Continental had the entire U.S. grain market, and not just 50 percent of U.S. exports, they would still have to face competition from Argentina, Australia, Canada and other members of the Cairns Group of agricultural exporting nations that lobby for agricultural trade liberalisation. IBM had to compete with Microsoft; both have to compete with Hewlett Packard, Dell, Toshiba and Hitachi. And if this mechanism fails we have the anti-trust authorities—people such as Joel Klein, the U.S. anti-trust tsar who recently went after Microsoft.

You are right to remind us that the small, local shopkeepers are an endangered species. But that does not create monopolies. As the little bookstores I loved in New York have disappeared, we have seen Barnes & Noble up against Borders and now Amazon.com.

What you are really mourning is the passing of the old. As technology, investment and migration span the globe, economic and social cultures evolve, change, even die. I share your nostalgia. I, too, would rather have the small bookstores, the intimate cafés, the fragrance of baguettes as you walk down the streets of Paris, and much else. And— like you I am sure—I happily put my hand in my wallet for bodies such as the National Trust and Unesco which salvage some of the precious things that time destroys everywhere.

Of course this simplifies the picture. We are not smoothly evolving towards a frictionless global system. There are big cultural differences which underlie many of the world's current trade disputes, both within the developed world (for example, different attitudes towards GM food in the US and Europe) and between the developed and developing world (tolerance of child labour in poor countries). It is part of the job of the WTO and its member governments to control these conflicts and make sure that they do not end in trade wars.

Pessimists like you will not be proved right on such conflicts. You are certainly wrong about the ability of non-dominant countries to profit from free trade. In 1961, when I visited Japan, I was told that the country could not export without the cartels which the US had outlawed, and that global integration could not be Japan's option. History proved otherwise.

Nor do I agree with your view that liberalisation in developing countries has been achieved mainly through threats from the Bretton Woods institutions. Far more important has been the successful example of east Asia's pro-openness approach. Of course the IMF has got things wrong, as it did in the first year of the Asian financial crisis. The World Bank also has not always looked after the interests of poor countries as well as it could have. For example, it pushed for intellectual property protection, which the United States wanted badly because of corporate lobbying rather than to support the interests of poor countries.

But such developed world interests are not always corporate interests. Today, for example, the Clinton-Gore administration is seeking a "social clause" in the WTO because it is beholden to the AFL-CIO trade union federation for money and support in the impending U.S. elections. The case for a clause is clearly flawed and is opposed by most developing countries. It is another case of western moralising disguising self-interest.

Yours,
Jagdish

Dear Jagdish,   4 November 1999

I am indeed nostalgic for the small cafés and shops of old, but it is not just out of nostalgia that I feel they must be restored. The supermarkets which have replaced them are a menace to the planet. They do not support local producers, but buy goods from all over the world, using transport which contributes to global warming—by far the biggest problem we face today. They use more plastic packaging, which is then incinerated, causing the dispersion of highly carcinogenic dioxins. They also provide three times fewer full-time jobs than the small shops did.

You argue that there is still healthy competition between the few companies that dominate particular sectors of the economy. But you forget that when you have a competition, someone will win. Darwin forgot this too. My concern is that as ever fewer giant companies control the sale of a particular commodity, they will see that it is less advantageous for them to compete with each other.

Already, large corporations are resorting to more vertical integration, controlling every step in the process in their respective fields: from the mining of minerals, to the production of goods, their shipping to subsidiaries in other countries, and their wholesaling and retailing to local consumers. Today about 30 percent of world trade is between big corporations and their subsidiaries. What is to prevent 50 percent, 60 percent, or even 80 percent of world trade from taking place within these organisations? We are heading towards a new era of global corporate colonialism. I wonder if it will still be called "free trade"?

Yours,
Edward

Dear Edward,   5 November 1999

Your worry about the supermarkets prompts a few sceptical thoughts. For example, agricultural trade liberalisation is bringing a shift from pesticide-intensive European agriculture to less environmentally unfriendly agriculture in the poor countries. This offsets whatever harm transportation may cause. Moreover, if there is a good macroeconomic policy that maintains full employment, then jobs lost through imports are replaced by (better) jobs in export industries. You cannot just look at one side of the ledger.

That is, of course, what many critics of foreign investment do. They see jobs exported to India, Guatemala and Mexico by big corporations but they do not consider the jobs coming in. In the Piedmont Mountains in South Carolina local people lost employment in the traditional textiles industry. But since then about 250 foreign companies, many of them German, have moved in and the workers are now earning nearly three times their former wages.

Looking around the world it is hard to find much evidence of persistent "excess" profits. But when you say that both Darwin and I forgot that someone wins the competition, and that, therefore, monopoly must follow, you miss the point I was making: winners cannot rest on their laurels if the markets can be contested by new entrants. Maria Callas, the greatest diva of her time, must worry about Renata Tebaldi if she drops a high note. The monopolist must always watch out. That's the beauty of it.

Yours,
Jagdish

Trade and Wages

11   Play It Again Sam: A New Look at Trade and Wages

11.1 Introduction

T. N. Strinivasan has written profusely, and profoundly, on both development economics and on international trade.[1] So, I could offer him my tribute by writing on either. But T. N. will appreciate, as the no-nonsense economist of integrity he has always been, that I must follow my comparative advantage and choose to write on trade. That I do today, tackling a question of immense topicality and great policy concern: to wit, and to put it strikingly, the effect of trade with poor countries on the poor in the rich countries.

Indeed, the prolonged decline in real wages of our unskilled workers, and the widely-shared sense that crystallized during the national debate over NAFTA that trade with Mexico would harm our workers have produced arguably the most animated and politically salient debate among economists on the question: *does trade with poor countries immiserize our unskilled workers?*[2]

Yet, despite the immense number of academic analyses, confusion reigns and general pessimism prevails. I propose here to remove the confusion and to reach a more optimistic conclusion.

11.2 Two Different Questions

In doing so, I first note that as Deardorff and Hakura (1994) and Bhagwati and Dehejia (1994) noted earlier, the question posed is ambiguous (these essays appeared in the volume edited by Bhagwati and Kosters

Originally published, as chapter 5, in *Trade, Growth and Development: Essays in Honor of T. N. Srinivasan*, ed. Gus Ranis and Laxmi Raut (Amsterdam: Elsevier, 1999), 57–70. Reprinted with permission.

1994). Different questions must be distinguished, each appearing at first blush to be like the other, while being quite distinct with different answers. In particular, I distinguish between two questions, both of importance and each corresponding in some way to what seems to agitate policymakers in some vague, if not inchoate, fashion. As it happens, I argue that the answer to each question, for different reasons, is not as alarming as in the popular perception of the threat from trade (with poor countries) to our workers.

Question 1 If the rich countries (the North hereafter) were to liberalize their trade with the poor countries (the South hereafter), or if the South were to liberalize its trade with the North, e.g., as NAFTA did for the US and Mexico, then would this reduce the real wages of workers in the North?[3]

Question 2 Can the observed changes in real wages in the North be explained by changes in trade (opportunities) coming from the South rather than by factors internal to the North?

As I will presently argue, Question 1 focuses exclusively on trade liberalization in the South and/or in the North and its consequences for real wages in the North. By contrast, Question 2 contrasts the effects on real wages in the North as a result of all factors (that would not be confined to trade liberalization alone but extend also to technical change and factor accumulation): these factors would then be grouped into those coming from the South and those coming from within the North, and interacting via trade.

In both cases, however, my answers are comforting rather than pessimistic. In each case, there are two steps involved in linking trade with real wages. The first step is to assert that the (relative) prices of labor-intensive goods have fallen within the North because of trade. The second step is then to argue that therefore, as in the Stolper–Samuelson (SS) theorem, the real wages of labor have fallen in the North. For Question 1, I show below (in the stylized 2×2 model) that step 1 certainly holds. But step 2, involving the empirical applicability of the SS theorem, is open to serious objections and the effect on real wages of all factors, including labor, could well be favorable. Therefore, one may well be optimistic on the impact of trade on real wages if the empirical relevance of the SS theorem is denied. As for the answer to Question 2, the answer I give below is decidedly optimistic in the sense that the first step itself cannot be taken: changes emanating from the South, in

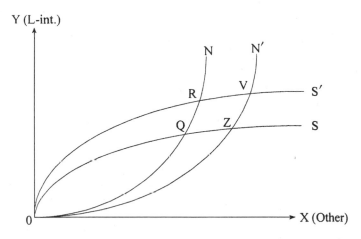

Figure 11.1

their totality (as distinct from merely trade liberalization in the South), will likely raise rather than reduce the prices of labor-intensive goods, ceteris paribus.[4]

11.3 "Exclusively Trade Liberalization" Question

This question refers to the effects of trade liberalization, whether in the South or in the North (vis-à-vis each other), on real wages of workers in the North. Thus, in a stylized 2×2 model where the South exports the (unskilled-)labor-intensive good Y while the North exports the capital-intensive good X, the answer to this question is straightforward.

In figure 11.1, depicting the offer curves of the South and the North, with tariffs in each region leading to the tariff-ridden offer curves intersecting at Q, consider trade liberalization by the South. This shifts its offer curve to OS' and the new trade equilibrium to R. Clearly, the trade liberalization will increase the supply of exports from the South at every relative goods price (i.e., terms of trade) and will reduce the world price of the labor-intensive good Y and hence, given any tariff in the North, also the *domestic* price of Y in the North.

If, however, the North liberalizes its trade, ON shifts to ON' while OS is unchanged, leading to trade equilibrium at Z. But while this raises the world price of the labor-intensive good Y, its domestic price will fall in the North (unless the Metzler paradox obtains, so we must rule it out).

Thus, whether the trade liberalization occurs in the South or the North, we can expect it to lead to a fall in the domestic price of the labor-intensive good Y in the North. Hence, it inevitably sets the stage for the Stolper–Samuelson (SS) theorem.

If SS reigns, the fall in the domestic price of the labor-intensive good Y will lead to a fall in the real wage of labor in the North. Thus, while the first step in the argument linking trade liberalization to decline in our real wages, via a fall in the price of labor-intensive goods, is *theoretically* satisfied (though, as argued in the next section, the stylized *facts* show that the prices of labor-intensive goods, whose behavior must reflect not just the trade liberalization we are discussing presently, actually rose slightly in the period when real wages declined), we still have to ensure that the second step, the applicability of the SS theorem, can also be taken.

But then we must recall that the SS theorem cannot be regarded as necessarily defining the empirical reality. In fact, the theorem became well-known precisely because it simply established a *possibility* when no one thought it possible to do so. In particular, these distinguished authors managed to show that under certain restrictive conditions, one could indeed infer an unambiguous effect on real wages from a change in the goods prices. Until Stolper and Samuelson did so, it was generally believed that while nominal wages would fall for workers intensively employed in the good whose price had fallen, the effect on *real* wages was ambiguous: it would depend on the consumption pattern of the workers, since a fall in the nominal wage could be offset by a preference in consuming the good whose price had fallen. The SS result, in showing that (given their model and its assumptions) we did not need to know what consumer preferences were in order to infer the impact on real wages, remained however a theoretical curiosum, as it were; few regarded it as an inevitable empirical reality or even as capturing a central tendency. Today, however, in a supreme irony, it seems as if it is regarded as our inescapable fate.

And that is a singular mistake. For, as discussed extensively in Bhagwati and Dehejia (1994), we must recognize that specialization in production will mean that instead of one factor being hurt while the other benefits from the change in the goods price, as in the SS case, *both* (of the two) factors will benefit from the price fall. Scale economies can also do this. Improvement in overall efficiency following trade competition can do it too. In fact, these "lift-all-boats" effects can kill the SS "redistributive" effect. As it happens, the calculations of Brown,

Deardorff, and Stern (1994) (with the aid of their well-known computable Michigan model during the NAFTA debate), allowing for the restrictive SS conditions not to be fully met, showed a real wage *improvement* for American workers from NAFTA. So, the asserted link between trade and real wage decline, as precisely postulated here, breaks down; the SS theorem, whose applicability is not inevitable or in my judgment even likely, is then not the dagger aimed surely at our workers' jugulars!

I might add that there is nothing in what I have said above about the Factor Price Equalization (FPE) theorem. The FPE theorem requires a great deal of added baggage: structure must be put on the South so as to make, for instance, its production functions identical to those of the North, to rule out factor intensity reversals, to assume identity of tastes across counties. Indeed, many of these assumptions are unrealistic (e.g., we know from the work in the 1960s by Minhas and Arrow–Chenery–Minhas–Solow that factor intensity reversals are not merely possible, since estimated CES production functions have different cross-sector elasticities, but also likely because endowments lie on different sides of the factor-intensity-crossover point). But that is no cause for concern, of course, unless we also wish explain what is happening in the South as a result of trade liberalization. All we need to do, in explaining the past and future link between trade (with the South) on the real wages of the unskilled in the North is to start from the fact that the South is a net exporter of labor-intensive goods and then to examine the effects of trade liberalization, as we have done, on goods prices in the North and therefrom on the real wages in the North. That is just what I have done here.

11.4 "Total Trade" Question

But then let me ask the altogether different Question 2, distinguished above, which relates to whether a shift in the offer curve of the South, arising from the *totality* of all relevant factors such as factor accumulation and not merely trade liberalization, can explain the decline in real wages in the North. Again, we would have to argue that this shift leads to a decline in the average world prices of labor-intensive goods, by augmenting their supplies (i.e., the offer curve shifts outward), and then again via the SS theorem to a decline in real wages. The second SS step runs into the same difficulties as with Question 1 in the preceding section. But so does the first step, because we must now reckon with factors such as capital accumulation and technical change as well, as I demonstrate presently.

The analysis of what happens to the offer curve of the South, as a result of several factors distinguished below, explains why the offer curve will not necessarily shift outwards so as to push down, ceteris paribus, the prices of labor-intensive goods in world trade (and hence be the cause of the declining wages in the North by triggering the SS theorem). In fact, it can be expected to exhibit the opposite tendency, reducing the overall excess supplies of labor-intensive goods and hence leading to a rise in their prices instead, *as seems to have happened*. It also explains a number of other stylized facts. I show this now, first by stating the stylized facts, and then developing the shift-of-the-offer-curve explanation.

11.4.1 *Stylized Facts*

A number of stylized facts have emerged in the empirical studies spawned by the trade-and-wages debate:

a. The most important fact is evidently the behavior of the prices of labor-intensive goods in world trade, which in the United States, fell in the 1970s but (slightly) rose in the 1980s and early 1990s. The latter phenomenon is now conceded by all serious scholars, including early skeptics such as the world class econometrician and trade economist Ed Leamer, who has done a considerable amount of careful empirical work on the subject.[5]

b. However, in an eyescan "refutation" of the SS theorem, U.S. real wages (of unskilled workers), defined first as "compensation per worker" and next as the less satisfactory "average hourly earnings," continued to rise during the 1970s while they fell by the latter measure and their rise was seriously moderated by the former measure, during the 1980s and early 1990s (see figure 11.2).

c. The wage differential between unskilled and skilled workers has risen not just in the US and other OECD countries, but also in some other countries, e.g., in Chile, Uruguay, Colombia, Costa Rica and Mexico in the last decade (see Robbins 1996).

Trade in labor-intensive manufactures of the poor countries has not only been a story of all these countries becoming larger exporters of such manufactures. Over time, per capita incomes grew more rapidly in some (e.g., East Asia in the 1970s and 1980s) as compared to

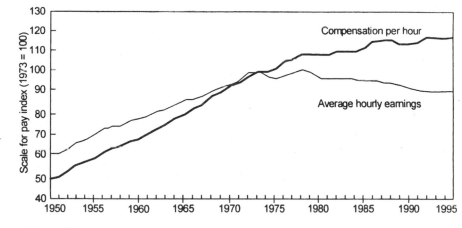

Figure 11.2
Real average hourly earnings and compensation. *Note:* Compensation per hour includes wages and salaries of employees plus benefits (employers' contributions for social insurance and private benefit plans). It covers the nonfarm business sector. Average Hourly Earnings does not include nonwage benefits. It covers production and non-supervisory workers in the private nonfarm sector of the economy. Both measures are adjusted for inflation using CPI-U-XI. *Sources:* Bureau of Labor Statistics, Economic Report of the President, 1996; M. Kosters, AEI, May 1996.

others. The former subset of poor countries then became net importers of labor-intensive manufactures themselves so that the net exports of the poor-countries group (constituted by the two subsets of countries taken together) to the group of rich countries grew less dramatically than many fear. The fear comes from an erroneous assumption that each poor country will become an increasing supplier of labor-intensive manufactures to the rich countries, leading to an avalanche of exports. International economists, among whom the late Bela Balassa deserves pride of place, have long understood this phenomenon empirically, calling it the phenomenon of "ladders of comparative advantage."

This more comforting picture is exactly what the Australian economist Ross Garnaut (1996) has shown in figure 11.3. There, the 1970s witness East Asia steadily increasing net exports of labor-intensive manufactures while Japan reduces them. The same pattern repeats itself in the 1980–94 period when East Asian (NIE) net exports decline from over 10 percent of world trade in labor-intensive manufactures to nearly zero while China goes almost in a crossing diagonal from around 2 to over 14 percent, the difference between the two leaving greatly reduced the net impact on what Garnaut calls the "old indus-

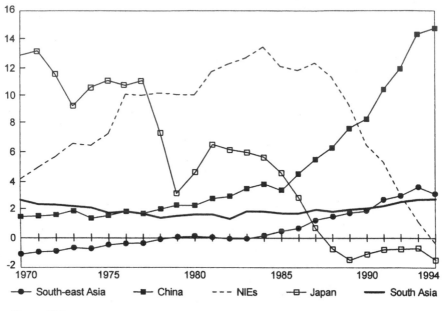

Figure 11.3
Ration of net exports to world imports of labor-intensive manufactures, East and South Asia 1970–94 (%). *Note:* South-east Asia includes ASEAN (including Singapore) and Vietnam; NIEs include Taiwan, Hong Kong, Korea and Singapore; and South Asia includes India, Pakistan, Bangladesh and Sri Lanka. *Source:* UN trade data, International Economic DataBank, The Australian National University.

trial countries" on the average. This is, of course, what I just recalled as the "ladder of comparative advantage" and countries climb up on it with growing per capita incomes.

11.4.2 Analysis

These stylized facts can be explained, and their underlying causes understood, by returning to the offer curve analysis. Essentially, I plan to answer Question 2 at the outset by analyzing immediately how the South's offer curve would shift as a result of various reasons such as capital accumulation. (In section 11.4, I will then go on to discuss the corresponding shifts in the North's offer curve as well, for identical reasons, seeking to tell the whole story of what happened in the recent period.)

The underlying changes that shift each offer curve are clearly: (1) capital and labor accumulation; (2) technical change; and (3) trade liberalization. (I say "trade liberalization" instead of the more generic "trade policy change" because we have been witnessing liberalization rather than growth of trade barriers in the last few decades.) Consider each of these three factors in turn.

1. When capital and labor accumulate at the same rate (say, $x\%$), the production of both goods will *expand* by an identical rate. But if capital accumulates more rapidly (say, at $y\%$), then we have to account for the effect of that extra non-uniform expansion of capital ($(y-x)\%$).

This latter effect, which international economists call the Rybczynski effect, reduces the excess supply of the labor-intensive good Y. It will thus contract or shrink the offer curve.

The net effect of factor accumulation will then depend on the relative strength of these two effects. But evidently, if capital accumulation is considerable, as it has been in East Asia for over two decades, that could well be a cause of their offer curve exhibiting a shrinking of their production of labor-intensive goods and their withdrawal from exports of such goods in world markets. (In fact, the East Asian "miracle" has been precisely in the "miraculous" investment rates that these countries have chalked up, as I have argued in chapter 4.)

2. If technical change is occurring and is contributing to the expanding per capita incomes as well, we can generally expect it to be occurring faster in the modern industries that use human and conventional capital intensively. In that case, one can expect again a pull of resources away from the labor-intensive industries towards the production of the progressive industries, thus contributing to a *decline* or shrinking of the South's offer curve rather than to its further outward expansion. (This tendency is conclusive when the technical progress is Hicks-neutral but may not be so decisive if it is biased.)

3. Trade liberalization, on the other hand, will *expand* the offer curve, as already discussed in analyzing Question 1. (I might add that import protection could, as emphasized by Paul Krugman in his classic work (1989), leads to export promotion eventually. This possibility is being ignored.)

Hence, there are two factors (trade liberalization and uniform expansion of all factors of production) which push the South's offer curve out, and two factors (beyond-uniform accumulation of capital and technical change) which pull it in. Very likely, the former two factors were more important than the latter two in the 1970s. In that era, the oil shock had generally depressed growth rates of per capita incomes in many developing countries while trade liberalization continued only at a moderate pace. From the early to mid-1980s through 1990s, however, the growth rates in developing countries were generally more robust, with the huge East Asian growth rates continuing more or less, while the "miracle" spread to other countries in Asia westwards. I would expect therefore that in the 1970s, compared to the later period, the expansion of the South's offer curve would be greater, and hence the downward pressure on the prices of labor-intensive goods, *ceteris paribus*, would be less. In fact, my stylized view, which I develop shortly, is that the later period, due to these effects, actually saw a *shrinking* of the net group offer curve of the South leading to a *price rise* of labor-intensive goods. Furthermore, the moderately *expanded quantities* of trade, despite that, are to be attributed to a simultaneous outward shift in the group offer curve of the North, as its demand for imports of labor-intensive goods rose for the same reasons operating in the North.

Given the asymmetries I have just argued for the South between the two periods, the 1970s and later, it is not surprising that the stylized facts on prices of labor-intensive goods show that the 1970s witnessed a fall in them, with opposite behavior in the later period.

Furthermore, if capital accumulation is a major factor in some Southern countries, one should expect the "ladder" phenomenon that Garnaut has documented (figure 11.3). And if conventional capital is a complement to skilled labor but a substitute for unskilled labor, the accumulation of capital would generally tend to widen the differential in reward in favor of skilled labor, as has happened in some of the better-performing countries.[6]

To recapitulate the main conclusion, therefore, the analysis of the factors that shift the South's offer curve shows that changes in trade with the poor countries, which arise from the *totality of changes* coming from them, can be plausibly argued to have been, in the recent period and on balance, benign as far as the fear of falling (average) world prices of labor-intensive goods is concerned. And if we then expect these forces to continue operating, with rapid growth diffusing through the developing world as broad economic reforms take root, then we can well expect that the future will also be benign.

Thus, the answer to Question 2, posed above, is essentially benign. The picture is dramatically different from the one we get (as when we discuss Question 1) if we focus exclusively on trade liberalization by developing countries:[7] a process which, in any case, is spread out over time in most cases and therefore is not likely to outweigh, at any time, the effect of rapid growth rates.

11.5   The Full Story

To grasp fully what happened in the recent period, however, we need to bring into the analysis the shift in the North's offer curve, a shift arising from the same constellation of causes that were discussed in relation to the South's offer curve.

When this is done, we are confronted with an interesting contrast: the factors that worked to reduce the supply of labor-intensive goods from the South work in reverse for the North's offer curve, since it *imports* labor-intensive goods. Hence, all factors tend to increase the North's demand for labor-intensive goods, reinforcing the upward pressure on the prices of labor-intensive goods that come from the South itself.

1. Thus, while uniform expansion of factor supply will push out the North's offer curve, further capital accumulation will reduce the output of labor-intensive goods and thus reduce their net supply and increase import demand. This will reinforce the outward shift in the offer curve.

2. A similar result would follow from technical change concentrated in the capital-intensive industries, disallowing complexities that can follow from biased technical change.

3. And trade liberalization, of course, will also shift out the offer curve.

So, we have a situation where all factors tend to reinforce one another, raising the demand for imports of labor-intensive goods and hence, *ceteris paribus*, raising their world prices. Associated with this, there would be expanded trade volumes. We would thus observe increasing "import penetration ratios" in the import-competing industries of the North as, in fact, we have. (Note that this outcome is a result of purely domestic factors, and is not to be attributed to an exogenous increase in export supplies from the South. In fact, as I argued above, my informed guess is that the export supplies from the South shrank, not rose, in the post-1980s period.) The world prices of labor-intensive goods would then be expected to rise with the North's increased demand for them, as in fact they have done.[8]

Insofar as these shifts in the two offer curves—one (for the South) shrinking and the other (for the North) expanding—translate into increased domestic prices for the labor-intensive goods and in the quantities traded, we are left with the question: what can we say about the accompanying effects on the real wages of unskilled labor in the North?

Clearly, if we ask a ceteris paribus question, namely, what is the effect of the shift in the South's offer curve on real wages in the North, then it has to be (if the SS theorem holds) positive. For it leads to a rise in the prices of labor-intensive goods, not a fall. If we bring both shifts into the picture, and look for a total answer, then clearly the answer has to be as follows: the factors underlying the North's expanding demand for labor-intensive imports may reduce the real wages of labor, ceteris paribus, but that fall will be *moderated* by the effect of the exogenous shift in the South's offer curve. In short, I would maintain this answer to Question 2 posed above: *trade with the South has moderated the adverse impact, such as may be, from technical change, on real wages in the North caused by technical change.*

To recapitulate the substance of my argument, if I was asked to put the most plausible story together from the previous analyses of the shifts in the South's and North's offer curves, it would be as follows. Based on a simultaneous shift in the offer curves of the South and the North (as in figure 11.1, where we go from an initial trade equilibrium at Q to V where both shifted curves ON' and OS' now intersect):

• Ongoing changes in capital accumulation and technical change, working alongside and offsetting the effects of trade liberalization, are likely to have been predominant in the world economy. These caused a mildly upward, instead of a substantial downward, shift in the average world prices of labor-intensive manufactures.

• The net effect of these forces has also been to raise the domestic prices of labor-intensive manufactures in the North as well.

• Insofar as the factors operating within the South and affecting its offer curve (i.e., the "trade opportunities" the South offers us or, in popular imagination, threatens us with) are considered, my conclusion is that they likely have been, on balance, increasing the average prices of labor-intensive goods in world trade during the years when real wages have fallen in the North.

• If, then, the SS theorem is invoked, the changes exogenously emanating from the South cannot be responsible for the decline of the real wages in the North: they push the goods prices in the wrong direction.

• But the overall increase in the world prices of labor-intensive manufactures also reflects a shift away from the production of labor-intensive goods in the North, a shift due to endogenous factors such as capital accumulation and technical change. By adding (as argued above) to the deterioration of the North's terms of trade—as the exogenous shrinking of the South's supply of labor-intensive exports entails—they further reduce the primary gain in income that these per capita income-augmenting fundamentals imply.

• Whatever the effect on real wages in the North, caused by the fundamental factors underlying the shift in import demands for labor-intensive goods in the North itself, there is no way we could argue that the forces shifting the export supplies from the South have had an adverse effect on them. Rather, they have made the real wages better than they would have been, if the SS theorem holds, since the ceteris paribus effect of trade with the South will be to improve the real wages in the North. Thus, it will have raised, and not lowered, the traded prices of labor-intensive goods.

I think that this conclusion is pretty plausible. It puts me on the side of those who deplore the usual declamations against globalization on the grounds that trade with poor countries hurts our workers. But it puts me right at the edge of that group since the most that they have said, in ways that I am not enthusiastic about analytically, is that the adverse effect is small or even negligible. I actually say that it is favorable, not adverse! And I expect it to remain so in the foreseeable future.

So, I claim the distinction of counting myself out of the "consensus" often asserted in Washington (especially in the think tanks distinguished by their armor rather than their grey cells, and even in the Bretton Woods institutions that seek amiably-agreed views) that economists "believe" that the adverse effect of trade on real wages is around 10–20 percent or 15–20 percent.

This was the range that Dani Rodrik recently concluded in his alarmist pamphlet on globalization for the Institute for International Economics; it is also to be found in an IMF pamphlet reported on in *The Economist*. The former was based on negligible work; the latter simply averaged, under instructions, all empirical studies on the subject and ignored the fact that, in science, the average of good and bad is bad. If

I am wrong, it will not be because of these forgettable contributions but because of the fault lines in my own argumentation. However, I hope to stand, alone for now, but not lonely for long.

Notes

1. My thanks go to Susan Collins, Don Davis, Alan Deardorff, Vivek Dehejia, Elias Dinopoulos, Robert Feenstra, Richard Freeman, Pravin Krishna, Paul Krugman, Robert Lawrence, Ed Leamer, Dani Rodrik, T. N. Srinivasan, and Martin Wolf for helpful conversations over the years on the issues discussed in this chapter.

2. In my view, this issue was created by NAFTA because bilateral trade agreements inevitably lead to a focus on the characteristics of products, endowments, governance, etc., of the specific country with whom you are negotiating. With Mexico being impoverished, with illegal workers streaming across the Rio Grande, it was inevitable that objections would arise as to how freer trade would indirectly hurt our workers the way illegal immigration from Mexico was allegedly doing. By contrast, there were no such questions raised vis-à-vis the Uruguay Round because the multilateral trade negotiations were with several countries, both rich and poor, and it would have therefore been simply absurd for anyone to object to them by raising the red flag over the implications of trade with countries such as India where there are even more poor than in Mexico! I have discussed this downside of regionalism, and more generally of PTAs (preferential trade agreements) in the course of discussing President Clinton's failure to secure fast-track authority from Congress in "Think big, Mr. Clinton," *The Financial Times*, Tuesday, November 25, 1997 (chap. 28 in this volume).

3. If wages are inflexible downwards, then unemployment would increase instead of wages falling. The former is assumed generally to happen in the United States, the latter in Europe.

4. Of course, if you believe that the SS theorem does not apply, so that the terms of trade improvement implied by falling world prices of labor-intensive goods will improve both national income and the real wage of labor, then a rise in the price of these goods is not a cause for celebration. The conclusion in the text is therefore comforting only if you believe in the stranglehold of the SS theorem on reality.

5. The only exception is provided by Sachs and Shatz (1994) in the in-house journal of the Brookings Institution. However, their evidence to the contrary is not compelling, in view of their regression failing to meet the requisite standards of statistical significance. Even then, these authors get their insignificant regression to show only a slight fall in the prices of labor-intensive goods, and that too by excluding computers without plausible justification.

6. The statement about the wage differential means, of course, that we depart from the 2×2 structure on factors and goods. But nothing qualitative that was derived within that framework needs to be modified.

7. The difference is in the first step of the two-step argumentation outlined above: the prices of labor-intensive goods may now be expected to rise, rather than fall, once factors other than trade liberalization are taken into account.

8. So would the domestic prices of the labor-intensive goods in the North, except when the cause of the change is trade liberalization by the North (as discussed in the analysis of Question 1).

References

Arrow, Kenneth, Hollis Chenery, Bagicha Minhas, and Robert Solow. 1961. Capital-labor substitution and economic efficiency, *Review of Economic Studies* 43: 225–50.

Bhagwati, Jagdish. 1994. Challenges to free trade: Old and new, 1993 Harry Johnson Lecture, *Economic Journal*, March.

Bhagwati, Jagdish. 1995. Trade and wages: Choosing among alternative explanations, *Federal Reserve Bank of New York Economic Policy Review*, January.

Bhagwati, Jagdish. 1995. Trade and wages: A malign relationship?, in: Susan Collins, ed., Imports, Exports, and the American Worker, Brookings Institution Press, Washington, DC, 49–99.

Bhagwati, Jagdish, and Vivek Dehejia. 1994. Freer trade and wages of the unskilled, in: Jagdish Bhagwati and Marvin Kosters (eds.), *Trade and Wages: Leveling Wages Down?*, The AEI Press, Washington, DC.

Bhagwati, Jagdish, and Marvin Kosters (eds.). 1994. Trade and Wages. *Leveling Wages Down?*, The AEI Press, Washington, DC.

Brown, Drusilla, Alan Deardorff, and Robert Stern. 1994. Protection and real wages: Old and new trade theories and their empirical counterparts, mimeo, Michigan, Ann Arbor.

Deardorff, Alan, and Dalia Hakura. 1994. Trade and wages: What are the questions?, in: Jagdish Bhagwati and Marvin Kosters (eds.), *Trade and Wages: Leveling Wages Down?*, The AEI Press, Washington, DC.

Garnaut, Ross. 1996. *Open Regionalism and Trade Liberalization*, ISEAS, Singapore.

Krugman, Paul. 1989. Import protection as export promotion, in: H. Kierzkowski (ed.), *Monopolistic Competition and International Trade*, Blackwell.

Robbins, Donald. 1996. HOS hits facts: Facts win; evidence on trade and wages in the developing world, Harvard Institute for International Development, Cambridge, MA.

Sachs, Jeffrey, and Howard Shatz. 1994. Trade and jobs in U.S. manufacturing, *Brookings Papers in Economic Activity*.

Samuelson, P. A. 1948. International trade and equalization of factor prices, *Economic Journal* 58 (June): 163–184.

Samuelson, P. A. 1949. International factor-price equalization once again, *Economic Journal* 59 (June): 181–197.

Stolper, Wolfgang, and P. A. Samuelson. 1941. Protection and real wages, *Review of Economic Studies* 9: 58–73.

12

Globalization: Who Gains, Who Loses?

12.1 Introduction: Some Conceptual Clarifications

1. The topic assigned to me presumes that globalization will lead to winners and losers. Let me therefore argue, at the very outset, that there need not be any presumption to that effect, either from policy changes or parametric shifts, for specific income classes within a country or for a country within the world economy.

In fact, the conventional presumption that we have in trade is precisely that noncoercive trade benefits all nations, leaving out envy that can immiserize oneself even as one gains relative to one's earlier position. This presumption concerning trade would seem to be violated for factor groups within a country by analyses such as that of Stolper and Samuelson which show, for instance, that freer trade will hurt (improve) the real wage of the factor that is intensively employed in the imported (exported) good. But even here, we should recall that these very authors noted that if, for example, nondiversification occurs, and the terms of trade improvement is substantial enough, *both* factors will gain: there will be no losers![1] (See figure 12.1 for an illustration of this proposition.)

So, everything depends on what one considers to be the relevant model(s) governing the process of globalization. This choice of models is, in fact, critically important, as I shall argue below, to the main question addressed in many papers: does globalization, while beneficial in the aggregate to the rich countries, harm the real wages of workers in these countries and, if so, by how much? I might say right out that I

Originally published in *Globalization and Labor*, ed. Horst Siebert (Tübingen: Institut für Weltwirtschaft an der Kiel, Universität; J. C. B. Mohr, Paul Sieback, 1999), 225–236. Reprinted with permission of Professor H. Lehment and Kiel University.

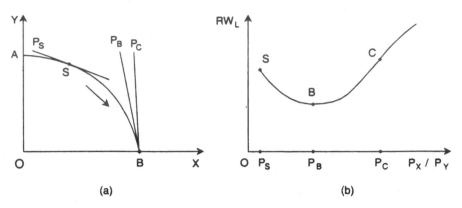

Figure 12.1
Real wages and specialization. *Note:* The real wage of labor at self-sufficiency is at S and declines due to Stolper–Samuelson reasons to B as the economy moves to specialization on good X as the relative price of the labor-intensive good Y falls to P_B. Beyond specialization, the real wage of labor now rises (instead of falling) as the price of Y falls further. The real wage of labor under free trade can then exceed that under autarky, as at C.

myself happen to have concluded, after years of reflection and research, that trade *benefits* workers (as a class) also.[2]

2. Next, no answer can be given to the specific income-distributional (i.e. who loses) question posed without first appreciating the fact that globalization can be on several dimensions: trade, equity (DFI) investments, short-term capital flows, and migration across borders. Some of these globalizations may be harmful even to aggregate welfare and, on that ground alone, may be objected to even as we support other forms of globalization that are beneficial. This is a distinction that has emerged forcefully today as many such as myself have stressed that they favor free trade but not necessarily free capital flows as in the form of capital account convertibility (see, in particular, Bhagwati 1998a).

At the same time, we must distinguish between globalization that proceeds independently of policy changes and that induced by them. Thus, for instance, at given levels of trade barriers, trade keeps expanding, even as a proportion of GNP, in the world economy. But it expands yet further because trade barriers are brought down by policy. The income-distributional effects of both types of globalization can be different, of course.

3. Moreover, policy is dictated by perceptions, quite regardless of the reality as seen objectively by scholars. Thus, even if there were a gen-

eral consensus among scholars that trade does not depress real wages of the workers, the perception may well persist among the public, as it seems to do in the United States, that it does and significantly to boot. This dissonance between facts and fears may be even more true for immigration issues.

4. Next, we need to distinguish between the winners-losers issue *within* a country and that *between* countries. A particular form of globalization may be mutually beneficial to countries, which then are all winners, while creating losers within countries.

5. Finally, the optimal policy responses to the income-distributional outcomes from globalization also divide into those that can be taken by *individual* nation states and those that require *concerted* international action. Thus, in regard to the former, it is clear that where a Pareto-better policy, such as freer trade, benefits one individual and harms another, we do say that the policy is still desirable in the sense that the winners *can* compensate the losers and still be left better off. As Ian Little reminded us, however, this welfare criterion for judging policies to be welfare-improving despite losers would be acceptable only if the losers were actually, not just potentially, compensated. This does mean that, in the presence of policy changes—such as freeing of trade or choosing not to close the door in the face of improving terms of trade—that create losers with significant immiserization, we would have to consider appropriate institutional response to moderate, if not offset, the immiserization (see figure 12.2).

Against this clarificatory, conceptual background, let me now turn to the precise task that I have been asked for. I will first recall the fears that many of the policymakers and intellectuals in the poor countries had, at the beginning of the postwar period, concerning the globalization process in the world economy, focusing on the notion that when the poor nations on the "periphery" integrated with the rich nations at the "center," the effect on the poor nations was harmful. In recounting these fears, I will concentrate on Labor Flows and on Freer Trade as the elements of globalization that the poor countries were freaked out over: both in terms of efficiency and growth, and regarding their internal and international winners-losers equation. Next, I will argue (as I have often done recently) that these fears have now been ironically transplanted to the "center" which regards globalization with the periphery to be inimical to its welfare, especially in regard to its

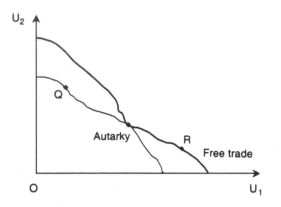

Figure 12.2
Utility-possibility curves for free trade and autarky. *Note:* The Kemp–Samuelson utility-possibility curves for free trade and autarky shows that under a specific equilibrium at free trade, at R, individual 1 (2) has a greater (lower) utility than under autarky at Q. Potential compensation can improve the utility of one individual, leaving that of the other unchanged, under free trade relative to autarky: for example, it can move the economy to north-east of Q under free trade. However, without such compensation, free trade leaves individual 2 as the "loser."

internal but also its international distributional outcomes. I will, finally, analyze the center's fear of trade in some depth and dismiss it as far less than compelling.

12.2 The Center and the Periphery: Fears of the Periphery

At the beginning of the postwar period ending in this millennium, the policy-makers and economists in many poor countries, which Raul Prebisch described as the "periphery," were fearful that (in the words of the Latin American intellectual, Oswaldo Sunkel) "integration into the world economy would lead to disintegration of the national economy." The periphery would find embrace of the "center," the rich countries, to its disadvantage.

Thus, in place of the conventional views of economists, who inclined to the view that such integration would be mutually beneficial, the view was that it would be a zero-sum game or a non-zero-sum game but with unequal outcomes where the center's gains from integration would be so disproportionate that the periphery would be left with losses. In the phrasing of Horst Siebert, the periphery would lose, the center would gain.

Almost twenty-five years ago, I characterized these views as providing, in contrast to the *benign-impact* approach of economics (where

noncoercive interactions on dimensions such as trade among different agents would produce mutual gains), a *malign-impact* view of the
world. I even went so far as to say that views such as the neocolonialism thesis represented a *malign-intent* approach where the immiserizing effect of such integration into the world economy, i.e. of what we
call today globalization, was not an inadvertent outcome of market
forces but an intended outcome of political forces that foresaw and
deliberately sought to exploit such possibilities. Thus, for instance,
foreign aid, instead of being thought of as a *benign-intent* flow from
the center to the periphery was seen as a *malign-intent* phenomenon
whose objective was to create dependency and continued exploitation
of the periphery.

The malign-impact ideas were, of course, the more fashionable than
the more radical malign-intent ideas; and they had great fascination for
many. Indeed, it is ironic that today the very same intellectuals who
held them have turned totally around and embrace the conventional
benign-impact views which stress the benefits the periphery stands to
reap from integration with the center. Thus, a notable example of what
I observe is President Cardoso of Brazil, the famous author of the
celebrated *dependencia* thesis, who provided enormously influential
support for the view that the periphery would be losers, who is now
presiding over Brazil's attempts at integration into the world economy
on the assumption that Brazil would be a winner!

So, let me, against this backdrop, recall how precisely these ideas
about the periphery being losers manifested themselves in relation to
globalization in the areas of labor flows and of trade; and how and why
these have generally changed to the view that the periphery would be
winners (as well, with the center) instead.

Labor Flows

The main concern over labor flows at the time related to the "brain
drain." The outflow of skilled people from the periphery to the center
was observed and deplored as leading to a deleterious effect on the
periphery: both in terms of losing skilled people and hence harming
aggregate welfare, so that the poor country would be a loser, while
also accentuating domestic inequalities within the poor country, making its unskilled losers in the process as well.

The huge analytical literature that developed on these issues in the
1960s and thereafter was addressed to examining, and generally dis-
counting, these fearful outcomes; and it would take a substantial paper

to just review it today. But the essence may be conveyed, in an incomplete but still illuminating way, by citing just a few offsetting arguments in favor of a brain drain:

i. the aggregate loss of welfare was exaggerated by confusing effect on GNP with the effect on the welfare of the non-migrants, the so-called TLBs (those left behind); and

ii. the outflow of skilled migrants could lead to remittances to countries of origin: migrants often retained their emotional and other affiliation to their origins; and

iii. these migrants again could contribute more to technological diffusion to their home countries if they migrated than if they stayed at home: "brains" are not static and need proper environments without which they may deteriorate, so a move to better environments, at the center such as the USA, would lead to more, say, Indian accomplishments and this in turn may stimulate other Indians to achieve more; and so on.

In fact, thinking about these aspects of the phenomenon of skilled outmigration, I shifted rapidly from worries about viewing the outward mobility of skilled people from the poor to the rich countries as a malign "brain drain" to seeing it more benignly in terms of what might be called a "diaspora" model, where the presence of one's nationals abroad has positive effects that outweigh the negative effects that a narrower focus concentrates on.

To strengthen the working of the *benign diaspora effects*, I then also focused my theoretical and policy analyses to two dimensions of international personal mobility: (a) an analytical examination of the question of extending income tax jurisdiction to nationals abroad so that the mere fact of working abroad would not enable a national to escape the tax *obligation* to his home country: this turned out to be a fascinating theoretical question, for instance, in the second-best theory of optimal taxation in the presence of international mobility of people, while also raising a host of important political and social questions;[3] and (ii) the exploration of the idea that the ability of nationals abroad to continue their attachment to the home country be simultaneously strengthened by improving their *rights* as well: i.e. through their ability to participate politically and economically in the home country: through dual citizenship, the facilitation of the ability to vote from abroad, etc.

Today, almost two decades after I opened up this set of issues associated with the diaspora way of looking at the problem of skilled outmigration, following upon the earlier focus on the brain drain view of the matter, the diaspora view has become the dominant one. The brain drain concern has receded; the outmigration of skilled nationals is regarded as an opportunity, not a peril, with institutional mechanisms being explored more systematically to exploit this opportunity to advantage.

Trade

Similarly, the notion that freer trade (and, for that matter, direct foreign investment [DFI]) would immiserize the countries on the periphery has generally receded from view. The fear here was manifold but would turn out to be unjustified:

i. It was feared that integration into the world's markets would consign the poor country to specialization on non-manufactures. We now know that this was not true. A huge import-substitution-strategy (IS) country such India wound up producing less manufactures in the end than a small EP (export promoting) country such as South Korea. By protecting the home market, IS slowed down growth and, in turn, industrialization.

ii. Autarkic policies, in fact, led to inefficiencies that deeply cut into efficiency and growth, as documented forcefully in the OECD project directed by Little, Scitovsky and Scott and in the NBER project directed by me and Krueger. A generic reference to "infant industry" protection to justify autarky, without serious examination of the way in which that argument may apply in specific cases, meant that markets were not allowed to operate in trade without good reason. Equally, the other argument used to justify the IS strategy, namely "export pessimism," was also seen later to be empirically untenable.[4]

Then, again, what about winners and losers *within* the poor countries from IS versus EP strategy? Here again, I would argue that the empirical consensus has moved against the proponents of the IS strategy. If the distributional problem is defined for poor countries, as I believe it should be, as the impact on the poor (rather than on somewhat abstruse notions such as the Gini coefficient and shares of income going to the top 5 percent: matters of little practical salience to the poor), then it is pretty clear by now that policies that handicap growth will draw fewer of the poor into gainful employment and hence will be harmful to the amelioration of poverty. By hurting growth, the IS strategy therefore created losers among the poor. Equally, by biasing the growth towards capital-intensive goods (when comparative advantage, indulged by freer trade, would have led to more production of the labor-intensive goods), the locomotive of growth was further undermined by the IS strategy.[5]

12.3   The Center and the Periphery: Fears of the Center

Today, therefore, the fears of the periphery regarding closer integration with the center have yielded to greater optimism. Many in the developing countries now think and act as if global integration will make the poor countries winners. And there seems to be less concern, and more optimism, that even within the poor countries, such globalization could assist, not harm, the poor. In fact, the poor nations clamour today for the rich countries to remain open to trade and inflow of immigrants (skilled and even unskilled). This attitude was obvious from President Salinas's approach to the United States, as represented by his determination to join NAFTA: where his predecessors had looked across the Rio Grande and had seen only a threat, he now saw unparalleled opportunity. Even Africa, so far tentative in light of her many problems and failures, has increasingly gained the confidence to be optimistic about becoming a winner through integration into the world economy.

But then the fears have now come to the center! These fears are, for the most part, not really about the rich countries becoming losers: national gains are expected from globalization, even with the poor nations. Rather, the fears are about the internal distribution of income, about their poor becoming poorer and the not-so-poor becoming poor. So, concerning free trade, it is not the old, and theoretically erroneous, pauper-labor argument (for protection). Rather, it is a new, and theoretically correct (but empirically unsound, as I shall argue), argument that trade with pauper countries will produce paupers in one's midst. In the following analysis, I will begin with the trade issue, then considering briefly the question of immigration of the unskilled, which has also raised similar fears in the rich countries.

Fears Concerning Trade and Appropriate Response

Perhaps, the greatest fear has related to trade. Unskilled workers in the United States have been agitated by the decline in real wages during the 1980s through early 1990s and then stagnation until very recently.

The European counterpart appears to have been high rates of unemployment instead due to labor market rigidities but, of course, reflect in some degree also macroeconomic factors.

The debate among economists in the United States has been quite intense on the subject. Generally, the labor economists have tended to assign a large role to trade as the cause of the decline in real wages. By contrast, the trade economists have been divided into three camps: (i) those, like Robert Lawrence, Matthew Slaughter and Paul Krugman, who conclude that the adverse effect of trade on wages has been "negligible" (though it is not clear what proportion of the decline in real wages would need to be attributed to trade to make it a negligible factor, and besides, their argument like that of most others does not seem to be based on econometric estimation based on properly specified models that allow for different factors among whom the causality is to be apportioned); (ii) those, such as Robert Feenstra and Gordon Hanson, who argue for a larger role; and (iii) I who argue that the effect of trade with poor countries on the real wages in the USA has been most likely been favorable, moderating the decline that would have occurred thanks to technical change.

If you believe that trade with the poor countries harms the real wages of the unskilled fairly seriously, then there is indeed a problem. Dani Rodrik of Kennedy School at Harvard, who recently wrote a small pamphlet entitled *Has Globalization Gone Too Far?* for Fred Bergsten's Institute for International Economies, with much of which I disagree,[6] said after a cursory analysis that there was a consensus about the adverse effect from trade being about 15–20 percent. The net effect has been that, given the Washington assumption that the combination of Harvard and IIE means that only truth and wisdom on trade can flow from this profound combination, the protectionist Congressmen have jumped onto this assertion of Rodrik's to argue that therefore we must go easy on freeing trade with the poor countries; and some have even argued that, therefore, protection is called for.

The more subtle response, however, which is also protectionist, has been that of what I call *intrusionism*. Faced with the fear of decline in living standards due to competition from the poor countries, confirmed recently by the Rodrik–Bergsten endorsement, those who do not wish to appear openly protectionist have taken for some years now to asking for the standards in labor and environment to be raised abroad so that their costs would rise and hence the force of competition would be reduced! Think of a bull charging at you. You can try to catch it by the horns: this is like *(import) protectionism* or *isolationism*. Or you can get around the beast and catch it by the tail, breaking the charge: this is like *(export) protectionism* or *intrusionism*.

And thus we get demands, driven by *competitiveness concerns*, for raising of standards in the poor countries, adding to the chorus of "unfair competition" demands that have proliferated on the trade scene for several years now as the force of competition has been felt around the world in a world increasingly globalizing. (Similar competitive concerns led, in the 1980s, to demands against the rich countries, especially Japan, which was asked to reshape its domestic policies and institutions, to seek restraints on its exports, to increase imports through import targets, so as to make our life comfortable. As Japan's trade threat has subsided, these demands, which some of us fought frontally and successfully as damaging to the world trading system, have also disappeared from view. But the threat is now seen from the poor countries instead!)

Needless to say, I find these *competition-driven demands* to be no more than disguised protectionism, as argued above, and I would strongly object to them, as I have in my many writings. But what happens when the same demands are being *driven by moral concerns* instead? Let me distinguish among two main types of moral concerns.

First, I may want to improve standards for workers in countries with which I have no trade, simply because of altruism. There is little doubt that some human rights groups, for instance, do think thus (even though sometimes one does wonder, as T. N. Srinivasan has argued, when the same groups (e.g., unions) that advocate moral concerns that transcend borders are also supportive of tougher immigration restrictions that reaffirm these very borders and when even NGOs inevitably display national priorities and prejudices that are not quite consonant with their profession of a symmetric moral viewpoint about humanity sans borders).

Second, I may want to object morally to certain processes being deployed to produce goods abroad, as leading to their being "defiled" and hence unacceptable to me as a consumer.

In both cases, we have demands for suspension of free trade. In the first case, it may be because we hope to use the suspension of trade, or its extension, as a tool to pry open better behavior. Or, even if we do not expect any results, then, as in the "defiled" product argument, we just want to be able to deny such products, made in ways unacceptable to us, access to our markets. How do we deal with these arguments which, while often not articulated clearly, are very much in the public domain today?

In both cases, the principal distinction for policy seems to be whether our moral preference is shared by many or is simply ours. In the former case, we can proceed by securing a multilateral consensus. The advantage of this procedure is that it is a good check on whether our professed morality is not simply masking other motives and whether it is sufficiently profound to hold general appeal. Racist apartheid clearly fit the bill. Once the multilateral consensus is built, we already have institutional mechanisms to deal with the suspension of market access: the UN embargo procedure and the GATT/WTO waiver procedures already allow for the consequent suspension of even a member country's total market access!

But suppose that we have a "boutique" or "niche" moral preference which others do not share: the love of the dolphins, to take the GATT case where the rulings were widely condemned by the NGOs, is among them. The problem and the solution in this case here seem to me to be exactly the way we set them out, more or less, in the 1991 *GATT Report on Trade and the Environment* which Richard Blackhurst directed and I helped to write.

Since moral preferences are strictly subjective, if GATT were to let any country suspend another's market access simply and automatically by asserting a moral preference, however democratically expressed, that could lead to a breakdown of predictable market access and disrupt the trading regime. At the same time, moral preferences cannot be trampled upon by international regimes: one cannot force a dolphin unsafe tuna down rejectionist American throats. So, the sensible procedure is to prevent automaticity of market access suspension and to allow for "compensation" to be paid when such suspension is undertaken despite its being declared WTO-illegal. Such compensation is best paid in the form of provision of another trade concession to the country. All this seems to me to be perfectly sensible.

Immigration

Parallel to the worry about the effects of trade (especially with the poor countries) on the real wages of unskilled workers in the rich countries has been the fear that unskilled immigration will also do the same. Indeed, that it has already been doing so. This question has become particularly pertinent in the United States, where alarmist conclusions to this effect have been drawn by conservative economists such as George Borjas, now at Kennedy School at Harvard, who then go on to oppose unskilled immigration (whether legal or illegal) in one fashion or another.

But their worries are again unsupported by proper analysis. The main argument against these pessimistic economists comes from the trade economists' standard but powerful notion that additional unskilled immigrants can be absorbed without a decline in real wages simply because the diminishing returns to unskilled labor from added unskilled labor need not arise, even with convex isoquants in each sector, because output shifts among sectors can absorb the added labor supply. In technical jargon, we call this the Rybczynski effect or alternatively the argument that as long as the overall capital-labor endowment ratio remains within the Chipman–McKenzie diversification cone, factor prices will not change. This has been known in the theoretical analysis of immigration for nearly a quarter of a century (see Bhagwati and Rodriguez 1995).

Recent empirical examination of the issue by Gordon Hanson and Matthew Slaughter has turned up evidence that broadly supports the view that the unskilled immigration into the United States has indeed been absorbed in this fashion, without hurting real wages of the unskilled. My own work suggests the same (Bhagwati 1998b). So, again, I would say that the alarm over unskilled immigration and its harmful effects on our workers appears to be unjustified and its influence in prompting proposals to undertake draconian measures to restrict legal and illegal immigration by often desperate measures is to be deplored.

Notes

1. Often, even sophisticated economists will not always allow for such complexity of argumentation. Thus, in a well-known article on trade policy reform, Dani Rodrik argues that the distributional effects for losers are quantitatively more important than the overall gains. But he rules out the possibility of there being no losers.

2. Cf. chapter 11.

3. There is a huge theoretical literature on the subject, the latest of which is Bhagwati and Wilson (1989). Also see several articles by me on the issue, reprinted in Irwin (1991: Part V).

4. The Indian resort to IS strategy was often justified in these terms and this harmful policy was defended against criticism by constructing models which were *closed-economy* models and therefore allowed ipso facto no possibility of an EP strategy! I have dealt with the deleterious role of economists in the unfortunate ruination of India's develop-

mental efforts in a *Times Literary Supplement* article on India last year: "A Machine for Going Backwards," August 8, 1997.

5. In India, we must add to these factors the harmful effects of the argument, formalized by Dobb, Galenson and Leibenstein, Bator and Sen, that capital-intensive techniques would harness more savings and would increase the growth rate. The conclusion followed strictly from the assumptions made; but that was no guarantee of its policy wisdom! Today, of course, in light of the experience of East Asian growth and Indian stagnation, both reflecting partly the huge rates of savings in the former group which did employ labor-intensive-goods EP strategy, it seems ludicrous that anyone should have been bamboozled by the models that argued otherwise (Bhagwati 1997).

6. For a brilliant critique of Rodrik's alarmist analytical assertions in this pamphlet, see Panagariya (1999).

References

Bhagwati, J. (1997). A Model for Going Backwards. *Times Literary Supplement*. August 8: 11–12.

——— (1998a). The Capital Myth. *Foreign Affairs* 77(3): 7–12.

——— (1998b). Bashing Illegals. *The Boston Review* 3(5): 21–22.

——— (1999). Play It Again Sam: A New Look at Trade and Wages. In G. Ranis and L. Raut (eds.), *Trade, Growth and Development, Essays* in Honor of P. N. Srinivasan. Elsevier Science.

Bhagwati, J., and C. Rodriguez (1975). Welfare-Theoretical Analyses of the Brain Drain. *Journal of Development Economics* 2(3): 195–221.

Bhagwati, J., and J. Wilson (eds.) (1989). *Income Taxation and International Mobility.* Cambridge, Mass.: MIT Press.

Irwin, D. (1991). *Political Economy and International Economics, Essays by Jagdish Bhagwati.* Cambridge, Mass.: MIT Press.

Panagariya, A. (1999). Trade Openess: Consequences for the Elasticity of Demand for Labour and Wage Outcomes. Mimeo, University of Maryland at College Park.

Rodrik, D. (1998). *Has Globalization Gone too Far?* Washington, D.C.: Institute for International Economics.

Moral Obligations and Human Rights

13   Moral Obligations and Trade

The question of moral obligation and trade is a multi-faceted one. Let me concentrate on a few salient points of central importance in today's debates concerning the reality of a global economy.

1. Most important, free trade is a moral cause. Why? Because, as Democrats here and Social Democrats and Liberals abroad fully appreciate now, our social agendas cannot be advanced without economic prosperity. Postwar experience worldwide, and not just classroom economics, have demonstrated persuasively that freer trade has been among the policies that have promoted rapid growth and economic prosperity. This has both reduced poverty enormously and also enabled governments to advance public health, education, and so forth. Where countries such as India, Egypt, Ghana, and much of South America turned to inward-looking trade policies, the result generally was low growth and often adverse impact on the well-being of the poor as well.

2. Ironically, the objections to free trade come today from fearful workers and other groups, among them some environmentalists, in the developed countries whereas the policymakers in the poor countries, which had embraced almost the same fears and objections to Free Trade at the beginning of the postwar period, have abandoned them. I call this the "ironic reversal." Our leaders in the OECD countries now have to wage battles against similar, counterproductive fears and objections, to avoid the mistakes that the poor countries made to the great disadvantage of their citizens, including the poorer segments of their societies.

Based on remarks made at Senator Bob Kerry's BACKPAK Conference on International Trade, Omaha, Nebraska, December 12, 1998.

3. The fear that trade with poor countries is producing paupers in our midst (an outcome, if true, should certainly arouse our moral sentiments in any decent society) is unjustified. Much research argues that the adverse effect of trade on the fall in real wages in the United States is negligible. My own research argues that, in fact, it has even been beneficial and that trade has actually helped to moderate the decline in real wages that would have followed from technical change. Unfortunately, the Clinton administration has failed to take this issue head on, confronting labor leaders such as John Sweeney of the AFL-CIO with economists on this issue.

The defining moment in the NAFTA win for Mr. Clinton was when Mr. Gore destroyed Ross Perot on television in the famous debate. In the absence of such a defining debate between Mr. Gore and Mr. Sweeney, for obvious political reasons, it is not surprising that Mr. Clinton lost the fast-track battle (though, as always, other factors, including those specific to Mr. Clinton, played a role as well).

4. Economic insecurity (which we can again regard as a moral concern) as a result of trade quite generally (as distinct from trade only with poor countries) is, however, a real problem in the global economy. Trade creates opportunities; but it also brings risks from increased flux (whether in reality or simply in terms of perceptions). We need therefore imaginative institutional change (which is not the same as more budget expenditures, since simply "throwing money" at problems is something we have learned not to do if we mean to get results) to assist those who cannot cope with the consequences of freer trade.

I have long pointed therefore to the need for measures such as Trade Adjustment Assistance (e.g., in my 1988 MIT Press book *Protectionism*, seventh printing), a theme that Robert Reich and others have endorsed. Portability of benefits, as labor turnover is expected to increase, including delinking of health care from employment (an unfortunate legacy from the Second World War), are among the kinds of adaptive policies that need to be increasingly identified and embraced.

5. Moral objections to free trade arise more frequently from the fact that other countries have different, often lower, environmental and labor standards than we do in specific industries. One objection is that it is "unfair trade" when others face lower burdens. But this is unpersuasive. Different countries have legitimate diversity in what industry-specific measures they will deploy, and in what sequence, even if they were to share (as they need not, since they can have different priorities

between different social agendas as well) the same commitment to labor or environmental standards. Congressman Gephardt is simply wrong in asking for equal burdens (as we bear) for the same industry in other countries. But then, we worry also that a "race to the bottom" will occur when others have lower standards and our corporations will move to locations with lower standards. This is empirically untrue. (Besides, we ourselves have lower standards than others in matters such as unionization. Our terribly low rates of unionization reflect not just a culture of "independence" but also a definite handicapping of the ability to strike in various ways.)

6. The second objection comes, not from our self-interest, but because we seek to push for better standards for altruistic reasons. But then, linking these altruistic agendas to trade treaties will generally undermine both freeing of trade and the advancement of the moral agendas, generally speaking. The best way to think about this is to recall our forebears' wisdom: you cannot kill two birds with one stone (except by fluke).

By seeking to create new "obstacles" to free trade, in shape of social and moral preconditions in trade negotiations and trade institutions, you undermine the freeing of trade: just recall how the linkage issue divided Republicans from Democrats and helped kill Mr. Clinton's fast-track request; and also remind yourselves that the poor countries remain deeply opposed to putting such agendas into trade treaties even if we were to get our own act together on such linkage. So, we miss one bird: the freeing of trade.

And we also miss the second bird: by mixing up trade, which inevitably reflects competitiveness/protectionist concerns, with our moral agenda, we also undermine our moral agenda by giving other countries the definite impression that we are using moral arguments to advance what is in effect a protectionist agenda. This impression is not irrational: just look at what we seek to include in a social clause at the WTO and we see that the items included are those where the poor countries, certainly not us, are fully expected to be defendants! As a citizen extensively active in human rights and social-agenda movements that reflect developing country concerns, I am quite aware of these problems that are totally missed in Washington and even by some of our own NGOs.

The answer then is to delink the trade agenda from the moral and social agendas that reflect altruism.

Our task as Democrats should then be to develop a second stone to advance proactively these other moral and social agendas, which we Democrats should take seriously. There are, in fact, several ways to do this.

The Clinton administration's failure has been to take this task with less than necessary determination and ingenuity. Instead, it has characteristically succumbed to the demands for linkage, undermining both freeing of trade and the advancement of our moral concerns in imaginative and more effective ways.

14 Trade Linkage and Human Rights

14.1 Introduction

Arthur Dunkel is widely, and properly, given virtually the entire credit for the success of the Uruguay Round since he nursed it through thick and thin. Without him, his successor Peter Sutherland would not have had the broad shoulders to stand on and grasp the prize soon after Dunkel's retirement from a most distinguished and defining term as Director-General of the General Agreement on Tariffs and Trade (GATT).

The Uruguay Round has now closed. And, as Lester Thurow pronounced with fanfare in Davos in 1989, *GATT is dead*. But it has died, not for his profoundly wrong reasons, but for Dunkel's profoundly right ones: it has been transformed, reborn, as the new and invigorated World Trade Organization (WTO). The important questions that arise now relate principally to the *new issues*, in particular, the linkage of trade with human rights; environmental and labor standards; competition policy; and how WTO obligations interface with national sovereignty.

I propose therefore to address here, so as to clarify an increasingly confused and confusing debate, the key question: should trade liberalisation or market access be linked to human rights, labor standards, environmental behaviour, and a host of "social" issues? This problem has acquired great salience recently in several contexts.

14.2 Trade Linkage in New Contexts

Trade with China has received the greatest attention. The renewal of most favored nation status (MFN) has traditionally attracted flak;

Originally published in *Uruguay Round and Beyond, Essays in Honour of Arthur Dunkel*, ed. Jagdish Bhagwati and Matthias Hirsch (Ann Arbor: University of Michigan Press, 1998), 241–250. Reprinted with permission of Springer-Verlag GMBH & Co.

now the economic and human-rights preconditions of China's entry to the WTO have also become a bone of contention on the domestic U.S. scene.

But the December 1996 Ministerial meeting of the WTO in Singapore was also marked by a sustained effort by the Clinton administration, allied principally with France and Norway, to insert a Social Clause into the WTO. Such a Clause would specify selected labor standards, like the non-use of child labor, as preconditions for gaining access to markets of WTO Members.

Similarly, regarding the administration's failed request for fast track authority to negotiate future trade agreements, Congressman Gephardt had written to his fellow Democrats in the house that no such authority should be granted unless agreements in regard to environmental and labor standards were built directly into the trade treaties, as distinct from the "side agreements" written into the NAFTA treaty. Besides, the position of Democrats generally was to stiffen these agreements whereas Republicans wanted to weaken, even delete, them altogether in future trade agreements. It is accurate to say that, in consequence, the administration failed partly because it could not resolve the linkage issue on the political scene.

14.3   Distinguishing between Linkage Issues

Evidently, if we are to analyse these demands and the appropriate way to deal with them we need to distinguish among them conceptually. For, similar as they are at first blush, and discussed in the media and in the U.S. Congress as if they were identical, they are in fact not so. The main distinction we must draw is between (a) the use of generalized trade sanction against offending countries and (b) the use of tactics such as suspension or denial of market access against specific products that offend a particular human right or standard such as the non-use of prison labor or of sweatshop workers in the manufacture of the product.

• *Generalized Trade Sanctions:* The UN-sanctioned embargoes against South Africa on apartheid or against Ian Smith's Unilateral Declaration of Independence in Southern Rhodesia qualify as generalised trade sanctions against a country whose human rights violations are widely deemed beyond the pale. The suspension or denial of MFN status to the Soviet Union over emigration rights or to China over its denial of multiple human rights to its citizens is another, admittedly less fierce, generalised sanction.

• *Preconditions for Trade in Specific Products:* Conversely, the NAFTA supplemental agreements on labor and environmental standards essentially provide for procedures to eventually fine and even suspend market access rights of firms or products that use proscribed standards or practices. Such agreements generally are not product-specific in content but are applied to specific offending products in practice. This applies also to the proposed social clause at the WTO: it would proscribe practices while a dispute settlement process would evidently apply in general to complaints about trade in specific products produced with the proscribed methods.

These two types of trade linkages to rights, standards and social issues are obviously different in character. They also raise somewhat different questions as to both efficacy and desirability. But, I shall argue here, the case for both is extremely weak, the latter even flawed.

14.4 Trade Sanctions

When we apply trade sanctions, we may not be deterred by the fact that they may not hurt enough so as to have a corrective, beneficial effect on the offending behaviour of the sanctioned country. In fact, we may even be willing to suffer economic harm ourselves while gaining no results. Thus, a moral absolutist may simply forego supping with the Devil even though the result is that she misses a free meal and the Devil does not shed his horns. There is little doubt that some of the human rights critics of China today, who would suspend China's MFN status and block its entry into the WTO, are in this moral camp. The American journalist Abe Rosenthal's columns in *The New York Times*, bursting with moral indignation at China's human rights violations and our economic engagement nonetheless with her, are certainly in this vein.

But few of us are entirely moral absolutists. Instead, most of us are consequentialists: we seek sanctions so that we get results. Here, there are two questions that an economist must raise: (a) are sanctions going to work; and (b) are there other methods that would work better (in the sense that the cost-benefit ratio is more favourable to us)?

• *Efficacy of Sanctions:* Clearly, anyone who claims that trade sanctions cannot work is wrong: the embargo on South Africa, for instance, is generally agreed to have been successful. What we must remember, however, are a few guiding principles which, if ignored, are likely to guarantee failure. A multilateral embargo, even a widely plurilateral one that includes the principal trading partners of the sanctioned country, is preferable to a unilateral one. It both reduces the likelihood of significant leakage and increases the psychological leverage. Even then, of course, defections are often observed and require extensive monitoring (which can be difficult) and penalties for defection (which can be hard to enforce). The efficacy of the embargo is greater if the target is a small country without leverage (such as Cuba after the collapse of the Soviet bloc and the ruination of the Russian economy) than if it is a large country with huge economic and political leverage (such as China today). It is a lot harder to maintain an embargo when the targeted country can exercise economic and political options to encourage defections: either within countries as when China can drive a wedge between our business and our human-rights groups or between countries as when it can play off the Europeans and the Japanese against the United States. The embargo will work better, therefore, when we target a country for practices that attract widespread condemnation, as with apartheid, as distinct from practices that are culturally specific to limited numbers of nations.[1]

• *Greater Efficiency of Alternative Policies:* But trade sanctions that can conform to these criteria and therefore have the prospect of being even moderately effective are likely to be a very small set indeed. In practice, we must therefore ask: are there not other ways in which we can prod or punish offending countries into changing their behaviour? Indeed, it is a question that must be confronted even when the trade sanctions might be considered to be an effective policy tool: for, the cost to us in terms of trade disruption and the gain in terms of effectiveness must also be evaluated and compared with those attending other ways of influencing the target country. A cost-benefit analysis is as appropriate here as in other areas of public policy.

In the modern world, with the phenomenal recent growth of civil society and of its institutions such as NGOs and media such as the CNN, our ability to zero in on morally offensive practices anywhere has grown hugely. Embarrassment, if not shame and even guilt, follow. Indeed, governments cannot escape scrutiny and the accusing finger from a variety of such quarters in the public domain.

Even international institutions such as the International Committee on Human Rights, the apex body that has its mandate under the international convention on civil and political rights which defines the basic human-rights law agreed upon by signatory states at the United Nations, become focal points at which these states must confront the consequences of their human-rights policies under procedures that, subject to certain conditions, grant standing to individuals against their governments. These inter-national institutions, besides, carry greater weight because they spare no nation, looking symmetrically at all (unlike national governments that often look at others while turning a blind eye to their own warts, a classic example being the annual, official U.S. evaluation of human rights that does not look at non-compliance within the United States itself). This impartiality also lends credibility, hence clout, to well known NGOs such as Human Rights Watch and Amnesty International: they report on police brutality in India only to follow up with an exposé of police brutality in New York.

The effectiveness of these institutions in prompting the desired changes cannot be overestimated. Instances abound, crowding our newspapers almost daily. A recent example is the influence exercised by American women's groups on the all-male hiring practice of the Vienna Philharmonic Orchestra by threatening to boycott their imminent U.S. concert tour. Faced with humiliation, if not the threat to the pocketbook, the orchestra caved in and hired a female member, thus changing a dishonourable, time-honoured tradition. By contrast, governmental actions including embargoes are likely to have been less compelling. The U.S. government, for instance, could not have effectively levelled the charge of sexism at Austria while its own society is not free from it: NGOs in the United States could effectively do so, however, and carry conviction because they equally target domestic sexism.

I would therefore argue that the better, if not the best, way to advance the agenda of human rights is to ask our governments to support NGOs at home and abroad working to advance the rights whose violation we deplore, with the government putting its money where its mouth is. And the vocal chords should indeed be exercised energetically in the existing international human rights groups.

Such a strategy could well find business groups allied in the effort, as contrasted with the case where trade sanctions are used and, because they endanger profits directly, business groups promptly tend to break ranks on human rights issues. The popular concern that détente and engagement change us rather than the offending countries, paralysing us into silence rather than prodding others into observance of human rights, derives wholly from the attempts to use trade sanctions as our weapons. By contrast, détente and engagement will yield results, perhaps slowly but surely, if we use them pro-actively, as I have argued, in the institutions of the new civil society to embarrass, shame and reform. Engagement then brings into the international arena, and hence into continual confrontation with the consequences of their violations, the nations that otherwise can be shielded by their isolation from this powerful process.

14.5   Setting Preconditions for Trade in Specific Products

The typical demands for fulfilment of particular labour (and often also environmental) standards, failing which market access would be denied or suspended to products utilising the proscribed processes, are of a different character altogether. For instance, they reflect not just moral objectives but a larger dose of *competitiveness* concerns. They are also generally more popular in the United States and in some European nations; but they are ill advised nonetheless.

These demands do not only come in the shape of the insertion of a *social clause* into the *multilateral* WTO, the incorporation of agreements on labour and environmental standards into extension of the *plurilateral and preferential* NAFTA to new countries, such as Chile, and the attachment of like strings to the renewal of fast track trade negotiating authority, but also in the shape of calls for *unilateral* enactment of legislation. This is particularly true of the *blue and green protectionism* bill proposed in 1994 by U.S. Congressman Richard Gephardt—blue refers to blue-collar workers and hence to labour standards, and green of course to environmental standards—and of the U.S. journalist Robert Kuttner's occasional demand for congressional approval of a *social tariff* on U.S. imports in the form of countervailing duties to offset the *social dumping* by countries with lower standards.

The principal reasons why these demands are unwise are that (a) they can be regarded, with some credibility, as protectionist in design, even though not necessarily in intent; and (b) a more effective way to pursue such agendas is again not through linkage in trade treaties and institutions such as the WTO but through other non-trade agreements and institutions such as the International Labour Organization (ILO) and UNICEF. In addition, there is much to be said for the view that freeing trade is about removing obstacles to trade whereas the demand for linkage is about putting up roadblocks to free trade instead: it is odd and ironic as well as intellectually incoherent, therefore, to introduce linkage into trade treaties and institutions.

14.5.1 Protectionist Design

The groups that seek such trade linkage are typically either those who fear international competition from countries with *lower* standards or those who want *higher* standards because they genuinely feel a trans-border moral obligation to extend such standards to people abroad.[2] It is useful to distinguish the two groups by their primary concern although it is possible for both objectives to be shared by an individual or a group and even though the public pronouncements of groups motivated by different concerns do progressively overlap as they ally with each other in their demands. Thus, if one scrutinizes the proponents of the social clause and of labor standards preconditions in regional trade agreements, the labor unions that are most vociferous include those in textiles, an industry exposed to fierce international competition from poor countries. At the same time, although human-rights groups focus on rights, not on competition, the language in which many U.S. Congressmen couch their support for such measures typically betrays a concern for *fair trade* and *unfair competition*, even if some of them speak of transnational moral concerns.

The Princeton economist Alan Krueger has suggested—based on statistical analysis of the constituency characteristics of Congressmen who sponsored the recently proposed Child Deterrence Act—that constituencies with a greater share of workers in his view more likely to suffer from foreign competition were not more likely to have sponsors. But this analysis basically ignores the central fact that, with grossly misleading and persistent propagation of the view that all child labor is automatically exploitative in the same sense as when children work in bondage and under hazardous conditions, the debate has been cleverly guided by those seeking relief from competition as one that equally derives from overriding morality. Thus, even those who speak from moral concerns have had these concerns aroused by tendentious and misleading characterisation of complex socioeconomic phenomena such as child labor in poor countries (whose solution does not lie in denying market access but in joining forces and deploying a set of policies whereby NGOs and governments work with impoverished families, employers, primary school authorities and the children themselves, as has been happening in India for example). It is as if the anti-abortion groups saturated the media with pictures of aborted late-term fetuses to distort and define the debate on abortion rights, to the exclusion of the nuances that are in fact at the heart of the debate. To run a statistical analysis on Congressmen's votes without going beyond the veil to ask pointedly whether their moral concerns have themselves been a result of active lobbying by the protectionist groups is to miss the point since the objective is precisely to investigate whether protectionism is playing a primary role in their vote. Just as Sherlock Holmes asked why the dog didn't bark, we must ask why these Congressmen have acquired the moral concern they have and why that concern takes the form of trade linkage rather than other methods.

The principal driving force behind these linkage demands has clearly been the fear of competition, as was abundantly evident in the United States during the NAFTA debate. Fearful of competition from the poor countries, protectionists such as Patrick Buchanan seek to turn to *isolationism*, withdrawing from the global economy. But an alternative response, equally designed to moderate competition, is what I call *intrusionism*. This takes the form of *unfair* trade demands addressed to the poor nations, seeking to raise their environmental and labour standards: this would presumably raise the production costs of rivals abroad in the South to levels that make their competition more tolerable. An analogy can drive this home. Faced with a charging bull, you may catch it by the horn (as with isolationism) or reach behind the beast and catch it by its tail (as with intrusionism). The intrusionist response however is no less of a folly than the isolationist option, though the foolishness is less transparent. It seeks to restrain trade, but from the other end: it is tantamount therefore to *export protectionism*, the mirror image of the conventional, Buchanan-variety *import protectionism*.

In fact, the protectionist intent, and more so the design, of the trade linkage may also be inferred from the fact that the contents of the social lause, for example, have been reduced to a *core*, where the defendants are fully expected to be only the poor countries, to the exclusion of the "social" issues where the OECD countries, chiefly the United States, are equally likely to find themselves as defendants. Thus, while the use of child labour sui generis (and not just the reprehensible practices of bonded child labor and the employment of children in hazardous occupations such as glassmaking and in cruel conditions of the type that inspired the impassioned writings of Chadwick, Engles and Dickens in nineteenth-century England and the subsequent protective legislation) is to be prohibited by such a clause, there is nothing for example about the rights of migrant labour where conditions of abject abuse are not uncommon in the United States itself if investigative TV reports arc to be believed. Again, while the *right to unionise* is to be included, there is no mention of restrictions on secondary boycotts for instance or the permitted hiring of replacement workers, which cripple the ability in the United States to strike and which doubtless have contributed to the emasculation of unions and to the phenomenal shrinking of unionised labour in the American garments industry. Again, the widespread use of sweatshops by the American garment industry on U.S. soil, with wholly inadequate enforcement, is evidently a violation of U.S. laws and of human rights aspirations, so that inclusion of this issue in a social clause in the WTO, with market access suspended for such an industry, would put the United States squarely into the dock, threatening its garment industry with virtual shutdown in world trade. So, where is the US on this issue on the social clause?

14.5.2   *Alternative Ways to Pursue Rights and Social Objectives*

The developing countries suspect then that, in pushing relentlessly for a social clause in the WTO, the Clinton administration is invoking ethics to secure relief from foreign firms in the competitive global age, wearing a moral mask on a face furrowed by the fear of competition.

An increasing number of economists, of all political persuasions, share this concern, albeit in a fairly nuanced way. They would de-link labour standards and other social issues from trade and thus terminate attempts at inserting them into the WTO, get away from selectivity aiming at the poor countries to include a far more comprehensive menu of concerns from the human rights agenda, and then address these concerns energetically in appropriate international agencies such as the ILO for labour issues and the UNICEF for children's issues. These economists therefore are not opposed to, and many indeed actively support, the pursuit of a human-rights agenda; they simply do not want to have it captured by intrusionists and protectionists who see this agenda (captured and defined by their extensive lobbying) as a splendid opportunity to advance their competition-moderating objective.

Again, such a de-linking of the moral agenda from trade treaties and institutions would enhance the credibility of the human rights and social-issues NGOs. The alliance with the protectionists distorts the agenda far too obviously in the direction of shielding the producers in the rich countries from competition from the poor countries. By asking for a proactive pursuit of these goals, they will be able to widen the agenda to a more substantial and symmetric menu of desired rights than a trade-dictated choice of menu must inevitably define.

Again, it is commonly asserted that ILO, UNICEF, and like institutions, do not have teeth. But this is the same as saying that the Pope has no troops. Surely, one does not need the rack to spread Christianity! It is easy to miss the fact that these institutions create the ethos and bring into a coherent framework the information about member states' performance in regard to rights and values that the NGOs seek to advance world-wide. In turn, this enables NGOs and governments to use this information to create the pressure points for progress,[3] thus leading in varying degrees to what I call the Dracula effect: expose evil to sunlight and it will shrivel up and die.

Thus, the ILO has the Committee of Experts on the Application of Conventions and Recommendations, whose distinguished members monitor annually the compliance of member states with the conventions they have ratified, while also taking up (one at a time) individual conventions and examining the member states' conformity to them *regardless of ratification*. The Trade Policy Review Mechanism at the WTO does much the same for Members' trade policy to great advantage, prodding the reviewed countries to move towards reforms even though there is no enforcing power at all. I have suggested that a World Migration Organisation could do the same for countries' overall policies concerning all forms of immigrants, legal and illegal, and refugees.

These are powerful techniques even if applied to others to the exclusion of one's own warts. But their power is vastly greater when they apply universally to all nations, playing no favorites. Thus, the ILO experts will catch the sweatshops in New York and the de facto slavery among migrant workers on American farms as much as they will highlight the prevalence of child labor in hazardous occupations such as rug-making in Pakistan and glassmaking in India.

14.6 Concluding Observations

All this strongly implies then that trade linkage in the form of a social clause for example is not an efficient way to advance a human rights or social issues agenda. It is also worth emphasizing that even the intrusionist lobbies that are fearful of international competition and push for the linkage as a precondition for freeing trade for that reason alone are mistaken in general. The belief in the 1980s that trade with poor countries produces paupers in our midst by hurting the real wages of our workers has been challenged effectively by a great deal of analysis that shows that the basic building blocks of the arguments leading to the fears are unsubstantiated: for example in the 1980s when real wages fell most, the prices of labor-intensive goods in world trade, and in the United States, rose instead of falling as required for the gloomy analysis of trade.[4]

Nor are the intrusionist lobbies, which fear that our own standards will collapse due to a "race to the bottom" as firms choose technologies and locations to exploit lower standards and governments compete to get the firms by lowering standards, on more solid ground. Numerous careful studies show that the empirical basis for these fears is hard to find; indeed, it does not exist.[5]

Therefore, it is mere folly to keep pushing for a social clause in the WTO. The proper course of action is to de-link the human rights and social standards issues from the trade agenda, and to pursue the former vigorously in appropriate institutions and by other means.[6]

Notes

1. Thus, the preservation of an endangered species such as the tiger is more likely to attract widespread condemnation than the elimination of dolphin-unsafe tuna fishing, which reflects concern for dolphins that is not grounded in a wider moral principle but reflects simply the fact that many Americans find dolphins cute.

2. These are not the only two motives that matter; but they are the principal ones of relevance to the policy questions discussed here. I have dealt with the question more fully in "Demands to Reduce Domestic Diversity among Trading Nations" in Bhagwati J and Hudec R (eds) (1996), *Fair Trade and Harmonization: Prerequisites for Free Trade?* MIT Press: Cambridge, Mass., chapter 1. Also see some of my writings on this subject in the media, reprinted in Bhagwati J. (1998), *A Stream of Windows: Unsettling Reflections on Trade, Immigration, and Democracy*. MIT Press: Cambridge, Mass.

3. These can include private boycotts, legally accepted in western jurisprudence. They can also generate voluntary labeling which enables consumers to vote with their dollars against practices they disapprove of.

4. I have dealt with these arguments in a series of papers, the latest being chapter 11. The occasional assertion that there is now a *consensus* that trade explains around 20 per cent of the decline in real wages is simply nonsense: I, for one, would now argue, on the basis of analytical reflection and study of evidence over several years, that trade *helps* workers. (Bhagwati, ibid.).

5. See the contributions by Arik Levinson and by Bhagwati and Srinivasan, in Bhagwati and Hudec, op cit., Volume 1.

6. This is the viewpoint I have advocated as a member of the Academic Advisory Committee of the Human Rights Watch (Asia) and was embodied in my writings and in the petition I organized opposing linkage in the renewal of fast-track authority that President Clinton unsuccessfully requested from the Congress last year. See, in particular, chapter 16; and Peter Passell, "Loading the trade agenda with divisive issues could backfire," *New York Times*, October 9, 1997.

References

Bhagwati J. (1997), "Fast Track: Not so Fast," *The Wall Street Journal*, September 10 (chap. 16 in this volume).

Bhagwati J. (1997), "Play it again Sam: Yet Another Look at Trade and Wages," Columbia University, mimeographed, February (chap. 11 in this volume).

Bhagwati J. (1998), *A Stream of Windows: Unsettling Reflection on Trade, Immigration and Democracy*. MIT Press: Cambridge, Mass.

Bhagwati J. and Hudec R. (eds.) (1997), *Fair Trade and Harmonization: Prerequisites for Free Trade?* Volumes 1 & 2, MIT Press: Cambridge, Mass.

Passell P. (1997), "Loading the trade agenda with divisive issues could backfire." *New York Times*, October 9.

15   On the Efficacy of Trade Sanctions

Jacob Heilbrunn both understates and overstates the case for unilateral trade sanctions against "tyrant" regimes.

He accepts uncritically the economic cost of these sanctions, recently estimated by an influential Washington think tank as "between $15 billion and $20 billion" and "250,000 jobs lost in 1995 alone." But the cost to us has to be estimated as the loss in the gains from trade, not the entire reduction of trade volume, and this is likely to be no more than a fraction of the total reduction in our trade. As for the assertion about jobs lost, this too is wrong: trade policy (whether theirs or ours) will generally not affect overall employment (as against, say, that of Boeing); only macroeconomic policy does.

At the same time, if we buy into the view that sanctions must be judged by a consequentialist ethic and deny ourselves the moral view that we will not sup with the devil, even if all we accomplish is the loss of a free meal for ourselves, Heilbrunn winds up being overly sanguine about unilateral trade sanctions by failing to consider that such sanctions must be judged against other policies to see if they give us the largest benefits for a dollar's worth of cost to us.

If we were to eschew trade sanctions, but instead proactively and publicly denounce rogue regimes for their egregious violations of civil and political rights, go after them at the international human rights agencies, deny them the gifts of aid and special trade privileges (such as trade preferences to developing countries), and assist their own NGOs at home (if possible) or in exile, we should surely carry most of our citizens and CEOs with us and exert moral pressure which, as Heilbrunn correctly states, even tyrants are not entirely immune from.

Originally published as a letter to the editor of the *New Republic* (June 29, 1998): 4. Reprinted with permission.

Where the Clinton administration fails us is in going easy on unilateral trade sanctions while assuming that détente and engagement alone should suffice to change these regimes. In the long run, it should work. But we can do better yet by activism of the kind I propose. If a woman is screaming for help because she is being beaten up by her boyfriend, you are not going to be credible if you tell her to hang in there; economic development will eventually lead to changes in the law to protect you. You have to do something right away to help!

The Design of the WTO and Trade Negotiations

Today President Clinton plans to ask Congress to renew the lapsed "fast-track" legislation. Fast-track authorizes the president to negotiate future international trade agreements on which Congress would then vote either up or down, without the prospect of the deal unraveling as its details are strenuously contested.

Fast-track is a brilliant political invention that was instrumental in the 1993 passage of the Uruguay Round of major international trade liberalization and the 1993 North American Free Trade Agreement. One can therefore only applaud Mr. Clinton's decision to seek fast-track now. Yet as the debate in Congress will soon reveal, the critical issue in fast-track renewal will not be the conventional tussle between free traders and protectionists. Rather, it will be over whether fast-track authority should contain a mandate that all future trade treaties submitted with fast-track status must include environmental and labor standards. In June 1994, the administration proposed such requirements. Yet in the face of Congress's strong preference for "clean" fast-track free from such preconditions, the administration abandoned fast-track altogether later in the year.

"Loaded" Authority

The administration has not really changed its mind on the "linkage" of environmental and labor issues to trade treaties. Whether the White House will succeed in outmaneuvering opponents in Congress to win "loaded" fast-track authority this time around is anybody's guess. But if it does, it will weaken the world trading system even as the administration claims to be strengthening it. For the arguments for linkage are weak, and many are wrong outright. In fact, if linkage is the price to be paid for fast-track, thoughtful free traders will want to side with protectionists against it.

Consider these five fallacious arguments in favor of loaded fast-track authority, which its proponents have found quite potent in public debate:

• *Trade is "unfair" if trading nations have different pollution and labor standards.* The truth, however, is that a diversity of standards is perfectly legitimate. The reason is simple: Different nations have different conditions and preferences. Thus, if Chile already has cleaner air and worse water than the U.S. does, it would only be sensible for it to have stiffer penalties for polluting water than the U.S., and smaller penalties for polluting air. Different regulatory burdens for an industry in different countries are therefore to be expected. Thus, when House Minority Leader Richard Gephardt (D., Mo.) talks of "equalizing burdens" on each industry across borders, he is advocating placing unjustifiable costs on producers abroad.

• *In competing to attract multinationals, countries will lower their standards.* This "race to the bottom" argument says the U.S. must seek harmonized international regulations in order to safeguard our own standards. The empirical evidence for this claim, however, is negligible. In fact, the economist Arik Levinson has shown that multinationals mostly use the most environmentally friendly technology. There are excellent economic reasons, including harm to their reputations, for companies not to exploit weaker standards. In addition, most poor countries are now democratic and have elements of an articulate civil society. It is hard to imagine their elected leaders trying to attract multinationals by inviting them to pollute their nations.

• *Products made with lower labor standards are morally unacceptable.* At first blush, it seems reasonable that we should want to exclude products made, for instance, in sweatshops. Shouldn't we then be able to say we will not trade with countries that fail to conform to our labor standards?

Such "values"-based denials of access to the U.S. market can surely open a Pandora's box, seriously disrupting trade. Because we think only of our values being imposed on others, we fail to see that the single worst aspect of some of our industries would be cited in efforts to curtail their international trade. For instance, many Americans strenuously object to the use of purse seine nets in tuna fishing because they kill dolphins. But what about the crowded U.S. hog farms? Or what if other nations want to suspend U.S. agricultural imports because of abuses against migrant workers in this county? Protectionist interests in other countries would quickly seize on such arguments, causing ever more economic damage.

• *Trade with poor countries is driving down U.S. workers' wages.* By now it has become commonplace to assert that up to 20% of the decline in real U.S. wages since the 1970s is due to international trade. Yet nearly all trade economists who have examined the issue conclude the adverse impact is negligible.

The conventional view is that U.S. wages must move in tandem with the prices of labor-intensive goods, which are increasingly produced in low-wage countries. Yet my latest research shows that real U.S. wages rose in the 1970s even though the prices of labor-intensive goods produced abroad fell, and U.S. wages fell in the 1980s while these prices rose. Indeed, I conclude that trade with poor countries has likely benefited U.S. workers.

• *We've done it before.* True, since the 1980s the U.S. has included environmental and labor regulations in bilateral and regional trade preferences. But we can correct a mistake, can we not? If we have grown a Frankenstein, must we live with him simply because our own misguided efforts created him?

The case for linkage is specious. Trade treaties should reduce trade barriers, not raise new ones. But the question remains: If our trade treaties do not include safe-guards against inhumane treatment of workers, for instance, how should the administration strive to improve other countries' labor and human rights standards? The answer: by proactive policies at institutions such as the International Labor Organization, the United Nations Environmental Protection Agency and Unicef, which already review, monitor and advance labor, environmental and child-welfare objectives. Trade negotiators and the World Trade Organization have no expertise in these complex areas.

Lazy Man's Answer

The efforts at using trade sanctions to eradicate child labor—which the ILO estimates involved nearly 250 million children last year—clearly illustrate the intellectual bankruptcy of quick fixes devised in a context like international trade, which is dominated by special interests. Linking liberalized international trade to a host of other goals is the lazy man's answer, unworthy of a great nation known for leadership on both trade and moral issues.

17 Short on Trade Vision

If we look to Washington for leadership on trade policy, as indeed we must, we should hold our breath. By ignoring opportunities, such as on a recent visit to Central America and the Caribbean, to make his stance clear, President Bill Clinton has begun his second term much as he started the first: sitting on the fence.

In his first term, Mr. Clinton finally abandoned his caution, embracing trade liberalisation and winning victories on the North American Free Trade Agreement (NAFTA) and on the Uruguay Round of the General Agreement on Tariffs and Trade (GATT), the forerunner to the World Trade Organisation. But now he seems paralysed.

He needs to provide a coherent trade policy, defined by both vision and an agenda, which rallies the free-traders behind it. At the same time, he must provide policies in pursuit of non-trade goals, for example on the environment and human rights. Currently activists in these areas focus on trade treaties and end up opposing them.

Mr. Clinton needs to declare that he supports fully the goal of multilateral free trade for the world economy. He should remind the U.S. Congress and Americans that multilateralism is alive and well; that the Uruguay Round was successfully completed; the WTO is working, with its dispute-settlement mechanism strengthened and widely used; and that he has secured valuable multi-lateral agreements in information technology and telecommunications. These agreements, together with one expected soon in financial services, have been applauded by U.S. export lobbies and therefore will meet no substantive obstacles in Congress.

In short, Mr. Clinton can make a resounding case for the WTO-centred multilateral trading system that reflects well on half a century

Originally published in the *Financial Times* (June 3, 1997). Reprinted with permission.

of U.S. leadership. But he should then set his sights higher. He could have an electrifying effect if he announced a goal of worldwide free trade by a date such as 2015—well into the next century to which he wishes to build a bridge—as many economists have advocated. Such a move would define a statesmanlike presidential vision without the requirement of getting Congress to sign up to it.

As the flip side to this embrace of a non-discriminatory, multilateral trade-liberalising agenda, Mr. Clinton also needs to abandon his administration's drift towards preferential trade agreements, such as Nafta and its extension to Chile, and to the proposed Free Trade Area for the Americas. With protectionist anti-NAFTA proponents such as Mr. Ross Perot, the billionaire and former U.S. presidential candidate, now off centre-stage, economists are increasingly saying what was unprintable in the 1980s—that free trade areas are really discriminatory trade agreements and that their proliferation is turning into a pox on the world trading system.

Mr. Clinton also needs to address the demands for human rights and for the improvement of other nations' labor and environmental standards that intrude on the trade scene. It is clearly a good idea to assert trans-border moral obligations and to identify with human rights in other countries. But the desire to link these objectives with trade, through the social clause at the WTO and setting environmental and labour standards preconditions during the fast-track renewal of trade treaties, implies cluttering up such treaties with new obstacles.

The human rights and social agenda would be better served, as I have little doubt the British government of Mr. Tony Blair would agree, if it were separated from trade treaties and pursued energetically in other ways.

Thus, in regard to improving labour standards and children's rights, for example, Mr. Clinton should seek instead to enhance research capabilities at the International Labour Organisation and Unicef, the United Nations children's fund, in order to strengthen the ability to monitor and review each member state's conformity to all ILO conventions and to the entire Convention on the Child respectively.

On these lines, Mr. Clinton could pursue a trade agenda that was ambitious in its pursuit of multilateral free trade but also practical in its pursuit of regional objectives and American values by non-trade means.

Dani Rodrik's article (*New Republic*, November 2, 1998) on "The Global Fix" prompts me to say: if you must fix what is broke, you need to know why it is. There is indeed much that is wrong with the world economic system. But it cannot be understood and its cures designed by invoking the celebrated Polanyi thesis, as applied famously to the growing integration of the world economy by the political scientist John Ruggie in 1982 when he argued that the New Deal had embedded liberalism of the marketplace into the "social order," making it tolerable and survivable, and that Bretton Woods had done the same for the world economy.

Rodrik would have us believe that the "Reagan and Thatcher 'revolutions'" have made us opt for a let-the-markets-rip strategy on "global capitalism" without attention to social and political contexts. In thus ignoring the Ruggie-Polanyi insights, we have imperiled the liberal international regime in two main ways: we have created "significant inequities, economic instability, or social disruption" and we have ridden roughshod over diversity of other cultures by indulging demands to harmonize away such differences in our capitalist pursuits. But neither charge is valid for, or reflects a correct understanding of the problems before, the world trading system for which Rodrik provides his "global fix."

As regards the first charge, Rodrik mistakenly transfers to *trade* the serious consequences of *financial* crises such as today's (which have come in any event from an *economic* miscalculation of the risks of freed capital flows, not from a disregard of the *social* context in which these

Originally published as a letter to the editor of the *New Republic* (Dec. 14, 1998). Reprinted with permission.

flows were set). This will not do. Free trade and free capital mobility are distinct phenomena and prescriptions: the former does not require the latter.

Rodrik's well-known misgivings about free trade's dire social consequences were shared by many fearful developing countries in the 1950s through 1970s but properly abandoned by them in light of the hugely documented postwar experience linking outward orientation in trade and direct foreign investment with success. They make little sense in the developed countries either, where they have resurfaced today in an ironic reversal.

As regards the second charge, Rodrik does no better. The harmonization demands that afflict us today are the product of important factors that have nothing to with the idea or ideology of mindless free trade. In fact, just the opposite is true.

Thus, international competition has intensified as the world economy has gotten more integrated. Firms have clamored therefore to iron out any "unfair" advantages that their rivals may enjoy from differences in their nations' domestic policies and institutions. But these are lobbying demands that reflect protectionism, masquerading under the guise of "fair trade," rather than ideological demands for free trade. Free traders such as myself have in fact spent years analyzing and unmasking them whereas politicians reflecting lobbying pressures have embraced them under the slogan: fair trade, not free trade.

But, a more worthy source of harmonization demands comes from socially motivated groups. The rapid growth of civil society, with its universalist aspirations, has meant that many wish to use trade policy and institutions as instruments of social change abroad. So, it is not that (Ruggie-Polanyi-ignoring) trade undermines the social agenda; rather, social agendas are pursued through the instrumentality of trade. But, precisely because trade is driven by economic gain, the moral and social agendas that are sought to be imposed reflect our competitiveness concerns and are distorted in the process. And the freeing of trade is undermined because trade treaties and institutions should be about reducing trade barriers, not creating new ones.

It is better then to free the trading system from such demands, leaving free trade to do its job of aiding economic prosperity, and to pursue social and moral agendas through a multitude of other, nontrade means. In short, kill two birds with two stones. The global fix that is called for, and which I have advocated, requires then, not that we abandon these social-agenda-driven demands altogether as in Rodrik's blueprint, but that we shift them to other nontrade areans and pursue them simultaneously with the passion and commitment that we bestow on the pursuit of free trade.

Fifty Years: Looking Back, Looking Forward

The fifty years of the multilateral trading system, which span from the birth of GATT at the beginning to the blossoming of the WTO at the end, merit unrestrained applause. Dividing the normal centennial celebratory period by half is truly appropriate: while much has been accomplished in the past fifty years, much remains to be done in the next fifty. I can add little to the experience and insights that my many friends at this symposium will present on this occasion.

But perhaps I can provide a unique perspective since I happen to combine contrasting personas. I was born in a developing country (India) but now am a citizen of a developed one (the United States). I am a scholar of trade theory but I also write on trade policy (unlike many who are not constrained by scientific pursuits and knowhow). I am an academic (and the epithet "professor" is occasionally thrown at me in debate as if it were an affliction) but have also been "on the inside" (since Arthur Dunkel made me Economic Policy Adviser to the Director General, GATT, during 1991–1993). I should not overdo this since I have limitations as well, which I was made aware of during the ill-fated negotiations for fast-track authority for President Clinton recently. I am informed that, on being faced by the U.S. Ways and Means Committee with my *Wall Street Journal* (September 10, 1997) op-ed. article arguing against linking fast-track to environmental and labor requirements, Ambassador Charlene Barshefsky is alleged to have remarked, Bhagwati (garbled: I admit it is a difficult name for lawyers, not for economists who have been exposed to it excessively) does not understand trade; he has never been in a trade negotiation. Since a good lawyer friend of mine teaches mock trade negotiations at

Based on a speech given at the 50th Anniversary Celebration Symposium on the World Trading System, organized by the WTO and the Graduate Institute of International Studies, Geneva, April 30, 1998.

my university, I hope to sit in on one of them in the near future and rid myself of this crippling limitation.

Looking Back

The achievements of GATT in liberalizing trade through reduced border trade barriers are too well known to need recounting. Successive rounds of multilateral trade negotiations (MTNs), culminating in the successful Uruguay Round, have brought down trade tariffs to dramatically low levels around the world. True, developing countries such as India still have tariffs that call for significant reductions. But it is a mistake to believe, as Mr. Bergsten has argued recently in *Foreign Affairs*, that the future task for the WTO will be to exchange "fair trade" disciplines offered by the developed countries for lower trade tariffs and restrictions by the developing countries. In agriculture alone, the tariffication brought about by the Uruguay Round has now led to sufficiently high tariffs in the developed countries that cry out to be reduced in reciprocal exchange in future MTN Rounds.

In the same vein, a steadily wider range of sectors with trade barriers has been brought under the GATT's axe. Take just two major examples. Agriculture, having escaped GATT owing to the 1955 waiver, is now back in the picture, with definite steps taken toward freeing trade therein with the Uruguay Round. And we now also have progress made on financial and other services in the GATT under the GATS umbrella.

Equally, the list of GATT's achievements must include the establishment of some, though woefully inadequate, discipline on "fair trade" rules. Economists understand only too well the misuse that has occurred of rules such as on antidumping (AD) measures, with continued capture of these ironically for "unfair" trade protectionism. It is an open secret that AD actions in reality have nothing to do with predation, and that the GATT has been unable to impose the necessary discipline in this area. On the other hand, it is not hard to imagine what chaos could have reigned in the absence of the GATT.

The Uruguay Round also must be credited with having brought about a single undertaking, with common rules and obligations for all members, with exceptions largely reduced to transitional periods for developing countries. We thus finally have a WTO that aims to have a single set of rules to govern world trade. This is a considerable achievement as few of us believe now, as many of us did in the 1950s through 1970s, that there should be special and differential (S&D) treatment for the developing countries. The earlier view was based on the belief that a different economics governed developing countries, requiring a different policy framework and special exemptions permitting readier resort to trade barriers for balance-of-payments reasons and on infant industry protection grounds, thus effectively exempting them also from the expected reciprocity in reductions of trade barriers in MTNs. Now, we believe that letting developing countries hold on to their trade restrictions is like letting them shoot themselves in the foot and that the same economics applies to them as to others. Their growing importance in world trade also makes it politically impossible to maintain huge asymmetries of market access. The imposition of the same rules on both sets of nations has therefore become the norm, implying a single undertaking. (In this context, the notion that the "least developed countries" should still be accorded S & D status is to ignore these fundamental lessons.)

Next, the WTO now has an effective dispute settlement mechanism. We have moved away from an ineffective system where a defendant could veto the adoption by the GATT Council of an adverse finding. This has removed the incentive to exercise "aggressive unilateralism" of the Section 301 variety in cases where the defendant did act this way, as in the soybean case where the EU had blocked two successive adverse findings at the GATT and then the United States had resorted unilaterally to retaliatory tariffs.[1] The strengthened dispute settlement mechanism has also led to increased resort to its impartial procedures to cool bilateral disputes that, as in the U.S.-Japan automobile case, were marked by acrimonious friction inherent to bilateral confrontations. The WTO resolution of the Eastman-Kodak-Fuji dispute has also served to underscore the fact that unilateral determination of "unfair trade" by national bodies such as the USTR, on the basis of complaints by interested national parties, and threats based thereon are simply an unacceptable way of proceeding in such disputes: the total defeat of Eastman Kodak shows how baseless the U.S. complaints against Japan are likely to have been, exactly as argued by some of us over the years in the teeth of assertions backed by few or no arguments. All this is to the good.

Environmental Problems

The environmental interface with WTO rules is also a matter of considerable controversy, and I believe that the time has come to take a concerted look at the problems that have emerged.

First, the basic idea that purely domestic, as opposed to global, environmental pollution should be dealt with by harmonization or upward movement of lower tax burdens abroad has an intuitive appeal. But, as I and Professor Srinivasan have argued,[2] there is a perfectly legitimate case for diversity in pollution tax rates for identical pollution across countries in the same industries (i.e., in cross-country intra-industry, tax burdens). Besides, the fears of a race to the bottom, which is theoretically possible, are unjustified by the empirical findings that corporations seem to use the more environmentally friendly technologies even where the requirements are more lax. So, the argument that free trade requires fair trade in the sense of harmonization or upgrading of foreign tax burdens with one's own is ill taken. Thus, most of the arguments advanced against free trade on this account, and the demands that the WTO should have "social dumping" clauses to permit countervailing duties when the foreign pollution tax burden is lower, are simply mistaken.

Next, this still leaves open questions of the type raised by the Shrimp-Turtle and the Dolphin-Tuna decisions. In all these cases, the GATT and WTO judgments are quite sound, in my view. Speaking very broadly, it makes little sense to legitimate unilateral assertion of environmental and social preferences and thereby suspend other WTO members' access to one's markets. It is surely more desirable to reach agreement on these matters through negotiations and, failing that, to suspend such trade while paying, if challenged at the WTO, suitable compensation for such unilateral suspension. If we do not do that, the road will open for everyone, making such unilateral assertions and disrupting trade in consequence. The issue requires accommodation of the kind embodied in the entire set of WTO procedures and ideas on how to handle such conflicts. The more militant environmentalists and NGOs such as The Public Citizen portray the WTO in demonized and distorted form on this question when, in fact, their own views are unbending, unaccommodating, and destructive.

Finally, I believe that, on the global environmental issues, we badly need to grandfather in the trade sanctions against defectors and free riders in the existing Multilateral Environmental Treaties, taking them (quickly) one by one to ensure that these potentially targeted nations have no justifiable case against such a procedure. (For instance, a pacifist in a war is a "conscientious objector," not a "free rider." My own impression, however, is that the MEAs have taken good care to carry most nations on board through suitable accommodations of the countries that may object.)

MAI

It is probably a heresy to say that the Multilateral Agreement on Investment (MAI), as presently drafted, and at the present time, is not a good idea and that it should be shelved temporarily. But the adverse reception accorded to the unveiling of the OECD-produced draft and the temporary withdrawal of it from any agenda indicate that there are basic problems with MAI. True, with trade and investment closely tied together today, an agreement on investment at the WTO seems a good idea.

But such an agreement must be balanced in at least two ways: first, it should not be just about removing obstacles to investment but also subventions and subsidies to it; and second, it must be formulated with the active participation of both developing and developed countries. Neither has been done.

Besides, tricky questions such as the use of state power against specific foreign firms with a view to extracting concessions from their governments have not been addressed. Thus, during the U.S.-Japan auto dispute, it was remarkable that the United States was threatening to zero in on Japanese auto firms' luxury model exports to the United States with punitive tariffs of 100 percent simply to impose import targets, component-purchase targets, and so forth. All this, while asserting in other contexts the need to leave multinationals free from political interference in matters of production and trade! Again, the United States was jawboning Japanese transplants into buying more U.S. components, virtually intimidating these firms into a "local purchase" policy, while pushing for the adoption of TRIMs outlawing the use of "local content" clauses by host countries for multinationals! MAI does not adequately come to grips with such transgressions by the powerful countries, while seeking to impose constraints on the weaker countries. But it should if it is to be credible.

In addition, I feel that the timing of the MAI is precipitous and bad. Developing countries are pushing their direct foreign investment (DFI) doors open quite dramatically on their own. If obstacles are created for inflows of foreign investment, a country will lose out in the race for attracting investment that all countries are engaged in. Why then get into devising MAI and selling it at the WTO when the market forces are already leading countries to several pro-DFI practices? By formalizing all this into an explicit MAI, we make this into a political issue, and invite the anti-DFI lobbies, the anti-WTO lobbies, and all the wackos in every country on to center stage. The WTO is in enough trouble from such lobbies, which played some role in President Clinton's defeat on fast-track renewal; it seems a foolish idea to add to them gratuitously. In fact, every informed scholar of the politics of international economic policy knows that the level of political difficulty escalates as you go from free trade in goods to free trade in services, to freedom of DFI, to freedom of all capital flows, to freedom of labor flows. We seem to have forgotten all this in the flush of the victory (still incomplete) of free trade forces at Geneva; but we do so at our peril.

Competition Policy

Finally, I believe that we have to get what Sylvia Ostry has called "system friction" under some form of managed control at the WTO. This involves getting into what is best called "competition policy." Two sets of problems in particular are important to distinguish. First, problems of market access in our exports, and predation by exporters in our imports, have come to the forefront, and we need to come to agreed parameters on what is acceptable practice and what is not.

Second, while we trade economists correctly view trade as the best antidote to domestic monopoly, it is also true that international cartelization can kill that therapeutic effect. Clearly, some form of agreed antitrust policy, which is not just "anti-big" on a kneejerk basis, has to be evolved. That is an important, unfinished task.

Notes

1. Section 301 actions where the United States is seeking to impose new obligations on others, not covered by earlier treaty commitments, are still a problem, however, for the U.S. administration if it wishes to abide by the spirit of multilateralism in the teeth of repeated attempts by U.S. lobbying groups, and Congress, to impose their demands on foreign nations. The distinction between these two types of 301 actions was noted and explored in contributions by me and Professor Robert Hudec in Jagdish Bhagwati and Hugh Patrick (eds.), *Aggressive Unilateralism* (Ann Arbor University of Michigan Press, 1991).

2. Bhagwati and Patrick, *Aggressive Unilateralism*, chap. 4.

On Thinking Clearly
about the Linkage between
Trade and the Environment

I Introduction

The question of linkage between trade and environmental issues, indeed between trade and labor standards and between trade and human rights, has reached center stage as several NGOs (nongovernmental organizations) have demanded that the WTO formally incorporate such a linkage through, for example, a Social Clause on labor standards in WTO and through as-yet-unspecified mechanisms as far as environmental standards are concerned.

Within the environmental arena, the GATT itself, and now the WTO (GATT's successor), have been the focus of much agitation by environmental groups that see this trade institution as an obsolete obstacle to environmental progress. The anti-GATT feeling materialized first when the celebrated Dolphin-Tuna decision was announced, declaring Mexico the winner in the dispute over the U.S. legislation that sought to proscribe access to Mexican tuna caught in purse seine nets. A throwback to that sentiment occurred recently when the Shrimp-Turtle Panel decision also went against the United States over its legislation that mandated unilaterally a denial of access to shrimp harvested without the use of TEDs (the turtle excluding devices).[1]

These cases reflected one of a number of different ways in which the work of the WTO interfaces today with the environmental questions and agendas. The main and unifying essence of both cases was this question: Should suspension of market access be allowed automatically to a nation that objects unilaterally (i.e., without obtaining a mul-

Based on a paper presented at the Conference on Environment and Trade at the Kiel Institute for World Economics, Kiel, Germany, Summer 1999, and at the Columbia University Conference on The Next Trade Negotiating Round: Examining the Agenda for Seattle, New York City, July 22–23, 1999.

tilateral consensus) to other countries exporting products to it when those products are made by using processes that the nation objects to on "values" grounds?

In the Dolphin-Tuna case, the U.S. government objected to the use of purse seine nets in harvesting tuna because these nets kill dolphins (which Americans have voted to protect, presumably because they are "cute" and a great draw at zoos) gratuitously and cruelly. In the Shrimp-Turtle case, the objection was similar: it related to what are called in GATT jargon PPM objections, namely, objections to process and production methods. Similar cases can arise if nations object in much the same way to the importation of, say, chickens produced in batteries, or hogs produced in crowded pens, or fur harvested from animals caught in leghold traps, and many more instances of what some nations, but not all or most, consider to be "values"-wise unacceptable PPMs.

But while these cases are the subject of high-profile, high-octane attacks on the GATT and the WTO, and they raise questions that necessarily involve an interface between the WTO and the environmental groups, other issues are equally the object of demands by environmental groups on the WTO but, in my view, are not necessarily ones that belong to a WTO or trade-treaty agenda. In particular, I believe this to be true of the demands for harmonization or upgrading of environmental standards in developing countries if they wish to export products, even when the pollution involved is "local" and has no global environmental externalities as with global warming or ozone layer depletion or acid rain.

Unlike in the popular debate, which tends often to blur necessary distinctions among different types of problems, and where the environmentally sensitive lobbies often are unwilling to make the distinctions anyway because they would weaken coalition building for political action, I propose here (since I am asked to address the "trade and the environment" linkage) to make these distinctions very sharply.

In particular, using these distinctions, I set myself the task of providing a road map that is aimed at dividing the current "linkage" demands between trade (whether institutions or negotiations) and environmental questions into those that are "necessary" and those that are not. In the latter case, as when trade access is used as a way of pushing environmental agendas abroad on altruistic grounds, I will also propose *alternative* ways in which such agendas may be pursued outside the trade context and institutions (e.g., in UNEP rather than

WTO), thus raising the question of what I like to call the design of "appropriate governance" (i.e., what agenda to pursue where).

II A Necessary Taxonomy

I first provide a necessary taxonomy so that the issues concerning linkage of trade and environmental questions can be analyzed with clarity and optimal policy solutions designed with the aid of such analysis. This taxonomy can be built essentially around two sets of distinctions:

i. whether the environmental damage or pollution is "domestic" or "international"; and

ii. whether the country addressing it follows egotistical (i.e., its own advantage) or altruistic (i.e., others' advantage) objectives.

The former distinction was introduced principally in the 1992 GATT Report on Trade and the Environment, though it must have been used simultaneously by many researchers, I am sure. If I pollute a lake in India that only (even then just a few) Indians have heard of, the pollution is of concern to Indians at risk. But if I pollute a river that flows into Bangladesh, or produce acid rain in the United States that goes across and hurts Canadians, the problem is clearly international. When global warming and ozone layer depletion are involved, the problem is actually global. The international/global problem is clearly one where externalities are at stake unless a "market" is already in place to internalize these externalities (e.g., by having tradable permits, suitably devised).

The latter distinction is appreciated by few, including economists who write about globalization, about fixing the world trading system, and so on without any real understanding of the complexity of the issues at hand.[2] Thus, we must distinguish between, say, objecting to the import of child labor–produced carpets from India because we object to being put at a competitive disadvantage with other nations because we prohibit, and they allow, cheaper child labor, and objecting to such imports instead with a view to reducing or eliminating the use of child labor abroad because we think that our cessation of such imports will help bring that about. In the former case, we are "egotistic": we are simply interested in maintaining our competing industries. In the latter case, we are being "altruistic" in thinking of children's welfare even though they are abroad in other nations, and we are using consequentialist ethics, hoping to effect change abroad. The latter is therefore a matter of seeking to advance social agendas abroad; the former is a matter of protecting our industries, for our own benefit. In assessing the demands for prohibiting the imports of products made with child labor, our evaluation of the proposal and the design of appropriate policy instruments will clearly have to be different, depending on which of these two motivations we are confronting.[3]

Once these two sets of distinctions are made, we have four sets of problems: domestic environmental problems with egotistic and with altruistic objectives by nations, and international environmental problems with egotistic and with altruistic objectives again. In this chapter, I devote myself to the domestic environmental issues, which are among the trickier ones where a great amount of confusion reigns.

The *international environmental issues* are understood much better, including in their interface with the WTO's functioning, and I shall eschew a discussion of them here. Let me just say, in regard to them, that the interface with WTO comes principally insofar as the MEAs (Multilateral Environmental Agreements such as Basel and the Montreal Protocol) seek to use trade sanctions against defectors and against free riders, and that these two sets of nations, when WTO members, could claim WTO-defined rights against the use of such sanctions. These questions are not easy to settle since we must raise questions such as: Is the MEA efficiently and equitably designed?[4] if the scientific evidence in support of it is disputed, can you treat a nation that does not wish to join as a free rider when in fact it may simply be opting out of getting on to the bus? In this context, let me say that, while Kyoto is a useful step forward (though I share some of the misgivings about its design that the economist Richard Cooper expressed in his recent article in *Foreign Affairs*,[5] and felt that Stuart Eizenstat's reply was lame, to say the least), I have been surprised that none of the models that I have seen seem to do the obvious if you know the domestic environmental scene in the United States:

• For the "stock" problem, that is, the damage done in the past, a clearly defined responsibility must exist for the polluters: this is a principle that has been accepted in the Superfund approach and in the torts claims addressed to past polluters for phenomena such as the Love Canal disaster. Why is it not accepted at the international level as well for past damage to the environment on global warming (principally, of course, by the developed nations)? The question then must be not whether there is responsibility for past environmental damage, but how to assess it and the specific ways in which the levy can be used to reduce the global warming problem—for example, by financing the creation of new environment-friendly technologies and their subsidized diffusion across the world.

• For the "flow" problem, as to what to charge for emissions, the conceptually clear answer has to be to put all such emissions (net of absorption services through, for instance, your forests) into the pot of world demand for such pollution and then to determine, with a suitable utility function defined positively on goods and services and negatively on pollution, the shadow price of a unit pollution. That would then define the cost that the nation must pay for its contribution to the global warming problem. Needless to say, that cost would be vastly higher for the rich than for the poor countries. Instead of doing this, the rich countries are opting for an international variant of the principle that we refer to in the United States as the "PSD" Principle—namely, prevention of significant deterioration. In plain English, this means that those who pollute a lot as part of the initial condition can get away with it: burdens are to be prorated to marginal changes in pollution!

So, what we have therefore in the global warming debate is a cynical and virtual denial by the rich countries of the Superfund principle whose incidence would hurt them, and an adoption of the PSD principle that would help them. Not bad, indeed. As I read the Kyoto arguments and policy papers, it seems to me therefore that the developing countries have an intuitive sense of what I am saying above but no conceptual clarity or technical work to back it. Instead they talk inchoately about how the *flow* burden should be far less on them both because the stock damage was due to the developed countries and also because they are poor and hence should not be asked to bear any burden. But as soon as they do that, arguing their case on these grounds, they are shot down in the U.S. Congress as countries that are doubly wrong because they wish to be free riders and are also guilty of trying to exploit the "guilt" angle!

Again, one needs to consider whether, given the hostility manifest between the more vociferous environmentalists and free traders on many other fronts, it would not be wise to "grandfather" the existing MEAs and to leave the contentious question of the WTO-compatibility of *future* MEAs to further consensus building among the WTO membership: we may prudently decide that this was one major battle from which we could withdraw. This is certainly an issue with which the WTO must come to immediate grips, preferably at the Millennium Round expected to be launched in Seattle in December 1999.

III   Domestic Environmental Issues

So, let me turn to the purely domestic environmental problems, dealing first with the egotistical objective and next with the altruistic one.

Egotistical Objective

Here, I deal with the following distinct aspects of the demands for "greening the WTO":

Contention 1

WTO should allow importing countries to countervail "social" dumping, namely, when a product is produced with differential tax burdens in different countries and the exporting country has a lower tax burden. This is what T. N. Srinivasan and I have called *CCII (cross-country-intra-industry) harmonization of tax burdens*.[6] Clearly, this is wrong. With different fundamentals, there is no good reason for such harmonization to occur or to be demanded. We may demand that every nation adopt a Polluter Pay Principle; but the pollution tax, for the same carcinogen in the same industry, will generally be different.

Contention 2

We nonetheless may object to others having lower tax burdens because that will result in a "race to the bottom" that hurts our standards even if we do not care otherwise what standards others have on a CCII basis. Therefore WTO should allow countervailing duties to offset "social dumping."

Unlike the previous argument, this is a theoretically sound one. But it is an argument for a cooperative solution that will nonetheless not be characterized in general by harmonization. Besides, a "race towards the top" can occur, as John Wilson points out in his chapter on the subject in the Bhagwati-Hudec volume.[7] Moreover, the argument depends on capital taxation being suboptimal. Finally, the empirical evidence for such a race does not seem to be strong since (1) multinationals do not seem to respond to lower environmental burdens (not just because the differences among different locations are small, since these could rise) for a variety of reasons including reputational ones (see the detailed discussion in Bhagwati-Srinivasan of the reasons why), though a couple of recent papers detect some elasticity of response to differential environmental burdens within the United States across states; and (2) the evidence that poor countries lower environmental regulations to attract MNCs is not plausible when democratic countries are involved: the competition for capital/MNCs is really through tax breaks, tax holidays, and land grants—all of which amount to a race to the bottom in taxation that hurts the competing countries, most analysts believe. Few democratic countries are going to offer facilities to pollute freely as a way of attracting MNCs.

So, *for contentions 1 and 2, the Gephardt-Bonior-Gore type of demand for harmonization and/or legitimation at the WTO of countervailing duties on socalled social dumping seems to me to be not the way to green the WTO. We should resist such demands.*

Instead, I recommend two other solutions:

1. I have argued that MNCs must be asked to adopt the environmental standards of their home countries when they go abroad. If they tend to do so anyway, as argued above empirically, then this mandate will not hurt and will buy environmentalists' approbation at very little deadweight loss.[8] I think now of this as a *mandatory code*, unlike the voluntary code approach discussed below that is complementary in my view.

2. We can also go ahead with devising *voluntary labeling schemes* like the SA8000 (whose pioneering originator, Alice Marlin, is at this Columbia University Conference), the world's leading code today that firms can sign on to and several have indeed recently. This defines conditions of work and includes independent monitoring. This means that all the signatory firms from every country would have to adopt the common minimum standards, whereas the mandatory Bhagwati-style code above would permit differences among firms from different countries.

"Values-Related" PPMs

Next, there is the Shrimp-Turtle and Dolphin-Tuna type of problem. U.S. consumers simply feel that the United States should be allowed to prohibit imports of products using morally objectionable PPMs. This question has also been dealt with in the Bhagwati-Hudec volume.

Evidently, we cannot force such imports down people's throats. Indeed, economists are well aware of the legitimacy of PPMs as something that enters our utility functions: after all, the way we produce something is part of the characteristics of the vector that defines a product. The problem is not that we free traders have not realized that PPMs are legitimate and must be dealt with,[9] but how do we deal with them when there is no consensus on that "value"? Do we allow automatic unilateral shut-off of such products?

Here again, the 1992 GATT Report, correctly in my view, argued that the grant of automatic market access suspension rights in such ethical or moral or "values"-related cases would be a slippery slope: how would we draw the line? Moreover, we do know that protectionist intent will occasionally underlie environmental legislation, often in the specifics of the design of the environmental regulation (as in the Dolphin-Tuna case and the Ontario-U.S. beer can case). Are we simply to ignore that by saying an environmentally aimed prohibition on imports cannot be challenged at all?

Therefore, I would say that the precise way in which the WTO deals with such values-related PPM problems should not be along the lines of automaticity. Nor should we accept an ill-considered proposal such as Rodrik's that an administrative procedure like antidumping be devised to ensure that the moral preference is genuine and widely shared within the country, after which the imports should be unilaterally shut off (as if the enactment of the Turtle and Dolphin legislation itself was not the expression of such a widely shared preference and as if an administrative body could sit in judgment over a legislative outcome).

Rather, we should proceed along the lines of *labeling*. This raises a number of questions that UNCTAD has been considering and that we know about from U.S. experience as well. For example, who determines the label, how "alarmist" or "realistic" should it be, and so on. Thus, in the hormone-fed beef case, the USTR Ambassador Barshefsky has suggested that it would be sufficient to label the U.S. hormone-fed beef as "Made in USA" since everyone knows that much of U.S. beef used hormones! Again, what are the problems for small producers in developing countries that have few facilities for such labeling? But it is still the way to explore and go, giving consumers information and choice.

Equally, I think it is necessary to ensure that, if the WTO continues to object to automaticity of such suspensions of access, as I believe it should, then the remedy when a country has lost such a case and still wishes to maintain the import suspension and is unwilling to accept a labeling solution should not be to slap on retaliatory measures (as the United States favors, if recent examples in the hormone-fed beef and the bananas cases reveal a trend) but rather to go for a cash compensation that reflects the gains from trade lost.[10] There is no point in disrupting trade yet further: it is time that the economists weighed in on this aspect of the dispute settlement procedures and remedies.

Other Forms of Linkage

I believe that the main ("egotistical") linkage questions of importance are the three I have listed and discussed above. But, in the classroom, we can certainly discuss other forms of "linkage" (in the sense of an interrelationship) that have little policy salience in my view. Two can be cited.

1. Suppose that I cannot use tariffs to exploit monopoly power. Then, I certainly can use other instruments (including pollution tax rates) to have a second-best improvement of my income through "inefficient" but still welfare-improving exploitation of monopoly power. This was at the heart of the Bhagwati-Ramaswami-Srinivasan, Kemp-Negishi, and related discussions in the early and mid-1960s.[11] Frankly, I do not think this sort of insight is particularly important in the trade and environmental interface discussion, any more than we want to get tied up worrying about dozens of possible policy instruments that may bear on trade indirectly. Cost-benefit analysis should encourage us to think of other things! But I could be wrong; or perhaps I should say: persuade me otherwise. (In fact, I should be personally happy as a scholar if I were wrong: after all, my own work in the 1960s helped define this linkage rigorously.)

2. Along the same line, scholars such as Brian Copeland have extended this type of argument to strategic interplay of environmental policies and to a demonstration of how environmental negotiations that complement trade negotiations can improve welfare outcomes.[12] In a recent paper, he takes egotistical governments maximizing utility. If tariffs are bound to zero, though each country has monopoly power in trade, each government then has an incentive to distort its environmental policy to manipulate the terms of trade in its favor. The country that imports the (only) environmentally dirty good in this model then has an incentive to stimulate the production of that good a little bit, in order to lower its world prices, and thus to relax its environmental regulation a bit (relative to the first-best, where the tax would just equal the environmental harm). The country exporting the dirty good has an incentive to restrict the production a bit to raise its world price, and hence to tighten its environmental regulation a bit (relative to its first-best). Therefore, without a free trade agreement, each country would set its environmental tax equal to the marginal environmental harm in that country; but with the free trade agreement, neither does. Hence, we can have further gains from negotiation, over environmental pol-

icy, once the free trade negotiation is done. Both countries can change their regulation in the direction of the first-best simultaneously, so that the terms-of-trade effects cancel out, and both countries therefore are better off because both have moved to giving individual polluters the right incentives.

But frankly, few developing countries have terms of trade to manipulate: they tend to be price takers in world markets (as empirical-cum-econometric analyses by Reidel and Panagariya have plausibly argued).[13] More important, I doubt if the Copeland-type argumentation really captures the spirit in which environmental regulations are set: I have seen no plausible evidence that the low environmental standards have been set by reference to trade-competitiveness considerations—the most extreme example being the case of abysmally low standards set by the former communist countries that hardly traded at all. My view rather is that the low environmental standards, set for trade-unrelated reasons, are in fact being used to advance protectionist agendas by the high-standard countries: the Copeland-type argument is, in that view, turning the reality on its head!

Altruistic Argument for Linkage

But suppose that we seek linkage because of altruistic reasons, treating trade treaties and/or institutions as mere instrumentalities through which we hope to effect change in morally offensive practices abroad.

Those who wish to use trade treaties and institutions to do this, as do the proponents of a Social Clause at the WTO, seem to me to use one instrument (i.e., trade policy) to achieve two targets (i.e., the liberalization of trade and the promotion of their social agendas). But typically, as we know from the theory of economic policy, we need generally two instruments to best achieve two objectives. A Social Clause illustrates this well. Dividing the supporters of trade liberalization into those who oppose and those who support the Social Clause undermines trade liberalization, as happened with the Seattle debacle. Making many, especially in developing countries, suspicious that the true objective of the proponents of a Social Clause is protectionism rather than advancement of social agendas also undermines the legitimacy of the morally motivated groups and their case.

Instead, I have proposed in chapter 7 that the social agendas are best pursued by nontrade means. This can be done at the ILO for child labor eradication, for example. In fact, the ILO has an excellent International

Program for the Eradication of Child Labour that does the heavy lift-ing necessary to do effective work on the problem, whereas the WTO has literally no competence in the area.

As elsewhere, I consider this issue best solved by assigning the reso-lution of a problem to an appropriate agency (rather than overloading one institution like the WTO with all problems); hence, I have called it a question of "Appropriate Governance" in my recent writings.

Such a policy would enable us to pursue both free trade (which I consider to be an important social and moral agenda as well, since the prosperity it brings is essential for removing poverty worldwide) and other social and moral agendas. To sacrifice one to the other gratu-itously, when both can be pursued together, would be inexcusable. It is time for our political leadership to act forcefully on that insight instead of succumbing to populist demands for solutions that yield less than the best.

Notes

1. In each of these cases, there have been more than one panel findings; in the latter case, the new Appellate Court also ruled after the initial panel finding. The precise grounds on which the United States lost in both the cases have therefore varied.

2. Here, the culprits include my good friend, Dani Rodrik, and his publisher, the Insti-tute for International Economics in Washington, D.C., which has published yet other authors such as the political scientist Mac Destler, whose knowledge of the economics of international trade policy questions seems to be exclusively based on reading what the institute brings out, advocating linkage to facilitate fast-track renewal and the start of the Millennium Round.

3. In this chapter, I cannot discuss these distinctions fully. A systematic and deep anal-ysis is provided in my and others' contributions to Bhagwati and Robert Hudec (eds.), *Fair Trade and Harmonization: Prerequisites for Free Trade?*, vol. 1, (Cambridge, Mass.: MIT Press, 1996); and also in three chapters in part VI of my recent book, *A Stream of Windows: Unsettling Reflections on Trade, Immigration, and Democracy* (Cambridge, Mass.: MIT Press: 1998).

4. Thus, in relation to the NPT and CTBT, India refused to sign them because it did not accept the division of the world into the status quo of those who had nuclear weapons and those that did not, and backed instead a *universal* nuclear disarmament plan. The moral incoherence of the nuclear nations is manifest from Britain's condemnation of India's nuclear tests when Britain, an admirable nation in other ways, holds on for no reason whatsoever to its own nuclear stockpile when it could instead make an impor-tant moral and effective gesture by bringing the great unilateral nuclear disarmament advocate Vanessa Redgrave (leader of the unilateral-British-nuclear-disarmament CND movement) out of the mothballs and putting her in charge of a rapid unilateral destruc-tion of Britain's stockpile! One might also note that the United States itself has not ratified the CTBT yet. The mere fact that a certain powerful group of nations, and its NGOs with their vast resources compared to those situated in the poor nations, support an MEA is

no proof that it is equitable, free from the power play that distorts priorities and burdens from an objective point of view, and that those who refuse to sign on to it are therefore "free riders" or "rejectionists." At least we economists need to look at such claims with a cynical eye.

5. See Richard N. Cooper, "Toward a Real Global Warming Treaty," *Foreign Affairs* 77, 2 (Mar./Apr. 1998).

6. See Bhagwati and T. N. Srinivasan, "Trade and the Environment: Does Environmental Diversity Detract from the Case for Free Trade?," chap. 4 of *Fair Trade and Harmonization*.

7. See John Douglas Wilson, "Capital Mobility and Environmental Standards: Is There a Theoretical Basis for a Race to the Bottom," chap. 10 of *Fair Trade and Harmonization*.

8. Bhagwati and Hudec, *Fair Trade and Harmonization*, 178–179.

9. Rodrik, in his IIE pamphlet on globalization, argues as if we are so unmindful. But this is to betray ignorance of the extensive debate over the problem, including that in the 1991 GATT Report on Trade and the Environment.

10. This suggestion is developed further in chapter 22.

11. See Murrray C. Kemp and Takashi Negishi, "Domestic Distortions, Tariffs and the Theory of Optimum Subsidy," *Journal of Political Economy* (1969): 1011–1013, and Jagdish Bhagwati, V. K. Ramaswami, and T. N. Srinivasan, "Domestic Distortions, Tariffs, and the Theory of Optimum Subsidy: Some Further Results," *Journal of Political Economy* 77, 6(1969): 1005–1010.

12. Without detracting from the importance of Copeland's analysis, I might mention that one of our Columbia students, in a dissertation that was awarded "distinction," Waseem Noor, developed precisely the Copeland-type argument, in the context of labor standards. I must confess that my reaction then was the same as now: that the argument is analytically beautiful but has no empirical salience in my judgment. Cf. Waseem Noor, *Labor Standards and International Trade: Four Essays*, Ph.D. diss., Columbia University, 1997.

13. See James Riedel, "The Demand for LDC Exports of Manufactures: Estimates from Hong Kong." *Economic Journal* 98, 389(1998): 138–148, and Arvind Panagariya, "Demand Elasticities in International Trade: Are They Really Low?" Mimeo, University of Maryland at College Park, 1999.

The Dispute Settlement Mechanism at the WTO

21   Mismanaging the Banana Dispute

In their attempt at being even-handed between the European Union and the United States ("The bad blood behind bananas," March 5), your editors let the United States off too lightly and chastise the EU too heavily.

True, the EU has "prevaricated for 17 months, using every conceivable legal device in the rich lexicon of international trade legislation" to put off the day when the WTO ruling against its banana regime would have to be implemented. But does a legitimate utilisation of dilatory procedures justify the deliberate use of unilateral actions by the United States? Indeed, the use by the United States of such unilateral threats and actions has earned it opprobrium over the years as a nation that believes in the law of the jungle, not the rule of law.

Nor can economists forget that, while the lawyers and the business lobbies prefer tight deadlines for both decisions and implementation, the economic effect can be disastrous in imposing the supreme folly of "shock therapy" on countries by legal means.

I must also deplore the inability of the leadership at the World Trade Organisation, International Monetary Fund and World Bank to come up with a compensation and adjustment programme that would, at a small fraction of their resources, adequately help the small banana exporters at risk from the WTO Panel, Appellate Court and Arbitration decisions dismantling the EU regime. Nothing in the doctrine of free trade requires that we ride rough-shod, at breakneck speed and with reckless regard, over the economies of the small and poor nations.

Originally published, under the title "U.S. Known as Nation that Believes in Law of the Jungle," as a letter to the editor of the *Financial Times* (Mar. 9, 1999). Reprinted with permission.

It is time to recognise that the WTO dispute settlement mechanism needs to be supplemented by co-ordinated efforts of the Bretton Woods institutions to ease the costs of implementing binding trade-related decisions when developing countries with substantial implementation costs are involved.

22

An Economic Perspective
on the Dispute Settlement
Mechanism

A few observations from an economics perspective are necessary in regard to the reform of the WTO's Dispute Settlement Mechanism. They are suggested by recent experience.

The tight timeframes we now have are generally excellent. But, as illustrated by the bananas case, they could also lead to what I have called (in chapter 21) substantial "shock therapy imposed by legal means" on countries that cannot cope with rapid and huge adjustment. In the bananas case, the countries required to really adjust on a significant scale are not the plaintiff or the defendant, which are huge in economic scale, but are rather small "third" countries, and the short-term impact on their economies is feared to be quite substantial. Besides, their fear is that the adjustment will proceed fairly fast, the schedule reflecting the rights of the successful plaintiff rather than the real economic difficulties of the true target of adjustment.

Therefore, I suggested in a letter to the *Financial Times* (chapter 21) that there must be explicit attention paid to two aspects of the problem in cases where the adjustment required is substantial if the WTO Panel finding so requires the following:

1. The Director General of WTO should *simultaneously* (as soon as a finding is made by the Dispute Settlement Panel) coordinate short-term relief from the World Bank and/or the IMF, while also getting the World Bank to direct some long-term aid to offset the loss of real income that can also be a major problem (as in the bananas case); and

2. The contracting parties should explicitly and fully reiterate that the adjustment period must reflect the economic problems that will ensue from implementing the adjudicated finding and that these problems

Based on remarks made at the Columbia University Conference on The Next Trade Negotiating Round: Examining the Agenda for Seattle, New York City, July 22–23, 1999.

may lie *outside* the economies of the legal parties to the dispute. I know that the existing agreement allows for a "reasonable" time for implementation; but that is set by legal considerations of expeditiousness (because the background to these provisions was dilatoriness used as a way of doing nothing) rather than by economic considerations that may require a slower process of dismantling the offending legislation that has been held WTO-inconsistent.

The traditional method of allowing trade retaliation as a "remedy" is even odder. For one thing, it compounds one trade barrier with another. Second, it seems to make little sense in cases such as the hormone-fed beef case where the EC legislation is consumer-driven and cannot simply be dismantled.

Does it really make sense to impose 100 percent duties on EU products for an equivalent amount of trade, which is tantamount to a huge amount of senseless trade disruption? (Incidentally, that "equivalence" is also economically silly: should we not be equating loss of gains from trade if equality of damage inflicted is desired? Also, what is the magic about 100 percent, which seems to be a number that recurs in all sorts of areas including Section 301-sanctioned retribution?)

I would suggest therefore that we rule out retaliation as a remedy but settle for "compensation" each time. That is best done as an impartial-tribunal-determined amount of lost gains from trade. That sum, in turn, could be passed on to the industry injured by the inability to dismantle the offending legislation, if the successful plaintiff country so desires. The original equation of retaliation with compensation is not meaningful and must be discarded. (I am well aware that the retaliation is often aimed at industries or products abroad where the successful plaintiff hopes to be able to generate political pressure on the losing defendant to repeal the offending legislation. But this is surely unlikely to work without actual trade disruption and, besides, in the cases where the repeal of the offending legislation is proving exceptionally difficult, surely the threatened retaliation is unlikely to work anyway, leaving only trade disruption in its wake. Moreover, monetary fines can also create the necessary pressure for change.)

Finally, wherever possible, we should turn to labeling, as distinct from proscriptive legislation, as a possible way of handling problems such as GM products, hormone-fed beef, child labor, sweatshops, exploitative migrant labour, and so forth. It is when these labeling solutions are not accepted that the remedy of compensation should be used.

Trade and Culture

Trade and Culture: America's Blind Spot

In June 1998, culture ministers from twenty-three countries convened in Ottawa at the invitation of Canada's Heritage Minister Mrs. Sheila Copps for a two-day international meeting on cultural policy. Their common target was the United States, which does not even have a culture minister. Their fear was that the United States routinely and aggressively sacrifices culture for free trade.

The immediate provocation was the loss by Canada to the United States at the WTO that struck down Canada's 80 percent excise tax on split-run editions of foreign (mainly U.S.) magazines. But the complaints range over several issues, among them:

• the U.S. trade negotiators' demands to eliminate audiovisual restrictions in the EU that limit show time for American films and TV programs in the asserted interest of protecting European culture;

• the attempts by us to roll back agricultural protection in the EU, Japan, and South Korea in spite of complaints that agriculture is a "way of life" and that therefore, as EU Commissioner Mr. Lamy said in Seattle at the failed WTO meeting, agriculture's "multi-functionality" must be respected;

• the U.S. insistence on the right to export hormone-fed beef and genetically modified (GM) products to Europe and Japan, which reject such products due to fears that are partly based on difference of culture between Americans and others; and

• the militancy with which, in the heyday of America's "diminished giant syndrome" and resulting Japan-fixation during the late 1980s and early 1990s the United States sought to rebuild Japan in its own image on several dimensions under the now-defunct Structural (i.e., read "cultural," broadly speaking) Impediments Initiative (SII).

Culture: Misunderstanding What Free Trade Really Means

Must culture necessarily yield to free trade? The U.S. lobbyists pushing for their agendas invariably invoke the doctrine of free trade in their behalf. Yet, this is wrong. Sophisticated economists who know the theory of free trade truly well also know that an important element of it is what is known as the theory of "noneconomic objectives."

Thus, free traders recognize the virtues of free trade but note that noneconomic objectives such as culture must also be accommodated. They also argue that it is important not to assume that free trade is incompatible with such objectives, however. Indeed, much of the theory of commercial policy in the presence of noneconomic objectives illuminates how domestic policies other than trade tariffs and quotas are often more efficient, least-cost ways of accommodating these objectives.

The lobbyists who understand little of the theory of free trade, but understand how to (mis)invoke it for their own advantage, are no friends of free trade. As Adam Smith rightly observed, and as conservative economists such as Milton Friedman have always emphasized, what business lobbies want and what social-good-minded economists want are often not the same thing. So, we must remember that the important issue in regard to maintaining culture when framing economic policy is not whether, but how.

Culture: America's Uniqueness

Of course, the lobbyists, who cry protectionism whenever foreign nations worry about threats to culture from free trade, work and flourish within an American culture that is unable to appreciate the cultural concerns of others and therefore encourages the presumption that these complaints must "really" be a mask for protectionism.

America is truly an exceptional nation. It is built on immigration, and immigrants are still a sizeable fraction of annual additions to the U.S. workforce. Multiple ethnicities are simply taken for granted; multiculturalism has a natural constituency that has only grown in recent years. In my classes at Columbia, it is difficult to find a true native American, born into U.S. citizenship: the faculty also come from everywhere, if not in the same numbers.

This translates into an openness to cultures. Indian music, Chinese acupuncture, a host of cultural influences freely work themselves into America's kaleidoscope. These cultural "imports" wind up fitted into an ever-expanding mosaic; they are not seen as a threat.

At the same time, America's enormous cultural vitality and techno-logical creativity, combined with hegemonic status in world politics, make her a net "exporter" of culture, giving her therefore no sense of threat from that direction either: it is *her* culture that spreads. But this spread of American culture threatens others to whom it goes. The spread of "low" culture, symbolized by McDonald's and Coke, accen-tuates intergenerational conflicts and reinforces the nostalgia that the old often feel about the loss of local culture. But the resentment extends to "high" culture as well. In particular, the United States is at the cut-ting edge of women's rights, children's rights, and much else that the more traditional, at times feudal or oligarchic, regimes elsewhere find threatening to their cultural and social order. America makes waves that threaten to drown them.

But that is not all. America stands out also because it is today the most experimental society in its attitudes toward technological change. When you think about it, it is not surprising that the consumer move-ments against hormone-fed beef and against GM products arose with intensity elsewhere and have only belatedly had an echo in the United States. A pill-popping culture that tends to see technical advances in an optimistic light contrasts with other cultures that are not quite so gung-ho about them. This contrast is depicted in a cartoon from *The New Yorker* (see figure 23.1) that shows a dissatisfied customer telling the waitress to take the broccoli back to the kitchen and "have it genetically modified": instead of laying traps in your path, GM processes aid you in your pursuit of happiness.

For all these reasons, therefore, the Americans find it difficult to see why trade is regarded by others as a threat to their culture; in con-sequence, they see the ugly hand of protectionism hiding behind such agitations and policy actions based on them. This only reinforces the cynical way in which lobbyists for industries such as Hollywood exploit and misuse the case for free trade to advance their own agendas.

Reconciling Trade and Culture

But then we must still ask whether protection is the ideal way to deal with a cultural concern. Two examples should suffice to show that it is not, generally speaking.

For instance, does it make sense to have audiovisual restrictions on the fraction of time allotted to showing foreign films rather than sub-sidies to make local ones? At the outset, with VCRs and cassettes, restrictions are likely to be an ineffective but expensive nuisance any-

*"Something's wrong with the broccoli. Please take it back to
the kitchen and have it genetically modifed."*

Figure 23.1
© The New Yorker Collection 1999 J. B. Handelsman from cartoonbank.com. All rights
reserved.

way. But equally, it makes more sense to have free imports of films
from Hollywood but to use subsidies to aid the production of French
films. That means more choice for the French and beneficial competition between French and foreign film producers.

This is a difficult lesson to teach since the typical gut reaction to the
flood of imported Hollywood films, and the decline of local films, is to
seek import bans or quotas. This may well be necessary as a temporary
measure to adjust to massive surges in imports. But it does not make
for a good long-run policy.

In this regard, the experience of South Korea is interesting to note.
Faced with the Korean government's capitulation to Hollywood's
demand to allow freer imports of Hollywood films, several Korean

actors, all clad in black, gathered in December 1998 to mourn their own deaths, staging a funeral marking the death of the fledgling Korean cinema.[1] Similar protests have been mounted in Mexico and Taiwan where import of Hollywood films is seen as a deleterious phenomenon that is destroying domestic cinema.

It is arguable that the better option for South Korea, Mexico, and Taiwan is indeed to permit freer imports, while subsidizing the making of local films. There is little reason to think that such promotion of local films will not work. It did in the case of Satyajit Ray's early films and has worked for other artistic "high-brow" films as well in India. South Korea has begun to subsidize film production as well, spreading $11 million over ten films in 1998. There are indeed audiences for well-produced local films, and not just for foreign films whether good or bad. In South Korea, *Swiri*, a local feature film (produced without a subsidy) attracted, four weeks into its release, a record 1.25 million viewers in Seoul alone, promising to rival the record attendances for Hollywood's *Titanic*. Pessimism about the ability to compete with Hollywood is exaggerated; promotion rather than protection seems the better solution, by and large.

The other example I might use to drive this point home against protectionism to shore up domestic culture relates to hormone-fed beef. Given the cultural dissonance between the EU and the United States, it is surely a good idea to see if, instead of simply banning the availability of such beef in the EU, we could persuade the EU consumers to accept a labeling solution. That would maintain market access for the American hormone-fed beef and make information available for EU consumers to avoid eating it if they fear its consequences for their health. This is clearly the direction in which we wish to move: labeling is in this instance a superior solution to outright prohibitions.

So, if we probe alternative policy options hard enough, we may well find ways to reconcile open trade with culture. Indeed, we often will. The challenge for policy is to find such solutions.

Note

1. I am indebted to an excellent essay by my student, In Kyung Kim, for the information on Korea's experience. The immediate cause of the protests noted here was the Korean government's proposal, under U.S. pressure, to change the quota that required theaters to screen domestic films for at least 146 days a year to one that reduced that quota to 92 days, starting in 2002.

Big questions demand big minds. To inquire into the wealth and the poverty of nations, to seek to comprehend "why some are so rich and some so poor," is no mean ambition, whether you are an economist or a historian. Indeed, while no economist is likely to attract critical attention investigating how soap is priced or whether the dollar is high, and no historian imperils his reputation by tracking the growth of the coal trade in nineteenth-century Ruhr, the risks are colossal when your canvas is outsized. And so are the rewards.

For this reason, the best among the economists and the historians have not shied away from the challenge of divining the alchemy of wealth and the secret of poverty. Adam Smith's *The Wealth of Nations* is the most celebrated example: the work virtually led Smith to found economics as we now know it, though it cannot be held to have ended the quest it defined as its task. Even a cursory glance at the two centuries since Smith's seminal work shows that the problem has continued to invite analysis, and to baffle the analysts.

Within economics itself, the notable efforts include that by Arthur Lewis, who broadened the Smithian inquiry about wealth to ask in 1977, in his *The Evolution of the International Economic Order*, "Why did the world come to be divided into industrial countries and agricultural countries," the former rich and the latter poor. And five years later, Mancur Olson published his influential book on *The Rise and Decline of Nations*. Olson had the interesting idea that pressure groups formed around industries that are related to successful development would eventually turn into a malignant iron fist that, unlike Adam Smith's benign invisible hand, would kill growth, and also that wars and

Originally published as a book review in *The New Republic* (May 25, 1998): 32–36. Reprinted with permission.

catastrophes that shook up this political kaleidoscope were a major source of renewed prosperity.

Historians, too, have been exercised by this great and urgent problem, often treating it within the context of the rise and fall of the empires that frequently went with the rise to prosperity and glory of nations; Gibbon on the Roman empire and Toynbee on Western civilization define the furthest reaches of the arena over which historians have wandered in their intellectual quest. And now today's premier economic historians, David Landes and Charles Kindleberger, have published important books addressing the same essential issues related to the economic rise and fall of nations, and drawing on the past as defined for Landes as an entire millennium and for Kindleberger as only (only!) its second half.

The timing could not be better. These books straddle between themselves the Asian financial collapse, which has shattered the canonical illusion that the twenty-first century would be Pacific, and replaced it with the inviting belief that it will continue to be American. The turbulent experience of the Asian economies in recent months has brutally exposed the fragility of our ideas and convictions about what triggers and sustains growth and what prompts and accelerates decline. We have learned again that reversals of fortune can be swift; and this is a reminder, too, that these economic historians tread on treacherous ground.

Landes is a historian who has crossed over into economics and Kindleberger is an economist who has crossed over into history. Landes puzzlingly sacrifices countless pages to interesting but peripheral issues; but there is certainly a clear thesis in his immensely learned book, and it is advanced with passion and certitude. It is that culture is the key. The Europeans triumphed economically owing to their culture; and they will continue to do so, as will others who imitate them effectively.

If we learn anything from the history of economic development, it is that culture makes all the difference.... Until very recently, over the thousand and more years ... that people look upon as progress, the key factor—the driving force—has been Western civilization and its dissemination: the knowledge, the techniques, the political and social ideologies, for better or worse. This dissemination flows partly from Western dominion, for knowledge and know-how equal power; partly from Western teaching; and partly from emulation.

For Landes, Western culture, with its associated "values," is the magic bullet, and, once you have it, you will be on a roll except for random contingencies. Kindleberger, by contrast, is a "rise-and-fall" man. He is taken more with the notion that nations come and go, even within the charmed orbit of Europe and the Western-values-defined diaspora. Drawing on the economic historian Joel Mokyr's contention that "no country has been on the cutting edge of technical innovation for more than two or three generations," Kindleberger is fascinated by the idea of a "national life cycle." He prefers a Buddenbrooks plot for the inevitable decline in a nation's fortune.

Where Landes displays an occasionally overbearing confidence in his judgments ("Big mistake." "Sacrilege." "Crazy." "Bad history."), Kindleberger's tone is more cautious. He concludes his inquiry with these words: "In due course a country will emerge ... for a time as the primary world economic power. The United States again? Japan? Germany? The European Community as a whole? Perhaps a dark horse like Australia or Brazil or China? Who knows? Not I." The two economic historians thus complement each other in temperament and in technique, Landes aiming at the sweeping, magisterial view that may be provided by the writing of history at its imaginative best, and Kindleberger deploying the focused, microscopic analysis that economics typically brings to the table.

Kindleberger offers a sensible and impeccable taxonomy of "influences," neatly classified into "internal" and "external," that bear on the likely prospect of economic decline in all prosperous nations; but it is Landes's far grander ambition to zero in on the essential mainsprings of wealth formation. He announces boldly that his "aim in writing this book is to do world history ... to trace and understand the main stream of economic advance and modernization." In his display of historical scholarship, Landes reminds me of Sakalanarayan Shastri, the legendary Indian scholar of Sanskrit grammar in the early twentieth century, who was asked "What have you read?" and reportedly replied: "Everything that has been written." Landes's erudition certainly pays off, but not completely. In the end his extraordinary enterprise is only partially successful.

Landes's central argument is that Europe's rise to economic preeminence since the fifteenth century was founded on a constellation of institutions, such as property rights. It also profited from phenomena such as the ability of Europeans to escape cities and nations that did not offer such opportunities to other cities and states, in geographical proximity within Europe, that did offer them. This ability to vote with one's feet meant that, within Europe taken as a whole, the dominant

pro-growth institutions held sway despite occasional lapses by particular locales.

What Eric Jones has called "the European miracle," and what Landes
calls "European exceptionalism," began, in Landes's account, with the
"luck" of geography. The Gulf Stream's warm current (whose origin
Landes describes at tedious length) had given Europe a "privileged"
temperate climate, consisting of "warm winds and gentle rain, water in
all seasons, and low rates of evaporation—the makings of good crops,
big livestock, and dense hardwood forests."

But then, why had Egypt and Sumer managed to get ahead even
thousands of years earlier? Landes argues that the hardwood forests in
Europe could not be cleared for cultivation because Europeans did not
have iron cutting tools until the first millennium before our era. The
Europeans thus had to settle in the less fertile areas such as lake-shores
and grasslands. But this does not quite answer the objection. Why
didn't the Europeans develop the iron cutting technology earlier? Why
could they not make more of these less fertile settlements?

After all, we know of numerous instances in which human ingenuity, resulting in great civilizations or rapid growth or both, has surmounted worse conditions than those of lakeshore and grassland
settlements. Think of Israel blossoming in the desert; or contrast North
Korea with South Korea, separated by war and political ideology but
not by geography (whether climate, weather, or natural resources).
Julian Simon has convincingly argued, against geographical determinism, that human beings are the ultimate resource. Place may impose
advantages or disadvantages, but it plays no more than a bit part in
the drama of development.

Indeed, Landes himself provides the best antidote to the thesis that
geography is destiny by proceeding to argue that what accomplished
the European miracle was in fact something else altogether. After the
terrifying invasions of the Vikings, the Saracens, and the Magyars had
been brought under control, "a new society was born" in Europe in the
tenth century. It was based on the principles of "popular sovereignty"
as opposed to those of oriental despotism, and on "private property" as
contrasted with the unprincipled principle of autocracy with its "ruler-
owns-all."

Landes draws a larger lesson from this. Only societies with "room
for multiple initiatives, from below more than from above, could think
in terms of a growing pie." It was this combination of popular sovereignty with the institution of private property that made economic

growth possible, and made it probable. Europe also profited from the rise of the semi-autonomous city, the "commune." Functioning economically as "governments of the merchants, by the merchants, and for the merchants," and exercising civil power, these communes provided the merchant, the "lever of riches" in Mokyr's evocative phrase, with the rights and the freedoms to live, to work, to accumulate, to prosper and to produce prosperity. Landes aptly adduces the medieval dictum: *Stadtluft macht frei*, or the city air makes one free.

Along with these fundamental economic and political freedoms came the ability to move to places where they were available, and the willingness of these jurisdictions to attract those who sought these freedoms. This accelerated the spread of these freedoms. The economic expansion that followed led, in turn, to the "commercial revolution" with all its associated codes, contracts, and the commercial infrastructure to support and to sustain trade and manufactures. Landes concludes eloquently that Europe "got thereby substantially enhanced security, a sharp reduction in the cost of doing business (what the economist calls 'transaction costs'), a widening of the market that promoted specialization and division of labor. It was the world of Adam Smith, already taking shape five hundred years before his time."

Landes cannot be faulted when he infers from this story (and from his account of Europe's boundless energy in the era of its outward expansion, in which it discovered the Americas and brought much of the world under its domain) that history is on the side of those who assert that institutions such as property rights, and the presence of flexibility of options when faced by restrictions on the freedom to work and to innovate, are important in improving the prospects for growth. To choose only one recent confirmation of the truth of this perception, anyone familiar with the economic collapse of the Soviet Union, which can be dramatically illustrated by a chart of Soviet growth rates in free fall, and which led Gorbachev into a half-baked *perestroika* with the unintended consequence of disintegration rather than rejuvenation, knows that the steady decline was caused precisely by the absence of the economic freedoms and institutions that Landes deduces from history as conditions conducive to growth.

Indeed, economists have long understood that these conditions are important. Surjit Bhalla argued trenchantly several years ago that "economic freedom," which includes property rights and the freedom to produce and to innovate, was associated with growth rates in a broad cross-section of countries; and the association has been reaffirmed by

number-crunching economists such as Robert Barro. Mediocre economists spend endless amounts of time and energy looking at such
statistical associations across countries, putting all kinds of countries
mindlessly on a "regression" that plots all kinds of variables against
growth rates, but they do serve the useful purpose of underlining
the conjectures of superior economists and gifted historians, such as
Landes and Kindleberger, whose ability to put their inferences into
the necessary context, and hence to reach sophisticated judgments, is
unrivaled.

If Landes had stopped there, it would have been splendid. He would
have reinforced, with the weight of sharp and detailed historical analysis, our current consensus in favor of political and economic freedoms,
of democracy and markets, as powerful institutions for promoting
prosperity. But he seeks to relate these pro-growth institutions to culture and values, seeking in turn to conclude that nations that do not
share this same culture and these same values are doomed to stagnation or to decline from earlier prosperity (which anyway must have
been due to fortuitous circumstance).

Landes wishes to link the European miracle causally, in the spirit of
Max Weber, to underlying values as defined by the Judeo-Christian,
and especially the Protestant, universe. Islam is held to be inimical to
a repetition of the European experience owing to its allegedly holistic
nature, with religion "in principle supreme and the ideal government
that of the holy men." Such assertions recur throughout the book. And
here Landes is stepping into quicksand. For it is nearly impossible to
relate culture or values to these pro-growth institutions and policy
frameworks, and hence to economic growth, in a causally tight way.

Landes rails against economists for being rejectionists on this front.
Among numerous assertions of the significance of culture, the most
amusing is his insistence that, despite the mirthful scorn of his economist friends, the use of chopsticks has led to East Asian dexterity with
doing microassembly in electronics. I must admit that I fit right into
Landes's casual empiricism: I can neither handle chopsticks nor fit
semiconductor boards. But surly electronics is one modern industry
that has spread *across* continents and cultures.

Economists have struggled with the culturalist claim and have given
up on it, for several good reasons. For a start, growth seems to be compatible with all kinds of values and cultures. Confucianism was long
held to be inimical to growth, but it became the mainspring of growth
when the Far Eastern nations—South Korea, Taiwan, Singapore, and

Hong Kong—became the winners in the race in the postwar period. And you have only to read the early literature on Japan to see how many foreign observers thought that Japan's culture was incompatible with growth. My favorite example is this comment by an Australian expert invited by the Japanese government in 1915:

> My impression as to your cheap labour was soon disillusioned when I saw your people at work. No doubt they are lowly paid, but the return is equally so; to see your men at work made me feel that you are a very satisfied easy-going race who reckon time is no object. When I spoke to some managers they informed me that it was impossible to change the habits of national heritage.

I have little doubt that many in Japan also shared this view, condemning Japan to low growth. (When the great Japanese novelist Natsume Soseki was contemplating a career as an architect, he was dissuaded from it at virtually this time by a friend who told him that, Japan being a poor country, he would have no opportunity to build anything splendid like St. Paul's Cathedral.)

Indeed, the early postwar period of developmental economics pitted the culturalists against economists who claimed that the role of culture was vastly exaggerated. A celebrated study by Edwin Dean in Nyasaland investigated the hypothesis that Africans react to prices differently from Western nations where "impersonal" cultural traits have squeezed such factors as tribal affiliation out of prices charged and received. Dean actually sat in on three markets, gathering data on prices to see whether, for instance, sellers belonging to the Likouba and the Bacongo tribes charged lower prices to buyers from their own tribes than to the others. The answer was that there was no statistically significant difference.

In light of such analyses, economists have generally taken three positions on the relationship between culture and development. As Walpole said, "every man has his price," and culture simply determines what that price is, not whether there is a price. Moreover, culture yields over time, and in necessary ways, to the profit motive. the sacred cow is sold by Hindus to Muslims for slaughter when the price is good. Then again, given a particular culture, we can still design incentives and policy frameworks (of the sort that Landes rightly extols) that will induce development; culture does not really confound or cripple an activist developmental policy.

In the end, Landes is the prisoner of the ambition that economists have generally renounced. Economists are usually content to explain growth by reference to proximate causes. Thus, the famous Harrod-Domar growth model that inaugurated postwar growth theory simply argued that growth was a function of your savings rate, which determined how much you increased your capital stock, and of the productivity of that increment in capital stock. So, if your income was $100 and your savings rate was 10%, so that you saved and hence invested $10, and the productivity of that investment was such that you would need 5 units of capital to get one unit of output, then income would grow by $(10/5) = \$2$, i.e., by 2%. And if these two parameters (the savings rate and the capital-output ratio) remained unchanged, then growth would continue forever at 2%.

Looking at this, a historian has famously remarked that it was like telling someone who had asked for a road map to just take the first left, then the first right, and keep repeating that until the end of time. Similarly, when W. W. Rostow wrote a book that sought to explain growth by discussing "propensities" to invest and to save and so on, the great economic historian Alexander Gerschenkron observed sardonically that Professor Rostow had explained growth by reference to the propensity to grow.

The wisecracks are funny, but they are off the mark. Economists will probe these parameters further. They will analyze, for example, how an inward-looking policy dampens the inducement to invest, and hence inhibits growth. They have even turned to investigating massively and systematically how the choice of economic policies is determined in the context of politics, breaking down the traditional wall between economists telling governments what they should do and political scientists analyzing what governments will do instead.

But they rarely wish to go further, peeling the onion down to the core, to discover why, "deep down," people exhibit different responses and make different choices when faced by identical institutions and incentives. They are not emboldened in the manner of historians. Consider India's Kafkaesque maze of bureaucratic controls, amounting to what we call here "industrial policy" but in a particularly virulent form. It almost killed India's economic growth for over a quarter of a century before India started economic reforms in 1991. Economists have shown how and why this regime hurt India's economic performance. They have also analyzed the role of economic ideology—the Fabianism which English-trained economists such as myself brought back to India in the late 1950s—and of the political structure and incentives that facilitated the rise and growth to robustness of this affliction.

But did Indian culture matter? I doubt it. After all, with the same overlay of culture in its broadest sense, different Indian states have experienced astonishingly diverse growth rates. Kerala's success, and Bihar's failure, have been attributed by analysts to factors such as the differences in the politics of an active, bottom-up mobilization of people by successive communist governments in the former, and a passive, top-down politics of feudalism in the latter. Did the fact that Kerala has more Christianity whereas Bihar has more Hinduism matter? If so, how? It is tempting to argue that Christianity has led to the greater emphasis on education. But it is well known that the Brahmins have traditionally valued education to an excess, and many Brahmins led the Indian Renaissance under British rule. Indeed, some have suggested, sometimes playfully and at other times out of exasperation, that it must have been gene mutation under centuries of the caste system, assigning each Indian to his immutable place in the social hierarchy, that led to the close embrace of an economic philosophy that assigns each industry to a hierarchy where goods are not just goods but some are better than others. If I wrote like Landes, I would say: Cute. Or, better still: Crazy.

I do not mean to deny culture any role. But the precise role of culture in economic behavior remains elusive. The encouraging truth appears to be that growth-inducing institutions, like hardy perennials that will grow in different and indifferent soils, are resilient and compatible with a range of cultures. And for a historian who is confronted with economic success in extremely diverse cultures, it is ahistorical to assert otherwise. Ironic.

IV

Regionalism,
Multilateralism, and
Unilateralism

25   Fast Track to Nowhere

Bill Clinton is almost certainly going to talk Congress into giving him the fast-track trade-negotiating authority he seeks. When it comes to striking political deals to get his way, the president's record speaks for itself. But the current synthetic controversy over fast-track is actually beside the point. The real question in trade policy lies elsewhere, drowned out by the political noise from Capitol Hill and the White House. What trade specialists in Washington—Fred Bergsten among them—should really be asking is this: do the president's trade goals made sense?

The administration's various actions and policy pronouncements —notably, its capitulation over the Helms-Burton act and its misguided efforts to insert a social clause into the World Trade Organisation (WTO)—raise grave doubts. Mr Bergsten offers the cliché that the United States is the "only plausible leader," and therefore an ideal architect, of the emerging world trading system. As somebody who believes passionately in the case for liberal trade, I am far less sanguine.

The administration says it wants fast-track authority in order to pursue "regional and global trade negotiations." The truth is that the president seeks it for regional agreements only. To be more precise, he wants to add Chile to the North American Free-Trade Agreement (NAFTA) and to move further towards creating a Free-Trade Agreement of the Americas (FTAA).

The president believes (and Charlene Barshefsky, the United States trade representative, has told Congress) that without fast-track he is "empty-handed" in trade talks with the Latin American countries. At stake, he says, are America's export markets to the south. The administration also notes that the European Union has lately been flirting

Originally published in *The Economist* (Oct. 18, 1997): 21–23. Reprinted with permission.

with the idea of its own free-trade agreement with Mercosur, and that other preferential trade arrangements are in the pipeline. Don't tie my hands at such a time, says Mr. Clinton.

This would be all right if there were any prospect that Mr. Clinton might lead bold new multilateral efforts to liberalise trade. If such efforts are under way or even under consideration, it is the administration's best-kept secret. Recent multilateral agreements on information technology and telecommunications, and the deal on financial services which the EU rescued and which may soon be brought to a conclusion, seem to suggest that multilateralism is alive and well. But it cannot seriously be argued that these agreements required fast-track, with its all-or-nothing vote. They are export-oriented "win-win" agreements in areas where America's competitive strength is not in doubt. Opposition to them was never likely to have been strong enough to trouble the White House.

If the president were indeed keen to embrace another round of multilateral trade negotiations, that would be a different matter. Many outside the administration have called for just such an initiative. But the president's advisers caution against it. These people are almost entirely of two kinds: litigators conditioned to see trade as a zero-sum game, or spin doctors who cannot lift their eyes from their latest poll findings. They have told the president to steer clear of a new multilateral initiative—despite the fact that Mr. Clinton was in fact the first G7 leader to moot the idea immediately after the end of the Uruguay Round.

Mr. Clinton has shied away even from the distant vision of a liberal trading world—or from any corresponding trade-policy goal, such as to dismantle all border barriers to trade by, say, 2010. Admittedly, considering the extent of trade protection in agriculture and the many high tariffs that remain even in the OECD countries today, that would take some doing (see figure 25.1). But the subject is no longer even discussed. The president's handlers dismiss calls for such initiatives as unimportant, impractical, untimely, even ludicrous. So much for American leadership on the multilateral front.

So we return to the short-run agenda that actually animates the administration: the FTAA. On this, I count myself among the many "purists" whom Mr. Bergsten deplores: I consider striving for an FTAA a great mistake. The reason is simple. Proliferating "free-trade areas" have become a pox on the world trading system. It is a mark of Washington's blurred vision and failure of leadership that, departing from a

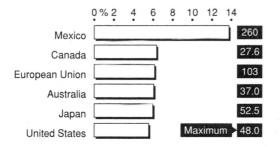

Figure 25.1
Average tariffs, 1996. Excludes those tariff lines with specific and compound duties.
Source: UNCTAD, forthcoming TRAINS CD-ROM.

half-century of steadfast adherence to nondiscriminatory multilateral-ism in trade, the administration has sought to build discriminatory free-trade areas instead.

The rationale advanced for this strategy in the early 1980s was that the turnpike of multilateral negotiations was unfinished and might long remain so. In the meantime, governments wishing to make progress towards liberal trade had to resort to the dirt road of regional free-trade areas. But that was before the great success of the Uruguay Round. The WTO created during the course of that round is the turn-pike that America and the other rich countries always said they wanted. Why not use it?

The administration's answer to that is to fudge the distinction between genuine, multilateral, non-discriminatory free trade and the inherently discriminatory free-trade agreements. Recalling Orwell's strictures on euphemisms in politics, let us call a spade a spade and henceforth talk not of free-trade agreements (FTAs) but of preferential trade agreements (PTAs). This may be helpful to lazy politicians, devoted to soundbites, who can absorb no more than two words at a time and therefore construe "free-trade area" as free trade.

Mr. Bergsten in fact fudges just as much as the politicians. In espousing "open regionalism"—meaning that new members will always be welcomed in—he fails to acknowledge that this is a protracted and tricky process, and in particular subject to votes in legislatures. The difficulty of adding Chile to NAFTA is a case in point. In practice, then, open regionalism is likely to prove a detour rather than a staging post on the path to liberal trade. I recall a meeting in Tokyo some years ago, when a Brazilian diplomat announced proudly that Mercosur practised open regionalism. This prompted a mischievous official from

Hong Kong to walk up to the stage and say: "Here is Hong Kong's application. When can we start?" No answer as yet.

This error of expecting more from PTAs than they can plausibly deliver has an ironic aspect. Mr. Bergsten compliments the United States for its perspicacity in forging PTAs that can be opened wider in due course—emphasising America's leadership, to be contrasted with the less public-spirited attitudes of the "inward-looking" EU. Yet to date the EU has actually signed PTAs with as many as 18 countries, many more than the United States has. If PTAs are a sign of trade-policy virtue, the EU, not the United States, sets the global standard. But that is nothing to boast about: in my view the EU is simply the greater culprit in the game of trade discrimination.

PTAS are an inferior policy to the multilateral freeing of trade not only because they deny trading opportunities to outsiders. They may well be worse for members too. This is because they can cause "trade diversion." Instead of importing goods from the countries that can supply most cheaply, the members of a PTA may choose to buy from fellow members. Thus, rather than merely creating trade where there was none before—which improves economic welfare—a PTA may redirect it from efficient sources to inefficient ones.

The distinction between trade creation and trade diversion was first drawn in 1950 by Jacob Viner, who was one of the great economists. Most other economists have since regarded it as essential in thinking clearly about whether regional trade-deals advance or retard economic well-being. Administration spokesmen such as Larry Summers (treasury deputy secretary and a distinguished economist in his own right) may say diversion is a "laughable" worry in practice, but it is now beginning to emerge in several empirical studies as a major concern.

For instance, Alexander Yeats, an economist at the World Bank, has found evidence of significant trade diversion due to Mercosur. Perhaps Americans can be forgiven for failing to notice what is going on in South America. But it is disappointing that commentators in the United States, where one expects a comparatively high level of economic literacy in public discourse, recently discussed the effects of NAFTA without mentioning the fact that Mexico too has almost certainly suffered from trade diversion to American sources.

Exports from the United States to Mexico increased by 45% between 1993 and 1996, and America's share in Mexican imports went up from 68 percent to 72 percent (see figure 25.2). At the same time, Mexico's tariffs on American goods were cut by an average of 7.1 percentage

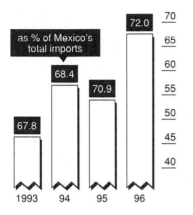

Figure 25.2
Mexico's imports from the United States, $bn. *Source:* IMP.

points. This resulted in "a ten percentage point average tariff advantage over foreign suppliers," according to a study commissioned by the administration and carried out by Data Resources Inc. This result was fatuously greeted as a proof of NAFTA's success. It suggests the very opposite. A provisional estimate by Arvind Panagariya of Maryland University suggests that Mexico's recent losses from trade diversion due to NAFTA could be as high as $3 billion a year.

The discovery of significant trade diversion in PTAs is hardly surprising. Recent work in the theory of political economy by Gene Grossman (of Princeton), Elhanan Helpman (of Harvard) and Pravin Krishna (of Brown University) shows how trade diversion is a pretty strong motive for lobbies to push for PTAs.

A Plague of PTAs

When President Clinton argued that NAFTA would help American firms to compete better with their (excluded) Japanese competitors, he was explicitly appealing to the trade-diverting aspects of the agreement—that is, to the welfare-reducing aspects. True, he was also exploiting the Japanophobia that his first term had fanned. In the main, however, he was simply deploying the most powerful special-interest incentive to choose PTAs over non-discriminatory trade liberalisation.

Presented with these arguments, the administration's proponents of PTAs fall back on the defence that they "lock in reforms" in countries such as Mexico. Robert Rubin, the treasury secretary, argued recently that, thanks to NAFTA, Mexico had reacted to the peso crisis by fore-going the use of tariff increases, unlike in previous crises.

In fact, Mexico put more than 500 of its tariffs up. Mr Rubin was right only about tariffs within NAFTA. (Many WTO tariff-ceilings, known as "bindings," were higher than the existing tariffs, thus allowing the tariffs to be raised legally under the terms of earlier trade agreements. In many cases this room for manoeuvre may well have been secured precisely because NAFTA put a lid on raising trade barriers against its members.) In other words, Mexico increased its relative protection against non-members of NAFTA, inviting more trade diversion. In-terestingly, however, many countries that are not part of significant PTAs, such as Thailand, have lately faced financial difficulties without raising their tariffs. So much for locking in liberal trade.

Nor is the argument that your reforms become "credible" if you join a PTA very compelling. The widely-noted reforms of New Zealand and Chile, for example, were credible without membership in a PTA. In fact, these countries undertook their major trade and other reforms unilaterally. And their policymakers and many economists I have talked to dismiss PTAs as a distraction from, and a drag upon, the domestic momentum towards reducing trade barriers unilaterally down to neg-ligible levels.

However, the biggest problem that Mr. Bergsten sidesteps and which increasingly bothers scholars of international trade is the "sys-temic" effect of proliferating PTAs. A few PTAs are just bad; in larger numbers, their bad effects multiply. Seen through Mr. Bergsten's rose-tinted glasses, the trade effects of a multitude of PTAs can be gauged simply by adding up, as it were, the series of partial liberalisations. A world with lots of PTAs, he supposes, has lower trade barriers and hence is moving towards global free trade. This is false economics: you cannot simply add these tariff reductions together. In principle, a pref-erential reduction of barriers can *increase* total protection in the world, in an economically meaningful sense, because of trade diversion.

On top of this, as PTAs spread, the world trading system comes to look like a spaghetti-bowl of ever more complicated trade barriers, each depending on the supposed "nationality" of products. As soon as trade barriers are differentiated by country, and the principle of non-discrimination is not fully adhered to, imported products must be assigned to a country to determine which duties and quotas apply.

The difficulty is acute for PTAs where members have different exter-nal tariffs. The United States made an issue of Hondas produced in

Canada, claiming that they were not Canadian enough in content to qualify for the lower NAFTA tariffs. But the problem arises also in customs unions with common tariffs—as when the French did not want to extend European Union trade benefits to Japanese transplant cars made in Britain. The rules on content and "transformation" that are commonly used to determine origin are inherently arbitrary, of course. They never made much sense; they make even less today, when production is massively globalised.

The absurdity of basing discriminatory trade policies on determinations of the origin of products was well illustrated by a previous U.S. trade representative, Carla Hills. She told Japan that cars produced by transplant factories in America were Japanese; exports of such cars back to Japan should not therefore count towards the import targets that America sought from Japan. Simultaneously, she told Europeans that the very same cars should be considered American—that is, they should not be subject to EU quotas for Japanese cars.

Note too that within each PTA different rules of origin often apply to different products, and that different PTAs apply different tariff-reduction schedules for different products. All in all, it is easy to see why a chaotic and discriminatory regime for global trade is developing, with a multitude of tariffs and quotas applying to particular products, all depending on administratively defined and inherently arbitrary definitions of the product's "nationality."

In the 1930s trade preferences and discrimination proliferated worldwide because of protectionism. Today we see them breaking out all over again—because of "free-trade areas." It is time to recall John Maynard Keynes's words in the House of Lords in the debates on GATT:

The separate blocs and all the friction and loss of friendship they must bring with them are expedients to which one may be driven in a hostile world where trade has ceased over wide areas to be co-operative and peaceful and where are forgotten the healthy rules of mutual advantage and equal treatment. But it is surely crazy to prefer that.

This message is well understood almost everywhere, it seems, except in Washington. Contrary to what Mr. Bergsten says, the Asian nations have chosen so far to reject American attempts to turn APEC into a PTA. Instead of "open regionalism," that empty phrase, they have chosen to make APEC a vehicle for unilateral, but concerted, trade liberalisation on a non-discriminatory basis, and for launching multilateral trade initiatives. Equally, the idea of a transatlantic free-trade area (TAFTA), proposed by Germany's foreign minister, Klaus Kinkel, has yielded to the non-PTA concept of a "transatlantic marketplace."

On to the Clinton Round?

Of these grand PTA schemes only the FTAA remains on the agenda. If the United States were to abandon it, this would put the last nail in the coffin of "large-scale regionalism." The energies of trade-policy makers around the world could once more be brought to bear on the multilateral regime and the WTO. Supporters of liberal trade in South America would rejoice, I am sure. Many are keen to return their countries to unilateral non-discriminatory trade liberalisation, and would like nothing better than to see the United States take the lead along that road at Geneva. South America's apparent enthusiasm for the FTAA is misleading. It is chiefly a response to Washington's own obsession with the subject. In this hemisphere, it often pays, one way or another, to feign enthusiasm for Washington's projects.

True, Mr. Clinton is out on a limb—committed to bringing Chile into NAFTA and then to building the FTAA, despite the growing doubts over PTAs among those concerned with the architecture of the world trading system. But if he is to exercise true leadership, and to justify Mr. Bergsten's hitherto unwarranted praise of his role in trade policy, it is time to think again. Mr. Clinton could and should return the United States to multilateralism, while continuing to pursue "regionalism" through a non-PTA mechanism, exactly as APEC has done so far.

Is that really so difficult, so implausible? Pursuing free trade in a non-discriminatory fashion in the WTO, while developing regionalism (in human rights, defence, security, democracy and so on) through APEC-style initiatives and institutions, ought to appeal to this president—just as it did to a distinguished predecessor. John F. Kennedy, Mr. Clinton's role model, adopted just this strategy. He followed multilateralism in trade, and even had a round of multilateral trade negotiations at the GATT named after him.

Mr. President, history beckons. Why fiddle with an FTAA when the Clinton Round is there for the making?

26 On the Perils of SAPTA

The Maldives summit of SAARC was yet another sign of the leadership that Indian Prime Minister I. K. Gujral is providing in foreign policy. By recognising that greater trade and economic interaction will facilitate regional peace, and that India as the major economic and military power must be prepared to make necessary concessions in bringing this about, Gujral struck the right note.

But Gujral is going down the wrong path if he buys the proposition that we need a Preferential Trade Agreement (PTA), the SAPTA, to pursue these objectives. In fact, the implementation of preferential lowering of trade barriers just among ourselves can be confidently expected to be extremely costly to each member country, compared to opening trade multilaterally for all nations and relying on the resulting expansion to increase trade volumes among ourselves. It is important, therefore, for South Asian nations to stick to multilateral trade liberalisation under the WTO auspices while pursuing the regional agenda in other ways. Let me explain.

PTAS among countries which have high trade barriers are almost certain to lead to what economists call trade diversion. When tariffs remain high on foreign countries while they are reduced for PTA members, imports of goods made more cheaply in outside countries are likely to become more expensive in our markets than the expensive imports from the PTA countries. So we are likely to import from one another at higher prices, hurting each other, when multilateral trade which does not favour one supplier over another can only lead to beneficial imports from the right sources.

Such a self-damaging trade diversion has occurred in Mercosur (the PTA among Brazil, Argentina, Uruguay and Paraguay). Studies show

Originally published, under the title "A Losing Proposition," in *India Today* (June 9, 1997): 65. Reprinted with permission.

how trade has been seriously diverted from external suppliers in favour of Mercosur members at great cost in the car industry which has high external tariffs. Similar costly trade diversion has been observed for other PTAS as well. NAFTA, among Mexico, the US and Canada, for example, has diverted textile exports to North America from the Caribbean countries to Mexico; the European Union (EU) has diverted imports from the Far East to European suppliers. Our fate will be far worse, given the enormous scope for trade diversion due to the high tariffs and high production costs in manufacturing and services in the region. Surely, our best bet is to continue liberalising trade on a non-preferential basis, using our leadership to urge other South Asian nations to do the same. We should do this both unilaterally, as is indeed desirable since our high tariffs have been harmful to our economic prosperity, and multilaterally, as we did at the GATT Uruguay Round.

Why do PTAs nonetheless appeal to even sensible statesmen such as Gujral? After all, he is not alone in embracing them. Indeed, there is an element of "monkey see, monkey do" in all this. With Mercosur, ASEAN and other PTAs breaking out in a witless race, it is no wonder that those who have not created or joined one feel that they are missing out on a good thing!

Besides, the US since the early 1980s, and the EU with greater frenzy in the past decade, have lent their blessings to the creation of even more PTAs. In fact, the US was opposed to PTAs throughout the post-war period, sticking to non-preferential tariff reductions at successive GATT negotiations. It has now abandoned that policy and is little different from the EU in that regard. Give the "hegemonic" status of the US and EU, the effect has been to legitimise the proliferation of such PTAs, regardless of the harm they do to member countries and to the world trading system on which they are now a pox. Multilateral bodies such as the World Bank, never free from the heavy hand of their more substantial members, have fallen in line instead of providing independent leadership on the question.

I suspect that SAPTA is also prompted by the traditional fear in our region of competition with the outside world, the sort of fear that led to three decades of autarky and wasted growth in the first place. Afraid of global competition, we would rather embrace trade with "equally inefficient" countries and then hope to shape up for competition with the outside world. I call this the "tricycle" theory: timid kids learn on a tricycle before getting on to a bicycle. The problem is that going with equally inefficient nations is a surefire recipe for maximising trade diversion and losses from trade liberalisation. Besides, the surest way to get better is to compete with people better than yourself: you do not improve your tennis by playing with opponents as bad as yourself!

Not going the SAPTA way, I should emphasise, is not to abandon regionalism. It is to abandon a particularly foolish form of regionalism. Gujral can pursue regional amity and his magnanimous help-our-smaller-neighbours initiatives without having to buy into SAPTA as well. For example, APEC is *not* a PTA and yet is proving to be a helpful "regional" initiative among the Pacific nations stretching from Chile to South Korea, promoting security, investment and other objectives. Similarly, the transatlantic trade initiative proposed by German Foreign Minister Klaus Kinkel as a preferential Free Trade Area, called TAFTA, has now been turned into a non-FTA venture instead.

Gujral will be exercising true leadership and also be in excellent company if, before SAPTA gets set in cement, he insists that South Asian nations progressively undertake trade liberalisation on a non-preferential, multilateral basis while pursuing regional initiatives in other ways.

The FTAA Is *Not* Free Trade

When the Clinton administration's spokespersons, or perhaps we should call them spin-masters, recently released the results of the commissioned study by the consulting firm DRI of NAFTA's economic effects, the public debate was so flawed analytically that one might as well have been witnessing it in a country populated by illiterates. Even the Lehrer News Hour, our justly celebrated intellectual news show, had Ambassador Mickey Kantor and Ms. Thea Lee debating the employment effect of NAFTA, when trade policy can generally affect employment only in specific sectors, not economy-wide.

But the public debate over NAFTA, then and now, has suffered from a worse, even crippling confusion. Few in the media, and fewer still in the administration and Congress, understand that there is a world of difference between a free-trade area (FTA), which moves to free trade only among its members, and free trade (FT), which lowers trade barriers for all. Indeed, there are now many well-known free traders among economists who oppose FTAs and consider them a pox on the world trading system, so that the widespread assumption in the policy debate over NAFTA and Free-Trade Area of the Americas (FTAA)— that free traders support them and protectionists oppose them—is rank nonsense.

As it happens, the idea of the expansion of NAFTA to Chile, and eventually of an FTAA, which the Clinton administration is wedded to, is a mistake. There is an alternative trade policy that would better fit free trade as well as our regional objectives. But it has failed to be debated because the administration has consistently fudged the distinction between FTAs and FT, and because of the legacy of Ross Perot

Based on a speech given at the World Bank Conference on Trade: Towards Open Regionalism, Montevideo, Uruguay, 1997, and published as *Trade: Towards Open Regionalism* (Washington, DC: World Bank, 1998), 13–19. Reprinted with permission.

during the NAFTA debate, when to be anti-NAFTA came to be popularly regarded as being protectionist.

This fall, as we move in the direction of the FTAA under the false banner of Free Trade, however, there is still a window of opportunity to introduce Washington to the real issues about FTAs and even to stop the train in its tracks: Ideas can be potent. I intend, therefore, to argue here why FTAs, including the FTAA, are a bad idea, and to outline the alternative trade policy that we should embrace.

Why Are FTAs Bad News?

An FTA, because of the *inherent* discrimination that it implies in freeing trade, is different from free trade. Indeed, its flip side is protectionist—protectionist against non-members, against whom the *relative* protection is increased because barriers fall in favor of members, while the ones against non-members remain in place. Recalling Orwell, therefore, serious economists have now abandoned the phrase Free Trade Agreements for one that reminds us of what they truly are: Preferential Trade Agreements (PTAs). Their *preferential* nature, and the huge growth in their number in the last decade, have raised alarms.

Trade Diversion

An important reason, first noted by Jacob Viner in 1950 in a pathbreaking study for the Carnegie Commission, is that the preferences create incentives to divert, not just create, trade. Thus, member countries, enjoying the enhanced protection vis-à-vis more efficient non-members, may replace them as producers and exporters within the PTA, distorting world trade and likely hurting themselves, since they buy imports more expensively from within the PTA.

The analytically informed proponents of PTAs have claimed that trade diversion is negligible in practice; Lawrence Summers, U.S. Deputy Secretary of the Treasury, has even remarked with characteristic forthrightness that he finds it "surprising that this issue is taken so seriously" and that it is a matter to "laugh off." But increasing numbers of empirical studies are now beginning to show that trade diversion is not a negligible phenomenon. Thus, World Bank economist Alexander Yeats' 1996 study of Mercosur (among Uruguay, Argentina, Paraguay and Brazil) turned up significant evidence of trade diversion.[1] The economists Jeffrey Frenkel and Sheng-Jin Wei have also concluded recently that the EU also has been characterized by more trade diversion than hitherto believed. The diversion of textile trade to Mexico from the Caribbean thanks to NAFTA, which excludes the latter and includes the former, has also been a source of discord.

Indeed, if one examines the administration-released DRI study of NAFTA's effects, one immediately finds prima facie evidence of trade diversion plaguing Mexico as well. Thus, according to the DRI study, while the peso crisis generally contracted Mexican domestic demand by 3.3 percent over the period, U.S. exports to Mexico increased by 36.5 percent (or $15.2 billion) from 1993 to 1996. U.S. share in Mexican imports thus went up from 69.3 percent to 75.5 percent. Equally, since NAFTA was signed the Mexican tariffs on U.S. goods were reduced by an average of 7.1 percentage points, resulting in "a 10 percentage point average tariff advantage over foreign suppliers." The Mexican government should itself worry about this strong evidence of trade diversion toward the United States, which is celebrated in the DRI Report as if it were evidence of NAFTA's success! In fact, a quick back-of-the-envelope estimate by University of Maryland economist Arvind Panagariya suggests that Mexico's annual loss from this trade diversion could be as high as $3 billion.

The growing empirical evidence of trade diversion in these preferential-trade agreements is, in fact, not surprising because there has been abundant evidence that many business lobbies prefer them-to genuine, multilateral free trade because they give them preferred access to foreign markets at others' expense. Just recall President Clinton's resort to Japan-bashing during the NAFTA debate: that it would give our firms a better access to Mexico over the Japanese. Economic theory, which often lags behind economic phenomena, has now demonstrated (in the work of Gene Grossman and Elhanan Helpman, and Pravin Krishna) that, under plausible assumptions, trade diversion provides the key motivation for opting for preferential-trade agreements. It is not remarkable, therefore, that those who indulge their preference for preferential-trade arrangements are seen also to use the preferences to their advantage!

It is also worth noting that the complacency about PTAs not leading to trade diversion has also been aided by the notion that the external trade barriers are no longer very high and that, therefore, preferences could not lead to significant trade diversion away from the non-members. But this is not true for several reasons.

To begin with, even trade tariffs are still very high, both in developing and in developed countries. In the latter, the Uruguay Round has still left several peak tariffs in specific products, whereas the tariffication of agricultural support has created truly substantial tariffs.

In developing countries, countries in South Asia and in Latin America are also not free from high trade barriers, making PTAs particularly dangerous.

Besides, the external trade barriers are today only a part of the protectionist story. "Administered protection," consisting of instruments such as anti-dumping (AD) actions, has become the favored policy of protectionists who cleverly use the appealing notion of "fair trade" to unfairly gain protection and advantage against successful foreign rivals. But then these instruments typically yield protection that is elastic and selective. Thus, AD duties, which bear little relationship to "predation" in the economic sense and hence have in practice no economic justification, are often based on adjusted prices that are estimated in ways calculated to find dumping or on inherently arbitrary "reconstructed costs"; the AD methodology compares not foreign and domestic prices, but foreign costs and domestic prices. Thus, within broad margins, it is arguable that AD calculations and actions will seek to accommodate the needs of the protectionist petitioners in the spirit of the story where the interviewing commissar asks candidates what the sum of 2 and 2 is, and the job goes to the candidate who answers: Whatever you want, sir. In addition to their being, therefore, *elastic*, AD actions are *selective* in the sense that they are mounted against specific countries and even specific firms within those countries. Thus, it is possible to use them to zero in against your most potent foreign rivals.

It follows then that, when internal competition among members breaks out, the temptation on the part of PTA members will be to protect each other with administered protection at the expense of non-members, unless such protection is severely regulated. In short, protection against non-members then becomes *endogenous* to the PTA. The consequence is that, as trade creation occurs within a preferential-trade agreement such as NAFTA, the endogenous raising of protection converts it into trade diversion instead. For example, as Mexico starts crowding out inefficient U.S. producers, the United States accommodates imports from Mexico by reducing imports from the most efficient non-member supplier, Taiwan, using AD actions against Taiwan.

Such a phenomenon is not an idle theoretical speculation. Important instances of such endogenous raising of protection against non-members have been observed. An example is the raising of tariffs on more than 500 non-NAFTA tariffs by Mexico during the 1995 peso crisis while the Mexican tariffs on NAFTA items remained on the downward path. The former could be raised because Mexico had bound tariffs above existing levels at the WTO; and it could be argued that the reason for taking such weak bindings was precisely that, with NAFTA, Mexico wanted to hold on to the freedom to raise some tariffs if deemed necessary, implying that the potential for trade diversion was implicitly built into the NAFTA treaty. Thus, Treasury Secretary Robert Rubin, in claiming (as does the DRI report) that, unlike 1982, NAFTA had made Mexico abstain from the use of trade restrictions to deal with the 1995 peso crisis, was wrong on two counts. Mexico did raise some tariffs, but on others and not on us, whereas Mexico has been no different from others in its policy reaction to a currency crisis: Trade restrictions as the knee-jerk, big-bang response to them are generally not seen as appropriate, whether a country has an FTA or not.

The French economist, Patrick Messerlin, has also written of the effect of the EU association agreements, leading toward eventual entry into the EU, had on the Central European countries' acceptance of obligations at the WTO. These nations, coming from the collapse of communism and the absence of significant protectionist lobbies in their midst, had embraced a strong policy of MFN-based trade liberalization. At the insistence of the EU, which was interested in getting preferred access to these markets, the eventual acceptance of WTO obligations by these countries was marked by a *raising* of their MFN tariffs!

The "Spaghetti-Bowl" Phenomenon

But if individual PTAs are flawed in this way, they have raised added concerns because of the "systemic" implications when many PTAs have emerged on the scene, as they have since the 1980s. These systemic implications arise because such preferential-trade agreements magnify the problems that arise, in essence, because we try to restrict or liberalize trade on the basis of which product comes from which country, or what I have called the "who is whose" problem. Thus, for instance, as soon as the United States wishes to liberalize preferentially the imports from Israel, it must decide whether an import coming from Israel is Israeli—i.e., it must establish a "rule of origin," which usually takes the form of some sort of "content" rule, such that a product is considered to be Israeli only if its Israeli content exceeds an arbitrarily specified share in gross value.[2]

The arbitrariness of this share *specification* is further compounded by the arbitrariness inherent in *computing* such content. Thus, consider the import of ingots of steel which, in conjunction with homogeneous domestically produced ingots, go into producing scissors and forks. How is one to determine which of these two products got what share of the imported as against the domestic ingots? Again, if forks need to be coated with plastics, we know that even if the plastics are immediately produced at home, their gross value would generally include imported intermediates at several stages of manufacture, which are impossible for the same reasons to identify and quantify meaningfully. Again, even if we were to estimate such imported shares meaningfully, the imports are likely in turn to include, in today's globalized production, intermediates produced by us and used by the producers abroad. The difficulties are myriad, even endless.

All of these problems, which inherently lead to absurd arbitrariness in trying to identify the origin of products, are particularly acute with an FTA where the different external tariffs inevitably require that the origin be established for virtually all traded products. In FTAs, the fear of non-member goods coming into one's territory at a lower tariff than one's own, simply by entering through another lower tariff member country, is palpable.

In reality, FTAs have created yet further problems by having many different rules of origin, varying by products (as in NAFTA, for instance) and by FTAs (when, say, the EU has FTAs with different rules with several different non-EU countries). The problems inherently posed by the rules of origin are further compounded since FTAs are on different schedules of tariff-cutting by sector and are not synchronized (having been negotiated at different points of time and with different schedules for reaching zero tariff outcomes), so that we typically find a large and chaotic set of applicable tariffs on the same good, depending on which source the good is assigned to.

The result is what I have called the "spaghetti-bowl" phenomenon of numerous and crisscrossing PTAs and innumerable applicable tariff rates arbitrarily determined and often depending on a multiplicity of sources of origin. In short, the systemic effect is to generate a world of preferences, with all its well-known consequences, which increases transaction costs and facilitates protectionism. In the guise of freeing trade, PTAs have managed to recreate the preferences-ridden world of the 1930s as surely as protectionism did at the time. Irony, indeed!

And thus in the debates on GATT, international economists who have been either ambiguous or complacent in regard to PTAs have acquired a proper appreciation of Keynes's famous words in the

House of Lords, extolling the virtues of multilateral MFN-based trade and rejecting the preferences he had earlier defended:[3]

> The separate blocs and all the friction and loss of friendship they must bring with them are expedients to which one may be driven in a hostile world where trade has ceased over wide areas to be cooperative and peaceful and where are forgotten the healthy rules of mutual advantage and equal treatment. But it is surely crazy to prefer that.

Two Qualifiers

Crazy to prefer PTAs, yes. But still, there are two circumstances where a staunch anti-PTA, multilateral free trader would make an exception:

First, if the PTA takes the form of deep integration in the form of an EU-core style Common Market, with common external tariff and internal factor mobility, and possibly even a parliament and attempts at a unified foreign policy, then the member nations are forming something close to the federal United States or India. In this case, the trade dimension cannot be judged in isolation from a very much bigger picture. Indeed, the overriding political need to countervail the nascent Soviet threat with a politically united Europe and the fact that the treaty would aim at deep economic integration in Europe and not just trade preferences the way an FTA does, were the reasons for the benign and supportive U.S. attitude to the 1957 Treaty of Rome, even though our view of PTAs was quite clearly hostile, as it had been about Britain's Imperial Preference during the GATT negotiations and had indeed been throughout our two-centuries' history as anyone familiar with George Washington's Farewell Address or with Woodrow Wilson's Fourteen Points will recall.[4]

Second, there is what international economists now call the "dynamic time path" justification for PTAs. This has to do with the possibility that, even though we seek worldwide multilateral free trade, multilateral trade negotiations (MTN) at the GATT, now the WTO, may not be the way to get there. We thus need to distinguish between "process multilateralism" and "outcome multilateralism."

The fact remains that the United States, faced in November 1991 with opposition by the EU and many developing countries to the declaration of another MTN Round to follow the Tokyo Round, felt that it had no option except to shift to PTAs, legitimate under GATT's Article XXIV, as a way of keeping trade liberalization going. Hence, came the

initiative under U.S. Trade Representative Bill Brock for CUFTA between Canada and the United States, the first break in our policy of un-
divided loyalty to MFN multilateralism. It is important to recall that
the motive, contrary to what it became later, was *not* regionalism in the
Americas. The motive, rather, was purely that of trade liberalization;
and the intention was to expand the FTA in *any* direction, whether in
our region or elsewhere. Bill Brock is regarded as having seriously considered adding Egypt and the ASEAN countries but found no takers.
We can be certain that if life had been found on the moon, and a government to negotiate with, Brock would have hawked an FTA to it as
well.

This second reason for FTAs then is simply that, if MTN is not working to liberalize trade worldwide, we will take the PTA route to freeing
trade worldwide, inefficient as PTAs can be en route. In short, if the
turnpike is not open, we take the dirt road.

No Excuse Now for PTAs by United States

But there is really no reason now for us to keep going on the dirt road.
The turnpike is open. The Uruguay Round concluded successfully.
GATT, pronounced by the summarily skeptical Lester Thurow to be
dead, did die but joined the blessed twice-born, appearing as the much
strengthened and institutionalized WTO. The unfinished business of
the Round, set on the negotiating agenda, has also been producing results: the telecommunication pact, the information technology agreement; and pretty soon, without doubt, there will be a multilateral
agreement on financial services. These multilateral agreements happen
to be backed by strong export lobbies that will profit from them, and
they have no countervailing import-competing lobbies arrayed against
them. So, in fact, the renewal of fast-track to get them through Congress is not necessary. Indeed, unless one goes for a new MTN Round,
which the Clinton administration has not committed itself to, there
seems to be no compelling reason to immediately renew fast track legislation as far as multilateral trade treaties are concerned.

There is also little evidence for the argument, often advanced, that
we should go for both MTN and PTAs because the latter will help the
former move forward. Fred Bergsten argues that the Seattle summit of
APEC moved the EU into settling the Uruguay Round by threatening
Europe with an American trade alternative of regionalism that would
exclude it from the trade game. But this is fanciful since there are

plenty of indications that the EU was about to settle anyway; besides, *we* made the key trade concession—in agriculture—which finally broke the logjam. Equally, APEC is cited as having led to the information-technology agreement three weeks before the first WTO ministerial meeting in Singapore; but this is nothing but a post-hoc-ergo-propter-hoc fallacy; our intensive work would have produced the agreement at Singapore even if there has been no APEC, for sure. Besides, APEC is a "regional" arrangement but is *not* a PTA.

On the other hand, there are disturbing examples of how PTAs have undermined the multilateral liberalization process instead, by holding up concessions by countries on an MFN basis because partner countries, especially hegemonic ones, in the PTA look for and get preferred access—as in the case of NAFTA and, more important, Central European countries that were already cited. Again, Sebastian Edwards of UCLA, who was the World Bank's Chief Economist for Latin America, recently argued in *The Wall Street Journal* that Chile's progress toward MFN liberalization had slowed down as a result of the different regional PTAs it was getting involved in. Thus, to those who say cutely that we will do well by following a "GATT plus" approach, using PTAs alongside multilateralism, I say: It is likely to work as well as the "marriage plus" approach worked with Demi Moore in the film, *Indecent Proposal*.

What about Regionalism for the Americas?

So, clearly there is no good case for us today to be pursuing trade liberalization through the NAFTA extension and through other FTAs. Indeed, FTAA remains at the moment the only "big-ticket" item on the PTA agenda with a possible political future.

Thus, the Asian members of APEC have refused to date to turn it into an Article XXIV-sanctioned FTA despite our clear desire in that direction. Instead, they have insisted on undertaking trade liberalization under APEC auspices only on an MFN basis. Partly this is because the successful Asian exporters have never wanted to go regional or subregional in trade; the whole world was their market. Partly, the politics of it would be absurd for them since an FTA would then exclude the EU, and hence the previous colonial powers with whom many Asian countries have a special relationship. Just imagine President Salinas entering into an FTA that excluded the United States. Then again, the Trans-Atlantic Free-Trade Area (TAFTA), floated by Foreign Minister

Klaus Kinkel of Germany and embraced by the Atlanticist Foreign Minister Michael Rifkind in Prime Minister Major's government, has given way now to a non-FTA transatlantic initiative.

In fact, a few weeks ago the European Council of Ministers, responding to the growing concerns about the proliferation of PTAs and its own role in creating this problem, resolved that the "current architecture" of its trading system would be frozen. In practice, it means that no new PTA initiatives will be undertaken without far more acute examination and skepticism than was the case to date. The WTO also has an active Committee on Regionalism whose task it is to analyze the working of Article XXIV in light of the growing tide of skepticism about PTAs.

One would think that the Clinton administration would take heed as well and desist from further indulgence of FTAs, reverting instead to multilateral trade initiatives. But it has not. Part of the reason, of course, is intellectual laziness. Partly it is also the fact that no international economists of repute have ever had access to the White House, where the main concern has been the politics of its trade policies, not their economics. Then again, there is the inertia of past decisions: The FTAA is in effect the legacy of the Baker transformation of the open, non-regional FTA initiative into a closed, regional initiative for the Americas.

But matching the American folly is much of South America's own misguided enthusiasm for the FTAA. It is remarkable that this continent, so rich in its literature, has been so deficient in its trade policy in the postwar period, having successively succumbed to the destructive strategy of import substitution, then fallen for the Generalized System of Preferences for developing countries, which many economists today believe to have been a mistake, and now enamored of the PTAs. It is sad to see the huge enthusiasm for free trade that has finally broken out there being channeled not into the multilateral freeing of trade, but into the politics and economics of PTAs.

But the South American enthusiasm is largely responsive to our own, seeing access to our markets as the gain they get from our preferred access to theirs. It also reflects the sense of solidarity, as against hostility, that is now more manifest in these countries toward us. "Regionalism" is then seen as a cementing bond, a glue to launch joint efforts for human rights, democracy, et al., in the Americas. But, it must also be recognized that the politics of PTAs in the Americas is also divisive and sidetracks free-trade sentiments into unproductive politics. This is true of the well-known rivalry between NAFTA and Mercosur as the leading lights of the trade-liberalizing movement in the Americas. Brazil, the dominant player in South America, sees NAFTA extension into FTAA as a hegemonic extension by the United States, and Mercosur is, at least in part, in response to NAFTA, just as the creation of APEC with U.S. initiative was in part a geopolitical response to Prime Minister Mahathir's Asian bloc initiative, which, in turn, was a response to our NAFTA. And so, with PTAs, politics tends to hijack and distort the freeing of trade, whereas the multilateral system tends to narrow it down to its economics—and permits more focused attention to the free-trade objective.

An Alternative for the Americas: Return to Camelot

The policy option for the United States is entirely clear. We should revert to exclusive focus on multilateralism and MFN-based trade liberalization, asking the South American nations to join in the multilateral opening of markets through a variety of initiatives, while pursuing "regionalism" and its separate objectives through non-PTA means. In short, we should renounce the FTAA gracefully, easing into an Americas Initiative that focuses, like APEC, on issues like security, democracy, human rights, drug trafficking, customs procedures and a whole host of issues of hemispheric interest, while becoming a regional platform for launching multilateral trade liberalization initiatives.

This is, in fact, the policy framework that President Kennedy had when he stayed loyal to non-discrimination in trade, eschewing our use of Article XXIV sanctioned PTAs while he launched the Alliance for Progress for South America for several non-trade objectives. Thus, in pursuing free trade through non-discriminatory trade liberalization and regionalism through the Alliance for Progress, he implicitly understood the chief lesson of policy making—that two objectives are usually achieved best with the use of two policy instruments. As our forefathers put it, one cannot (generally) kill two birds with one stone. It is surely not too late to return to Camelot.

Eliminating Preferences

On the general question of PTAs, some would even like to roll back existing PTAs to rid the world trading system of this pox. That is utopian, but a standstill, a freeze, is more doable. There is, however, a simple solution to ridding the world of the preferences that existing PTAs burden us with. Since preferences relative to zero are zero, one can effectively eliminate them also by reducing the MFN tariffs down to zero. Hence, many economists have allied themselves to the goal that Martin Wolf of *The Financial Times* first proposed for the trading nations to announce: that, by a date such as 2025, the world be rid of all border trade barriers.

So far, the U.S. administration has poured cold water on the idea, arguing that concrete trade pacts are necessary, not a vision. That is like saying that it is enough to go around filling potholes as one finds them, that a road map is unnecessary. But then what can one expect from an administration where trade policy is run by politicians watching the polls, and where lawyers, with their adversarial mentality, implement it?

Notes

1. Mercosur is a customs union (CU), which is different from an FTA, because it also has a common external tariff. A Common Market is additionally characterized by free mobility of capital and labor among the members. All are PTAs.

2. The U.S.-Israel FTA does not have any value as a precedent and signifies no change in trade policy since it was dictated purely by the politics of our "special relationship."

3. John Maynard Keynes, Speech to Parliament, in 24 *The Collected Writings of John Maynard Keynes: Activities 1944–1946: The Transition to Peace*, pp. 623–624 (Donald Moggridge, ed., 1979).

4. See the interesting historical account of our commitment to "equality of treatment" in trade and hence to nondiscrimination or MFN in trade in David Palmeter, "Some Inherent Problems with Free Trade Agreements," *Law and Policy in International Business*, The International Law Journal of the Georgetown University Law Center, Vol. 27 (4), pp. 991–997, Summer 1996.

Palmeter, a distinguished trade lawyer, also expresses astonishment at the fact that "there has been virtually no debate—vigorous or otherwise—on the current retreat from the United States' historic commitment to nondiscriminatory multilateralism" (page 993). Of course, he means a *public* debate; within *scholarly circles* in the universities, there has indeed been a vigorous debate where I have witnessed an increasing hostility to PTAs emerge in the last few years, when there was really little when I started writing in 1991.

Bill Clinton's recent rout in the U.S. Congress over fast-track trading authority came at a particularly bad time. Leaders of the Asia-Pacific region are meeting in Vancouver just when Asian countries are needing to boost exports dramatically in order to grow out of trouble. In these circumstances, the world requires U.S. leadership in pushing for free trade more than ever.

But haven't Mr. Clinton's trade troubles with Congress ruled that out? The answer is no—at least, not for a future president.

Even though Mr. Clinton himself was only playing public relations when he defiantly promised his foes in Congress that he would try again, he was basically right: fast track—and by extension U.S. leadership in multilateral trade—is not beyond presidential reach. It is true that it may be beyond him now and later—especially if the Asian turmoil widens and temporarily strengthens the hand of some openly protectionist members of the Congress. But when the crisis has been contained, as it eventually will, matters will change. The prize remains within the presidential grasp if the deeper "systemic" causes of his failure are understood.

There were many aspects of the fast-track defeat that were specific to President Clinton. As he sensed defeat, he lost his amiability, and, it seemed, his political touch. But what brought the vote in Congress so close in the first place was not a sudden outbreak of protectionism which, as all empirical studies show, is hard to sell in times of general economic prosperity and the elevation of the United States to the status of top dog on the street of world competition.

Rather, it had to do with the president's fundamental error in interpreting the true meaning of the passage of the North American Free

Originally published in the *Financial Times* (Nov. 25, 1997). Reprinted with permission.

Trade Agreement (NAFTA) through Congress. The president had clearly inferred wrongly from his heroic NAFTA struggle and success that he could always get his way in Congress on trade, no matter what.

Instead, NAFTA had been a Pyrrhic victory, changing the U.S. trade scene for the worse and making the passage of future trade liberalisation, especially with developing countries, immeasurably more difficult than before.

By equating what was essentially a bilateral, preferential trade agreement between the United States and Mexico with multilateral nondiscriminatory free trade almost worldwide, the president (and George Bush before him) had reduced the issue of free trade, with its expansive promise, to a petty level.

In seeking fast-track authority without linking it to a compelling objective, such as Sir Leon Brittan's "millennium round" idea for discussing global trading issues and the worldwide freeing of trade, the president came across as interested only in a pettifogging agenda such as the extension of NAFTA to Chile. As his former adviser George Stephanopoulos virtually said, most Democrats failed to see why they were being taken to the trade well again, for prizes so small.

But if NAFTA damaged fast track by making petty and discriminatory freeing of trade look like the real thing and by setting U.S. trade ambitions so low as to appear hardly worthwhile, it also served to bring on to the agenda a whole host of new trade-unrelated lobbies (comprising mainly environmentalists, unions and human rights activists). These lobbies would afflict all future liberalisations.

The problem with bilateral trade deals is that those who oppose the liberalisation of trade will use any shortcomings in the partner country to attack the trade treaty.

This is what happened with Mexico. The state of its democracy, and the dominance and corruption of the governing Institutional Revolutionary party became a reason for denying NAFTA; so did Mexico's apparent environmental degradation and neglect of labour standards. Soon, these had become "trade" issues and then, in short order, preconditions for the freeing of trade.

Equally, the fear of trade with poor countries became politically salient in the US largely because of NAFTA. The sight of impoverished Mexicans crossing the Rio Grande and fears of their effect on real wages fuelled the fear that NAFTA would do the same indirectly through freer trade.

By contrast, the Uruguay Round of multilateral trade negotiations had the direct advantage of moderating, and even preventing, such focuses of concern by diffusion over a wider area: there were simply too many countries and too many issues.

Now that NAFTA has predictably left this legacy, any president seeking fast track will have to deal with these new lobbies that seek linkage to trade treaties. But this leaves the politics divided between the Republicans who will properly not have linkage—for it creates new obstacles to trade when trade treaties should eliminate them—and the Democrats who wish more of it.

The only solution is for the Democrats to be brought on board by diverting these lobbies away from the trade agenda and to devise alternative ways of advancing their beliefs. This, Mr. Clinton failed to do.

The lesson is clear. The United States's chances of exercising leadership on trade will involve raising the president's ambitions to progress on the grand, multilateral trading front. And the trade-unrelated lobbies will have to be satisfied in other ways that are credible. Both are eminently achievable.

In Favor of China's Entry into WTO

China has replaced Japan as the Lex Luthor in America's imagination and in its public-policy domain. It is facile, however, to conclude that we need an enemy to feel comfortable and that the end of the Cold War has left us with a withdrawal symptom that makes us yearn for a devil to fear and a monster to slay.

Yes, China is truly off the curve regarding its economic organization and its civil and political regime. Its economy, despite the massive inroads made by capitalist roaders, is marked by residual features of the extensively planned system by which it had been managed since the triumph of the communists almost a half-century ago. At the same time, having put *perestroika* (economic restructuring) ahead of *glasnost* (political liberalization), the Chinese communists have continued to preside over an authoritarian regime that violates all conventions of a civil and civilized society, offending not merely the human-rights groups, but anyone with a moral sense and a social conscience.

The question of China's entry into the World Trade Organization, or WTO, thus has been caught up in the acute reactions that China provokes among some trade-policy elites and virtually all of the human-rights activists. In one of those rare alliances that make politics ever fascinating, these groups, normally in unison only in their distrust of each other, have come together in opposing China's entry into the WTO. But I believe they are fundamentally mistaken. In fact, the goal of getting China to conform more to rules-based and market-determined trade and to respect human rights will be reached more quickly by admitting her to the WTO.

Among the many fallacious arguments advanced by the opponents of China's entry, three stand out. Foremost among these is the claim

Originally published as part of a symposium in *Insight* (Dec. 1, 1997): 24–27. Copyright 1997 News World Communication, Inc. All rights reserved. Reprinted with permission.

that China does not have a market economy. It has been claimed that the WTO requires that member states be "market economies," since they must accept meaningful obligations in regard to matters such as access which cannot be implemented if the economic system does not permit markets.

But put this claim in perspective. The General Agreement on Tariffs and Trade, or GATT, already permitted communist states— Czechoslovakia and Poland—to join. We therefore face a genuine question: Is China, which surely has moved away from communism to markets in a dramatic (though incomplete) fashion, to be considered less favorably than previous members which had not made the move at all? The best, and not necessarily partisan, Sinologists are divided on the question of how far markets have gone in today's China. But there is no debate about the fact that markets are indeed here and that they are steadily increasing in scope.

Take import markets: Already in bilateral negotiations with the United States (often backed by threat of sanctions and counterthreats by the Chinese), the People's Republic has proceeded to make pledges to publish the rules and procedures American exporters must follow, while reducing or eliminating import licenses, quotas and other controls that impeded access to China's markets.

The same is true of state trading. Here again, we should recall that GATT traditionally accommodated occasional state trading, adding safeguards to ensure, however imperfectly, the preservation of market-access obligations and nondiscrimination between different exporters. True, China presents a more difficult problem because of the preponderance of state-owned companies. But even here, profound change is on the way. With the economic realities of inefficient state enterprises all too evident to the Chinese authorities themselves, the latest Chinese Communist Party Congress finally has resolved to reduce them to a negligible share of the economy.

Indeed, the Brookings Institution's China expert, Nicholas Lardy, has shown fairly conclusively that China's goods markets have been liberalized in farming and distribution sectors as well, whereas the labor markets also are functioning to allocate labor in the rural and small-scale manufacturing sectors.

Thus, the traditional practice of GATT in admitting truly nonmarket economies and the complex reality of the Chinese economy, which has manifold and growing aspects of the market in it, indicate that it is folly to exclude China from the WTO on what only can be regarded as de facto ideological grounds.

A second faulty argument against China's WTO membership is that China runs huge external surpluses, exporting far more than it imports. Critics claim that this is incontrovertible proof that China's markets are unfairly closed. The charge, however, is wrong—both factually and conceptually.

China has, since 1978 when its reforms began, run overall deficits—and not just surpluses. Currently, its surplus in balance of trade is small (though the bilateral surplus with the United States is large). But it also must be said that, in economic logic, these balances have nothing to do with whether a country is open or closed. Surpluses and deficits are macroeconomic phenomena: They reflect not trade policies, but domestic differences between aggregate spending and income (which are influenced by fiscal and monetary policies).

The same fallacy, inferring trade openness from deficits and closedness from surpluses, was rampant in Washington during the period of Japan-bashing. It managed to survive obvious contradictions: For instance, Japan had run deficits when it was less open for decades after World War II and only surpluses since the eighties, when it clearly had opened much wider.

A third argument of the critics is that China cannot be expected to abide by the rules of WTO when it has no rule of law. But that is a non sequitur. True, China has no rule of law as we understand it. But this has not prevented us and others transacting with China in gargantuan terms: Her total trade already is close to $200 billion.

And in 1993, she was attracting direct foreign-investment flows of more than $25 billion, putting her ahead of all other developing countries, even as we were threatening China with retribution due to her lack of protection for intellectual-property, or IP, rights and seeking to persuade her implausibly that she would lose foreign investment if she did not do so! The absurdity of the notion that China would cease to attract investment in the absence of IP protection was brought home to me when I was at a meeting at the Commerce Department, where many of America's top chief executive officers were being briefed by scholars, just before boarding the plane for China on then-commerce secretary Ron Brown's jaunt to Beijing in search of trade and investment opportunities: Nothing like the absence of the rule of law, including nonexistent IP rights, was going to deter these gentlemen from that gigantic market!

Some critics charge that China cannot enforce internally the disciplines it accepts bilaterally or multilaterally. Thus, in regard to lax enforcement of IP agreements, some China specialists pleaded that

Beijing could not effectively enforce what is enforced elsewhere. This is a ludicrous claim: Try telling that to the Tibetans, or just see how much better the enforcement is now that China sees that it is necessary if she is to get our support in getting into the WTO.

Besides, if any member of the WTO fails to deliver on a commitment that immediately exposes it to the binding Dispute Settlement Procedure and hence to retaliation in the shape of withdrawal of trade concessions to the offending country. So, China would be subject to the WTO's rules-based discipline which itself inevitably would create the incentive for China to exercise discipline internally.

In fact, precisely because the WTO imposes discipline on its members, with built-in punishments for deviant behavior, we confidently can predict that China's entry into it will help the United States to advance our trade and our human-rights objectives.

WTO entry will multilateralize the demands that we have made bilaterally on China for new and further reforms. So far, we have asked, with only moderate success, that the Chinese change their nontransparent import procedures, state trading and production, inadequate IP protection and a host of other unacceptable practices. But, as a precondition of WTO membership, China will have to accept these and other demands simply as part of its membership obligations as long as we insist, as we have done so far, that China get no special exemptions.

Besides, the lesson from our clumsy attempts during the eighties to use our clout to get Japan and the European Union bilaterally to accept new trade obligations is that typically these big players tell us to get lost when we demand new concessions bilaterally but accept them when the same demands are made multilaterally. The U.S.-Japan auto dispute, begun by us with dire threats of tariff retaliation against Japanese auto firms, ended in ignominious failure on our part as the Japanese drew a line in the sand. Japan plays far more pliably within the multilateral WTO. So will China.

In fact, I would urge that China also be required to sign the optional WTO Government Procurement Agreement as a condition for WTO accession, even though developing countries (except for Singapore and Hong Kong) have not accepted it. Given the current preponderance of state enterprises in China, despite the announced intention to reduce it drastically, it is important that politics be taken out of their functioning so as to ensure fairer market access. Human-rights groups also should welcome this since China, unconstrained by WTO discipline, typically has tried to switch orders away from those who criticize its human-rights record. Everything that makes Chinese enterprises stick to WTO principles of nondiscrimination in purchasing would make such Chinese threats less credible since they could be immediately challenged, if translated into action, at the WTO.

In the end, contrary to the fears often expressed that China will wreck the WTO, it is the WTO that will help change China. It will be the bull in the China shop. As China moves herself out of the old economic and political order, benefiting her own multitudes while also suiting our own objectives, the WTO will provide a nudge in the same direction.

30 Free Trade without Treaties

President Clinton and seventeen other Asian-Pacific leaders are meeting today in Vancouver. Rather than the convivial photo-op they'd planned, however, they must contend with worrisome trade news. A spate of Asian currency devaluations has raised the specter of renewed protectionism around the world. South America's Mercosur trade bloc, led by Brazil, just raised its tariffs some 30 percent. And Congress turned its back on the president and refused to approve fast-track authority for him to negotiate further free-trade accords.

In light of all this dismaying news, what are the prospects for free trade? Is the future bleak, or will the postwar trend of dramatic liberalization continue to accelerate despite these setbacks?

On the Ropes?

The immediate prospects for more U.S.-led multilateral trade accords do indeed look grim after the defeat of fast-track. But that doesn't mean that free trade itself is on the ropes. A large portion of the world's trade liberalization in the last quarter-century has been *unilateral*. Those countries that lower trade barriers of their own accord not only profit themselves, but also often induce the laggards to match their example. The most potent force for the world-wide freeing of trade, then, is unilateral U.S. action. If the United States continues to do away with tariffs and trade barriers, other countries will follow suit—fast-track or no fast-track.

To be sure, the General Agreement on Tariffs and Trade, the World Trade Organization and other multilateral tariff reductions have greatly contributed to global wealth. The WTO has become the international institution for setting the "rules" on public and private practices that affect competition among trading nations. Much still needs to be done in that mode, particularly on agriculture tariffs, which remain too high around the world. A future U.S. president, if not Mr. Clinton, will certainly need fast-track authority if another multilateral effort, such as the "millennium round" called for by Sir Leon Brittan of the European Union, is to pursue these goals.

But the good news is that even if organized labor, radical environmentalists and others who fear the global economy continue to impede fast-track during Congress's next session, they cannot stop the historic freeing of trade that has been occurring unilaterally world-wide.

From the 1970s through the 1990s, Latin America witnessed dramatic lowering of trade barriers unilaterally by Chile, Bolivia and Paraguay; and the entire continent has been moving steadily toward further trade liberalization. Mercosur's recent actions are a setback, but only a small one—so far.

Latin America's record has been bettered by unilateral liberalizers in Asia and the Pacific. New Zealand began dismantling its substantial trade protection apparatus in 1985. That effort was driven by the reformist views of then-Prime Minister David Lange, who declared, "In the course of about three years we changed from being a country run like a Polish shipyard into one that could be internationally competitive."

Since the 1980s, Hong Kong's and Singapore's enormous successes as free traders have served as potent examples of unilateral market opening, encouraging Indonesia, the Philippines, Thailand, South Korea and Malaysia to follow suit. By 1991 even India, which had been astonishingly autarkic for more than four decades, had finally learned the virtue of free trade and had embarked on a massive lowering of its tariffs and nontariff barriers.

In Central and Eastern Europe, the collapse of communism led to a wholesale, unilateral and nondiscriminatory removal of trade barriers as well. The French economist Patrick Messerlin has shown how this happened in three waves: Czechoslovakia, Poland and Hungary liberalized right after the fall of the Berlin Wall; next came Bulgaria, Romania and Slovenia; and finally, the Baltic countries began their unilateral opening in 1991.

The currency crisis roiling Asia—which has just led South Korea to seek a bailout from the International Monetary Fund—hasn't disturbed this liberalizing trend yet. Unlike similar currency crises of the 1980s, the countries that have been forced to devalue their currencies in the 1990s—whether Mexico in 1995 or the Southeast Asian tigers today— are not rushing to raise tariff barriers. Leaders of developing countries know that without expanded international trade, they cannot maintain their "miracle" economies' impressive achievements, and indeed cannot avoid further economic catastrophes.

U.S. leadership is crucial to maintaining the trend toward free trade. Such ultramodern industries as telecommunications and financial services gained their momentum largely from unilateral openness and deregulation in the United States. This in turn has led to a softening of protectionist attitudes in the European Union and Japan.

These developed economies are now moving steadily in the direction of openness and competition—not because any officials in Washington threaten them with retribution, but because they've seen how U.S. companies become much more competitive once regulation and other trade barriers have fallen. A Brussels bureaucrat can argue with a Washington bureaucrat, but he cannot argue with the markets. Faced with the prospect of being elbowed out of world markets by American firms, Japan and Europe have no option but to follow the U.S. example, belatedly but surely, in opening their own markets.

The biggest threat to free trade is not the loss of fast-track per se, but the signal it sends that Americans may not be interested in lowering their trade barriers any further. To counteract this attitude, President Clinton needs to mount the bully pulpit and explain the case for free trade—a case that Adam Smith first made more than two hundred years ago, but that continues to come under attack.

Debunk the Protectionists

The president, free from the burdens of constituency interests that cripple many in Congress, could argue, credibly and with much evidence, that free trade is in the interest of the whole world, but that, because the U.S. economy is the most competitive anywhere, we have the most to gain. The president could also point to plenty of evidence that debunks the claims of protectionists. The unions may argue that trade with poor countries depresses our workers' wages, for example, but in fact the best evidence shows that such trade has *helped* workers by moderating the fall in their wages from technological changes.

Assuming that the president can make the case for free trade at home, the prospects for free trade world-wide remain bright. The United States doesn't need to sign treaties to open markets or, heaven forbid, issue counterproductive threats to close our own markets if others are less open than we are. We simply need to offer an example of openness and deregulation to the rest of the world. Other countries will see our success, and seek to emulate it.

V   The Debacle in Seattle

Seattle will no doubt be sizzling despite the mild weather at the end of November. For that techno-trendy city is the site for the World Trade Organization's Inter-Ministerial Meeting and more specifically, the place where the WTO's 134 member nations will attempt to kick off a new round of negotiations for liberalizing global trade.

Why the ado? This is, after all, the young organization's first trade round. What's more there will, no doubt, be an intense (if polite), public relations tussle over what the round should be called. If you're an American, the choice is between the Clinton Round, an opportunity that the President appears to have blown by procrastinating over whether he wanted a round at all, or the uninspired Seattle Round. If you are not an American, the preference, following the suggestion of Sir Leon Brittan, Europe's trade minister, is for the Millennium Round—and that's to just because it is apt to take a millennium to complete it.

But the reason the whole world will be watching is that both free trade and the World Trade Organization are under siege. Worse, the forces that threaten further trade liberalization under WTO auspices come from two altogether different directions.

Start with labor unions and other nongovernmental organizations—in bureaucratese, the NGOs. The NGOs, constituting the civil (or as cynics would say, the uncivil) society, vary from the skeptical to the deeply hostile, calling into question the value of free trade (or "globalization" as they like to call it) and its premier institution, the WTO.

True believers want the WTO plowed under. They see it as the wicked arm of multinationals that want to impose the horrors of glob-

Originally published in *The Milken Institute Review* (Fourth Quarter 1999): 4–7. Reprinted with permission.

alization upon us all. Lesser extremists oppose any new liberalization, preferring to de-fang the WTO rather than bury it.

Those in the moderate camp do not oppose the WTO or trade liberalization. But they would exact a considerable price for cooperating—namely, the obligation to link freer trade to labor and environmental standards, human rights and assorted social agendas. A big catch, of course, is that they do not all share the same views on what those agendas should be: One man's minimum living wage is another's right to starve.

More pointedly (and with greater consensus) the moderate NGOs are angling for a slew of procedural changes. These would include revising the WTO's dispute-settlement mechanism to allow NGOs to file "friend of the court" amicus briefs and to require environmental impact statements with every proposed trade pact.

Not all of the moderates' demands—particularly those for linkages to non-trade issues—are sensible. But many of them do lie within the bounds of a constructive debate over the trade-liberalizing agendas that most governments and economists will want to consider at Seattle. You can be sure, though, that the extremists will garner the bulk of the attention.

Reporters are already salivating at the rumor that some activists plan to march the streets of Seattle in turtle suits to demonstrate against the WTO's recent decision in the Shrimp-Turtle case. (In case you missed that one, the WTO is not happy about United States legislation unilaterally suspending rights to market shrimp harvested without the use of "turtle-excluding devices.") And do not rule out Japanese monster look-alikes—GATTzillas—or streakers aiming pies at the WTO Director-General, Mike Moore. First reports predicted that more than 10,000 NGO and union-backed warriors were to storm Seattle; by late September, that number had jumped to more than 100,000.

The Shape of Things to Come

What NGOs can't manage to create in the chaos department, governments probably will. There are deep divisions within member governments, economists and policy wonks over the agenda in Seattle. In particular, there are strikingly different conceptions of its design and contents:

A core round focusing on conventional business—items that have been near the top of the free traders' agenda since the General Agreements on Tariffs and Trade was started after World War II. That would include further reductions in barriers to commerce in agriculture, manufacturing and services, as well as repairs to the dispute-settlement mechanism. The need for the latter has become manifest in view of the nasty squabbles between the United States and the European Community over bananas and hormone-fed beef.

A core-plus round that would include some of the "new issues"—the ones that fuel the ideological fires of assorted NGOs, labor unions and governments. Linkage of environmental and labor standards to WTO-protected market access tops this list, but it also includes issues dear to the hearts of Western policy wonks—agreements on rules for international investments and policing competition. (The Uruguay trade round itself had new issues: intellectual property protection, liberalization of trade in services and agriculture. These, for better and worse, have now become "old" issues for the WTO.)

It is fair to say that governments are divided between the two conceptions. India opposes a new round—which boils down to a very conservative view of what the core agenda should be in the next negotiations. The United States is not far off, differing from India mainly on the linkage of labor standards. Democrats, with the elections looming and the AFL-CIO commanding a huge campaign war chest, cannot but be craven to the union demands. By contrast, the Europeans, led by Sir Leon Brittan, are enthusiastic about the "core-plus" agenda.

Leaving aside politics, which is necessarily somewhat fluid, one might ask which of the two alternatives should be pursued. I would argue that the core agenda makes more sense.

Plenty of Old Issues to Fight About

Some analysts urge a broader negotiation on the grounds that it would put more on the table to haggle over, as in, "I give you access in services, you give me intellectual property protection."

Indeed, Fred Bergsten of the Institute for International Economics in Washington has argued that we have now reached the point where the rich countries have very few trade barriers and the poor countries have too many. So the tradeoff between rich and poor countries cannot be achieved on trade liberalization alone.

That is simply not true. Economists, among them Arvind Panagariya of Maryland, have demonstrated to my satisfaction that there is plenty to bargain about without adding fresh grist for argument. Some stiff industrial tariffs remain in place, notably in textiles, and the rich-country tariffs on agriculture are appallingly high. Moreover, the liberalization of trade in services has barely begun. If, as Director-General Moore has urged, we can be generous in reducing trade barriers of special interest to developing countries, so much the better.

Add, of course, the much-needed reform of the dispute-settlement mechanism (where consensus is going to have to be forged on contentious issues such as how to handle genetically modified products), and we have a really compelling agenda for the next three years. That three-year time frame, incidentally, fits well into Moore's schedule, since he must split the six-year director-general's term with Dr. Supachai Panitchpakdi of Thailand.

Second, we no longer have the "GATT is Dead" threat from regionalism—the argument that without new issues at the multilateral level, all the liberalization action would end up in regional trade negotiations. Regionalism is even regarded by many as a cancer to be suppressed because proliferating regional preferences are undermining the economic logic of open trade. At the very least, then, there is regionalism-fatigue. And the World Trade Organization is more prized an institution than the General Agreement on Tariffs and Trade ever was.

Third, there is little prospect that any consensus could be hammered out on the new issues. A pact on investment policy, drafted by the rich countries at the Organization for Economic Cooperation and Development, is bitterly opposed by the NGOs. It is, in fact, overly ambitious in laying down the rights of multinationals while underplaying both the rights of host countries and the obligations of multinationals to local employees and communities.

Note, too, that the OECD investment proposal is a voluntary code. If blessed by the WTO, it would become mandatory and the objections to it would become even more vociferous. It is therefore a non-starter for Seattle.

Competition policy is really a North-North issue, prompted mainly by Washington's unhappiness with Japan and the difficulty in penetrating its clubby markets. However, the main division here comes between the Untied States Department of Justice, which would like to handle the problem through antitrust laws, and the Europeans who would like to see the WTO tackle it. It is unlikely that these fundamental differences, already closely identified with powerful political personalities, could be resolved in a three-year time frame.

If you think investment and competition would be tough nuts to crack, linkages aren't even worth attempting. The primary opposition comes from the poor nations—from their policy intellectuals and even some NGOs who see links between trade and environment and labor-standards as a back door form of protectionism. Many of them would opt for what I have called "appropriate governance" from alternative institutions such as the International Labor Organization, UNICEF, UNEP, and other agencies set up for the job.

Opposition to the core-plus agenda needn't be based on where you stand on the new issues, but on whether you think change is possible. It seems highly unlikely that any compromise can be struck any time soon on the new issues—whether or not rich-country activists strut around Seattle in turtle suits. I, for one, am not sorry.

The most practical approach, then, is one in which negotiations advance on two tracks. The first track—the one that actually defines the new round—would stick to what I have labeled the core issues. Then there could be a separate track, where more contentious issues including the dismantling of the abominable "anti-dumping" laws, inescapable conflicts between trade and environmental values and the right to file amicus briefs in trade disputes can continue to be explored without holding the trade round hostage.

With free traders on the defensive, it is easy to lose perspective. The fact is, though, the most solid grounds for agreement on trade liberalization—mutual advantage—still exist. Now as before, the real problem is assembling coalitions with the power to get the job done and the wisdom to compromise in the name of the greater good.

32

Labour Standards and the WTO: The Case for Separate Agendas

Last month, a number of Third World intellectuals and NGOs issued a sharp and pointed statement, drafted principally by me but worked upon by a few others from prominent NGOs in the Third World, arguing against the linkage of labour (and environmental) standards to WTO and to trade treaties. This meant that these signatories were also against the Social Clause being included in the WTO. Besides, their arguments implied clearly that they were for the questions relating to Labour Standards (or Rights) to be transferred wholly to the ILO, with the WTO kept substantively out of these issues. This is exactly what the first WTO Ministerial at Singapore had resolved, despite enormous pressures and threats from the United States: "The International Labour Organization (ILO) is the competent body to set and deal with [labour] standards." The only ambiguous concession, wrung from a generally hostile set of nations opposed to linkage by pretending that it would help close the Singapore meeting without amounting to anything substantive, was a weasel sentence at the end of the resolution about collaboration between the ILO and WTO secretariats.

Now, the United States, under obvious pressure from its labour lobbies, chief among them the AFL-CIO on whom the Clinton-Gore administration closely depends for election support, has escalated the issue to a demand for a Working Group of the WTO, not of the ILO, which would report within two years on these complex issues which simply do not belong to the WTO. And Chancellor Schröder of Germany has also turned around on the matter, shifting the balance of forces within the EU closer to a support of the Social Clause and the U.S. demands. He too is trying to pacify the restive left wing of his party, after the Lafontaine departure and the difficulties in which he

Originally published in *The World Trade Brief*, Agenda Publishing and the WTO, Seattle, Seattle, November 1999. 123–125. Reprinted with permission.

finds his reformist proposals for a German embrace of the so-called Third Way of Tony Blair. But in throwing a bone at the left wing and the unions, Mr. Clinton, Mr. Gore and Mr. Schröder are really throwing a bone down the gullets of the Third World nations and the WTO.

No wonder the developing countries see these shifts on the Labour Standards at the WTO as a breach of good faith. It also gives substance to their fears that the United States in particular cannot be trusted to advance the social good, despite its claims of leadership and altruism, and is simply a prisoner of its special-interest lobbies. It also justifies their fears that, given a foot in the door, it will cynically muscle its way past the door.

So, let me say why the developing countries' intellectuals and NGOs, (indeed several economists in all parts of the world as well), see the injection of Labour Standards into the WTO or other trade treaties and institutions of lesser importance, as both inefficient and dangerous because of its capture by labour groups seeking to moderate the force of international competition in any way they can. Let me also remind the reader that this campaign, and statement (known by its acronym: TWIN-SAL, for Third World Intellectuals and NGOs: Statement Against Linkage), should disabuse the media and the governments in the developed countries of the self-serving notion, widely accepted by the mainstream media in the rich countries because of natural but lazy acceptance of the stories put out by rich-country lobbies and compliant governments, that those who oppose Linkage are corporate interests and malign governments.

At the outset, it is important to understand that the demand for Linkage via a social clause in the WTO (and corresponding preconditions on environmental standards for WTO-protected market access) is a reflection of the growing tendency to impose an essentially trade-unrelated agenda on this institution and on to other trade treaties. It is the result of an alliance between two key groups:

i. Politically powerful lobbying groups that are "protectionist" and want to blunt the international competition from developing countries by raising production costs there and arresting investment flows to them; and

ii. The morally driven human rights and other groups that simply wish to see higher standards abroad and have nothing to do with protectionist agendas.

The former groups are not interested in improving the wellbeing in the developing countries; they are motivated by competitiveness concerns and hence are selfishly protective of their own turf. This is manifest, for example, in the selective nature of the contents of the proposed Social Clause: only issues, such as Child Labour, where the developing countries are expected to be the defendants rather than plaintiffs, are included. Thus, enforcement against domestic sweatshops, which is notoriously minuscule and lax in the United States where they abound in the textiles apparel industry, is not in the Social Clause; nor are the rights of migrant labour which is subject to quasi-slavery conditions in parts of U.S. agriculture.

Nor does the Social Clause look askance at yet other unpleasant social facts in the developed countries. For example, the United States has almost as little as 12 to 14% of its labour force in unions today. As a country that insists on measuring the trade openness of Japan by looking at "results" (i.e., actual imports), the United States ought to be equally willing to treat the absence of unions in an industry as a prima facie presumption that there is some de facto deterrence to union formation. As it happens, unionization in the United States has almost certainly been handicapped, among several factors, by legislation (on matters such as the right to hire replacement workers during a strike) that has impaired unions' chief weapon, the ability to strike.

Nor has any developed-country proponent of the Social Clause proposed that the developed countries ought to take a far greater commitment to labour rights than the developing countries that are at a much lower stage of development. Thus, while unionization must surely be permitted in developing countries, should not the United States require, in the interest of genuine economic democracy, union representation on Boards of Directors the way some European nations do? Ironically, in the United States, one cannot even begin to do this in a meaningful way since unions are absent from most factories in the first place. Thus, in these ways, we see that the moral face of these developed-country lobbies agitating for higher labour and environmental standards in the developing countries, whether they are labour unions or corporate groups, is little more than a mask which hides the true face of protectionism. They stand against the trading and hence the economic interests of the developing countries and are in fact advancing their own economic interests. They need to be exposed as such.

On the other hand, there are also morally driven groups that genuinely wish for better standards for labour and the environment in the Third World; and they must be fulsomely applauded. But their demands for linkage, i.e., the inclusion of provisions for improvements in standards as preconditions for trade access in the WTO and other trade treaties and institutions, while not deceptive and self-serving, are nonetheless mistaken and must also be rejected. Superior ways of advancing these objectives and agendas exist, which lie outside of the trade context and can be pro-actively pursued instead. Thus, consider:

Self-Serving Selectivity: Contaminating the Moral Agenda

If we treat these standards from a moral viewpoint as "social" and "ethical" agendas to be advanced everywhere, we still confront the fact that the agendas will continue to be selected from the viewpoint of trade-competitiveness concerns. Therefore, they will inevitably tend to be selectively biased against the developing countries. They will also protect the developed countries from symmetric scrutiny of their own violations of non-selected social and ethical "human rights" norms that have been incorporated in international agreements such as the United Nations International Covenant on Civil and Political Rights, and the United Nations Covenant on the Child.

This has already happened. What a neutral and universal approach to the use of trade sanctions requires instead is that their use in the case of all significant human rights norms be subjected to an agreement among nation states. Thus, the possibility of juvenile capital punishment in the United States, an egregious violation of the Covenant on the Child that offends the moral sense of nearly all civilised nations today, should equally be a subject for suspension of trade access to U.S. products generally.

If trade proscription against the United States is rejected, as we should all agree, on the ground that it cannot proscribe even the widely condemned possibility of juvenile capital punishment because it is politically extremely difficult to do so, how can the inability of India and Bangladesh to effectively eliminate (even "exploitative") child labour, an immensely more difficult economic and social problem, become a subject for rapid-fire proscription via the Social Clause?

Surely, it makes sense to treat all such lapses from the human rights covenants, by every country, in their total economic, political and social context, and then to advance sophisticated and nuanced public policy programmes that enable sustainable progress to be made on implementing the desired change. Besides, this approach should be symmetrically applied to the problems endemic to the developed countries as much as to those afflicting primarily the developing countries. In short, the human-rights approach must reflect a genuine commitment to the entire slate of important human rights, treating the matter of sanctions impartially and symmetrically sans borders and without favouritism towards the rich and the powerful nations.

It is distressing that one sees no evidence that, except for a few groups such as Amnesty International, this symmetric approach is taken to the issue of trade sanctions. The developing countries, looking at the Social Clause for instance, cannot but regard it as having therefore been contaminated by the selectivity imposed by the rich nations.

And this is not a matter for surprise. For, deep down, this selectivity reflects the competitiveness concerns that inevitably dominate trade negotiations and treaties and institutions: competitiveness is the name of the trade game! You cannot expect anything but hard play if you go to a poker game; to expect the poker players to burst into singing hymns while they drink whisky and utter profanities is to be naïve.

You Cannot Kill Two Birds with One Stone

By thus contaminating and devaluing the moral objectives, even though the subset of groups advancing them have truly a moral rather than a disguised competitiveness objective, we wind up harming both trade liberalisation (which is the true objective of the WTO) and advancement of the social and moral agendas.

Thus, the proponents of trade liberalisation divide over the appropriateness of these agendas: developing countries oppose them and developed countries end up with internal division. In the United States, we have Democrats who want to go after the developing countries on their standards even more vigorously than the Clinton administration and many Republicans who instead oppose Linkage altogether. Not surprisingly, the Clinton administration failed to get fast-track authority for trade liberalisation renewed for the first time in U.S. history last year.

At the same time, the advancement of the social and moral agendas gets held up because it is being pursued (under protectionist pressures) in an evidently cynical and self-servingly selective fashion by the developed countries that push for it, mainly the United States and France (and now Germany). So, we undermine both of these important tasks that progressive intellectuals and NGOs in the Third World would indeed like to see advanced in a nuanced and sustainable fashion. The underlying reason for such an unsatisfactory outcome is that you are trying to kill two birds with one stone. Generally, you cannot. So, trying to implement two objectives, the freeing of trade and the advancing of social and moral agendas, through one policy instrument such as WTO, you will undermine both. You will miss both birds.

Alternative Proposal: Get Another Stone

This leads to the main proposal of the Third World Intellectuals and NGOs. Linkage is like trying to kill two birds with one stone, so we need another stone or a whole slew of sharp pellets. That stone has to be a pro-active set of agendas, at appropriate international agencies such as the ILO, UNICEF and UNEP; moral and financial support for NGOs in the developing countries; and so on. The opponents of this idea argue that the ILO, for instance, lacks teeth. But the teeth fell out because the ILO was sidelined when the United States had pulled out of it. Today, if we are serious, the US and other rich nations can open ILO's mouth and give it a new set of teeth.

The ILO can be asked, like the WTO with its built-in trade reviews under the Trade Policy Review Mechanism (TPRM), to bring out annual Review Reports on member countries' conformity to the ILO conventions; UNICEF could do the same for Children's Covenant; UNEP for Environmental Standards; and so on. Appropriate agencies putting out such impartial reviews would enable numerous NGOs to build their crusades on impartial analyses that are truly symmetric, just the way the WTO has managed with the TPRM. Do not underestimate the value of information and exposure as long as it is impartial between nations. The Dracula Effect—expose evil to sunlight and it will shrivel up and die—can be very potent indeed.

Therefore, it is intellectually compelling to argue that Linkage be buried. It should be replaced by Appropriate Governance at the international level, where each agenda is pursued efficiently in appropriate agencies.

This does not mean that there are no necessary interfaces. This is especially true between UNEP and WTO to address inherently overlapping problems: e.g., the solution to conflicts between trade-sanction provisions in MEAs and WTO obligations, and the "values"-related unilateralism on sanctions that led to the contentious Dolphin-tuna and Shrimp-turtle cases. It is important to remember, at the same time, that these interfaces can be addressed often by imaginative solutions that can be pursued without sacrificing either trade or the environment.

In lieu of the confrontations that have become common now between groups pushing for trade and those pushing for the social agendas, it is time at Seattle that we banish the Linkage issue from the WTO agenda. Instead, we must devote all energies to these "necessary-interface" questions (that inhere on the environmental, not labour, questions) with goodwill and creative solutions.

If the developed countries' governments, intellectuals and NGOs are allowed to do otherwise, the Third World will have to bear the burden. This is evident from what happened to the successful crusade to get In tellectual Property Protection (IPP) into the WTO. This subject does not really belong to the WTO whose organizing principle must be the basic attribute of free trade: that each member benefits since trade liberalisation is a mutual-gain policy. By contrast, the WTO Trade-Related Intellectual Property Rights or TRIPs Agreement, which enshrines IPP into the WTO, essentially redistributes income from the developing to the developed countries. We cannot even claim that the TRIPs Agreement advances the world good: nearly all economists agree, for instance, that the 20-year Patent length, which was built into the TRIPs Agreement, is almost certainly inefficient and exploitative of the vast majority of the developing-country nations. But it got into the WTO, as part of the Uruguay Round agreement, simply because it was backed by developed-country power as reflected in Special 301 retaliations by the United States, and also because of endless repetition in the public arena (despite economic logic to the contrary) that it was good also for the developing countries (an assertion in which the World Bank economics leadership joined, evidently under the shadow of Washington). The intellectual objections of Third World economists, and the negotiating objections of some of their governments, were simply brushed aside.

The same is likely to happen on Linkage unless the Third World unites and is vociferous. This time, however, the NGOs of the developed countries, like the developed-country corporate lobbies under IPP, are unfortunately into the game instead. In fact, they now argue that, having delivered IPP to corporations, the WTO must now give Linkage to Labour and for Nature. So, having been successfully harmed once, the poor nations are to be harmed again for equity among the lobbies of the developed countries. The NGOs pushing for Linkage need to be reminded that IPP was pushed into the WTO, not for corporations everywhere, but for *their* corporations!

It is time to raise our voices from the developing countries and call a spade a spade. The WTO's design must reflect the principle of mutual-gain; it cannot be allowed to become the institution that becomes a prisoner of every developed-country lobby or group that seeks to advance its agenda at the expense of the developing countries. The game of lobbies in the developed countries seeking to advance their own interests through successive enlargement of the issues at the WTO by simply claiming, without any underlying and coherent rationale, that the issue is "trade-related," has gone too far already. It is time for us to say forcefully: Enough is Enough!

33

The World Trade Organization's second ministerial meeting in December promises to be a real happening—the most entertaining thing to hit Seattle since Hollywood sent Meg Ryan there. Militant labor, environmental and other nongovernmental groups, some keen to destroy the WTO and others bent on killing trade and globalization, plan to invade the city. Though by the most generous estimate they represent only a few million people, they hope to wreck a meeting desired by 135 WTO member nations, nearly all with democratically elected governments, representing more than 3 billion of the world's people.

But the threat to the multilateral trade negotiations comes not just from these protesters. There are fundamental problems that divide the governments themselves. Chief among them is the question of including in the new round's agenda an issue with as many fissures as an earthquake-ravaged city: labor standards.

The Clinton-Gore administration's current demand that the Seattle agenda embrace labor issues puts a deep divide between the United States and many developing countries. It creates a gulf between the administration and the many economists who strongly counsel against linking trade and labor issues, particularly at the WTO. And it separates Republicans from Democrats, and even centrist Democrats from ultraliberal Democrats. The administration is calling for the formation of a WTO working group that would report in two years on the relationship between international trade and employment, social protection and so-called "core" labor standards, including child labor. That is a bad-faith violation of the understanding reached at the WTO's first ministerial meeting in Singapore in December 1996.

Originally published in *Newsweek* (Nov. 22, 1999): 37. Reprinted with permission.

The Singapore Declaration clearly stated what numerous economists believe to be the case: "The International Labour Organization is the competent body to set and deal with these standards." The United States did manage to append a weaselly concluding statement saying that "the WTO and ILO Secretariats will continue their existing collaboration." But such collaboration was perfunctory at best; the statement was a small bone for U.S. Ambassador Mickey Kantor to take home and throw to the labor unions. Yeo Cheow Tong, Singapore's minister and chairman of the meeting, was careful to clarify the matter in his concluding speech, saying that the text would *not* lead the WTO to undertake further work on the relationship between trade and core labor standards. And yet here we are, with the United States demanding that the WTO do precisely that!

We should not take at face value the reassuring whispers from Washington that this is just another "talking" exercise, aimed at co-opting the unions. Indeed, the next thing will be the ultimate prize that the unions seek: a social clause that will prevent countries from trading freely if they did not meet tough labor standards.

The social clause is a terrible idea with a single merit: it shows just how counterproductive it is to impose agendas essentially unrelated to trade on the WTO. As proposed by the United States and France (among other countries), the social clause sets "core" labor standards, including the right to unionize, and nonuse of child labor. It is the product of an alliance between two groups: financially flush and politically powerful labor unions, whose motivation is mainly protectionism; and morally driven human-rights and other groups.

For evidence that the unions care mainly about guarding their own turf, consider the selective nature of the proposed social clause. Only issues such as child labor, where the developing countries are expected to be the *defendants* rather than the plaintiffs, are included. So enforcement against domestic sweatshops, for example—which is notoriously minuscule and lax in the United States—would not be included.

To be sure, there are also groups that genuinely wish for better standards for labor everywhere. They must be applauded. But their demands for a social clause at the WTO are nonetheless mistaken, because there are superior ways of advancing their objectives and agendas. By mixing up moral and social issues with trade, we make those important concerns captive to protectionism. You cannot get poker players, drinking whisky and telling bawdy tales, to burst into singing hymns! If we try, we inevitably devalue our moral concerns, and slow down trade liberalization as well.

Why try to kill two birds with one stone, when a second stone is handy? The new, dynamic head of the ILO, Juan Somavia of Chile, is eager to move the cause of labor rights forward—but without resort to trade sanctions. Let all nations seeking to advance progressive agendas take them to appropriate institutions: labor issues to ILO, environmental issues to UNEP, children's issues to UNICEF, and so on. That way lie both "appropriate governance" and more rapid fulfillment of our shared objectives.

34 Did Clinton Take a Dive in Seattle?

Seattle sizzled on Monday and fizzled on Friday. The third ministerial meeting of the World Trade Organization was expected by many to witness the launch of the WTO's first multilateral trade negotiation. But despite upbeat press briefings by U.S. Trade Representative Charlene Barshefsky, who insisted that things would come together in the end, the representatives of 135 nations returned home declaring failure. What went wrong?

Serious and irreconcilable differences among the member countries on the conventional trade agenda may have derailed the talks. Or the administration may have unwittingly been guilty of gross mismanagement.

Then again, perhaps President Clinton willingly sacrificed and scuttled the talks to pursue a short-run political agenda, this so-called "political failure" actually constituting a political triumph for him. I believe that the evidence points much too convincingly to the last hypothesis.

Differences on the trade agenda did kill the launch of an earlier negotiating round in 1982 in Geneva. But the European Union was adamant at the time in refusing to put agriculture and services on the bargaining table. No such deep divisions on narrowly defined yet broadly pertinent trade matters existed at Seattle.

The real problems lay elsewhere, in the city rather than the state of Washington. The administration had literally done nothing to prepare Seattle for the ruckus that erupted. Everyone knew for weeks that disruptive demonstrations were being planned and by whom. On Tuesday, when the formal negotiations were supposed to begin but were held up by mayhem, I saw groups of hooded demonstrators. I asked a young woman why they wore masks, to which she replied truthfully: "We are anarchists."

Originally published in *The Washington Post* (Dec. 7, 1999). Reprinted with permission.

The riot started about an hour later. Where were the plainclothesmen who could have asked what I did—even if they had not read Bakunin, I assume that they would have heard of anarchists—and done what was necessary to cut off the riot at its inception? Why was Seattle left to its own home-grown devices when Washington should have brought its federal expertise into the town?

But if the violent demonstrators were kept out of mind, the administration had done nothing either to engage the peaceful demonstrators from nongovernmental organizations in reasoned dialogue. Attempts to assuage their misguided concerns about globalization, free trade and the WTO should have been made long before Seattle. Recall that the turning point in the equally supercharged NAFTA debate came when Al Gore demolished Ross Perot's ill-informed assertions concerning the perils of NAFTA in a famous television debate.

This time, however, Clinton joined in the anti-globalization frenzy, endlessly repeating the witless sound bite that "globalization needs a human face," implying as its flip side that it lacks one. The great communicator was on the wrong side. Indeed, the overwhelming scholarly evidence on the effects of freer trade and direct foreign investment is favorable, if only he would look at it.

Evidently, Clinton could not alienate his labor constituency in this election season. Indeed, he was unwilling to lend his efforts to launching a round at Seattle until a few months ago.

Then came the U.S.-China accord, cynically timed just two weeks before Seattle. If there is any country that arouses ire among the anti-globalization groups, it is China. So Clinton was waving the red flag—pun intended—before the raging NGO bulls, making Seattle's success ever more problematic. Why wasn't the accord with China announced *after* Seattle instead?

Finally, just as the poor countries were properly objecting to the setting up of a Working Party on "labor rights"—defined in a cynically protectionist fashion so as to target the poor countries exclusively—and were seeking to shift the question to an appropriate agency such as the International Labor Organization, Clinton arrived and said that he wanted trade sanctions against the poor countries on the issue. That blew it.

So, Clinton emerges having won the minds and cash of the business community with his China deal, and having won the hearts and cash of the unions with his destructive grandstanding at Seattle on labor rights. Not bad for the Democratic Party. The WTO and freer trade are another matter.

Was the debacle in Seattle the triumph of non-governmental organisations over free traders? Is it the dawn of a new era of "people
over profits"? Many Americans believe this. They could not be more
mistaken.

Poor countries drew an altogether different lesson from the World
Trade Organisation meeting in Seattle: that, unless their governments,
their intellectuals and their NGOs stand together, the WTO will be
hijacked by the NGOs and lobby groups of rich countries.

Even as the negotiating governments were reaching accommodation
on a conventional agenda of trade liberalisation, poor countries drew a
line in the sand and scuttled the trade round over the insistence of the
US on including a working party on labour standards in the WTO.
True, many developing countries had indicated strong opposition to
the U.S. proposal before they arrived. But why did they refuse to yield
a little for the larger cause of a new trade round?

Poor countries were startled by the spectacle in Seattle. Not just
in the streets but also in the debates held by peaceful NGOs. It was
clear to them that the anti-globalisation and anti-WTO crusade had
been captured by groups whose mindset was to take aim at the poor
countries.

Consider just two of the widely reported symbols of the NGO
protests.

First, the Associated Press photograph of a young boy, perhaps ten
years old, carrying a placard saying: "Tell the WTO No Child Labour—
would you want your child working to death?" Aside from the irony
that the child was made to carry the poster instead of attending school,

An abbreviated version of this chapter appeared, under the title "An Unjustified Sense
of Victory," in the *Financial Times* (Dec. 21, 1999). Reprinted with permission.

one could retort that the correct message should have been: "Would you want your child starving to death?"

Starvation is what children would face if poor parents were simply proscribed from sending children to add to the family income. As Clare Short, Britain's minister for international development, noted at the WTO-sponsored NGO symposium: child labour is a "development, not a trade, problem."

The inclusion of the issue of child labour on the WTO agenda would do nothing to solve a complex and long-term problem. Rather, it is a calculated move to shelter America's labour-intensive industries from competition from poor countries. It is protectionism hiding behind moral rhetoric.

Second, take the demonstrators marching outside the Seattle meetings in seaturtle costumes and denouncing the WTO as anti-Earth. The costumes were a reference to a long-running turtle-shrimp controversy. In October 1998, the WTO upheld the US approach to protecting turtles against four Asian plaintiffs, which had objected to being forced to employ Turtle Excluding Devices (TEDs) when fishing for shrimp.

However, in the same ruling, the WTO objected to the selective and discriminatory way in which U.S. legislation was designed. In particular, the United States had given only four months' notice to India and the other plaintiffs to adopt US legislation on use of Teds. The US had also unreasonably suspended all shrimp exports from India even though farmed (rather than sea-harvested) shrimp were the bulk of Indian exports.

To India, it was apparent that the ethnocentric NGOs, active agitators on the U.S. side, were displaying arrogance and disdain for poor nations—a fact that was all too obvious in Seattle.

It is therefore understandable that developing country representatives, even before they arrived, were alarmed at how the developed world was trying to distort the WTO agenda. The protests there only gave a sharper edge and clarity to developing world concerns.

After all, poor countries had already been bamboozled at the Uruguay round in 1993 into accepting intellectual property protection in the WTO even though it was clearly not a trade issue and despite it obviously being a dagger aimed at the poor countries. This time, it is labour issues that are being used in the same fashion—a bone thrown to labour unions in the rich countries and down the gullets of the poor countries.

Figure 35.1
Among the ironies at the demonstrations at the WTO meeting in Seattle was this child, taken away from school on a Tuesday, marching to condemn child labor. The child had no way to understand that poverty drives much of child labor in the poor countries, that child labor is a developmental and not a trade problem, and that he was likely a pawn in the insidious game of rich-country protectionism. AP Photo/Itsu Inouye. Reprinted with permission of the Associated Press.

The last straw was when President Bill Clinton—seeking the labour vote in an election year—announced that the U.S. objective was to set up trade sanctions against poor nations if they did not respect labour rights. Predictably, the poor nations responded by walking away from the launch of a new trade negotiating round.

The NGOs would like to believe that their "unified" movement must be credited with this "success" in preventing a new trade round, and that they have now emerged as a significant anti-WTO force.

How untrue. Instead, by taking over an anti-poor nations agenda of issues unrelated to trade, rich-country NGOs have stimulated the developing world into mobilising its own NGOs and intellectuals into defending against a WTO takeover by rich countries.

VI

Investment and Immigration

Owen Fiss makes my day. For some years now, in a series of essays, book reviews, and op-ed articles,[1] I have argued for an immigration policy that would shift enforcement to the border while effectively reducing, or at least freezing, the current level of internal enforcement aimed at punishing employers of illegals (via employer sanctions) and the illegals themselves (via ID cards, INS raids with a view to detection, detention, and deportation, et al.). A bipartisan consensus, however, has moved increasingly in the opposite direction—by zeroing in on the illegals already in our midst, not just through punishments but even (for many) by denial of access to social benefits assured to all Americans. Despite this trajectory, I remained optimistic that I would not be lonely for too long. Frankly, however, I had expected fellow economists and political scientists to move in my direction. Instead, Fiss brings constitutional law to bear on the issue, lending me a wholly unforeseen and entirely welcome ally.

Two Policy Objectives

Enlightened Americans broadly share two principal objectives in their conception of an appropriate policy towards illegal immigration: to reduce the illegal inflow; and to treat people who are here, whether native or naturalized or alien, with the basic decency that each of us owes to others within the community. This fundamental good sense defines our obligations as much as their rights.

The first objective is typical of nearly all societies: borders are commonly defined to exclude and borders out of control simply do not sit

Originally published in *The Boston Review* 25, no. 5 (October/November 1998): 21–22. Reprinted with permission.

well with the body politic. But the second objective is, at least in intensity, uniquely American. Other modern societies also exhibit elements of it, but rarely with our passion and consistency.

The explanation lies in our history: the absence of an identity defined by shared memories that define "us" against "others," and a history of immigration that leads the culture to pride itself on ensuring chances for each and all. Our sensibility is offended at its core when we contemplate that any group, any individual, is denied fair access to the opportunities that our country offers.[2] The notion that we can thus live alongside an underclass of humanity, denied access to social benefits and economic betterment simply because its members are illegal aliens, violates our fundamental sense of decency and morality.[3]

A False Start

Our legislators have typically tried to achieve these twin objectives by eliminating illegals who are already here: the first objective having been fully achieved, the second followed as well since you could not ill-treat illegals if there were none. To that end, efforts have been made since the 1986 legislation to reduce the stock of illegals through an amnesty program, and to reduce the flow of illegals through employer sanctions that would eliminate the magnet of employment opportunity.

Predictably, amnesty left many still in illegal status. More important, employer sanctions could not reduce the flow. Even in Germany and Switzerland, government analyses had warned, such sanctions face serious enforcement problems since few judges would impose the necessary penalties against employers whose only sin was hiring (as against ill-treating and exploiting) the illegals. Our strong civil liberties traditions and groups raised the enforcement hurdle even higher. Besides, the difference in prospects at home and in the United States are so vast that employer sanctions could not seriously reduce incentives to attempt illegal entry.

In effect, then, the illegals continued in our midst, with little change in the attempted entries: the first objective was hardly advanced. At the same time, INS harassment increased with the enhanced domestic enforcement, pushing yet more of the illegals into the underclass. So, the second objective was even set back. The 1986 consensus on policy had been plainly wrong.[4]

Current Follies

The answer therefore must be to turn the policy on its head. Try to control immigration at the border. To be sure, this strategy will not work too well since more than half the illegals are now estimated to come across in difficult-to-monitor ways other than crossing the Rio Grande. But such enforcement will produce the satisfaction, at low cost, that "we are trying to control the influx." As to the illegals who are in: leave them alone, more rather than less. And treat them like us, enjoying our social and economic rights.

But instead, we have again worked ourselves up into a frenzy, seeking ever more domestic enforcement. In addition to employer sanctions, there have also been increasing demands to deny the illegals (even legals at times) access to social benefits in the tired and false expectation that these policies will significantly reduce the incentive for attempted entries. So, we see the prospect of more domestic enforcement that will do little to reduce illegal inflows and much to drive the illegals into an underclass that degrades them and offends our moral sensibilities, while also violating the constitution, according to Fiss's analysis.

Pete Wilson Meets "Harvard Square"

Two recent developments have hastened this movement to the brink. First, whether Pete Wilson was also motivated by his own animus against illegals and/or a low-politics pandering to his constituents' animus, there is no question that California had fiscal problems, analogous to those in Texas and Florida. While illegal immigrants create a net (if mild) fiscal surplus, immigration studies reveal a distributional problem: the federal government gains net revenue, and the states lose it. This fiscal problem for states results in part from the educational expenditures which were in contention in *Plyler v. Doe* (see Fiss's article for analysis of this case). Efforts by state legislatures to exclude illegals from social benefits might, then, be viewed as a political strategy aimed at generating federal assistance for these states. Because immigration policy is a federal matter, I should think the federal government does have constitutional responsibilities in this area. But let me leave it at that.

Far more worrisome is the unfortunate intellectual role played by economists and sociologists. Two of their arguments have helped turn the illegal immigration "phenomenon" into a "problem": (a) because illegals are typically undereducated and unskilled they have been a contributory factor in the decline in real wages of our own unskilled since the 1980s; and (b) inner-city problems have been accentuated by immigrants who have taken jobs that would otherwise have gone to natives. As it happens, many of these social scientists are located currently in Cambridge and can be aptly described as the "Harvard Square" school of naysayers. Among the economists is George Borjas of Harvard's John F. Kennedy School of Government, who drew media attention as Pete Wilson's adviser.[5] Among the sociologists are Orlando Patterson and Kathleen Newman, now at the Kennedy School. Patterson has drawn on Borjas's economics to urge President Clinton to take on illegals more strenuously. Newman's remarkable work on the inner-city problems has correctly emphasized the importance of economic opportunity for blacks, but is unfortunately often interpreted as implying a substitutional relationship between blacks and unskilled immigrants.

I have no space to say why these arguments are unconvincing: Francisco Rivera-Batiz and I are just finishing a book entitled *In the Eye of the Storm: Targeting Illegal Aliens*, where we refute these alarming contentions, both conceptually and empirically.

But I may add that many of these intellectuals have been led to the *non sequitur* that we must encourage skilled immigrants at the expense of the unskilled ones. This proposal is not merely economically indefensible (since it is impossible to make a convincing case that the skilled immigrants will produce greater benefits for us) but also violates our deepest moral sense. Suppose we had only one place for an immigrant, and could give it to a rich doctor from India or an impoverished peasant from Haiti. Suppose you are to vote entirely on the basis of whom you wish to assist and not a whit on which immigrant will do *you* good. Which would you choose? I have little doubt that the average American would choose the impoverished peasant. The Statue of Liberty does capture that essential truth about us; and it is that truth which is obscured by focus in the scholarly debate on what is materially good for us and by the unconvincing economics often deployed to support alarmist views.

Notes

1. Several of these have been reprinted in my latest book, *A Stream of Windows: Reflections on Trade, Immigration and Democracy* (Cambridge, Mass: MIT Press, 1998); see especially chaps. 31–34 and 39.

2. Yes, there are serious lapses, especially in regard to blacks. But here too, the strength of the civil rights movements, and our ability to make steady if inadequate progress towards equality of access for the black community, are reflections of what I argue in the text. So is the fact that, when seized by panic over the rise of Japan in world trade, the Europeans simply erected significant barriers against them without any *angst* whatsoever whereas we had to go through a song and dance about how "unfair" the Japanese were in trade, thus first convincing ourselves that if we were to strike the Japanese with trade sanctions and barriers, it was a 'fair' move on our part! On the Japan question, and how we handled it as described, see again *A Stream of Windows*, esp. chaps. 14–16 and 18–21.

3. This sentiment surfaces in a much weaker sense in other civilized societies, simply because it is difficult to come down hard on hapless humanity. I have often cited a telling quote from the Swiss novelist Max Frisch who, on observing how West Europeans found it extremely difficult to send home the *gastarbeiteren* (guestworkers) even though they had been brought in on the explicit understanding that they could be sent back, remarked: "we imported workers and got men instead."

4. This is just what I had anticipated; see my *Wall Street Journal* article of February 1, 1985, reprinted as chapter 33 in *A Stream of Windows*.

5. Where Borjas has been arguing that the unskilled immigration has harmed our workers' wages, Dani Rodrik of the Kennedy School has endorsed the fraternal claim that trade with poor countries has harmed our workers in his 1997 pamphlet, *Has Globalization Gone Too Far?* I have challenged both assertions in my own recent research.

Why Borjas Fails to Persuade

I should say at the outset that, much as I have found his empirical research on immigration into the United States to be a most useful and valuable addition to the many important contributions made over the years by U.S. immigration experts such as the late Julian Simon and the pioneering researcher, Barry Chiswick, I intend to express in a friendly and scholarly way my almost total disagreement with Borjas's analysis of the impact of immigration and, even more, with his views on immigration policy. I believe that my differences derive from several reasons, as follows:

1. I started thinking and writing about immigration questions a quarter of a century ago and in the context of *general equilibrium* models that we trade theorists typically use[1] whereas Borjas got into the subject much later and from familiarity with the labor economist's typical use of *partial equilibrium* tools instead.

2. The theorists and empiricists of immigration in the last quarter of a century considered a range of theoretical and policy issues (e.g., the conceptual question of how to define the social welfare function for a country in the presence of migration,[2] the question of optimal income tax policy in the presence of international personal mobility,[3] or the differentiated modeling of migration depending on the kinds of skills involved[4]) which are missing from, and hence handicap, Borjas's analysis[5];

3. A sensible discussion of immigration policy requires in my view that the economic analysis both reflect, and be situated squarely within the context of, ethical and sociological analysis whereas Borjas typi-

Originally published in *Social Dimensions of U.S. Trade Policy*, ed. Alan Deardorff and Robert Stern (Ann Arbor: University of Michigan Press, 2000), 87–94.

cally ignores these aspects and hence is handicapped by his narrow focus.

4. Like the late Julian Simon, I am strongly biased in favor of a relaxed view of immigration whereas Borjas inclines, I believe, towards a more cautious and skeptical, if not hostile, view of the matter.

5. I find both morally unacceptable, and economically unconvincing, his view that we ought to favor skilled over unskilled immigrants.

Whose Welfare?

Let me begin with Borjas's definition of how we must evaluate the effects of migrants on U.S. welfare. Borjas, unlike in his earlier writings, now distinguishes clearly, as we learned to do in the 1960s,[6] between the welfare of the "migrants" and that of those already here (whether native-born or naturalized or legal and illegal aliens), namely, "us." That is all to the good.

But he is wrong to argue that we in the United States must be concerned only with the economic effect on us. This is sociologically and ethically an untenable viewpoint. As I have long argued, whether one treats migrants' welfare as part of "U.S. welfare" depends on the nature of the migration and also on the moral nature of our society. With permanent immigrants, it is likely that we will view their welfare as part of U.S. welfare: after all, the immigrants are joining our society. On the other hand, it is perfectly possible that, especially with the temporary and the "yo-yo" migrants who move back and forth, as with the guestworkers programs of Western Europe, some societies may not think so (though, even here, recall the solidarity expressed by some German labor unions with the guestworkers, the *gastarbeiters*, in their famous slogan: *ihr kampf ist unser kampf*).[7] With illegal immigrants, the willingness to consider the welfare of immigrants as part of social welfare may be even more tenuous (though I plan to explore that too below). Equally, it is possible, in an analysis that embraces both the sending and the receiving countries, that the migrants' welfare will be considered part of neither country or as part of both countries' welfare.

Borjas therefore is wrong to think that the only plausible view to take is for our national economic welfare function to be defined purely on us and this, in turn, to be evaluated in terms of available goods and services as affected by the inflow of the immigrants. He considers that this is how Americans view immigration politically. I do not think so at all.

Thus, I believe that Americans, whose society has been uniquely formed by immigration, do have morally informed views on *both* which kinds of immigrants they would favor (thus implicitly indulging in interpersonal comparisons) *and* how immigrants must be treated, whether legal or illegal, once they are in their midst.[8] And, on both counts, *disregarding wholly the altogether separate question of how different immigrants will affect "our" economic welfare*, American are typically likely, even today, to show both decency and good moral sense.

Take the question of which kind of immigrants we would favor. Conduct a mental experiment. Assume that we have one immigrant visa to offer and there are two applicants: a skilled and well-heeled doctor and an unskilled and impoverished peasant. Banish all thoughts as to which of the two will add more to our economic welfare: it might help to think of either being settled sight unseen on a remote "paradise island" and being out of our lives before and after our choice. Whom would we then choose for the largesse? I have little doubt that most Americans would take in the peasant. *That* is what the Statue of Liberty is all about: taking in those whose needs are the greatest. In virtually ignoring this essence of American moral sensibility, Borjas unwittingly reduces the Statue of Liberty, with her outstretched hand holding the torch of liberty, to a monument instead to New York's subway rider with her raised hand holding on to the overhead strap as the train lurches along the labyrinthine tracks.

Nor does Borjas's focus on considering only *our* economic welfare come to grips with what I take to be the dominant American moral sense when he fails to consider also the immigrants' welfare once they are in our midst. In deciding how we should deter illegal immigration, for example, Borjas's focus would make us gladly put up with one or all of measures such as employer sanctions, the use of ID cards, deprivation of schooling for children[9] et al. which are likely, almost certain, to propel the illegals in our midst towards an underclass status without access to many of the economic and social "goods" enjoyed by the rest of us. In doing so, he and others so inclined discount the fact that, as I have argued recently in the *Boston Review*:[10]

The explanation [of the American sense that we should "treat people who are here, whether native or naturalized or alien, with the basic decency that each of us owes to others"] lies in our history: the absence of an identity defined by shared memories that define "us" against "others", and a history of immigration that leads the culture to pride itself on ensuring chances for each and all. Our sensibility is offended at its core when we contemplate that any group, any individual, is denied fair access to the opportunities that our country offers. The notion that we can thus live alongside an underclass of humanity, denied access to social benefits and economic betterment simply because its members are illegal aliens, violates our fundamental sense of decency and morality.

I would even add that, in this regard, I have been struck particularly by a possible parallel between the way we wish to treat equally well all in our midst, and the absence in our culture of the Cinderella complex, the differentially advantaged treatment of one's natural over that of one's adopted or acquired children. I hazard the view, based on my casual observation of other cultures, that there is no particular opprobrium there in discriminating in favor of one's natural children, whereas in our culture, this is simply beyond the pale: all children, once in one's fold, are the same.

Economic Effects on Us

Having therefore rejected as indefensible for U.S. immigration policy analysis the exclusive Borjas concern with "our" economic welfare, let me now accept this focus and still disagree with his analysis and conclusions. There are three main issues I wish to comment on.

1. *Aggregate Income versus Income Distribution:* Borjas seems to accept that immigration will improve our welfare, in the aggregate.[11]

The problem is that, despite Borjas's conviction that unskilled immigration, which has to be largely illegal immigration (which is almost exclusively of the unskilled) but also includes some who come in on the refugee entries and others admitted under the familial programs, affects the real wages of our unskilled workers adversely, I would maintain that this case is hardly proven. The original Mariel boatlift study of David Card had first indicated that the effect of the influx of roughly 100,000 Cubans into Miami had left the average wages unchanged. What had happened then to "diminishing returns"? There were two answers to this puzzle once the partial-equilibrium habit of mind was abandoned. First, the normal influx of other migrants into Miami and the efflux of Miami residents elsewhere could have adjusted to the Cuban inflow and offset it. Second, the Cuban inflow may well have left Miami within the Chipman-McKenzie diversification cone, killing the diminishing returns as we well know from general-

Table 37.1
Comparative educational distributions of outmigrants and Mexican immigrants, 1990, California, Texas, and New York (persons 25 years of age or older)

Educational distribution	Native outmigrants 1985–90 (%)	Mexican immigrants 1980–90 (%)
California		
Less than high school	14.6	71.0
High school diploma	26.7	12.5
Some college	34.9	11.7
College or more	23.8	4.8
Texas		
Less than high school	16.0	69.5
High school diploma	27.8	12.8
Some college	30.6	12.1
College or more	25.6	5.6
New York		
Less than high school	13.2	46.2
High school diploma	22.3	26.6
Some college	30.9	20.8
College or more	33.6	6.4

Source: Data from U.S. Department of Commerce, 1990 U.S. Census of Population and Housing. Francisco Rivera-Batiz, "Migration and the Labour Market: Sectoral and Regional Effects," paper presented at the OECD Seminar on Migration, Free Trade and Regional Integration in North America, Mexico City, January 15–16, 1998.

equilibrium analysis (explained simply in chapter 38 as the "output-mix" effect). By now, the labor economists understand these possibilities but wrongly discount them.

Thus, Borjas claims that the local effects in the states such as Florida, to which the unskilled and often illegal immigrants go, are masked by the net outflow of previous residents from these states, with the implication that the "problem" of adverse effect on wages is simply exported elsewhere, thus presumably is likely to surface there. But Rivera-Batiz (1998) has produced reliable refutation of Borjas's argument, which is based on shaky evidence from a sociological study. Breaking down the outflow by skills, it can be seen in table 37.1 that the states receiving the unskilled immigrants have largely experienced outflows of skilled residents. In itself, therefore, the failure to show serious adverse impact in the states of immigration on wages from the unskilled immigration cannot be explained away in the fashion Borjas seems to favor.

But Rivera-Batiz's calculations suggest strongly that the diversification-cone argument may be the overriding reason why we have not observed the enduring and adverse impact anywhere on the wages of the unskilled here. It is obvious that the different labor markets around the country are connected, so that the diversification cone needs to be defined on more-than-local endowments. If it is defined over national endowments, and we reckon with the fact that capital accumulates at a rate more or less commensurate with the growth of the labor force (inclusive of all immigration) and of the unskilled labor force by itself as well, all at the national level, it becomes harder to expect that the immigration we have observed to date can be a source of any noticeable adverse effect on the wages of the unskilled. If so, the Borjas concerns about income distribution are simply exaggerated, at best, and ill-founded, at worst. In either case, we ought to dismiss them from the public discourse.

2. *Revenue Distribution:* The income distributional implications can arise also in a different sense which is fairly important, however. I believe that while there is some persisting disagreement whether immigration, on balance, leads to a drain on public revenues, the arguments going back well over a decade and raising a number of conceptual and measurement differences, there is general agreement that the center tends to gain net revenues and the states of (immediate) immigration tend to lose them.

The problem then is that, even if the former gain dominates the latter loss, if nothing is done to compensate the losers, then the Governors of those states will have a huge political incentive to seek transfers by way of "compensation". Failing that, they will try to turn immigration, and the "drain on their exchequers" into a political issue. The competition for schools and health services will become an issue. In fact, I would venture to say that Texas earlier, and California Governor Pete Wilson later, may well have chosen to opt for truly offensive proposals to deny schooling to children of illegal immigrants as a strategic political ploy to bring the entire issue to center stage, rather than because they genuinely believed that this ought to be our policy. What this points to, of course, is that the federal responsibility for revenue transfers must match the federal immigration policy: the states should not be left in the lurch.

3. *Skilled versus Unskilled Immigration:* Let me conclude with the Borjas preference for skilled migration. I have already said why it offends our moral sense about what types of immigrants we ought to prefer. But I

am presently addressing the separate issue: which type of immigrant is *better for us*.

Here, if we assume that migrants earn the value of their marginal product, there is little impact on the rest of us, one way or the other. So, the answer must be: we ought to be indifferent among different levels of skills, on economic grounds. But that is where you get into the question of (uncompensated) externalities. Are these externalities to us greater from the skilled? As skilled members of the elite, we are naturally disposed to vote for that proposition! But frankly, how do we know? I can readily imagine all sorts of externalities of importance from letting in a Haitian maid, or having her come in illegally, enabling women to go into the workforce in New York and yielding the social value of increased facilitation of female participation in the workforce. Again, unskilled immigrants who create economic opportunity for themselves in inner cities in all sorts of ways may well have a demonstration value for blacks who may otherwise take too seriously the notion, not entirely wrong of course, that the inner cities "lack economic opportunities." This demonstration value itself is an externality, lifting enlightened black leaders from defeatism into hope and action. One could go on.

In fact, the whole problem with externalities is that, as we have known from the industrial policy debates, they are the first refuge of the scoundrels. What I find ironic is that Borjas, who I suspect is suspicious of arguments based on externalities on industrial policy issues, appears only too happy to assert them when it comes to favoring the skilled migrants! I believe therefore that the growing fetish for the skilled immigrants is just that, and we need to look at it straight in the face for the morally unacceptable, and economically unjustified, prescription for changing our immigration policy that it is.

Notes

1. There were important contributions in this literature by Harry Johnson, Herbert Grubel, Tony Scott et al. For a synthesis and review of that literature, see Bhagwati and Rodriguez (1976).

2. I take up this question immediately below.

3. There is thus a huge literature in public finance on this question. See, for example, Bhagwati and Wilson (1989), Bhagwati (1991), Wilson (1982a;b), and Mirrlees (1982).

4. Several theoretical models of professional migration and its consequences were developed by Koichi Hamada, myself and others in Bhagwati and Partington (1976), for instance.

5. It is perhaps indicative that Borjas's references are almost entirely to himself (a failing that I share) and a narrow set of his associates, suggesting disregard of not merely the earlier literature by Johnson, Grubel-Scott, Berry, myself, Hamada, Mirrlees and many others, but also of recent literature by Barry Chiswick, Harriet Orcutt, Kar-yiu Wong and many others.

6. Again, the first to draw this important distinction was Harry Johnson. It then became standard in the formal discussions of the so-called 'brain drain' that stimulated much of the theoretical and policy writings in the 1960s and 1970s.

7. Translated, the slogan means: Their battle is our battle.

8. Of course, Americans differ in what they think we owe to legal as distinct from illegal immigrants. Some, like me and Owen Fiss, the constitutional lawyer at Yale, would treat both pretty much the way we treat ourselves; but others would treat illegals less favorably. See chapter 36.

9. Borjas himself does not approve of the deprivation of education for children. But he approves of nearly everything else, as far as one can tell from his public writings. E.g. see his *New York Times* op-ed article, "Punish Employers, Not Children," July 11, 1996.

10. See chapter 36.

11. I find it difficult to see, however, why he is unwilling to put a figure on this gain, considering he shows no shyness in turning out estimates that require even more heroic empirical assumptions. Such empirical estimates would help define the empirical trade-off between the income gain and the distributional problems that Borjas believes, but which I shall argue below to be implausible, to be the outcomes of current unskilled immigration, and hence also enable us to consider more meaningfully whether "compensation" to the damaged parties could be financed from the gains that the immigration brings.

References

Bhagwati, Jagdish. 1991. "International Migration and Income Taxation." In Douglas Irwin (ed.), J. Bhagwati, *Political Economy and International Economics*. Cambridge: MIT Press.

Bhagwati, Jagdish. 1998. "Getting Policy Wrong." *Boston Review* 23: 21–22.

Bhagwati, Jagdish, and Martin Partington (eds.). 1976. *Taxing the Brain Drain: A Proposal.* Amsterdam: North-Holland Publishing Company.

Bhagwati, Jagdish, and Carlos Rodriguez. 1976. "Welfare-Theoretical Analyses of the Brain Drain." In J. Bhagwati (ed.), *The Brain Drain and Taxation: Theory and Empirical Analysis.* Amsterdam: North-Holland Publishing Company.

Bhagwati, Jagdish, and John Wilson (ed.). 1989. *Income Taxation and International Mobility.* Cambridge: MIT Press.

Borjas, George. 1996. "Punish Employers, not Children." *New York Times*, July 11.

Borjas, George. "Economic Research and the Debate over Immigration Policy." In A. Deardorff and R. Stern (eds.), *Social Dimensions of U.S. Trade Policy*. Ann Arbor: University of Michigan Press.

Grubel, Herbert, and Anthony Scott. 1966. "The International Flow of Human Capital." *American Economic Review* (May).

Hamada, Koichi, and Jagdish Bhagwati. 1976. "Domestic Distortions, Imperfect Information and the Brain Drain." In Bhagwati and Partington 1976.

Johnson, Harry. 1965. "The Economics of the 'Brain Drain': The Canadian Case." *Minerva*.

Johnson, Harry. 1967. "Some Economic Aspects of Brain Drain." *Pakistan Development Review* 3.

Mirrlees, James. 1982. "Migration and Optimal Taxes." *Journal of Public Economics* 18: 319–42.

Wilson, John. 1982a. "Optimal Linear Income Taxation in the Presence of Emigration," *Journal of Public Economics* 18: 363–80.

Wilson, John. 1982b. "Optimal Income Taxation and Migration: A World Welfare Point of View." *Journal of Public Economics* 18: 381–98.

38

A Close Look at the Newest Newcomers: Immigration Debate Takes Skill

The United States, George Borjas observes, is "heaven's door," through which much of the world's humanity wishes to pass. Mr. Borjas would like to man that door, waving through the most virtuous petitioners and, no less important to him, minding heaven's capacity at the same time.

But frankly, he lacks the qualifications for the job. For one thing, he does not appreciate fully one characteristic of American exceptionalism: that we are a nation of immigrants. However shopworn the phrase may be, it is also a defining principle of American identity. Even when we are inclined to surrender in times of distress to mean impulses, moving to close "heaven's door" or to serve our own economic ends in narrow (and often counterproductive) ways, Americans never seem to lose their innate empathy for the immigrants who seek to join them.

No less important, Mr. Borjas advances economic arguments that are critically flawed—on current evidence—making his qualifications as a gatekeeper even more dubious.

Mr. Borjas's principal thesis is this: Thanks to the 1965 Immigration Act, which shifted the national origins of legal immigrants toward poor countries, we have been attracting immigrants who are increasingly unskilled. Through wage reductions, this new population is producing a massive shift in income distribution away from unskilled native workers.

What is more, the assimilation rate of these new poor-country immigrants—and hence the rate of improvement in their incomes—is slower than that of earlier immigrants, adding to ghettoization and ethnic friction. National interest thus requires that we undo the damage of the 1965 Act and turn to a point system, like Canada's, which would give people more qualifying points for entry if they are skilled.

Luckily, Mr. Borjas's alarmist analysis, presented at length in *Heaven's Door*, is less than persuasive. Take the crucial question of skills. In earlier writings, Mr. Borjas had virtually asserted that the absolute skill levels of legal immigrants had declined since the 1965 act; he was promptly refuted, convincingly in my view, by the late Julian Simon, who showed, in a co-authored paper, that the immigrant education levels at entry had in fact risen from the 1960s through the early 1990s.

Now Mr. Borjas has retreated to arguing for only a *relative* decline in the skills of immigrants—relative, that is, to the skills of native workers. Here, a devastating blow has just been dealt by three well-known immigration experts: Guillermina Jasso, Mark Rosenzweig and James Smith. They have used INS (instead of Census) data to show that the absolute skill levels of immigrants have exceeded those of natives for much of the period 1972–95 and that the relative skill levels of immigrants have also risen since the mid-1980s.

Mr. Borjas's larger economic claim, that immigration drives down wages, does not survive scrutiny either, Most reputable labor economists, in fact, have long puzzled over the *minuscule* effect on wages of even large-scale immigration (if there is any effect at all, which is debatable). We now have an explanation.

Added workers can be absorbed in two ways. Either wages decline so that every cost-conscious producer increases the labor-intensity of production, substituting labor for capital and adding workers. Or, in an optimistic scenario, extra workers are absorbed without such a substitution. Economists call this scenario the "output-mix effect." Insofar as it operates, wage decline is avoided or, at the very least, moderated. As it happens, the economists Gordon Hanson and Matthew Slaughter have recently demonstrated that significant output-mix changes, favoring labor-using activities, have been associated with increased immigration. Thus wages are not driven down as Mr. Borjas suggests.

Mr. Borjas's assertions about ethnic ghettos, in another part of "Heaven's Door," seem compelling until one notices that his view is terribly static. It was perhaps inevitable that, as the American population diversified to include more non-English-speaking non-Europeans, new immigrants would turn to one another more than previous immigrant generations had. But this "ghettoization" has also been encouraged by the ideology of liberal multiculturalism, which has produced (along with some positive effects on the core college curriculum) misguided programs, like bilingual education.

Already, though, a counter-response is evident. Last year, Hispanic parents in California overwhelmingly supported Proposition 227, which brought bilingual education in that state to an end. As Hispanics grow in numbers, and become politically more active, their perceptions of American possibilities will sharpen, increasing their resolve to join the mainstream. In short, economically motivated assimilation will reassert itself.

Not surprisingly, Mr. Borjas, who teaches at Harvard's Kennedy School, has become a kind of beacon to anti-immigrationists, especially in certain precincts of the Republican Party. Alas, since he plays the "our-poor-get-hurt" tune, he has now begun to seduce liberal Democrats as well. This is a pity. If we are to revise our legal immigration policies yet again, it is important that the charges leveled at them are based on robust empirical arguments. Mr. Borjas's claims, I'm afraid, do not meet that test.

Response to Borjas's Letter to *The Wall Street Journal*

In regard to George J. Borjas's Sept. 30 Letter to the Editor in response to my review of his book "Heaven's Door" (Leisure & Arts, Sept. 28): He is naturally upset that, for pro-immigrationists, I have driven a stake through his heart, and for anti-immigrationists, I have nailed him to the cross. Either way, he would like to rise again. But he cannot, at least on the basis of his disingenuous and shopworn "you do not know the facts" response.

That he had "virtually implied" that the absolute skill levels of immigrants had declined is amply documented, with many quotes from Mr. Borjas himself, by Julian Simon and Ather Akbari in their joint paper that I cited. Take Mr. Borjas's words and let your readers judge for themselves his assertion that he never "made [the] claim" that the absolute skill level of immigrants had declined: "In short, the new immigrants are less skilled than the old"; "more recent immigrants admitted into the country are relatively less skilled than earlier waves"; and a few more, should these not be enough.

As for Proposition 227, Mr. Borjas quibbles. At the end, the widely reported overwhelming Hispanic support was reduced, as a result of the $3 million advertising blitzkrieg by the Spanish language television network, Univision. But the estimated supporting vote was still as large as two out of five, simply confirming my view that Mr. Borgas takes too static a view of the assimilationist process among these groups. If I had even a minuscule fraction of the space in my review as Mr. Borjas had in his book, I would have been happy to note these well-known details.

His judgments on the important studies that I cited as being at variance with his assertions (on which he critically bases his case for reopening the legal-immigration debate) are simply wrong. The Hanson-Slaughter studies extend even to Israel, where substantial output-mix effects (which can explain the lack of significant adverse effect on wages) were observed under very large post-Soviet-breakup immigrant influx. And their reservations about drawing conclusions at the aggregate U.S. level from their cross-regional analysis, despite the strong documentation of output-mix effects, relate primarily to an excessively scrupulous concern for the extremely remote technical possibility that relative prices of goods might change as a result of immigration as well.

As for his strictures on the Jasso-Rosenzweig-Smith study, Mr. Borjas cites the well-known problems with INS data, but forgets to note the problems with the Census data he himself relies on. He also omits the key point that the great virtue of the INS data is that they enable the analyst to link (as one must for a persuasive analysis of the effects of the legal immigration regime that is sought to be evaluated) the immigrant outcomes with the visa system that the immigration regime works with. But all this pales before Mr. Borjas's total misrepresentation and indeed inversion of these authors' findings: he refers to figure 1a where he should refer, as do the authors in their analysis and conclusions, to figures 1b and especially 2b. The reader can judge Mr. Borjas's methods for himself.

39

Who Needs the Multilateral Agreement on Investment?

Sir, Your editorial "A case of MAI culpa" (October 20) on the desirability of shelving the Multilateral Agreement on Investment, especially now that France has opted out, makes eminent sense. But more must be said.

The MAI, in its current form, is unbalanced in three ways. It argues for eliminating restrictions on the functioning of corporations, presumably to ensure efficiency in world allocation of resources. But it fails to extend the proscriptions to subventions to attract corporations: but these distort efficiency equally!

The MAI more generally is conceived as a set of rights of corporations, instead of systematically including also their obligations. The latter would also require that notions such as the "stakeholder" obligations of corporations to the communities they operate in should also be laid down in the agreement.

Moreover, the MAI makes little concession to the political sensibilities of the host countries and to their own definitions of their economic interests.

These deficiencies may well be fixed if the MAI is negotiated at the World Trade Organisation, as you recommend. But, even then, there are powerful reasons to have the matter dropped altogether from the WTO agenda. First, the WTO is now a "single undertaking" so that the revised MAI would still be mandatory on all WTO members. The issues it touches are inherently controversial, will take the WTO gratuitously into the politically supercharged domain, and endanger its real mission: to free trade.

Originally published, under the title "Powerful Reasons for the MAI To Be Dropped Even from WTO Agenda," as a letter to the editor of the *Financial Times* (Oct. 22, 1998). Reprinted with permission.

Many of us have been arguing that labour and environmental agendas be pursued (proactively) by means other than trade treaties and institutions, leaving the WTO to pursue free trade instead. But it is hard to tell the lobbies seeking to push these agendas into the WTO to get off its back even as the MAI is sought to be worked into the WTO. It was bad enough to work Intellectual Property Protection—an issue of enforcement of asserted property rights against essentially poor nations rather than of trade where all gain—into the WTO as the Uruguay Round closed.

But with IPP and the MAI both in, it would be hard to refute the charge that what is good for "capital" at the WTO is not considered good for "labour" or for "nature."

VII   Globalization

40

But Mr. Clinton, Globalization *Has* a Human Face

President Clinton will play the host at the November Ministerial Meeting of the WTO in Seattle that is expected to launch the millennium round of multilateral trade negotiations. However, unlike his role model President John Kennedy, whose name graces the sixth such round, he has already missed the bus. It could have been his—the Clinton—Round for the asking if only he had responded enthusiastically and early to the cascading calls by many of us to do so.

But then, it may be just as well. For, it would have been odd, perhaps even a travesty, to name the next round, designed to free trade further and to extend globalization, for a president who reportedly embraced, at the University of Chicago recently, the stereotypical critique that "globalization needs a human face."

Doubtless, that is what he hears from his pollsters who report such complaints from their "focus groups." And it is also what he surely hears from his and Vice President Gore's constituencies: the fearful labor unions and the militant nongovernmental organizations (NGOs) that are not merely oblivious to the benefits of, but are hugely hostile to, foreign trade and investment.

But, in saying that globalization needs a human face, Mr. Clinton concedes that it lacks one! So, he surrenders before the battle is joined, even though he is on higher ground. Indeed, globalization *has* a human face. Oh sure, it needs cosmetic surgery on one cheek and a trinket in an ear: even the most glorious face can be prettified. But the central reality is that the glow in the face that makes it human, rather than a mere mask on the wall, comes from the fact that it is joined to a human body that takes sustenance from a set of beneficial policies that definitely include globalization rather than national isolation.

An abbreviated version of this chapter appeared in the *Financial Times* (Aug. 18, 1999) under the title "Cheap Liberal Talk." Reprinted with permission.

Indeed, one could vigorously challenge virtually every charge that has recently been leveled at the freeing of trade and direct foreign investment. But take just the most common such misconceptions: that trade and foreign investment produce poor in the rich countries; that they bypass, even worsen, poverty in the poor countries; that the multinationals, major players in the world economy today, exploit foreign workers; and that they also harm women at work. How simplistic, even contrary to the facts, all this is.

Starting in the 1980s when the real wages of U.S. workers declined, interrupting the robust upward trend in the postwar years of prosperity, the unions in the rich countries have feared that the culprit must be globalization in shape of trade with poor countries and the outflow of direct foreign investment to them. The more sophisticated among the unions therefore support free trade only among "like-wage" countries: they were relatively quiet in the United States when the preferential Free Trade Agreement was with Canada but were agitated when it was with Mexico.

The majority, however, have unabashedly asked for protection or opposed new trade liberalization with the poor countries. Alternatively, many have sought to increase the cost of production of their rivals there by asking for "level playing fields" through raising of the labour and environmental burdens there to levels similar to their own (in the absence of which they allege, without economic logic, that "social dumping" occurs.) Of course, the former is classic import protectionism or "isolationism"; the latter is a form of "export protectionism," much like Voluntary Export Restraints, or what I have called "intrusionism," which is equally aimed at restraining free trade. Remember: if a beast is charging at you, you can either stop it by seizing its horns or break its charge by reaching out behind it and catching it by its tail.

But the fear of globalization that prompts this protectionist politics, building on the notion that Marx who unsuccessfully predicted the immiseration of the proletariat in the nineteenth century is striking again with the aid of globalization, is itself unfounded. A principal element in the antiglobalization case is the assumption that the average (relative) prices of labor-intensive goods have steadily fallen, causing the real wages of the workers to fall: the celebrated Stolper-Samuelson argument of trade economists. But, the facts show that the opposite occurred: the argument cannot even get off the ground!

This sounds counterintuitive since one is inclined to say that, as increasing numbers of countries among the poor ones have exported more over the years, the total supplies must have vastly increased and the prices of labor-intensive goods must have fallen drastically in world trade. The fact of the matter, however, is that the poor countries that have become richer, especially the Four Tigers at the outset and then the ASEAN countries, have gone from labor-intensive exports to capital-intensive exports. Hence, the "net" exports of labor-intensive exports from the poor nations have not added up immensely; they have not been coming at us blockbuster style. Thus, Ross Garnaut of Australian National University has calculated how Japan withdrew from such exports in the 1970s, largely offsetting the rising labor-intensive exports of the Four Tigers, whereas the latter yielded to and fully accommodated the entry of China in the 1980s through mid-1990s. To put it another way, even though trade liberalization will tend to increase labor-intensive exports from the poor countries, rapid capital accumulation and technical change in capital-intensive industries will offset this and tend to raise, not lower, world prices of labor-intensive goods. No surprises there, except for the unions. Indeed, the surprise, if you take this argument to its logical conclusion, is that trade with the poor countries may have even been a beneficial influence on the real wages of workers in the rich countries, *moderating* instead of accentuating the fall in real wages induced really by technical change that reduces demand for unskilled labor.

Nor should we be browbeaten by the frequent contention that direct foreign investment has undercut the well-being of our workers. Aside from anything else, the argument focuses only on outbound flows, forgetting the inward flows. In a BBC debate on globalization some time ago, I was treated to a clip that had the French mayor of the town that lost Hoover to Britain raging against multinationals; I could not help remarking that there had been no complaints when Hoover, a U.S. firm, had come to his town in the first place. In the 1980s, when real wages were under greatest pressure, the United States got almost as much investment as it made abroad. A telling example is provided by the *Wall Street Journal* reporters Bob Davis and David Wessel in their recent book, *Prosperity*, where they recall how Interstate 85, going through Piedmont Mountains in North Carolina, a traditional textile stretch of country, has now been nicknamed the Autobahn. The textiles lost abroad have been replaced by the influx of nearly 250 foreign firms, several of them German, such as BMW and Hoechst. The workers are doing hugely better than when they were stuck with employment in textiles.

But does globalization work in the poor countries? True, policy-makers have shifted from their postwar fears of integration into the global economy and now see it as an opportunity rather than as a threat. President Cardoso of Brazil, a renowned sociologist who sounded the alarm with his *dependencia* thesis, is now at the forefront of efforts at globalization in Latin America. But the fears that have now, in an ironic reversal, shifted to the rich countries, have tended to be embraced by the NGOs and the unreconstructed left in the poor countries. Liberal reforms that necessitate opening the economies to more trade and direct investment are decried as beneficial only to the rich and actually harmful to the poor.

But here again, the reality is different. Autarkic policies, as practiced by India for over three decades, produced abysmal growth rates, hand-icapping the creation of jobs that would have pulled the poor into gain-ful employment. Both India and China, when they have experienced rapid growth, have managed to dent poverty in a sustainable fashion; and rapid growth has been associated with a policy framework that has, in varying degrees, included globalization.

Rapid growth also generates, at given tax rates, the tax revenues that must be found if more schools are to be built, if health care is to be ex-tended to the villages, if clean water is to be provided, and if much else is to be done for the poor. Without these revenues, liberal talk comes cheap; and it costs the poor dearly when intellectuals who properly decry "abysmal poverty" improperly oppose globalization and liberal economic reforms whose absence only accentuates poverty.

Indeed, even phenomena such as the continuing high rates of illit-eracy in India, where often parents do not send children to schools even when available, can be traced back to low growth: poor parents will not find it attractive to forego children's incomes when the pros-pect of finding jobs for them after schooling are dismal with poor growth of the economy.

Equally at variance with facts is the frequent charge that multi-nationals "exploit" foreign workers. The growing "living wage" movement on U.S. campuses by students who typically denounce mul-tinationals ignores two facts. Few workers are going to work, except under duress or in the gulag, for a "dying wage." Also, as it happens, the economists working on multinationals typically confront the phenomenon known as the "wage premium"—that is, multinationals usually pay more than the going wage, thus treating the workers better than their apparent opportunity cost. In fact, in my experience,

Figure 40.1
Students, wild placards in their hands and screaming mouths distorting their faces, denounce corporations on the campus of the University of Michigan. They are typical of the ill informed militancy characterizing the small but noisy anti-globalization groups that have arisen on U.S. campuses today. Time Magazine/Steve Liss. Reprinted with permission of *Time Magazine*.

it is the aspiration of both skilled and unskilled workers in the poor countries to get into multinationals.

In my view, therefore, the condemnation of multinationals that earn profits for themselves and also bring economic benefits to both their employees and certainly to their host countries is entirely misplaced. Media reports also reveal that much of it in the United States today is due to the labor unions, which oppose the outward flow of investments by multinationals and are therefore advancing their agendas through an energetic and well-financed recruitment of young activists.

Thus, John Sweeney, President of AFL-CIO, has poured "more than $3 million into internships and outreach programs meant to interest students in careers as union activists" (*Time*, April 12, 1998). Many of these students have become antimultinational activists on campuses across the United States (see figure 40.1), and their proximity to the unions is manifest from the fact that they typically object to multinationals using sweatshops (often mistakenly confused with firms and factories paying low wages that naturally reflect the fact that these countries are poor and have low wages) in Guatemala while ignoring the many sweatshops (properly defined as those in violation of safety standards, minimum wage laws, legislated working conditions, etc.) within the United States itself. I once offered a couple of such students, who were sitting at a table on College Walk on the Columbia University campus and waylaid me with complaints about our corporations exploiting labor in sweatshops abroad, to use my Metrocard subway pass to go down to the garment district where there were many sweatshops indeed and to do something about *them* forthwith! Evidently unaware that we had the real sweatshops right here, they had been snookered into agitating instead against our investment abroad.

While, again, globalization is typically charged with hurting women—as when multinationals, for example, are accused of exploiting female labor in the Export Processing Zones—the opposite may in fact be true. Thus, economists Sandra Black and Elizabeth Brainerd have argued recently that globalization has helped reduce the gender wage gap in the United States. Drawing on Gary Becker's idea that increased competition means that a firm would find it increasingly difficult to indulge its "taste for discrimination" such as hiring equally productive men at higher wages and yet survive, they show that increased import competition in the shape of increasing import shares in industries during 1977–1994 is associated with greater reduction in the men-women wage gap.

And, as for women's employment in the poor countries, surely the correct take on it is that it is the protectionist policies in the rich countries in industries such as textiles and garments that help reduce the demand for female labor in the poor countries and thus contribute to keeping them poor. More important, without the benefit of suitable employment and income that alone can give them the economic independence, even women's rights cannot be advanced meaningfully. For, it is easy enough to pass socially progressive legislation and yet accomplish little: you may legislate against men beating up their wives, but if the battered wife cannot walk away and support herself with a job, then the legislation's potency is unlikely to be compelling.

None of this is to deny that we must have today what I call "appropriate governance," both domestic and international, to sustain and manage the world economy and the world polity. But we are bound to get its design all wrong if our political leadership lazily buys into the uninformed fears and the raging passions that drive the antiglobalization groups today.

41

Globalization,
Sovereignty, and
Democracy

Introduction

Like everyone else, economists like to break out of the narrowness of their discipline and speculate on a larger theme, painting on a bigger canvas. Like John Kenneth Galbraith, they may even make money while having fun. In the process, they may even illuminate and inform, doing good while doing well.

The task I have been assigned is an intellectually challenging one: does the growing globalization of the world economy and the presumed growth then in interdependence promise to constrain national sovereignty; and, does it equally threaten to compromise democratic accountability within nation-states? I feel daunted by the task: it is both extremely broad in scope and at the same time inadequately amenable to conventional analysis within any discipline. My analysis, while grounded in my understanding of the globalization process that is ongoing, must therefore remain essentially speculative in character. Few such speculations, especially those that contain within them a prognosis of the future, have turned out, if the past is any guide, to stand the test of time (though, I derive comfort from the fact that the worth of an idea lies in what it stimulates, even if by provocation, even while it is itself wildly wrong).

Since a major element of the globalization process today is international trade and since we economists tend to think of international trade as essentially a technology (in the sense that it adds to one's productive potential yet another way of transforming goods into one another, via external exchange), the great failure of such speculation

Originally published, as chapter 12, in *Democracy's Victory and Crisis*, ed. Axel Hadenius (Cambridge: Cambridge University Press, 1997), 263–281. Reprinted with permission.

that comes to mind, of course, is that of the celebrated pessimists George Orwell and Aldous Huxley. The authors of *Nineteen Eighty-Four* and *Brave New World* imagined modern technology as the enemy of freedom and the unwitting tool of authoritarianism; things, however, turned out for the better, not worse. Modern technology was supposed to make Big Brother omnipotent, watching you into submission; instead, it enabled us to watch Big Brother into impotence. Faxes, video cassettes, CNN have plagued and paralyzed dictators and tyrants, accelerating the disintegration of their rule. As a wit has remarked, the PC (personal computer) has been the deathknell of the CP (Communist Party).[1]

But closer to home, both to me and to the broader theme of this conference, has been the failure of the early intellectual thinking on the relationship of democracy to development.[2] Thus, when reflection on strategies for the newly liberated countries began in the 1950s, there was considerable skepticism about the ability of democracies to compete in the race against totalitarian regimes. In fact, it seemed evident that democratic ideas and countries were fated to suffer a disadvantage in this contest. To understand why, it is necessary to recollect the mindset at the root of the conception of development that then prevailed.

The Harrod–Domar model, much used then, analyzed development in terms of two parameters: the rate of investment and the productivity of capital. For policy-making purposes, the latter was largely treated as "given," so debate centered on the question of how to promote investment. This approach favored by mainstream economists coincided with the Marxist focus on "primitive accumulation" as the mainspring of industrialization and also with the cumbersome quasi-Marxist models elaborated in the investment-allocation literature that grew up around Maurice Dobb.

But if the focus was on accumulation, with productivity considered a datum, it was evident that democracies would be handicapped vis-à-vis totalitarian regimes. Writing in the mid-1960s, I noted "the cruel choice between rapid (self-sustained) expansion and democratic processes" (1966: 204). This view, which the political scientist Atul Kohli has christened the "cruel choice" thesis, was widely shared by economists at the time (1986: 155). Later emphasis would shift away from raising the rate of savings and investment (dimensions on which most developing countries did well) to getting the most for one's blood, sweat, and tears (dimensions on which developing countries performed in diverse ways). Indeed, by the 1980s it was manifest that the policy framework determining the productivity of investment was absolutely critical, and that winners and losers would be sorted out by the choices they made in this regard. Democracy then no longer looked so bad: it could provide better incentives, relate development to people, and offset any accumulationist disadvantage that it might produce. Indeed, as Kohli has emphasized, the growth rates of democracies have not been noticeably worse than those of undemocratic regimes (1986).[3]

I also think that the common view, that the undemocratic nature of the regimes in South Korea, Taiwan, Singapore, and Hong Kong was the key to their phenomenal growth, is false. This is a *non sequitur*, a choice example of the *post hoc ergo propter hoc* fallacy. These regimes owe their phenomenal success to their rapid transition to an export-oriented trade strategy (which first enabled them to profit from the unprecedented growth in the world economy through the 1960s, and then positioned them to continue as major competitors in world markets),[4] as well as to their high rates of literacy (which economists now generally acknowledge to be an important "producer good"). Both of these growth promoters were present in part because of the geographic proximity of Japan and the power of its example. Similarly, I would argue that the dismal performance of India owed to her poor choice of developmental strategy, with excessive reliance on import substitution and degeneration into mindless bureaucratic controls, as also low rates of literacy (whose roots lie in social and political factors discussed insightfully by the political scientist, Myron Weiner, in his recent book [1991]), the former failing to be blamed in large part on the intellectual affinity that its governing classes harbored for both Fabian politics and Cambridge economics.[5]

East Asian authoritarianism and Indian democracy are thus not the key to explaining their relative performance: the proponents of the contention that democracy aids, or at minimum does not hamper, development have little to fear from the comparative performance of these two regions.

Clearly, then, the "cruel choice" thesis was wrong; and, for us who value democracy, the error hurts our ego while warming our hearts. Here we have therefore an excellent illustration of how speculation grounded in the best thinking of the time failed the test of time, simply because we were using the wrong road map. I am therefore conscious, as I address the tasks before me, that some years down the road, the reality that I seek to grasp will have proven to be elusive again.

The Questions

The central questions that I will address now are:

• Is sovereignty being lost by nation-states because of the interdependence implied by the increased globalization of the world economy?
• Is there also a decline, for this and other reasons, in the democratic accountability that national governments owe to their citizens?

Environment vs. Trade: An Illustration

These questions have acquired considerable political salience today. They are readily illustrated, though neither in all their complexity nor with the analytical rigour that I hope to use below, by the often-acrimonious debate between the proponents of free trade, the General Agreement on Tariffs and Trade (GATT) and the World Trade Organization (WTO), on the one hand, and many environmentalists, on the other.

To a large extent, of course, this conflict is inevitable. It reflects partly differences of philosophical approaches to nature that are irreconcilable. Several environmentalists assert nature's autonomy whereas many economists see nature as a handmaiden to mankind. The environmentalists' anguish at the effect of human activity on the environment is beautifully captured by Gerald Manley Hopkins when, in *Binsey Poplars*, he writes:

O if we but knew what we do
*   When we delve or hew—*
Hack and rack the growing green!
*   Since country is so tender*
To touch, her being so slender,
That, like this sleek and seeing ball
But a prick will make no eye at all,
Where we, even where we mean
*   To mend her we end her,*
*   When we hew or delve:*
After-comers cannot guess the beauty been.
*   Ten or twelve, only ten or twelve*
*   Strokes of havoc unselve*
*   The sweet especial scene,*
*   Rural scene, a rural scene,*
*   Sweet especial rural scene.*

It is indeed hard to find an echo of Hopkins in the utilitarian, cost-benefit calculus that many economists bring to bear on the question of the environment.

Then again, the conflict reflects other contrasts. Thus, trade has been central to economic thinking since Adam Smith discovered the economic virtues of specialization and of the markets that naturally sustain it, whereas markets do not normally exist to protect the environment and must often be specially created. Trade therefore suggests abstention from regulation, whereas environmentalism suggests its necessity. In turn, trade is exploited and its virtues extolled by corporate and multinational interests, whereas environmental objectives are embraced typically by non-profit organizations which are generally wary of, if not hostile to, these interests.

In the end, however, the hostility of the environmentalists to trade and the institutions such as the GATT that oversee it arises from precisely the two issues posed earlier: the threat that trade, increasingly resulting from the globalization of the world economy, poses to sovereignty and to democratic accountability.[6] Let me elaborate.

Thus, concerning sovereignty, the environmentalists feel that their ability to maintain the High Standards that they have achieved in their countries will be constrained and eroded by free trade and free capital flows with the Low Standards countries. Their concern is reminiscent of the classic problem of "socialism in one state." Just as capital and labour outflows will undermine the socialist objectives in a country going it alone, so will environmental (and labor) standards erode if they are lower elsewhere. In economists' language, the "political equilibrium" will shift in favor of those who oppose High Standards as industries decline through competition with foreign rivals operating under Low Standards. Moreover, there may ensue an interjurisdictional competition to attract capital and jobs through lowering environmental (and labor) standards, so that the trading countries may wind up with an inferior Nash equilibrium, characterized also by lower standards in one or all jurisdictions, than would emerge in a cooperative equilibrium.[7]

The environmentalists also fear the undermining of their High Standards via the alternative route of the Low Standards countries challenging the High Standards as "unscientific" or as "closet protectionism." In this instance, when the High Standards are subject to such challenge at the GATT (and now, the WTO which is replacing the

GATT) by other trading nations, the environmentalists see the problem as the second one posed above: the undermining of democratically enacted legislation by "faceless bureaucrats" at the GATT. Again, they argue that "the process of negotiating international agreements [such as the GATT's Uruguay Round of multilateral trade negotiations, concluded in April 1995 at Marrakesh] is less subject to public scrutiny, and therefore a threat to democratic accountability."[8]

In fact, some environmentalists have gone even further and alleged that trade liberalization is in part a strategy for circumventing the health and welfare regulations legislated democratically within the nation: the title of a celebrated article by Walter Russell Mead in *Harper's Magazine* (September 1992), embracing this thesis, is: "Bushism, Found: A Second-Term Agenda Hidden in Trade Agreements."

Thus, the questions concerning the impact of globalization, and the integration of one's economy into the world economy, on sovereignty, and on democratic accountability are central concerns in the political arena. A systematic examination of these questions is manifestly necessary. I will therefore turn to each of these questions. But, prior to doing so, I will consider briefly the nature and extent of globalization to date.

Globalization

The process of globalization of the world economy has occurred on several dimensions: trade, capital flows, human migrations (voluntary and involuntary). I will sketch these with great brevity.

Trade flows have dramatically increased in the last two decades, with most countries doubling the share of their trade in GNP and more. The increased trade reflects the continuing reduction of trade barriers with successive multilateral trade negotiations and also, in the case of developing countries, a substantial amount of unilateral, nonreciprocal trade liberalization which can be attributed to a mix of aid-conditionality and self-enlightenment in light of the postwar example of successful outward-oriented countries.[9]

A contribution to this phenomenon has also been made by the expansion of transnational production by multinational firms to a point where many have now made the claim that it is impossible now to say whether a product is American or Japanese or European: a claim that is perhaps premature but certainly destined to be validated in the near future. The trade flows have expanded, not just in manufactures, but explosively in services. In turn, that has meant, because services must be supplied often by taking the provider to the user, that the trend towards foreign establishments and (temporary) migration of skilled labor such as lawyers and accountants has greatly accelerated.

Investment flows have increased. True, we forget that the East India Company and the Dutch East Indies Company dominated commerce and the economic life of their countries, so in the long historical sweep, it is probably untrue to talk of the increased dominance of direct foreign investment (DFI). But, in recent decades, it has certainly grown; and its composition is now more evenly balanced between rich-to-poor and rich-to-rich countries. Much DFI occurs now in services, partly piggybacking on manufacturing DFI from their home country. Again, while DFI leads to trade, trade leads to DFI; the entry of Spain into the EC triggered a substantial influx of DFI to access the EC market and President Salinas realistically hoped for a similar bounty for Mexico from the North American Free Trade Arrangement (NAFTA).

The growth of the international flow of *short-term funds* is perhaps the most dramatic change in the world economy. Their staggering size and their volatility that recently devastated Mexico is a continuing and painful reminder, of the vulnerability that they equally bring, to the finance ministers and Central Bank chairmen and governors of even powerful countries like France, England, Japan, and the United States.

By contrast foreign *aid* flows have continued to shrink in real terms. But they remain important, bilaterally from the triad (the EU, USA, and Japan) and multilaterally. (They bring explicit conditionality with them, unlike the private funds which exact only the implicit conditionality that the task of wooing them or else losing them implies.)

An important dimension on which countries interface has been humanity itself. *Illegal* flows have become dramatic as, now that information and networks exist, the rich countries have become targets for entry. Immigration controls have been evaded, as controls invariably are; it is not too farfetched to say that borders are getting to be beyond control.

The problem is compounded for the *refugees*, both as narrowly defined in UN Covenants, and in terms of the wider definition of flight from civil wars and mortal danger. The UN High Commissioner for Refugees finds her hands full and her purse empty as the refugees have multiplied with civil wars brought about by ethnic strife, famine, and deprivation.

Conventional Concerns: Benign versus Malign Impacts

Economists generally see the increasingly interdependent world, with its growing exchange of goods and services and flows of funds to where the returns are expected to be higher, as one that is gaining in prosperity as it is exploiting the opportunities to trade and to invest that have been provided by the postwar dismantling of trade barriers and obstacles to investment flows. This is the conventional "mutual-gain" or "on-zero-sum game" view of the situation. I would argue that it is also the appropriate one.

But it is not a view that has had a clear run at the best of times. That integration into the world economy is a peril rather than an opportunity, that it will produce predation at one's expense instead of gain, has never been wholly absent from the policy scene. The substance of the disagreement among policy makers and among mainstream economists has, however, been defined by disagreements concerning the impact of such integration or globalization on conventionally defined economic welfare whereas only recently have broader concerns about sovereignty and democratic accountability risen from the fringe to command attention in policy circles.

An Irony

But I must point to an irony: where the developing countries (the South) were earlier skeptical of the benign-impact view and the developed countries (the North) were confident of it, today the situation is the other way around.

(i) The Earlier Situation

Thus, if you look back at the 1950s and 1960s, the contrast between the developing countries (the South) and the developed countries (the North) was striking and made the South strongly pessimistic about the effects of integration into the world economy while the North was firmly optimistic instead.

The South generally subscribed, not to the liberal, mutual-gain, benign-impact view, but to *malign-neglect* and even *malign-intent* views of trade and investment interactions with the world economy.[10] It was feared that "integration into the world economy would lead to disintegration of the domestic economy." While the malign-neglect view is manifest most clearly in the famous *dependencia* theory that President Cardoso of Brazil formulated in his radical youth as Latin America's foremost sociologist, the malign-impact view was most vividly embodied in the concept and theory of *neocolonialism*.

Trade thus had to be protected; investment inflows had to be drastically regulated and curtailed.[11] The inward-oriented, import-substituting (IS) strategy was the order of the day almost everywhere. Only the Far Eastern economies, starting mainly in the early 1960s, shifted dramatically to an outward-oriented policy posture: the results, attributable principally to this contrast in orientation to the world economy but partly also to initial advantages such as inherited land reforms and high literacy rates, were to produce the most remarkable growth experiences of this century (and, as I shall presently argue, to facilitate by example the reversal of the inward-looking policies in recent years). But, at the time, the developing countries were certainly in an inward, cautious mode about embracing the world economy.

By contrast, the developed countries, the North,[12] moved steadily forward with dismantling trade barriers through the GATT Rounds, with firm commitment to multilateralism as well, subscribing essentially to the principles of multilateral free trade and of freer investment flows as the central guiding principles for a liberal international economic order that would assure economic prosperity for all participating nations.[13]

(ii) Role Reversal: The Turnaround

Today, however, the situation is almost reversed. The fears of integration into the world economy are being heard, not from the developing countries which see great good from it as they have extensively undertaken what the GATT calls "autonomous" reductions in their trade barriers, i.e., unilateral reductions outside the GATT context of reciprocal reductions. Of course, not all these reductions, and increased openness to inward DFI, have resulted from changed convictions in favor of the liberal international economic order and its benefits to oneself, though the failure of policies based on the old pro-inward-orientation views and the contrasting success of the Far Eastern countries following the pro-outward-orientation views have certainly played an important role, especially in Latin America and Asia. But some measure of the shift must also be ascribed to necessity resulting from the conditionality imposed by the World Bank and, at times, by the International Monetary Fund (IMF), as several debt-crisis-afflicted countries flocked to these institutions for support in the 1980s, and equally from their own perceived need to restore their external viability by liberal domestic and international policies designed to reassure and attract DFI.

But if the South has moved to regard integration into the world economy as an opportunity rather than a peril, it is the North that is now fearful. In particular, the fear has grown, after the experience with the decline in the real wages of the unskilled in the United States and with their employment in Europe in the 1970s and 1980s, that by trading with the South with its abundance of unskilled labour, the North will find its own unskilled at risk.[14] The demand for protection that follows is then not the old and defunct "pauper-labor" argument which asserted falsely that trade between the South and the North could not be beneficial. Rather, it is the theoretically more defensible, income-distributional argument that trade with countries with paupers will produce paupers in our midst, that trade with the poor countries will produce more poor at home.

Now, it is indeed true that the real wages of the unskilled have fallen significantly in the United States during the previous two decades. In 1973, the "real hourly earnings of non-supervisory workers measured in 1982 dollars ... were $8.55. By 1992 they had actually *declined* to $7.43—a level that had been achieved in the late 1960s. Had earnings increased at their earlier pace, they would have risen by 40 percent to over $12" (cf. Lawrence 1994). The experience in Europe has generally been similar in spirit, with the more "inflexible" labor markets implying that the adverse impact has been on jobs rather than on real wages (*Employment Outlook* 1993).

But the key question is whether the cause of this phenomenon is trade with the South, as unions and many politicians feel, or rapid modern information-based technical change that is increasingly substituting unskilled labor with computers that need skilled rather than unskilled labor. As always, there is debate among economists about the evidence: but the preponderant view today among the trade experts is that the evidence for linking trade with the South to the observed distress among the unskilled to date is extremely thin, at best. In fact, the main study by labor experts that first suggested otherwise has been shown to be methodologically unsound in not appreciating that if real wages were to fall for unskilled labor due to trade with the South, the goods prices of the unskilled labor-intensive goods would have to have fallen (see Bhagwati 1991a); and subsequent examination of the U.S. data on prices of goods shows that the opposite happened to be true.[15]

While therefore the consensus currently is that technical change, not trade with the South, has immiserized our proletariat, the fear still persists that such trade is a threat to the unskilled. In Europe, there has thus been talk of the difficulty of competing with "Asiatic ants"; such talk leads to talk of protectionism, in turn.

Alongside this is the fear that multinationals will move out to take advantage of the cheaper labor in the poor countries, as trade becomes freer, thus adding to the pressure that trade alone, with each nation's capital at home, brings on the real wages of the unskilled. Of course, this too is unsubstantiated fear: but it has even greater political salience since the loss of jobs to trade is less easily focused on specific competing countries and their characteristics than when a factory shuts down and opens in a foreign country instead. As it happens, I suspect that, at least in the United States, the flow of capital also is in the wrong direction form the viewpoint of those who are gripped by such fear. For, during the 1980s, the United States is estimated to have received slightly more DFI than it sent out elsewhere, both absolutely and relative to the 1950s and 1960s. Besides, if foreign savings are considered instead, the 1980s saw an influx, corresponding to the current account deficit that has bedeviled U.S.–Japan trade relations for sure.

The fears in the developed countries are fairly potent, nonetheless, and drive a number of other demands, such as those for harmonizing and imposing higher environmental and labor standards on the poor countries: not primarily because of moral concerns reflecting a sense of transborder moral obligation but often with a view to somehow and anyhow raising the costs of production in the poor countries to reduce the pressure of competition that is feared to depress one's wages and take away one's jobs. I will return to these aspects of the question below.

Globalization and Sovereignty

Evidently then, I regard the foregoing critiques and fears of the globalization process in the developed countries to be unsound, and the reverse enthusiasm for globalization among the developing countries today to be sensible. In fact, I embrace (with necessary nuances) the current "Washington consensus," which I embraced in fact long before it reached Washington, that successful and robust development requires two pillars: democracy (whose merits I began my analysis with) and markets (which, in turn, imply integration into the world economy).

But there are new concerns which have arisen, which cut across the rich and poor countries and in fact afflict the latter even more pointedly, concerning the loss of sovereignty as also of democratic accountability following the globalization phenomenon. These are important concerns, especially since, if integration into the world markets for trade, investment, and people is undercutting democracy, then the two legs on which the Washington consensus seeks to walk will be pulling in different directions. These concerns therefore need to be carefully assessed.

Let me begin with the question of sovereignty. Two different ways can be distinguished in which this question may be approached. Both concern the poor nations more than the rich nations, since the latter are politically and economically the stronger.

Increased Cost of Certain Policy Options

One way is to consider sovereignty as adversely affected if the globalization, while welfare-improving, increases the cost of certain policy options so dramatically as to impair, in effect, our *ability* to adopt them.

Thus, the increasing trade opportunities and flows of funds and of DFI in today's world economy are increasing the ability of different countries to achieve greater income or even significantly accelerated growth rates. At the same time, however, the increased reliance on trade, external funds, and DFI may constrain the ability of individual nation-states to pursue social agendas.

This may happen, for instance, because the politically weaker nations may find themselves unable to pursue more egalitarian agendas, for example, without serious consequences such as outflows of capital. This used to be, in fact, the problem of "socialism in one state": if you went socialist, while the world around you was not, your capital and people would exit, forcing such immense economic costs that the option of socialism was effectively ruled out.

Then again, to recount a more pertinent problem today, consider the Mexican debacle in early 1995. Integration into the capital markets of the world through capital account convertibility aided Mexico's prosperity for sure by enabling her to gain from short-term capital inflows and by avoiding the efficiency losses that exchange control restrictions entail. But then such integration and openness to volatile short-term capital inflows demands extremely difficult fiscal and monetary discipline in whose absence the economy becomes seriously vulnerable. When things go wrong, as they did in Mexico, putting the economy on the rack to restore credibility with Wall Street becomes Hobson's choice: the alternatives are even worse. Policy options shrink dramatically before and during crises.

One may well ask: if governments choose to integrate and take these risks and corresponding constraints on their policy options, is this not a calculated and rational surrender of sovereignty? By and large, I think that this is a valid way to look at the question. But some observations are in order.

Governments may not adequately grasp the full implications of globalization when they choose to integrate in specific ways into the world economy. Evidently the many macro-economists, who have dominated Mexico's recent politics, did not. Then again, even if they did, they may overdiscount the downside scenarios, leading to a regret phenomenon.

Unfortunately, the reversal of mistaken policies may not be easy. It is hard to imagine that Mexico will be able to get out from under Wall Street's yoke now that it is financially crippled thanks to embracing Wall Street with abandon.

Besides, governments are not unitary actors. A decision to integrate, for example, that constrains (by increasing greatly the cost of such a shift) the ability to shift to more egalitarian policies down the road may weigh greatly on some groups. These groups will then continue to regard and to oppose the decisions to integrate the economy into the world economy as a surrender of sovereignty even when the decision is taken democratically and is best seen as a welfare-improving one.

These groups also see several recent institutional arrangements underlying and embodying the globalization as being explicitly designed to *preempt* future options to reverse the integration process. Thus, during the NAFTA debate in the United States and Mexico, the most popular argument for NAFTA's passage by the US Congress was precisely that, once Mexico had entered NAFTA, it would politically "lock in" Mexico's markets-oriented and outward-looking proglobalization reforms. Presumably, the cost of withdrawal from NAFTA would be so great that no political party could succeed in reversing the reforms which were integral to the NAFTA arrangements. The political ability to reverse the "reforms" later would be constrained, signifying to those who wish to work for such reversal that there has been a loss of "sovereignty" in this sense.[16]

Strategic Action by Governments and Non-governmental Organizations (NGOs)

What I have said so far suggests reasons why globalization is seen as reducing sovereignty, even though it increases efficiency, income, and wealth, simply because it is felt to be reducing the ability to exercise certain policy options. This reduced ability is, however, simply a reflection of the market forces as reflected in the globalization process. No "conspiracy" or "strategic" behavior by any foreign governments or agents is involved; the country is simply a victim of autonomous, "structural" developments in the world economy.

But strategic behavior impacting on one's sovereignty also may be an increasingly important factor in a globalized economy. Thus, the strong nations, exploiting their increased leverage through globalization, may successfully impose on the weak ones demands that improve the distribution of gains from trade and investment in their favour, either bilaterally through aggressive actions that reflect the increased vulnerability of internationally integrated weak nations to such threats (as in the case of the use by the United States of market-access-closing threats under the Special 301 provisions of its trade legislation against selected developing countries that do not accept the maximalist US version of desirable intellectual property protection) or multilaterally (as when socially suboptimal, excessive intellectual property protection was demanded and successfully translated into concessions by the weaker nations in multilateral trade negotiations at the Uruguay Round which culminated in the transformation of the GATT into the WTO).[17] In these instances, the weaker nations are forced into renouncing policy options that are clearly useful in the pursuit of their interest: the integration in to the world economy and the dependence brought by it increases the cost to the weaker countries of not yielding to such demands for the abandonment of their welfare-improving policy options.

But such strategic behavior also comes today through the proliferating NGOs, many of which have active international agendas (aimed at exploiting the leverage implied by the increased globalization of the world economy through trade, private capital and DFI flows, foreign aid programs, etc.), not with a view to shifting *economic* advantage in their constituents' favour, but motivated instead by *moral* considerations. Today, there is a veritable explosion of NGOs around the world, even among the developing and the former socialist countries.[18] But there is little doubt that, on the international stage, as it impacts on national sovereignty, the well-financed and organized NGOs of the rich countries, whose impassioned one-page advertisements in leading newspapers such as *The Financial Times* and *The New York Times* cannot have missed catching your attention, call the shots. And the efforts of these NGOs are often aimed at the developing countries: e.g., at Mexico's environmental standards, at India's Narmada Dam, at Thailand's safety standards, indeed at an increasing number of issues.

A noteworthy aspect of these NGO efforts at intruding on the sovereignty of nations in regard to matters which the NGOs are targeting is that it reflects an enhanced sense of the obligation that we as human beings owe one another, transcending national borders. In turn, this phenomenon has contributed to an important shift in the current approach to questions of sovereignty: namely, that the nation-state is no longer accepted by many as necessarily the legitimate and exclusive arbiter of its citizens' welfare.

The sense of transborder moral obligation is of course ancient, long predating the modern nation-state. As John Dunn, the Cambridge political theorist, has reminded us eloquently in tracing the origins of the notion of a "human community," and the consequent answer to the question of what human beings owe one another:

an old answer [to the question of what we owe to others] with deep Greek and Christian roots, is that there is just one human community, "that great and natural community"..., as John Locke called it, of all human beings as natural creatures, whose habitat is the whole globe and whose obligations to one another do not stop at any humanly created—any artificial—boundary. Locke had a very powerful explanation of why this was so, an explanation which tied human obligations immediately to the purposes of God himself.... A pale shadow of Locke's conception, with God tactfully edited out, still lives on in modern secular understandings of human rights ... and, even more diffusely, in anthropocentric interpretations of the collective ecological imperative to save a habitat for the human species as a whole. (Dunn 1993)

Obligation implies rights. If then transborder obligations to others elsewhere are accepted, so must the notion that these others have rights which *we* are expected to sustain.

It follows then that the assumption in international relations since the Treaty of Westphalia, that nation-states have exclusive domain over their subjects such that treatment of these subjects is a matter of domestic sovereignty and international relations therefore must respect moral pluralism, is no longer acceptable. As Raymond Plant has put it succinctly: "The principle of cuius regio euius religio may have been central to the Treaty of Westphalia but the principle of cuius regio, eius jus is not compatible with the idea that there are basic human rights the moral authority of which crosses frontiers" (1993).

The problem, of course, is that the mere assertion of morality does not automatically put these NGOs on higher ground. Often, the demands they make are culture-bound and have no overriding moral force as when environmentalists in the United States seek to attack Mexico with trade sanctions for using purse seine nets to catch tuna and killing dolphins in the process; surely these demands appear to Mexicans to be morally defective in putting dolphins ahead of the Mexican poor (since purse seine nets are more productive). Also, Mexicans may well wonder why there is no equivalent condemnation of equally cruel hog farming or chicken batteries within the United States itself, suggesting compellingly that there is no morally coherent approach here to the issue of cruelty to animals and of animal rights.

Often the NGOs, based in the North, also focus on the failings in the South rather than admitting the commonality of these failings everywhere and turning the spotlight equally on the moral turpitude in their own backyards. Thus, for instance, the labor-standards lobbies have typically used the example of a deadly fire in a toy factory in Bangkok, Thailand, where several women workers died, unable to use the exit doors which had been closed to prevent theft. But a similar fire had occurred in North Carolina in a chicken parts plant, with exit doors closed again to prevent theft, and was a far more serious matter since it was in the world's richest country. Why not use that example instead or alongside? Then again, the demand to include a Social Clause in the WTO has also been couched overwhelmingly in terms of the developing countries indulging in practices leading to unfair competition rather than focusing on the universality in practice of the failures in regard to the practices (such as, for instance, virtual slavery through bonded labor, say in India, and through cruel abuse of migrant labor, say in the US) chosen to be put in the Clause. Equally, one fails to see good faith efforts to include within the Clause practices where some of the developed countries would be more serious culprits (e.g., in regard to the effective as against the notional right to unionize, the right to worker representation in management, the treatment of immigrant labour, etc.).

The feeling has steadily grown, therefore, among the developing countries that the morality that many of the NGOs advance to override national sovereignty via the use of trade and aid sanctions is selective, aimed at the developing countries rather than universal, is often a mask for protectionist intentions, and is hypocritical in throwing stones at other countries' glass houses while building fortresses around one's own.[19] The NGOs' efforts are therefore unlikely to succeed until these fundamental flaws are fixed, as I optimistically expect that they will eventually as the NGOs mature and their activities and influence expand.

Globalization and Democracy

The arguments above about the effect of the globalization process on national sovereignty have an obvious relationship, of course, to the ability of citizens to participate effectively in the democratic choice of policies within the nation-state. On the other hand, there is much that is positive for the spread of democracy in the developing countries when globalization is seen on the dimension of freer mobility of people and of ideas that goes with greater integration. The idea of democracy itself has spread through the postwar period, a role being played in the dramatic turn of the Third World to democracy by the increased awareness among the peoples there of the institutions of democracy in the developed world. Trade and investments have drawn the elites, the bourgeoisie, into deeper contacts with the democracies and have surely prompted their successful demands for democracy in their own countries.

Also, the *quality* of democracy has certainly improved with the increased trade and investments that, alongside the growth of foreign education and the availability of information through the medium of television (which brings telling images of individualism, political freedom, liberated women, etc., to vast audiences via CNN, BBC and other worldwide services), are serving as catalysts for bringing ever more of the traditionally peripheral groups such as women increasingly into an assertive, and often a political, role in their own societies. To give just one telling example: the enormous expansion of Japanese multinationals in the European Union and in the United States in the last fifteen years, and the accompanying explosion in the number of corporate wives and children living in the West, has been a source of cultural change in the direction of modernizing the elite women (and men) of Japan and encouraging their inclusion in Japan's strengthening democracy and polity.[20] I can only applaud such outcomes.

Notes

1. In Huxley's instance, the irony is greater still when one contemplates that mescalin was seen by him as opening the doors of perception when today its progeny, LSD, etc., are seen as closing these doors.

2. For a short commentary on this question, see Bhagwati (1992), and, in particular, see the extended analysis in Bhagwati (1995a).

3. This conclusion is certainly not refuted by the more intensively statistical chapters in this volume on this subject. While Surjit Bhalla appears to deduce that "political freedom," or democracy, has a benign influence on growth, Przeworski and Limongi are more skeptical of this benign relationship. Neither concludes, however, as the cruel-dilemma thesis did, that democracy harms growth.

4. The question of the reasons for the East Asian "miracle" have been the subject of much controversy among economists recently. My own view, developed in many writings, is that their external orientation since the late 1950s enabled these countries to raise their investment and hence savings rates to phenomenally high levels, while the high export earnings and high investment rates meant that imports of new-technology-embodying capital goods also increased dramatically, enabling these countries to profit additionally from the technological inflow.

5. I have discussed the role of these intellectual antecedents, and of misplaced economic theorizing by some of India's leading economists, on India's dismal economic performance (Bhagwati 1994a).

6. The threat to sovereignty was also a principal objection to signing the Uruguay Round accords by many legislators in the two democracies, India and the United States. Ironically, the former feared that the weak countries would lose sovereignty to the strong ones, the latter feared that the strong countries would lose it to the weak ones.

7. The theoretical aspects of this argument, which has attracted a huge economic literature, have been nicely reviewed and synthesized by Wilson (in Bhagwati and Hudec 1996).

8. This claim is quoted in Robert Hudec's excellent article (1993), containing the proceedings of a conference on "The Morality of Protectionism" at the New York University Law School in November 1992.

9. This value of example has certainly worked in South America and in India, where such unilateral trade liberalization has occurred. It would have greatly pleased Cobden and Bright, leading lights in Britain's repeal of the Corn Laws, who were unilateral free traders and felt that the example of British success from her free trade, rather than reciprocity, would effectively spread free trade elsewhere. Cf. Bhagwati (1988).

10. These different economic-philosophical positions are discussed in depth in Bhagwati (1977: chapter 1).

11. This attitude extended to other areas too: the outward flow of skilled manpower was thus considered a "brain drain" rather than an opportunity for one's citizens to train and work abroad that would lead to a beneficial impact as this diaspora expanded.

12. They were called the West, of course, then. The changing nomenclature of the poor and rich countries reflects a shift from a historical, cultural, and imperial divide into East and West to a contemporary, post-colonial and development-related divide into South and North.

13. See, for example, Bhagwati (1988), on the question of free trade, and Bhagwati (1991b) on the issue of multilateralism.

14. The evidence in support of this phenomenon in the 1980s, both for the United States and for several other countries, is reviewed and synthesized nicely by Marvin Kosters (in Bhagwati and Kosters 1994: chapter 1).

15. This empirical work by Robert Lawrence and Matthew Slaughter is reviewed in Bhagwati and Dehejia (1994). A subsequent empirical study by Sachs and Schatz (1994) claims to overturn the Lawrence and Slaughter findings by taking out computers (a procedure that is debatable at best). Even then the coefficient with the changed sign is both small and statistically insignificant. So, while Noam Chomsky has educated us that two negatives add up to a positive in every language, it is wrong to claim that the two negatives of a statistically insignificant and small parameter of the required sign add up to a positive support for the thesis that trade has been depressing the real wages of the unskilled! The work of Adrian Wood (1994) argues in support of the trade-hurting-real-wages-of-the-unskilled thesis but his arguments have been effectively criticized by Lawrence (1994). See also the most recent review of the theory and evidence in Bhagwati (1995c).

16. Mind you, this is not the same thing as Ulysses chaining himself voluntarily to resist the sirens; here, he is chaining also others who have no such fear of the sirens.

17. On these questions, see Bhagwati (1991b).

18. Salomon (1994) calls this the global "associational revolution" and studies the diverse cultural and political roots of this phenomenon.

19. I have dealt with these problems in greater depth, in the context of environmental and labour standards demands at the WTO, in several writings. See, for example, Bhagwati (1995b).

20. I have dealt with this question of Japan's political, economic, and cultural evolution and convergence in the context of a critique of the Clinton administration's Japan policy (Bhagwati 1994b).

References

Bhagwati, Jagdish. 1996. *The Economics of Underdeveloped Countries*. London and New York: Weidenfeld and Nicolson and McGraw-Hill.

———, ed. 1977. *The New International Economic Order: The North–South Debate*. Cambridge, Mass.: MIT Press.

———. 1988. *Protectionism*. Bertil Ohlin Lectures, 1987. Cambridge, Mass.: MIT Press.

———. 1991a. "Free traders and free immigrationists: strangers or friends?" Working Paper No. 20. New York: Russell Sage Foundation.

———. 1991b. *The World Trading System at Risk.* Harry Johnson Lecture. Princeton: Princeton University Press.

———. 1992. "Democracy and development," *Journal of Democracy* 3: 37–44.

———. 1994a. *India in Transition.* Radhakrishnan Lectures, Oxford University, 1992. Oxford: Clarendon Press.

———. 1994b. "Samurais no more," *Foreign Affairs* 73: 7–12.

———. 1995a. "Democracy and development." First Rajiv Gandhi Memorial Lecture, delivered on October 22, published in *Journal of Democracy* 6: 50–64.

———. 1995b. *Free Trade, "Fair Trade" and the New Protectionism.* Harold Wincott Lecture, 1994. London: Institute for Economic Affairs.

———. 1995c. "Trade and wages: choosing among alternative explanations," *Federal Reserve Bank of New York Economic Policy Review* 1: 42–47.

Bhagwati, Jagdish, and Vivek Dehejia. 1994. "Freer trade and wages of the unskilled—is Marx striking again?," in Bhagwati and Kosters 1994.

Bhagwati, Jagdish, and Robert Hudec, eds. 1996. *Fair Trade and Harmonization: Prerequisites for Free Trade?.* Cambridge, Mass.: MIT Press.

Bhagwati, Jagdish, and Marvin Kosters, eds. 1994. *Trade and Wages: Leveling Wages Down?* Washington, DC: American Enterprise Institute.

Dunn, John. 1993. "The nation-state and human community: life chances, obligation and the boundaries of society." Mimeograph, King's College, Cambridge.

Employment Outlook. 1993. Paris: OECD.

Hudec, Robert. 1993. " 'Circumventing' democracy: the political morality of trade negotiations," *Journal of International Law and Politics* 25: 311–322.

Kohli, Atul. 1986. "Democracy and development," in John P. Lewis and Valeriana Kallab, eds., *Development Strategies Reconsidered.* Washington, DC: Overseas Development Council.

Lawrence, Robert. 1994. "Trade, multinationals, & labor." NBER Working Paper No. 4836. Cambridge, Mass.: National Bureau of Economic Research.

Plant, Raymond. 1993. "Rights, rules and world order." Mimeograph, University of Southampton.

Sachs, Jeffrey, and Howard Schatz. 1994. "Trade and jobs in US manufacturing," in *Brooking Papers on Economic Activity* 1: 1–84.

Salomon, Lester. 1994. "The rise of the nonprofit sector," *Foreign Affairs* 73: 109–122.

Weiner, M. 1991. *The Child and the State in India: Child Labor and Education Policy in Comparative Perspective.* Princeton: Princeton University Press.

Wood, Adrian. 1994. *North–South Trade, Employment and Inequality.* Oxford: Clarendon Press.

As reforms in economic policy—generally centered on dismantling inward-looking policies on international trade and attracting equity investment—and the privatization of many public-owned enterprises have swept across the developing world, critics have charged that these reforms are inimical to the reduction of poverty. Thus, it is not unusual for a long-standing proponent of these reforms like myself to get into recurring debates on the question. Only a few months ago, I and Martin Wolf of *The Financial Times* teamed up to face two rather impassioned opponents in a BBC debate. Our opponents claimed that pro-globalization policies are responsible for the accentuation of poverty, while we argued exactly the opposite.

In fact, this debate is only a replay of the debate that we Indian economists and planners had almost four decades ago, with occasional argumentation thereafter, when we began planning for national poverty amelioration. India at the time had (and still has, precisely because of the policies that presently call for pro-globalization reforms) the misfortune of having a comparative advantage in poverty. Since policy economics is like literature and reflects the immediacy of one's experience, Indian economists have not surprisingly been at the forefront of debates about how to reduce poverty.

As I shall presently argue, this debate in India was precisely between those who maintained that growth reduced poverty and those who argued that it bypassed or even increased it. Proponents of the pro-growth strategy were divided into those who came to see the inward-looking import-substitution (IS) model toward trade and direct foreign investment (DFI) as the culprit that crippled growth and hence accen-

Originally published in the *Journal of International Affairs* 52, no. 1 (Fall 1998): 447–459. Copyright The Trustees of Columbia University in the City of New York. Reprinted with permission.

tuated poverty (a minority in the 1960s and 1970s), and the vast majority that continued to cling to the increasingly implausible notion that these anti-globalization strategies were in fact pro-growth policies, despite compelling theoretical arguments and a growing body of evidence suggesting the opposite.

Since the 1980s, a majority of policy economists around the world have begun to favor economic reforms that increase global integration, in the strong belief that such reforms would, *ceteris paribus*, promote growth and would, both directly and indirectly (by raising resources for spending on social programs and in other ways discussed below), help to improve living standards among the poor. Today, the widespread view among Indian intellectuals and policymakers is that the absence of pro-growth economic policies for nearly three decades only served to accentuate Indian poverty. Ironically, the growth-retarding and hence poverty-enhancing policies in place throughout this time were adopted at the urging of those very economists who claimed that they were the virtuous ones who wished to attack poverty, while the rest of us were interested in growth for itself.[1]

Against this backdrop, I argue that pro-globalization and pro-privatization economic reforms must be treated as complementary and indeed friendly to both the reduction of poverty and social agendas. I maintain that poverty reduction and advancement of social agendas require not merely a policy focus on schooling, public health, etc., but also *simultaneous* attention to reforms aimed at improving the economic efficiency and growth of the economy. More precisely, I shall argue specifically in this chapter that:

• Growth (or "development") has been regarded for several decades as a principal *instrument* for reducing poverty, rather than as an *objective* in itself. Hence the contention in some influential developmental circles and international agencies that poverty reduction has only recently been designated as an objective of development, displacing the earlier preoccupation with growth per se, is totally off the mark. The falsity of this argument is a cause for concern insofar as it encourages the harmful ethos that somehow growth is irrelevant, if not inimical, to poverty reduction and to the promotion of social agendas. Growth is, in fact, an important force for poverty alleviation and has been regarded as such, at least in Indian planning and policy circles, since the 1950s.

• Growth is properly regarded as an instrumental means of reducing poverty because, generally speaking, it moves poor unemployed and underemployed people into gainful employment. Growth can still have varying degrees of efficacy in terms of its impact on poverty, depending on the "structural" forms that poverty and growth take and on the political and social contexts in which the growth process unfolds.

• Increased integration into the global economy (through trade and DFI) and other reforms (such as privatization) currently being proposed in poverty-ridden countries can be fully expected to assist in poverty eradication.

• Growth attacks poverty in yet another way: economic prosperity alone increases tax revenues which, in turn, can be used to finance conventional anti-poverty programs such as the building of schools and the provision of clean water, electricity and health facilities for the poor. Without revenues, these expenditures cannot be sustained, let alone expanded. But this requires that these agendas be on the radar screen of governments: the availability of funds is no guarantee that they will be used for the right purposes.

• In this respect, there is a clear role for democracy to guarantee effective political participation among peripheral groups, nongovernmental organizations (NGOs) and social activists. There is also a profound need for a combination of government and private NGO work to maximize the impact of governmental expenditures on social and economic programs that target the poor. Growth will also support social and poverty-reduction agendas, since it will enhance the effectiveness of legislation aimed at helping the poor.

Thus, in conclusion, those who viscerally oppose economic reforms today as anti-poor are misguided and unfortunately accentuating poverty instead. We need to build bridges between economic reformers and anti-poverty campaigners, not burn them.

Growth as an Anti-Poverty Strategy, Not as an Objective in Itself

In the mid-1970s and 1980s, I began to encounter assertions, from the International Labour Organization (ILO) and elsewhere, that growth had long been the primary objective of development planning and that poverty had been recognized as worthy of attention only recently. Such claims profoundly surprised me. A few dramatic examples of some of the untrue statements I was exposed to are illuminating.

First, I remember reading a biographical sketch of one of the South Asian architects of the Human Development reports of the United Nations Development Programme (UNDP). The thrust of these reports is that the UNDP deals with human beings, and hence with poverty and social agendas, whereas those of us who have worked at encouraging growth over the years are somehow tangential or inimical to those objectives. Such assertions prompted me once to mischievously inform the affable and dynamic UNDP head, Gus Speth, when he asked me at a party what I did, that I worked on Inhuman Development. The biographical sketch amusingly claimed that this particular economist had "dethroned the goddess of GNP from her pedestal."

I recall another example that took place several years ago when I was giving the keynote address at the twenty-fifth anniversary celebration of the Center for Development Studies in Antwerp, Belgium. In response to my comments on poverty, the Dutch economist Louis Emmerij (who had run the program on poverty at the ILO) said somewhat sarcastically that it was good to see Professor Bhagwati finally talking, not about free trade and growth, but about poverty and inequality. I could not resist retorting that I might have agreed with the statement were it not for the fact that, apropos of my speech that day, I was reading my best-selling 1966 book, *The Economics of Underdeveloped Countries*. The first chapter of that book is entitled "Poverty and Income Distribution."

In fact, many social scientists have responded with strongly disapproving commentary to the claim of some early development economists that pro-growth economists and policymakers ignored poverty. To cite one eminent sociologist, Gilbert Etienne, who has worked for decades on India's villages: "The claim that developmental strategies in the 1950s and 1960s overemphasized growth and increases of the GNP at the cost of social progress is a surprising one!... Equally peculiar is the so-called discovery of the problem of poverty."[2]

Growth: A Pull-up, not Trickle-down, Strategy for Removing Poverty

So, let me explain why we perceived growth at the time, and must continue to do so almost four decades later, as an effective anti-poverty strategy. This is because in countries such as India, where the poverty is immense, there are no simple answers like income redistribution (even if feasible politically) to bring poverty down. The problem is that redistribution would have little impact on poverty, even in the short-term. As the eminent Polish communist economist Mikhail Kalecki told me in India in 1962, the trouble with India is that there are too many exploited and too few exploiters. Moreover, governments need to pursue a sustained attack on poverty rather than a one-shot approach. With a rising population and stagnant growth, any favorable effects of redistribution on poverty would quickly erode.

Hence, Indian planners saw rapid growth as the principal component of an anti-poverty strategy. The idea was an activist program which would raise domestic savings and investment, assisted where possible by the influx of foreign funds through aid and investment in order to achieve accelerating growth that would move increasing numbers of people into gainful employment. The theoretical rationale was embodied in the well known Harrod–Domar growth model, in which employment rises with increasing capital stock and the chief policy instrument is a fiscal strategy to raise domestic savings.

All this was a far cry from the conventional liberal view in domestic debates within OECD countries, where growth is often presented as a *passive*, "trickle-down" process. Indeed, we thought of our strategy as an *active*, "pull-up" strategy requiring extensive savings mobilization, with the state playing a major (interventionist) role in that effort. Clearly, this was no conservative option.

Of course, not all growth has identical effects. Economists are ingenious enough to construct all kinds of scenarios. Thus, I am known for having demonstrated that growth can actually diminish economic well-being, as when it leads to losses from worsened terms of trade which outweigh the primary gains from growth.[3] To take another example, if rich farmers implement technical change, output increases and prices fall—and the poor farmers who did not innovate are hurt. For this reason, we used to say that the Green Revolution (which brought in new high-yield seeds) might lead to the Red Revolution! But these downside scenarios can be ruled out by suitable accompanying policies: in the former instance, an optimal tariff is the answer; in the latter, the government could adopt a price maintenance program or a policy to raise national investment, which would lead to a matching increase in demand for the added output of the high-yield grains.

Then again, it is obvious that growth may simply bypass certain pockets of poverty. Thus, for example, if tribal areas in India are not integrated into the main economy, growth occurring in the latter will not touch the former. This may well be the case internationally if an impoverished nation is not linked to the growing world economy and hence to profits from either trade or DFI. Indeed, such is the situation for many of the smaller, impoverished nations today (though, I would say, these "non-linkage" afflictions are, at least to some extent, a result of bad inward-looking policies over the years, and not an unfortunate external calamity of which poor countries are simply victims). Once again, supplementary programs are needed to accompany growth, so that it can act more effectively as a locomotive lifting people out of poverty.

If the efficacy of the locomotive depends on the nature of growth, there is enough evidence by now that the IS strategy harmed the poor, not just by slowing growth but also by affecting the horsepower of the locomotive. In a project for the National Bureau of Economic Research (NBER) that I and Professor Anne Krueger directed in the 1960s, we found that the IS strategy tended to reduce employment by biasing growth toward capital-intensive projects and choice of techniques, seriously limiting the assault on poverty as a result. This finding was reinforced by Krueger in a subsequent NBER Project, which focused more directly on the employment effects of the IS and the export pro-moting (EP) strategies.[4] Thus, the Far Eastern economies, with strik-ing growth rates over nearly three decades, had a substantial positive impact on the living standards of the poor because the development was based on labor-intensive production and exports. In India, on the other hand, the impact on poverty was handicapped, not merely by abysmally low growth rates, but also by the fact that the Indian eco-nomic planners—under the impetus of counterproductive theorizing that legitimated the use of capital-intensive techniques and the promo-tion of huge white elephants in heavy industry—biased the growth of the economy away from employment-creation.[5]

We may still ask whether the evidence demonstrates that in India, for instance, growth has pulled people out of poverty. After much de-bate, it seems that by now evidence of a favorable link has become more compelling. In the 1980s, when the Indian growth rate picked up from a range of 3 to 3.5 percent to around 5 percent, poverty reduc-tion accelerated.[6] Evidence on the Green Revolution's spread has also shown it to be linked to improvements in poverty.

Pro-Growth Reforms: Globalization, Privatization, and Market Reforms

Against this backdrop, the recent wave of economic reforms in much of the developing world and in formerly socialist economies is to be regarded as an important long-run input toward the elimination of poverty. There are, however, two important caveats. First, the short-term effects of a *transition* to globalization, in which economies are opened up to integration into the world economy, may well exacerbate poverty. This is sometimes glossed over by ideologues. See, for example, the World Bank's 1996 *World Development Report* on the transition problems that the former-socialist countries face, entitled *From Plan to Market*. This report virtually dismisses, and even ignores, the problems concerning unemployment and income distribution that attend such transitions. Moreover, it asserts without any serious response to the arguments advanced by scholarly opponents of the shock therapy model propounded by Jeffrey Sachs that these effects are desirable.[7] On the other hand, serious scholars of such transitions—chief among them Padma Desai of Columbia in her recent book, *Going Global: Transition from Plan to Market in the World Economy*, and John McMillan of the University of California at San Diego—have insightfully analyzed these problems associated with attempts at global integration.[8]

The second caveat is that all forms of globalization are not equally desirable, even from the viewpoint of efficiency and growth. Thus, it has become evident recently that the IMF's determination to push for capital account convertibility around the world has been hasty and, in fact, dangerous. The Asian financial crisis since 1997 has radically shifted opinion in the direction of halting the aggressive spread of such convertibility. Hence, the IMF is now conscious of what I have always argued, that free trade in widgets is not the same as free trade in dollars.[9] Unfortunately, public perception has likewise confused these two forms of globalization (goods vs. dollars); and now that the latter has once again caused a crisis, with incalculable economic and political consequences for the countries caught in the aftermath, there has been a tendency to condemn globalization per se, condemning the good form of globalization for the sins of the bad one.[10]

I would stress that the postwar experience has amply demonstrated the mutual gains to be made from trade liberalization. This is also true of equity investments, which bring into a country the benefits of capital, skills and technology. I would add the caveat, however, that energetic regression-prone economists such as Harvard's development experts Robert Barro and Sachs do not help us by turning out endless cross-country associations between growth rates and trade indicators. They even persuade financial journalists to reproduce these results as if they "proved" that globalization in trade, for instance, is immensely beneficial to liberalizing countries. In fact, they do not really do this.[11] My faith in the advantages of freer trade and eased restrictions on DFI inflows derives instead from sophisticated and nuanced studies of countries in which trade liberalization and DFI inflows are put into the appropriate context.

I should also add that privatization is now widely seen as conducive to economic efficiency. This view is not ideological, as it was when we were embarking on development and many of us had not pondered the deep-seated incentive problems that public enterprises would face, given the political context within which they would be operating, especially in developing countries. Political staffing, often excessive and of middling quality, the ability to ride out losses by resorting to subsidies and the absence of effective incentives for workers and managers to perform are among the key and ineradicable defects of public enterprises. Some unreformed proponents of the Marxist and Fabian preference for public ownership insist that suitable reforms could still salvage public enterprises as efficient economic entities. This logic, however, is like saying that if we put stripes on an elephant, it will become a zebra.[12]

Growth: Added Revenues to Support Anti-Poverty and Social Agendas

Let me then turn to another reason why growth, aided and accelerated by reforms like those outlined above, can help. Without prosperity, the government will fall short of the funds needed to advance literacy, secondary schooling, health, sanitation, and a host of programs aimed directly at the poor and conventionally described as "anti-poverty" programs in donor agencies and recipient countries. Of course, because it pulls the poor into gainful employment, growth is also to be seen as an indirect anti-poverty program, as I have already argued, and it is wrong to think otherwise. Indeed, to those who use the cliché of "development with a human face," I respond: "Yes, indeed. But remember that the face cannot exist by itself, except as a mask in a museum. It must be joined to the body; and if the body is emaciated, the face must wither no matter how much we seek to humanize and make it pretty."

For those who doubt this, it is perhaps necessary to reflect how, faced with a budget deficit, President Clinton turned away from social programs requiring funding, enraging in the process his liberal supporters who concluded that he had abandoned liberalism. As soon as the budget turned into a surplus, however, his liberal voice became loud and clear.[13]

Growth, Poverty, and Social Agendas: All Bedfellows

Though revenues resulting from prosperity allow for spending on anti-poverty programs and on social agendas, this does not guarantee that they will be so spent. For this, it is necessary to identify processes and institutions that will generate and sustain the right "preferences," not just culturally but in terms of effective political demand. This is where we recognize the importance of democracy, with effective participation among the poor and minorities. Their vote enables their voice to be heard.[14] The introduction of democratic politics into poor countries should therefore be seen as "political reform" that complements the "economic reforms" that I have discussed so far.

The specific forms that such democratic politics may assume can be diverse. One important aspect is the growth of NGOs, which Indians call Social Action Groups. These NGOs help to ensure that in poor communities, still emerging in some cases from feudal social and political structures, the voice of peripheral groups is not silenced by intimidation despite formal democratic practices. I might add that the role of female education in the development of civil society has been phenomenal. In the early 1960s, when I was working on poverty at the Indian Planning Commission, I recall discussing with the great Indian planner, Pitambar Pant, the immense growth of women in higher education and wondering where they would all go and with what consequences. We came up with images of women engineers, doctors, scientists and scholars. But we had no idea that several of them would wind up as active members of NGOs, pushing social agendas in all directions. Indeed, both in rich and in poor countries (with higher education), NGOs are increasingly dominated by women.

In addition, it is important to emphasize that growth seriously enhances the efficacy of social legislation and anti-poverty programs. Take literacy, for instance. Political scientist Myron Weiner has beautifully noted that literacy has usually required that the incentive of poor parents to put children to work rather than sending them to school is outweighed by countervailing values. In the Lutheran religion, for example, everyone needed to know how to read the Bible instead of relying on a priest to act as a liaison to God. For economists, this countervailing pressure can come from the prospect of earning higher income as a result of education. Higher income, however, will come only when growth provides economic opportunities that allow increasing numbers of children to travel down the educational road. The few schools that do exist in India have had problems with attendance and thus work below potential output, largely because low growth over the decades has drastically reduced the chances that improved incomes will result from sending children to school.[15]

Moreover, in some instances, it can be argued that social agendas follow economic growth. Thus, for example, many political scientists and sociologists, among them Barrington Moore and Ralf Dahrendorff, have maintained that democracy emerges when growth has produced a middle class that seeks democratic rights. Similarly, movements for environmental protection, for children's and women's rights, etc., seem to gather steam as economies grow and their populations acquire information and ideas from other countries further up the development ladder.

I should note that this tendency is sometimes used by economists to argue, totally without justification, that economic growth will eventually take care of social and poverty concerns and that we therefore do not need to address them directly. I have a simple answer to that. If a hapless woman is being beaten by her husband and screams for help, it would be a bit ludicrous to say to her to hang in there, because growth will eventually change values and laws so that husbands are no longer able to abuse their wives. What you will want to do is immediately nail the guy to the wall. And so must social agendas for the poor and minorities move ahead, hand in hand with the growth process.

One final remark on the positive relationship between growth and poverty reduction is worth making. Sometimes, expenditures aimed at removing poverty can in turn promote growth. Thus many economists have recently argued that if credit market imperfections prevent the poor from investing in health, education and enterprises, then this can impede growth. Again, a malnourished labor force cannot be conducive to higher productivity: the "efficiency wage" theory, associated with economists James Mirrlees and Harvey Leibenstein, formalizes the idea that firms will sometimes pay more than the going wage if a productivity boost results from better nutrition enabled by higher incomes.

Concluding Observations

And so, in many ways, the current reforms in developing countries must be seen as significant inputs into the important fight against world poverty. Unfortunately, in countries that face serious poverty, this is still not understood and reforms are considered to be a luxury for the rich and irrelevant to the poor. Having begun this essay with relevant reminiscences about India in the 1950s, let me conclude it with pertinent remarks about India in the 1990s.

Specifically, as we Indians try to move ahead with economic reforms to finally reduce poverty through rapid growth, let me express my astonishment, anguish and outrage over the following all-too-familiar criticism of reforms made by two influential economists:

Debates on such questions as the details of tax concessions to multinationals, or whether Indians should drink Coca Cola, or whether the private sector should be allowed to operate city buses, tend to "crowd out" the time that is left to discuss the abysmal situation of basic education and elementary health care, or the persistence of debilitating social inequalities, or other issues that have a crucial bearing on the well-being and freedom of the population.[16]

Mindful of the damage that such attitudes have done to the cause of poverty reduction in India over a quarter of a century, I was moved to respond, in a review essay:

Much is wrong here. No one can seriously argue that there is a crowding out when the articulation of Indians is manifest in multiplying newspapers, magazines and books and the expression of a whole spectrum of views on economics and politics; this reviewer has noticed no particular shyness in discussing social issues, including inequality and poverty in India.... But, more important, the put-down of attention to multinationals misses the point that India's economic reforms require precisely that India join the Global Age and that India's inward direct investments were ridiculously small in 1991, around $100 million, and that this was an important deficiency that had to be fixed. The reference to Coca Cola is no better, serving as a cheap shot against multinational investment; but it also betrays the assumption that Coca Cola is drunk by the elite or the Westernized middle class, not by the truly poor. It is more likely, however, that the former derive their caffeine from espresso coffee as well whereas the poor are the ones who must depend on Coke instead![17]

In fact, the contemptuous reference to the privatization of bus transportation in cities could only come from elitist economists who travel by private car and are unaware that the common people (especially the poor) travel by buses whose efficiency needs to be improved by privatization. In short, we confront here the spectacle of economists, who espouse the cause of the poor, becoming unwitting accomplices in the perpetuation of poverty. Ironic indeed.

Notes

1. See my critique of these economists and the hugely deleterious effects they had on India's poverty even as they were identified in the public eye as economists "more genuinely" concerned about poverty, in Bhagwati, "A Machine for Going Backwards," in *Times Literary Supplement*, reprinted in Bhagwati, *A Stream of Windows: Unsettling Reflections on Trade, Immigration, and Democracy* (Cambridge: MIT Press, 1998) chapter 56.

2. The Etienne quote is cited in my 1987 Vikram Sarabhai Memorial Lecture on Public Policy and Poverty, printed in *World Development*, 16, no. 5 (1988) pp. 539–555 and reprinted in Bhagwati, *Political Economy and International Economics*, ed., Douglas Irwin (Cambridge: MIT Press, 1991) chapter 25.

3. Bhagwati, "Immiserizing Growth: A Geometrical Note," *Review of Economic Studies*, 25, no. 3 (June 1958) pp. 201–205.

4. The volumes from the first project were published in 1978 by Ballinger and for the second project by University of Chicago Press in 1982. In addition, much important research-project-based work along these lines was done, in particular, by I.M.D. Little, Maurice Scott and Tibor Scitovsky for the OECD Development Center in the 1960s and by the late Bela Balassa for the World Bank. The findings of these projects and other research have been reviewed in Bhagwati, "Export-Promoting Trade Strategy: Issues and Evidence," *World Bank Research Observer*, 3, no. 1 (1988) pp. 27–57, reprinted in Bhagwati, *Political Economy and International Economics*, chapter 24.

5. Here, I have in mind the work on the choice of techniques in the 1960s by economists such as Amartya Sen, which did incalculable harm to the cause of growth and hence of poverty reduction by emphasizing the role of capital-intensive techniques in accelerating the growth rate by increasing savings. These conclusions came, of course, from the assumptions underlying the models built. But logical rigor is no substitute for wisdom; and, as the Oxford economist Thomas Balogh, adviser to Prime Minister Harold Wilson, used to say, rigor can lead to rigor mortis.

6. For a generally favorable assessment of the effect of growth on poverty reduction in India, see the recent World Bank Country Study, "India: Achievements and Challenges in Reducing Poverty" (Washington DC: 1997).

7. In fact, one looks in vain even for references to the contributions of academic scholars who have opposed shock therapy.

8. Padma Desai, *Going Global: Transition from Plan to Market in the World Economy*, (Cambridge: MIT Press, 1997).

9. See Jagdish Bhagwati, "The Capital Myth," *Foreign Affairs*, 77, no. 3 (May/June 1998) pp. 7–12. In explaining why free trade in widgets and in dollars were equated without justification, I also advance the view that a role has been played by what I call the "Wall Street-Treasury complex," an idea that has been picked up by the political scientist Robert Wade and others and needs further scholarly investigation.

10. A particularly good example of this is a recent *Los Angeles Times* story by Tom Plate (May 12, 1998), citing my *Foreign Affairs* article on "The Capital Myth" and saying: "This Columbia University professor still swears allegiance to free-market philosophy in other respects [than free capital flows as with capital account convertibility], but his defection on this issue is on the order of a Vatican bishop turning up at a Presbyterian pulpit." The

irony is that, not merely are the two forms of globalization, in free trade and in free capital flows, quite distinct from each other, but I have always been skeptical of free capital flows (as distinct from the advantages of equity investments).

11. In fact, such regressions are double-edged, since those opposed to trade can also play around with them, often leading to reversals of the "findings" by adding more variables, changing proxies, altering time periods or country coverage, etc. We are faced then with mutually assured destruction by opposed groups, each claiming scientific rectitude that serious econometricians and scholars would find unacceptable.

12. None of this is to say that all forms of privatization are good. Recently, for example, there has been much criticism of the Russian privatization. But few of the critics have faced up to the problem that all privatization programs must be politically and economically feasible, and unless they offer a better and feasible alternative, their critiques are not compelling. See, for example, Desai, "Russian Privatization: A Comparative Perspective," *The Harriman Review*, 8, no. 3 (August 1995) pp. 1–34; and her review of Maxim Boycko, Andrei Shleifer and Robert Vishny, *Privatizing Russia* (Cambridge: MIT Press, 1995) in *Journal of International Economics*, 42, no. 1/2 (February 1997) pp. 244–246.

13. Of course, nothing is uni-causal in the world of politics. Clinton's personal problems may have also intensified his need to rally the liberal Democrats around him. But he simply could not have done that without the necessary revenue surplus.

14. See my Rajiv Gandhi Memorial Lecture on "Democracy and Development," reprinted in Bhagwati (1998) chapter 40.

15. As is always true, the full explanation of India's appalling illiteracy is more complex. Thus, in some cases, it is the teachers who do not turn up.

16. Jean Drèze and Amartya Sen, *India: Economic Development and Social Opportunity* (Oxford: Clarendon Press, 1995) p. vii.

17. Jagdish Bhagwati, *Economic Journal*, 108 (January 1998) pp. 198–199.

Growth Is Not a Passive "Trickle-Down" Strategy

James Wolfensohn, president of the World Bank, appears twice with Joseph Stiglitz, his chief economist, in the *Financial Times* of September 22, once pointing a finger at him ("Economist rebuked over views on Russia") and the other time joining hands with him in an assault on your editorial writers and on your columnist Martin Wolf ("Growth is not enough"). But whatever the merits of Mr. Wolfensohn's critique of Mr. Stiglitz's "open-mouth" proclivity, the demerits of their joint critique cannot be ignored.

I find it puzzling that these distinguished gentlemen, whose acquaintance with developmental issues is relatively recent, think that they are to be complimented for departing from "the old approach of an exclusive focus on growth" and on "trickle-down" economics. This is no more than the old fallacy of putting up a straw man. Or perhaps the answer is simpler: it is plain ignorance.

Growth, from the 1950s, was seen in India, to take one notable example, as an instrument that would actively "pull up" the poor into gainful employment, not as a passive "trickle-down" strategy. Nor was it treated in isolation from land reforms, spending on education and public health, extensive community development schemes and the promotion of progressive social agendas through appropriate legislation.

Nor can Mr. Wolf or your excellent leader ("The Bank's development," September 16), which these gentlemen deplore, be read as a demand for "exclusive" reliance on growth for development. Where the World Bank today can be faulted, as the leader rightly does, is in continually losing sight of the fact that growth is a critical and hugely important component of any strategy to promote development in the poor countries.

Originally published as a letter to the editor of the *Financial Times* (Sept. 27, 1999). Reprinted with permission.

The protestations of Messrs. Wolfensohn and Stiglitz are hardly credible. And your leader does ask properly: is not something lost by taking the Bank in all sorts of directions, however important in themselves, under the umbrella of slogans such as a "holistic" approach to development? One can end up doing all things badly and nothing well. And is there not something like what I call "appropriate governance" in terms of what different international institutions should be doing? Thus, many of us want labour rights to be addressed; but many of us equally oppose their inclusion in the World Trade Organisation rather than the International Labour Organisation.

In regard to the World Bank and Mr. Wolfensohn, I was surprised to learn from Thomas Friedman's recent book on globalisation, *Lexus and the Olive Tree*, which I recently reviewed for the *Wall Street Journal*, that Mr. Wolfensohn was now handing out moneys for supporting local cultures. But is that not what Unesco, aided by bilateral programmes and foundations, with real expertise in the area, is supposed to be doing?

Should Mr. Wolfensohn, like Evita Peron and President Taubman of Liberia, be handing out (our) moneys to his favoured cultural programmes and whatever else he considers worthy of support? These are serious questions which cannot, should not, be swept under the carpet by pretending that those who raise them are "narrow, growth-only" ignoramuses.

By now, neither the illiterates who sit in front of their TV screens nor the literates who look into their PC screens can have failed to hear about "globalization." Indeed, the concept—in caricature form—is constantly invoked these days to explain nearly everything.

Thomas Friedman, a reporter who has risen to be a columnist for the *New York Times*, is not immune from this affliction. In *The Lexus and the Olive Tree* (Farrar, Straus & Giroux, 394 pages, $27.50), he attempts to explain a great deal. Sadly, the book's failings match its ambition.

It will come as no surprise to Mr. Friedman's readers in the *Times* —where he calls the world's statesmen, the Bills and Bibis, by their first names—that he crowds his book with puffy quotations from the mighty. Worse, we also hear from his college pals, his brother-in-law and his 79-year-old mother, who plays bridge on the Internet with three Frenchmen to the evident delight of her son.

And then there are the ceaseless attempts at phrase-making; "Globalution" (for the revolutionary effects of globalization); "Glocalization" (for reconciling the world with local culture); and "DOS Kapital" (for Internet-aided investment).

The cuteness turns into silliness when Mr. Friedman propounds the "Golden Arches Theory of Conflict Prevention": i.e., no two countries with McDonald's (and hence with much to lose from a disruption in the prosperity brought by globalization) will ever go to war. This short-lived theory has been disproved by the war between Belgrade and NATO.

And that is where Mr. Friedman's book really goes astray: on substance. For starters, he keeps finding globalization where none exists.

Even an old Vietnamese woman weighing passers-by on a ramshackle scale for money makes him think of it. But such sights have been routine in underdeveloped countries for decades. He sees globalization in a rural Chinese election when the winning candidate promises economic opportunity. Surely such stories testify instead to the universality of the profit motive.

Mr. Friedman offers a holistic vision of the globalization process: Faxes, e-mail and the Internet ("Lexus") have put the world economy into the fast lane, helping along the global integration of trade and capital flows. Nations now have no options, he argues, only a Hobson's choice to join in and prosper or be marginalized. But, he adds, globalization creates social and cultural tensions—the "olive tree" that defines (threatened) local turf for this former Mideast correspondent.

But Mr. Friedman is too much of a technological determinist. Consider trade and equity investments, both enormous sources of global prosperity. They have grown at cruise-control speed throughout the postwar period. Why? Policy decisions removed barriers, not technological advances. Or take short-term capital flows. True, their pace and scale have grown astonishingly with modern communication. But few would deny the role of Wall Street lobbyists—with the acquiescence of Treasury officials—who pushed for breaking down capital-account restrictions world-wide and helped precipitate, among other things, the Asian financial crisis.

Politics, in short, matter. To take yet another example: Our business lobbies have often bullied U.S. administrations into riding roughshod over the cultural concerns of other nations. Thus we have tried to remake Japan in our own image under threats of retaliation (threats that Mr. Friedman once approved of); and we have objected ferociously to the Canadians and the French when they have tried to defend their movies and magazines from competitive pressures.

Mr. Friedman is also unduly simplistic about the cultural effects of globalization. Although he properly underlines how globalization can lead to unequal outcomes—enriching some, harming others—he strains credulity when he starts worrying about the McDonald's and Pizza Huts he sees as he travels around the world. They are just the latest manifestations of the international transmission of "low" culture that has always been with us. Most cultures survive and even flourish through such cross-fertilization. McDonald's in India offers "veggie" burgers.

Mr. Friedman fails to see that the threat to local cultures today comes in quite a different way. Our "high" culture—that is, our values-driven push for human rights, freedom and individualism—challenges conventional and nondemocratic regimes around the world. It would do so even if there were no Internet.

Mr. Friedman's oversimplifications harm a worthwhile project. The problem, in the end, is that Mr. Friedman relies too much on the "talk and travel" method of research and too little on the "read and reflect" technique. Stories can embellish analysis; they cannot substitute for it.

Thomas Friedman, in his column (Op-Ed, February 2) on the appropriate ways to think about the "Global debate," writes about the subject
with much insight but more must be said.

Friedman divides the debate on global integration into a matrix with
four cells, obtained by combining in alternative ways those who want
to integrate "faster or slower" (i.e., sign "more or fewer free-trade
agreements") and those who would integrate with or without intervention to provide a "safety net." Bill Clinton then falls into the cell
that opts for faster integration with a safety net and Newt Gingrich into
the cell, however, that mixes faster integration without it.

But this matrix fails to confront the reality that those who fear the
force of integration into the Global Economy and wish to moderate it
are typically divided today into those who would go slower into freer
trade (with some, like Pat Buchanan, going ballistic and wanting to
unravel existing free trade treaties as well), and who are thus not
ashamed of being condemned as protectionists; and those, like the
Clintonites, who favor faster freeing of trade but who, using slogans
such as "fair trade" and "level playing fields," opt instead for forcing
our rivals abroad to raise their costs so as to moderate the force of the
competition at source.

Thus, for instance, in its insistence that the WTO adopt a social
clause under which the poor nations, in effect, are to be denied
access to our markets unless they adopt a set of highly-selective labor
standards which will make their competition "fair," the administration
has opted for "intrusionism" in lieu of the "isolationism" that conventional protectionism implies. The former protects our industries by

Unpublished letter to the editor of *The New York Times* (Feb. 2, 1997). Reprinted with
permission.

moderating competition at source; the latter, through familiar import barriers, at destination.

The Republicans who favor freer trade are opposed to imposing a variety of such intrusionist prerequisites for freeing trade, many seeing a protectionist motive in the Clintonites' desire to introduce environmental and labor standards requirements, for example, into free trade treaties such as the WTO. So do an increasing number of economists of all political persuasions, who would delink trade treaties from such intrusionism and would pursue social and human-rights agendas instead at appropriate international agencies such as the ILO, UNICEF, and UNEP. On the issue of the revival of fast-track authority to negotiate more trade-liberalizing treaties, the divide between Democrats who wanted more intrusionism and Republicans who wanted none has already led to a policy paralysis.

Mr. Friedman's matrix thus needs to be revised. Instead, we need a matrix that reflects the division of the debate into those who, on the external front, favor moderating the impact of global integration, dividing in turn into isolationists and intrusionists, and those who instead accept the impact but divide in turn into those who wish to design domestic institutions to cope with it and those (libertarians) who would go with laissez-faire instead.

If you thought globalization is the fastest-growing phenomenon today, think again. Books about globalization are. *A Future Perfect* is only the latest in a torrent of writings on the subject, chief among them being *The Lexus and the Olive Tree* by Thomas Friedman. Yet it stands as one of the rare exceptions to the law of diminishing marginal utility; its many merits far outweigh the sense of déjà vu that afflicts most books taking yet another look at globalization.

It is not just that, like the best Oxbridge graduates, Micklethwait and Wooldridge (both of *The Economist*) write gloriously. As journalists, they have also learned the art of making a point vividly by buttressing it with an apt anecdote, a striking interview, or a telling quote. Yet the book's substance is what really makes it stand out. The authors neatly sketch and defend globalization, examine its pitfalls, and analyze how to avoid them. Given such an overwhelming agenda, they cannot hope to paint on this immense canvas without incurring minor blemishes of detail and errors of judgment. But judged in its entirety, with all its ambition and achievement, the book is a spectacular success.

The authors' predilection for free markets makes them skeptical of the many populist critiques of globalization. Yet they often manage to turn these critiques on their head to show the exact opposite—that globalization can work to lift overall prosperity and reduce poverty. Indeed, Micklethwait and Wooldridge are at their most eloquent and persuasive when they broaden the scope of their case to include liberty and democracy as globalization's additional benefits.

Then again, since the authors are historians by education, they are aware that globalization had been halted in the past and that it can

Originally published as a review of John Micklethwait, *A Future Perfect: The Challenge and Hidden Promise of Globalization* (New York: Crown Business, 2000) in *Foreign Affairs* 79, 4 (July/Aug. 2000): 134–139. Copyright 2000 by the Council on Foreign Relations, Inc. Reprinted with permission.

run into rough weather again as it did in the first half of the twentieth century. Therefore, they analyze at length the nature of growing anti-globalization sentiments, which in turn leads them to suggest how globalization should be "managed" if it is to survive and deliver on its immense promise for humankind.

Motley Crew

No one can escape the antiglobalists today. One can simply turn on the TV, read the news reports on the street theater in Seattle last year and in Washington, D.C., this year, or read profiles of the professional anti–World Trade Organization (WTO), anti–Bretton Woods, anti-globalization agitators in *The Wall Street Journal* (Lori Wallach of Public Citizen) or *The New Yorker* (Juliette Beck of Global Exchange).

This motley crew comes almost entirely from the rich countries and is overwhelmingly white, largely middle class, occasionally misinformed, often wittingly dishonest, and so diverse in its professed concerns that it makes the output from a monkey's romp on a keyboard look more coherent. But it has become powerful enough to force many rich-country politicians to play along. Micklethwait and Wooldridge excoriate the latter as sellouts, contrasting them unfavorably with great leaders such as Robert Peel, who took huge political risks to liberalize Britain's trade in 1846. It has now become customary among politicians—particularly those who claim to share others' anguish but whose own anguish relates primarily to the votes they seek—to say that "globalization needs a human face." This implies, of course, that it lacks one. And there starts the rot—an implicit surrender, in the face of logic and evidence, to the worst fears and loudest rhetoric of globalization's critics. In response, Micklethwait and Wooldridge insist that our leaders debunk the myths.

Statesmanship requires that politicians say, "Globalization has a human face; it works wonders in all sorts of ways. Sure enough, like every gigantic force or phenomenon, it has a few downsides. But what this simply means is that the indisputably human face of globalization needs a trinket in one ear and cosmetic surgery on the other."

History's Lessons

Only a little knowledge of postwar history on attitudes toward globalization is needed to toughen up politicians' spines: it shows that

Figure 46.1
Unlike Prime Minister Robert Peel, who bravely liberalized Britain's trade by repealing her Corn Laws, today's politicians are too often sellouts to the protectionist cause. Portrait of Prime Minister Robert Peel, by Franz Xavier Winterhalter, Royal Collection © 2000. Reprinted with permission.

policymakers who succumbed to antiglobalization fears lost out to contrary experience—and are consigned by the now eagerly globalizing poor countries to the dustbin of history, to be returned to center stage only when their sorry images are invoked to underline what went wrong.

In the postwar period there has been an ironic reversal of attitudes toward globalization. Rich-country politicians embraced globalization in the decades following World War II, forging the liberal international economic order. By contrast, poor countries walked away from it, treating it as a peril rather than an opportunity. But today, mainstream policymakers in poor countries are busily abandoning autarkic attitudes while rich-country lobbies and responsive politicians are reinventing for themselves the very fears that the now-chastened policymakers in poor countries consider to have been disastrous for their well-being.

For example, concerns over trade and incoming foreign direct investment (FDI) provoked the poor countries' battle cry from the 1950s through the 1970s: that "international integration leads to national disintegration" (in the words of Chilean intellectual Osvaldo Sunkel). And the "benign impact" models that economists espoused—which portrayed international trade and direct investment as mutually beneficial for all countries involved—were replaced by contrary and deeply pessimistic approaches. "Malign impact" models fretted that interaction with the "center" countries would harm the economies of the "periphery" (the developing world). Other "malign impact" arguments contended that the periphery was being put at political risk through an unwitting loss of sovereignty to rich nations and their corporations (the celebrated *dependencia* thesis of the then-sociologist and now Brazilian president, Hernando Cardoso). And "malign intent" models of neocolonialism asserted that globalization of trade, aid, and investments was no more than a calculated reimposition of colonialism by other means.

These arguments should sound familiar to anyone watching the news today. If the poor countries once worried about the outflow of their skilled—the brain drain—to the center, scholars like George Borjas and Orlando Patterson and the unions now fear the inflow of the unskilled from the periphery. Poor countries once worried that trade with the center would harm their nascent industrialization and development; today, trade with the periphery strikes terror in the hearts of the center's unions, who believe their wages will be reduced to Chinese levels. Whereas the periphery once resisted the inflow of FDI, rich-country unions now resist its outflow. If the periphery once opposed being dominated by the center, the center now fears losing its identity to the periphery. And the examples run on.

Clueless

In the face of these cascading complaints, today's rich-country anti-globalists must be taught the same lesson before damage is done—what the poor-country anti-globalists had to learn painfully years ago from the policy choices dictated by their doctrines. And since there is almost always a morsel of wheat underneath the abundance of chaff, the residual, legitimate complaints of the antiglobalist camp must also be addressed. The energy that drives the antiglobalist campaigns stems from four different types of fallacies.

The Fallacy of Aggregation

Micklethwait and Wooldridge's account beautifully describes how globalization raises many diverse issues, including culture, national identity, and economic organization (e.g., whether big corporations will displace the small mom-and-pop outfits). It is particularly fascinating when it describes in loving detail the growing tribe of "cosmocrats"—graduates of rapidly homogenizing business schools who circumnavigate the globe with cell phones and laptops, our noisy neighbors on planes and trains, a throwback to the "ugly Americans" of yesteryear. They aptly note that the gulf, indeed the chasm, that separates these ceaselessly orbiting elites from their own local communities creates tensions that feed the antiglobalist paranoia.

But they fail to emphasize that globalization attracts gratuitous criticism because few care to analyze its anatomy. That failure, which leads critics to commit the fallacy of aggregation by visiting the sins of one type of globalization on all others, is most manifest in the reactions to the Asian financial crisis. It has been widely assumed that if freedom of capital flows had caused a devastation in Asia, free trade must be judged a mortal peril as well. But as every serious student of globalization knows, important similarities exist among freer trade, freer capital flows, and freer migration. Yet there are also striking dissimilarities, both economic and political. For example, it would be fanciful to imagine that free trade could lead to the kind of upheavals wreaked by financial liberalization.

The Fallacy of Misassigned Blame

The antiglobalists also make the mistake of attributing to globalization the blemishes of other faces. To take the most telling example, many workers and unions fear that the deterioration, then stagnation, of unskilled workers' real wages in the 1980s and early 1990s resulted from trade and foreign investment. That would appear to be another black mark against globalization—except that the argument cannot be sustained. Most of the empirical work of the last decade suggests that trade with the poor countries has not produced paupers in our midst. Marx, who wrongly predicted the proletariat's immiseration in the nineteenth century, is not striking again courtesy of globalization. Recent work suggests that trade may have moderated rather than accentuated the decline in real wages (especially in the 1980s) that other factors such as unskilled-labor-saving technical changes were forcing.

This tendency to blame globalization for the evils of the world that are attributable to other causes is evident all too often. The literature of the radical groups in Mexico's Chiapas, which has endured poverty for more than a century, would have one believe that the 1993 North American Free Trade Agreement had much to do with it instead.

The Fallacy of the Wrong Question

Then again, some critics ask the wrong question. The United Nations Development Program and the World Bank have fallen prey to repeating endless condemnatory variations on the theme that globalization has led to greater income inequality. But even if such a causal relationship could be established—and it has not been—they do not explain why should it matter, given that inequality's consequences will differ hugely across countries, from negative to positive effects.

To illustrate, if George Soros makes another $1 billion while the poor earn no more, inequality will increase in New York: the top five percent of households will earn a greater share of total income and the bottom five percent will earn less. Yet the poor may not even notice this—or they may even see it like an increase in the lottery of the American Dream. Similarly, if Bill Gates makes $30 billion, he may spend $25 billion on charitable contributions to eliminate disease in Africa and thus truly help the poor. If this income had been earned in a more egalitarian fashion by the multitude or shared in smaller sums among his rivals, the impact on the redistribution of well-being would have been worse from a cosmopolitan-egalitarian viewpoint. Without these deeper forms of sociological and economic analyses, the antiglobalization bureaucratese remains empty and the liberal talk around it little more than populist rhetoric.

The Fallacy of Inappropriate Solutions

Compounding these errors is the fallacy of inappropriate solutions to globalization's alleged problems, Micklethwait and Wooldridge illustrate this beautifully through their discussion of culture and globalization. For instance, the French and the Koreans have been sensitive about Hollywood's overwhelming their cinema. The European Union has opted for audio-visual restrictions that impose quotas on time allotted to U.S. films, thereby restricting the scope of free trade. But it would be more sensible to opt for a subsidy to French cinema while maintaining free trade in films. That way, French cinema can be encouraged while free trade indulges consumer choice and allows healthy competition between Renoir and Spielberg.

The debates over hormone-fed beef and genetically modified (GM) foods represent another divide. Europeans have turned dramatically against what they term "Frankenfoods," whereas the United States has not. But this difference might well stem from cultural attitudes. After all, the United States is a protechnology, pill-popping country, a land of silicone implants and Viagra—or, as one wit put it, a nation of artificially enhanced women chased by artificially aroused men. It is wrong for the United States to insist that, short of "scientific evidence," Europe must accept GM foods and hormone-fed beef. To pretend that the Europeans are protectionists when they make a cultural choice in rejecting these foods misses not only the point but the bus.

The same goes for contentious issues such as child labor. Methods other than trade sanctions are far more appropriate to reduce child labor; hence, the International Labor Organization, not the WTO, is the preferred institution to go through. Many nongovernmental organizations in the poor countries where child labor is a concern consider trade sanctions to be counterproductive—and regard the Clinton administration's endorsement of the AFL-CIO demand that the WTO embrace a "social clause" as politically motivated protectionism hiding behind a mask of moral concern. Aided by the administration, meanwhile, unions stand uncorrected and unexposed while taking the ostensible higher ground to target the WTO and globalization.

Keeping the Faith

Micklethwait and Wooldridge conclude with a final, grand question: Who should run to the barricades to save globalization, and with what weapons? They exhort politicians and business groups to fight for the cause. Indeed, they must. But surely this is not enough. The primary role in defending globalization will have to be played by the intellectuals. Until the myths and half-truths spread about globalization are destroyed with pointed argumentation, until wrong policy proposals are publicly and continually challenged and right policies advocated in their place, the average politician cannot be expected to stand up and fight for the common good. John Maynard Keynes, the authors' favorite intellectual, wrote famously of the power of "defunct economists" over today's policies. Today's economists and public intellectuals must be more ambitious. They must roll up their sleeves and get into the battle, fighting to influence policies while they are still alive and kicking—not after they are gone and defunct.

Index